THE COLONIZATION OF MI'KMAW MEMORY AND HISTORY, 1794–1928

The King v. Gabriel Sylliboy

In 1927, Gabriel Sylliboy, the Grand Chief of the Mi'kmaq of Atlantic Canada, was charged with trapping muskrats out of season. At appeal in July 1928, Sylliboy and five other men recalled conversations with parents, grandparents, and community members to explain how they understood a treaty their people had signed with the British in 1752. Using this testimony as a starting point, William Wicken traces Mi'kmaw memories of the treaty, arguing that as colonization altered Mi'kmaw society, community interpretations of the treaty changed as well.

The Sylliboy case was part of a broader debate within Canada about aboriginal peoples' legal status within Confederation. In using the 1752 treaty to try and establish a legal identity separate from that of other Nova Scotians, Mi'kmaw leaders contested federal and provincial attempts to force their assimilation into Anglo-Canadian society. Integrating matters of governance and legality with an exploration of historical memory, *The Colonization of Mi'kmaw Memory and History* offers a nuanced understanding of how and why individuals and communities recall the past.

WILLIAM C. WICKEN is an associate professor in the Department of History at York University.

WILLIAM C. WICKEN

The Colonization of Mi'kmaw Memory and History, 1794–1928

The King v. Gabriel Sylliboy

UNIVERSITY OF TORONTO PRESS
Toronto Buffalo London

© University of Toronto Press 2012
Toronto Buffalo London
www.utppublishing.com
Printed in Canada

ISBN 978-1-4426-4279-9 (cloth)
ISBN 978-1-4426-1155-9 (paper)

Printed on acid-free, 100% post-consumer recycled paper with vegetable-based inks

Library and Archives Canada Cataloguing in Publication

Wicken, William Craig, 1955–
    The colonization of Mi'kmaw memory and history, 1794–1928 : the King v. Gabriel
Sylliboy / William C. Wicken.

Includes bibliographical references and index.
ISBN 978-1-4426-4279-9 (bound)   ISBN 978-1-4426-1155-9 (pbk.)

1. Micmac Indians – Colonization – Nova Scotia.   2. Memory – Social aspects –
Nova Scotia.   3. Collective memory – Nova Scotia.   4. Sylliboy, Gabriel, 1874–1963 –
Trials, litigation, etc.   5. Great Britain. Treaties, etc. Micmac Indians, 1752 Nov. 22.
6. Micmac Indians – Government policy – Nova Scotia – History.   7. Micmac Indians
– Nova Scotia – History.   I. Title.

E99.M6W49 2012   971.6′00497343   C2012-900879-6

University of Toronto Press acknowledges the financial assistance to its publishing
program of the Canada Council for the Arts and the Ontario Arts Council.

University of Toronto Press acknowledges the financial support of the Government of
Canada through the Canada Book Fund for its publishing activities.

This book has been published with the help of a grant from the Canadian Federation
for the Humanities and Social Sciences, through the Aid to Scholarly Publications
Program, using funds provided by the Social Sciences and Humanities Research
Council of Canada.

For my grandfather Clinton Clause (Claus), 1890–1964
Who chose in 1920 to be 'Indian' no longer

Contents

Conclusion   229

Acknowledgments

Research for this book began while I was preparing a report on the Maritime treaties for the Royal Commission on Aboriginal People in 1993 and continued the next year, while I was an employee of Nova Scotia Aboriginal Title, an organization that was funded through the Confederacy of Mainland Micmacs and the Union of Nova Scotia Indians. My thanks go to both organizations for giving me the opportunity to pursue my research.

Over the next several years this project lay dormant, as I began teaching at York University, testifying in a series of court cases, and working on a much revised version of my Ph.D. research. Only in 2004 did I again begin working on it.

Along the way, I have received the help from a number of people. Foremost among them are archivists at the Library and Archives of Canada and Nova Scotia Records and Archives Management. I have also benefited from the friendly advice of those who kindly agreed to read individual chapters of the manuscript. My thanks go to Rusty Bitterman, Bettina Bradbury, Carolyn Podruchny, John Reid, Nicholas Rogers, and Anders Sandberg.

Thanks are due to a number of people at the University of Toronto Press and people in their employ, some of whom I know, and many more I do not. Foremost, I owe a debt of gratitude to Len Husband, who continued to believe that this project was worthwhile, and encouraged me to make the necessary revisions. As well, I would like to thank Frances Mundy, who has guided this manuscript through its final stages, and Harold Otto, whose expert reading of the manuscript has improved the book's final version.

As well, I would like to thank Carolyn King of York's Geography Department, who prepared the two maps of Nova Scotia, and Stacey Alexopoulos, who did the index.

I would also like to pay my respectful dues to the anonymous reviewers who took the time and energy to carefully read and to comment on the original manuscript and then the revised version. Although some of the comments were initially harsh, I realized, after setting aside my ego, that there was some justice in what was said. This spurred me to make the necessary revisions and then to listen again as another reader made other valuable and pertinent comments. The final product, I think, is a much improved and better written manuscript than the one I originally submitted. This process made me understand that peer review does work when people take the time. The reviewers' insights helped immeasurably, and to these anonymous people I owe an enormous scholarly debt. If I have erred, it is perhaps in not doing enough to make the manuscript even better. Any errors that remain are my fault alone and not the responsibility of others.

Finally, my greatest debt lies with my family, Jane, Keelin, and Marcus Greenlaw, who have contributed in different ways to the completion of this book.

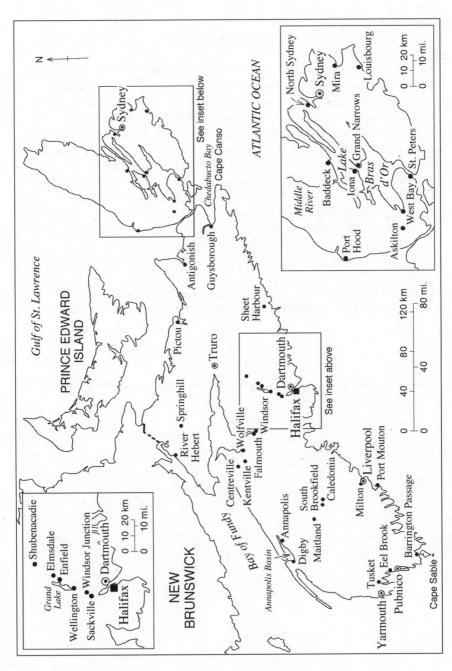

Contemporary map of Nova Scotia

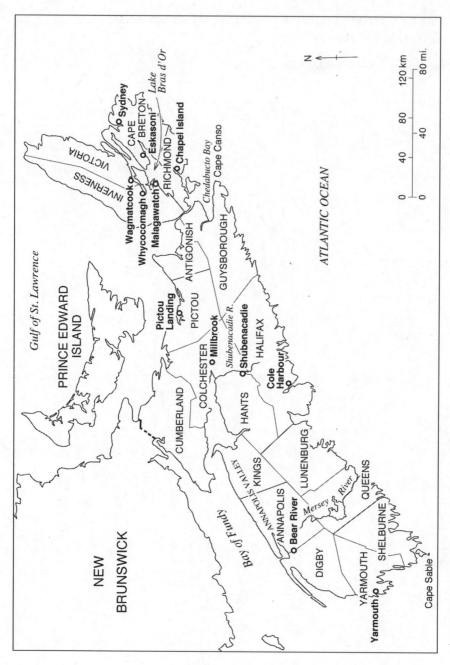

Mi'kmaw reserves and counties of Nova Scotia

THE COLONIZATION OF MI'KMAW MEMORY AND HISTORY, 1794–1928

The King v. Gabriel Sylliboy

Introduction

The problem is that people remember. People always remember. But what is remembered is shaped by the historical context in which a memory is formed. Although that memory may be transmitted to future generations, how they remember will be shaped by the historical context in which they receive the memory. The result is a subtle change, but one that will widen with each succeeding generation.

How, why, and in what form succeeding generations of aboriginal people have understood historical events is the subject of this book. I believe that aboriginal people formed an understanding of events that differed from the understanding of others because of the particular circumstances in which colonization affected them. One consequence was that the memories they formed, and which were remembered and transmitted to later generations, differed from how other Canadians created, remembered, and conveyed other memories about the past.[1] I believe that today the difference in how such memories are remembered is a source of friction between aboriginal people and government officials and exacerbates difficulties in resolving disputes between them.

There was a time in the late nineteenth and early twentieth centuries when such conflicts might have been softened. This was a time when Canada emerged as a transcontinental nation and also a time when it became something more than just an assemblage of its diverse parts. It was a time when the railway reached from sea to sea and a time when aboriginal people were shunted aside. It was at this moment when government might have chosen a path that would have harnessed rather than marginalized aboriginal people. But they did not, perhaps because they could not. The result was that aboriginal people formed and transmitted memories about the past, which have persisted until today and which have affected current disputes. Most aboriginal people in the early twentieth century did not have a choice but to be Indians and from their lived experiences, they remembered and retold a history that stressed the oppressive character of government policy, folding the history of the more distant past into their present. In this book, I explore this issue by reference to one aboriginal community in Canada, the Mi'kmaq of Nova Scotia. I do so by examining why, how, and in what form, five Mi'kmaw men in 1928 remembered a treaty their ancestors had signed with the British Crown in 1752.

My reference is the prosecution of the Grand Chief of the Mi'kmaw people, Gabriel Sylliboy, who in 1927 was charged with trapping musk-rats during closed season. He might have simply paid the fine or done jail time, as others had done before him. But Sylliboy challenged the government's right to restrict when and where he could hunt, claiming that the 1752 treaty superseded provincial legislation. To prove his point he had a lawyer speak for him. When the magistrate found him guilty, Sylliboy did something no other Mi'kmaq had done: he appealed the decision to the County Court.

At the appeal trial in July 1928, he and five other Mi'kmaw men told Judge George Patterson how they interpreted the 1752 treaty. Sylliboy said, 'since I was boy heard that Indians got from King free hunting and fishing at all times ... Under treaty get from Gov't blankets and flour and some shoes & long coats. Still get them.' Andrew Alek testified that 'Mic-macs had right to fish all they cd eat or sell at all seasons of year.' Francis Gould was more explanatory: 'Remember my grandfather going to Sydney & getting blankets long coat corn (3 bushels) gun powder flour sometimes seed corn beads for moccasins, He told me he got these from the King. Under the Treaty. We promised to keep Treaty & got these things in return. That is what my grandfather told me.'[2]

In his September 1928 decision, Judge George Patterson of the Nova Scotia County Court rejected the men's testimony and confirmed Sylliboy's conviction. Patterson outlined three main reasons for his judgment. First, he said that because Sylliboy was from Cape Breton, he could not claim protection from the 1752 treaty, because it had been made with the chief of Shubenacadie, a community on mainland Nova Scotia. In other words, the treaty would only protect Sylliboy if he was from Shubenacadie. Second, Patterson said that even had Sylliboy been from Shubenacadie, the treaty had no legal force. Echoing the tenor of the Ju-dicial Committee of the Privy Council's decision in St Catharine's Milling (1888), Patterson stated that treaties were made by 'independent powers' but the Indians were never regarded as such. 'A civilized nation first discovering a country of uncivilized people or savages held such country as its own mark until such time as by treaty it was transferred to some other civilized nation. The savages' right of sovereignty even of ownership were never recognized. Nova Scotia had passed to Great Britain not by gift of purchase from or even by conquest of the Indians but by treaty with France, which had acquired it by priority of discovery and ancient possession; and the Indians passed with it.' In Patterson's view, Mi'kmaw rights ended with European settlement in Nova Scotia. France had been the first to settle Nova Scotia and that, Patterson implied, ended the Mi'kmaw community's right to do anything except what was dictated by the French colonial government. With the British conquest of Acadia in 1713 power passed from the French to the British and so too did the Mi'kmaq. For this reason, the 1752 'treaty' was an agreement – not a treaty – and 'was made by the Governor and council with a handful of Indians giving them in return for good behaviour food, presents, and the right to hunt and fish as usual.' That agreement could be unilaterally altered and could not restrict government from legislating in the public interest. Finally, even if both of these issues were decided differently, the Mi'kmaq could not continue to enjoy the treaty's benefits, because soon after its signing they had abrogated it by warring upon the British. According to Judge Patterson, once abrogated, the treaty could not be resuscitated.[3]

The Sylliboy case was one of many instances in the early 1900s when aboriginal people challenged the government's interpretation of their status within Confederation. Disputes focused on four main legal issues: the relationship of treaties to provincial and federal legislation, the federal government's responsibility towards aboriginal people under Section 91(24) of the British North America Act, the government's power under the Indian Act of 1876, and finally, and much less commonly, the rights of aboriginal people who had not surrendered their land to the Crown. These challenges were premised on similar principles: that aboriginals retained a jurisdiction, although sometimes limited, over their community and resources. This included the rights of access to land that had been surrendered but on which they still exercised harvesting rights, to use unsurrendered land, to practise their own customs, and, in some cases, to resolve internal disputes. Even in instances where surrenders had been obtained, some communities said that they had not done so, and if they had, that they had not surrendered a right to hunt and to fish and to use off-reserve resources. In addition, aboriginal communities

Gabriel Sylliboy, 1930 (Nova Scotia Museum, Halifax: P113/73.180.615; N-15, 068)

contested Ottawa's right to unilaterally reduce reserve land. Sylliboy's action therefore was not an isolated case of 'lawbreaking' but was part of a broader response by Canada's aboriginal population to economic expansion onto lands and resources they used and to government and missionary efforts at assimilating them into Anglo-Canadian society.[4]

The Sylliboy case occurred at a critical time in this contested terrain, coming just after Parliament had passed an amendment to the Indian Act that made it more difficult for aboriginal people to hire lawyers to represent their interests.[5] Judge Patterson's decision therefore assumed an importance it might not otherwise have done. Occurring after the lockdown on lawyers, the case became an important precedent in Maritimes jurisprudence, which only ended after the passage of the Constitution Act of 1982 and the subsequent Supreme Court decision in *R.* v. *Simon* (1985).[6]

Sylliboy was also important because it reinforced the ideological framework established in the *St Catharine's Milling* case of 1888, when the Judicial Committee of the Privy Council had said that aboriginal people had lacked the legal capacity to negotiate with the European powers. This opinion was part of a more generalized vision of non-European people within the British Empire and, as Edward Said pointed out, was part of a 'structure of reference and feeling' that the British used to justify colonialism. 'Neither imperialism nor colonialism,' Said wrote in the early 1990s, 'is a simple act of accumulation and acquisition. Both are supported and perhaps even impelled by impressive ideological formations that include notions that certain territories and people require and beseech domination.' Such notions, he contends, also led to conceptualizing non-Europeans as wanting in the attributes European elites had retrospectively identified as essential characteristics of human life.[7] Judge Patterson's belief that the eighteenth-century Mi'kmaq were a savage and uncivilized people was characteristic of this ideological framework in which governments justified the colonization of aboriginal lands and the regulation of their communities.[8]

In an earlier book, I discussed the treaties that were the subject of Judge Patterson's decision. Then, my principal emphasis was to understand how the eighteenth-century Mi'kmaq understood the written treaty texts they had made. I concluded that from the time the first treaty was signed in 1726, the British referred less to the oral discussions that had been part of the negotiations and more to the written texts. This dissonance, which grew in correlation with British power in the region, I suggested, was at the basis of later disagreements about how the treaties should be interpreted.[9] In this book, I continue that story by examining how succeeding generations of Mi'kmaw leaders understood these same treaties.

The differences between that book and this one are many and are mainly to do with the time period studied. My previous book examined the era before 1760, in a region of the North Atlantic world relatively unpopulated and where it was still possible for aboriginal people to live outside the purview of European sight and pen although never completely hidden from them.[10] In contrast, this study examines the 1790s to the 1920s, years when Mi'kmaw access to land and to resources declined. In 1761, when the last of the major treaties was signed, the Mi'kmaq retained use of a greater part of mainland Nova Scotia and Cape Breton, while British settlement was confined to coastal outports and to farmlands along the Bay of Fundy. By the time of the Sylliboy appeal in 1928, however, most Mi'kmaw families lived on reserve and were subject to government policies aimed at assimilating them into Anglo-Canadian society. Although this process of dispossession and civilization had begun in the early 1800s, it reached its zenith with the institution of the 1876 Indian Act and a federal bureaucracy intent on enforcing the adoption of Anglo-Canadian norms of behaviour. [11] Duncan Campbell Scott, the deputy-superintendent of Indian Affairs from 1913 to 1932, expressed this policy in 1914: 'The happiest future for the Indian race is absorption into the general population, and this is the object of the policy of our government. In the Indian communities now under discussion we see the natives advanced more than halfway towards the goal, and the final result will be this complete absorption. The great forces of intermarriage and education will finally overcome the lingering traces of native custom and tradition.'[12] In other words, the purpose of Anglo-Canadian policy was to disempower the Mi'kmaq as a distinctive people and to create in their place a new proto-typical native who, to paraphrase Said, could be 'put to work.'[13] This meant changing not only what people did but also what they thought.

What transpired in Nova Scotia from the 1760s to the 1920s was not unique but was part of an 'Angloboom' that swept the globe. In this time-frame, James Belich says, the population of the Angloworld exploded, increasing sixteen fold between 1780 and 1920.[14] Nova Scotia was caught in this tidal wave and so too were the region's indigenous inhabitants, the Mi'kmaq, even though the growth of the white settler population was not always as precipitate as in other regions.[15] As a generation of scholars has pointed out, this world was 'British,' and however that culture and identity was transmitted from the metropole or was reproduced outside, the effect was palpable.[16]

This colonial world spawned a worldwide network of interlocking webs, which imperceptibly affected Jane Austen's consciousness as it did that of the Mi'kmaq. The English novel, Said argues, became a standard to identify Englishness and also helped to shape norms of behaviour in England and in its gradually widening empire of colonies, of which nineteenth-century Nova Scotia was a part, if only, a poor one. By positing what was English, the novel assisted in shaping what was not and those in need of reform, a group, which included in its ever-widening embrace, the Mi'kmaq.[17] This was, as Catherine Hall argues, a reciprocal process in which each defined the other.[18]

In the same way that the imperialist impulse for property and wealth created an ideological construct that infected the English literati, so too did it afflict those subject to its dictates. However, understanding the ways in which it did is not quite as easy as dissembling a Jane Austen novel. The Mi'kmaq were not English, nor were they often literate, and if they were literate, they did not write novels. Understanding how colonialism affected their consciousness is not easily accomplished because there are few written records we can use.

Mi'kmaw recollections of the treaties beginning in 1794 and ending with the Sylliboy case in 1928 offer one way to tackle this issue. In this book, I focus on these memories to examine how British and Canadian colonization influenced Mi'kmaw consciousness. The men's testimony at Sylliboy's trial, when combined with other documentation, shows that at regular intervals Mi'kmaw leaders complained that the government was not honouring promises made in the eighteenth century. This process of remembering was shaped by the circumstances of the men's lives, and by the circumstance of their parents, grandparents, and great-grandparents' lives. Colonization framed their lives and if read within the broader context of Nova Scotia's ascension from colony to province, these recollections illustrate how colonialism affected Mi'kmaw memories, gave those memories its force, and shaped the people who remembered them.

Colonization shaped Mi'kmaw memories from 1794 to 1928 in three ways. First, it created the conditions in which they could be remembered. Colonization isolated the Mi'kmaq economically and reinforced cultural and social bonds among individuals and communities. By linking the improvement of life with material progress, policy-makers demanded that the land be confiscated and that the Mi'kmaq and others adapt to the region's political economy of private ownership and commercial exploitation.[19] Those families who were unable, were unwilling, or were deemed incapable, were marginalized or forced to move. For the Mi'kmaq, the effect was the cohesion of social and political networks with other communities inside of Nova Scotia and outside of it. Spearheading this movement was the Grand Council, which from the early to mid-1850s worked to foster these connections. Although the council is little known, they, like other indigenous political organizations in the British World, reformed themselves in opposition to settler society. They also created linkages with other indigenous peoples associated with the Roman Catholic Church and which were the product of earlier historical relationships with the French Crown.[20]

Second, colonization shaped peoples' social relationships with non-aboriginals. The treaties and how Mi'kmaw leaders remembered them became part of this process. Like their neighbours, the Mi'kmaq also professed a loyalty to the Crown but the way they did so was differently conceived. For them, loyalty meant obeying the treaty their ancestors had signed. In the same time period that Britons, writ large, created images and models of patriotism, which included identification with the Crown, and radiated outward to the other parts of the British World, the Mi'kmaq did the same, but in different ways.[21] This process did not begin with Jane Austen's novels, but with how the Mi'kmaq understood the past, in a period when the British Empire was nowhere near as omnipotent as it would later become, and a history that the Empire was later less willing to remember. The Mi'kmaq, like other subaltern members of this world, created alternative ways of thinking about loyalty, but unlike the unruly Scots, Irish, and Acadians, their voices were less visible but more persistent, as the reforms meant to homogenize values were less successful in reforming their loyalty. Colonization therefore shaped a Mi'kmaw identity within a framework linked to the British Crown but which differed from how other Nova Scotians perceived that relationship. This jaded 'Englishness' persisted after 1867 and became the principal motif through which Gabriel Sylliboy and the other five men who testified at his appeal expressed their relationship to central authorities.[22] However, that identification was with an older vision of the Crown as benefactor and omnipotent lord whose promises could be reincarnated despite the new political and cultural boundaries created after 1867.

Finally, how leaders remembered 'the treaty' changed from generation to generation. These modifications occurred in response to colonization, which had included the imposition of a legal and institutional structure and the incremental economic changes that had forced families to seek alternative sources of income and different ways of living. This process of actively remembering the treaties reveals the evolving character of the colonial state and shifts in Mi'kmaw consciousness.[23] However, since the colonial state changed, so too did Mi'kmaw memories. To see colonialism as an all-powerful behemoth, which imposed its rule on the Mi'kmaq consistently from the 1760s, is to overestimate the power of the British Empire and of its successor in Nova Scotia, the Canadian state. The state's power was historically contingent, and so in evaluating Mi'kmaw recollections of the treaty we must pay attention to the limitations of the state's reach and power.

In the immediate aftermath of the Seven Years War, heterogeneity was the pragmatic starting point for British policy-making. It could not be otherwise, because the British government lacked the manpower to staff its ever-growing dominions and so depended on maintaining a welter of relationships with Blacks, South Asians, and Native Americans, not to mention the Scots and Irish. And it also meant not privileging one to the exclusion of others, a point, says Linda Colley, that helped fuel colonial American enmity towards British policy-makers. This created permeability between Englishness and otherness, inducing British policy-makers to view with jaded discomfort the white Englishmen who were the Empire's most visible legionnaires. As a result, the ability of white officials and colonial adjuncts to impose their will on a region's indigenous inhabitants was limited.[24] While the 1760s therefore witnessed the emergence of Britain's global empire, it was also a period of uneasiness when policy-makers and military officials held an unsteady grip over a far-flung empire, the nature of which was demonstrated by the secession of the thirteen colonies in the American Revolution.

Mi'kmaw leaders sensed this limitation and played on this weakness in their discussions in the 1790s with English officials such as the Lieutenant Governor, John Wentworth, and the Superintendent of Indian Affairs, George Henry Monk. But such expressions, while underlining Mi'kmaw independence from British authority, also signaled changes in the community's perceptions of their political position and that families exercised a relative 'liberty,' and not an absolute one.

The British government's uneasiness towards those they governed outside the British Isles continued into the early 1800s and only abated in the 1820s as a result of a concerted political and military effort to marshal the nation to maintain and to extend its overseas dominions. This was accompanied by the creation of a 'cultural framework' that viewed Englishmen as 'worthy' and culturally more advanced than others and acted, as Said says, as a justification for imperialism. This was enhanced by a broadened understanding of the country's demographic growth, underwritten by Thomas Malthus's *Essay on Population* and by nationally organized censuses that demonstrated the country's growth and vitality. By the 1850s, uneasiness about the nation's health or its military capacity to keep its empire had been banished as Great Britain emerged as the world's wealthiest industrial economy.[25] This ascension to power racialized subject peoples, like the Mi'kmaq, in ways that had not been true before, and this affected how they perceived their relationships with British officialdom. This change was visible in how a new generation of leaders recalled the treaties in the 1820s when they began emphasizing the integration of the Mi'kmaq into Nova Scotian society, made with the assistance of overseas adjuncts of a metropolitain-centred humanitarian movement. By the 1850s the tone had changed again and leaders now pleaded the poverty of their people and begged for the Crown's assistance. This plea, however, was less welcomed than earlier petitions, reflecting the diminished influence of humanitarians, a change in how their proponents now viewed non-whites within the British world, and the British government's movement away from responsibility for its colonial possessions in North America.[26] Mi'kmaw leaders and their supporters in Nova Scotia sensed this change in metropolitain sentiments and began viewing the eighteenth-century treaties as legal documents which represented the King's law and to which the monarch should hold civil officials accountable, an issue that exposed the contradiction in colonial jurisdictions and the historic conflicts between the Crown and Parliament.[27]

Colonization evolved after the confederation of Canada, New Brunswick and Nova Scotia in 1867, and later inclusion of the Northwest and British Columbia. This new stage of colonialism was partly the result of industrialization and of the enhanced economic and political unity forged by the completion of the Intercolonial Railway in 1876 and the earlier provincial railway system.[28] It also stemmed from the centralization of power in Ottawa that led to efforts to assimilate aboriginal peoples into Anglo-Canadian society, which by the late nineteenth and early twentieth centuries, had become more firmly entrenched as the dominant national motif. Assimilation had always been implicit in British colonial schemes but only in the late nineteenth century did this idea reach its apogee with the transformation of Canada into a new transcontinental free trade zone. The change in British North America's economic and political status stemmed from changes in the British world. These changes included Great Britain's dismantling of mercantilist tariffs, the growing power of the United States, industrialization, and the transportation revolution introduced by railways. This made aboriginals a subject of more pressing concern than before and mainly because the settlement of the Northwest necessitated the state's intervention in a more forceful manner than in the more settled regions, where Indians had been subdued, if only imperfectly. Despite these differences the change in responsibility towards aboriginals as wards of the new federal state, and its escalating financial and political power, made the Mi'kmaq a subject of government attention in a manner that had not been seen before 1867.

With more Mi'kmaw families living on or frequenting reserves after 1867, governments were more successful in reshaping their values and attitudes. Although people resisted government fiats, their ability to do so was circumscribed by economic impoverishment. In response, the Grand Council developed new strategies of resistance, although such efforts were always tempered by accommodation. By the early 1920s, this had led Mi'kmaw leaders to use the courts to assert its interpretation of the eighteenth-century treaties. This was only possible, however, because of jurisdictional disputes between provincial and federal governments. The Mi'kmaq were able to use this favourable situation to challenge Nova Scotia's claims to determine the use of non-reserve lands and resources. By the early 1900s therefore, the treaties had become a source of rights and were part of a broader debate about the place of aboriginal people within the nation state. The King's law continued to form the basis of Mi'kmaw appeals as it had the century before, but resolution was now sought through domestic courts and not through reference to external institutions, such as the Colonial Office. This change in orientation altered Mi'kmaw memories, as leaders were now forced to consciously adapt their memories to the directives of a text-driven court system, a pattern that has continued to shape how later generations have understood their history.

Because memory and its transmission play an important role in this study, some preliminary remarks about these two issues are necessary. Studies that employ memory as an analytical tool have assumed various forms.[29] One approach is to examine collective memories. 'Collective memories' concern how a society or a community remembers the past or a past event. Those who study collective memory might anaylse how and why such memories are formed, sometimes tracing their development over generations, at other times focusing on specific events or historical periods to elucidate broader cultural trends.[30] In Canada, the most common approach has been the study of commemoration. This entails deciphering a commemorative event or a historical figure to chart how various generations have remembered history, people, and events. The resulting analyses are useful for understanding how memory became subject to manipulation as well as for evaluating changing norms, including attitudes about aboriginal people. Coates and Morgan, Knowles, Nelles, and Pope, for instance, all explore how aboriginal peoples were perceived in the late nineteenth and early twentieth centuries and show how succeeding generations obscured or rationalized the appropriation of aboriginal lands and justified assimilationist policies. As Pope explains about the commemoration of Cabot's landfall, 'The whole point of the landfall myth was that discovery was a precedent: North America was meant to be British; conquest was merely incidental. At least in public, the history of discovery was a substitute for other histories, a useful diversion from the issues of ethnic dominance, coercion, and dependency that we cram clumsily into the concept of conquest.'[31]

In contrast, my interest is in the inter-generational remembering of a collected memory. I focus on how a small group of men remembered what they had been told about an event in their people's history. My subjects are five of the six men who testified in Sylliboy's appeal. As Jeffrey Olick points out, a collected memory approach has distinct advantages. First, it potentially avoids the reification of a particular set of memories as is true of commemorative studies, which focus on a subset within a group and usually on individuals with access 'to the means of cultural production, or whose opinions are more highly valued.' Although Bodnar's distinction between official and vernacular memory is one way to avoid this problem, the emphasis on charting societal norms renders detailed understandings of individual memories unworkable or if the focus does switch to the individual, does not obviate reification. Second, a collected memory approach does not necessarily assume the existence of a collective memory and allows for differences in how memories are remembered. Finally, focusing on individuals allows the use of psychology and neuroscience.[32]

The disciplines of psychology and neuroscience provide ways to think about and to analyse the transmission of memories across generations. As Daniel Schacter shows in his overview about how people remember the past, the act of remembering is always an active process, in terms of what individuals choose to remember, how they encode the information, and how they recall it.[33] In Olick's words, the brain does not act as a perfect repository of data from which memories can be instantly recalled. Rather, storing memories in the brain is 'an active process of construction and reconstruction in time.'

Mnemonic devices can help to recall an event and so minimize the agency of remembering. Although the Mi'kmaq did use mnemonic methods to recall past events, I have assumed that the five men remembered the treaty mainly through what they had heard and what they had witnessed even though they probably did have access to other texts. Indeed, when first accosted by a forest ranger in November 1927, Sylliboy said that he was protected by treaty and could show the ranger a copy of it. However, neither Sylliboy nor the other four men referred to a text in their testimony. Nor did they refer to any other 'text.' In the absence of evidence, I have centred my analysis on their testimony, which suggested that their understanding of the treaty was formed from personal memories.

These memories consisted of two types. Sometimes, the men spoke of time-specific memories and at other times of memories spanning years. Both of these we might call part of their long-term memory, which psychologists often distinguish from short-term or working memory.[34] The men also referred to different kinds of events. As David Lowenthal tells us, memories are intensely personal, relating specific incidents, feelings, and smells that are intrinsically are own. For this reason, memories are also 'crucial for our sense of identity. To know what we were confirms that we are.'[35] The psychologist Daniel Schacter explains there is a structure that underlies the stories we tell about our lives. This structure divides our autobiographical memories into three layers. At the most general level are the stories that might span years or decades, the next level relates events covering days, weeks, or even months while the final level recounts time-specific events that might last only minutes or hours. In retelling stories about their lives, individuals usually intersplice all three different memory types.[36] In their testimony, the men related lifetime stories from their childhood but also recounted stories that could only have lasted a day or two. As well, such memories are usually tied to specific individuals. As Irving Hallowell found after living among the Aninshinabeg of northwestern Ontario in the 1920s and 1930s, events that occurred in the past are correlated 'with the life-span of certain deceased relatives or other deceased persons.'[37] This is also true of the men's testimony.

In contrast to such memories, other parts of the men's testimony relate information they had received from their parents or from others.

Joe Christmas said that he heard that the Mi'kmaq got the right to hunt and fish from 'our grandfathers.' Andrew Bernard said that his father had told him that the Mi'kmaq got the right to hunt and to fish from the treaty while Francis Gould said he heard about the treaty from his grandfather. Gabriel Sylliboy, on the other hand, said 'Since I was boy heard that Indians got from King free hunting and fishing at all times,' suggesting that his memory came from a community-held memory and was not associated with a specific individual.[38] Although these memories are also private, they purport to describe inter-generational oral transmissions. Because these memories do not deal with specific events or individuals we might term them 'semantic memories.' Geoffrey Cubitt defines semantic memories as those that contain 'factual or conceptual information, of a kind that can be abstracted from the circumstances of its acquisition.'[39]

The men's testimony therefore contains multiple layers, which must be analysed in different ways. Some memories, which relate to specific events in their lives, had become intermeshed with a history of the treaty. For instance, each of the men believed that the act of receiving goods was a confirmation of the treaty's validity. But that memory was different from what their parents and grandparents had told them. Thus, in analysing the men's testimony, we will need to distinguish between the men's active ways of remembering and other memories that recall conversations with relatives.

This analysis is only possible because of the age of the men, their residency, and because of additional documentation linking their memories with the generations before. Five of the men had been born in the mid- to late 1800s, had lived their lives in Cape Breton, and had assumed positions of leadership within each of their communities. Four of the men were born between 1850 and 1854 and were between 74 and 78 years of age in 1928. Gabriel Sylliboy was born in 1875 and so was 53 years old. Although each man came from Cape Breton they were from different communities; Andrew Alek was from Chapel Island, Andrew Bernard was from Wagmatcook, Joe Christmas was from Sydney, Francis Gould was from Eskasoni, and Gabriel Sylliboy was from Whycocomagh. The way they had lived their lives also differed. Some had always lived in the same community, others had moved, some to the city. Regardless of their personal life stories, however, each of the men had assumed leadership positions and was connected to the Grand Council, a political body uniting reserve communities throughout Cape Breton and mainland Nova Scotia. In 1928, Gabriel Sylliboy was the Grand Chief, Andrew Alek was the Putus, or adviser and keeper of the treaties, while Joe Christmas had previously served as an assistant to the Grand Chief. Thus, there is much about the men that links them and makes their memories reflective of broader community understandings.

The men also represent a generation who were less affected by the reform movement, which in the late nineteenth and early twentieth centuries reshaped the attitudes, values, and consciousness of aboriginal men and women. This reshaping of Mi'kmaw interior life assumed many different forms, but included material changes, such as the introduction of on-reserve housing, cultural changes such as the beginnings of compulsory education, economic changes such as the integration of men and women into the wage labour economy, and political changes that would revolutionize how band governments were elected and how they functioned. Because the men were less affected by these changes, their testimony is a unique opportunity to examine what a group of men born before industrialization and before the introduction of a pervasive school system thought and remembered about their peoples' history.

Through all of this I have assumed that memories about the treaty were affected by the social and cultural context in which they were transmitted. As Geoffrey Cubitt explains, this approach assumes that 'individuals always remember in social contexts, and the ways in which they remember cannot be coherently understood unless the influences that govern those contexts and the terms of their engagement in them are thoroughly examined.'[40]

The idea for this book developed in the months after the Supreme Court of Canada's September 1999 ruling in *R.* v. *Donald Marshall Junior*. Marshall, a Mi'kmaw man from Cape Breton Island, had been charged with fishing and selling fish without a commercial license. At the time he was charged, Marshall was required by statute to buy a license from the federal government to sell fish to commercial vendors. The Nova Scotia Mi'kmaq challenged the government's legislative authority, arguing that the eighteenth-century treaties provided them with a right to fish and to sell fish. They accepted the government's prerogative to regulate the fishery, but they believed authorities did not have the unilateral right to determine how, where, and when Mi'kmaw people could fish. The government disagreed and said that in signing the treaties, the Mi'kmaq had agreed to live within Canada's legislative system. This was necessary, said the government, because only it had the ability to work in the interests of all Canadians and to ensure that fish stocks were preserved as a renewable resource. If the government did not regulate the number of commercial licenses and the amount of fish each licensee harvested, then the fish stocks would be destroyed. This was as true for eels as it was for any other species, including crabs, lobsters, and scallops. The Mi'kmaq countered that the present-day fishery had only come about because their ancestors had agreed to make peace with the British. Therefore, the government should honour the spirit of the treaties before determining who should have the right to fish and to sell fish. In other words, as the signatories to the treaties, the Mi'kmaq had a prior right to Atlantic Canada's fishery and this right should be honoured before determining other peoples' rights. The government said everyone should have an equal right but prioritized those who already had made a financial commitment to the industry by purchasing a license. The Mi'kmaq had neither and so they tended to interpret the rhetoric about 'equal access' as a legal justification to exclude them.[41]

On 19 September 1999, the Supreme Court released its decision. In a 5–2 decision, the court set aside Marshall's conviction and found federal fisheries legislation to be an infringement on his treaty rights. The court focused its attention, not on the 1752 treaty, as Sylliboy had done in 1927–8, but on a series of treaties the Mi'kmaq and British had signed in 1760 and 1761. Drawing on its previous rulings,[42] the Court found that eighteenth-century officials had implicitly promised that the Mi'kmaq would have a right to sell their fish at British run truckhouses. This right, said the Court, was protected by the Constitution since the government had not abrogated the treaties before 1982 when the Constitution was formally patriated. Federal fisheries statutes legislating Mi'kmaw fishermen to purchase a license from the government were therefore an unreasonable burden and interfered with those constitutional rights.[43]

The implications of the decision were clear: the government would have to allow Mi'kmaq to fish commercially. This meant changing the present regulations. Since the Mi'kmaq were coastal fishers any new arrangement would hurt non-native fishers. The result of the Supreme Court's decision therefore was to bring the Mi'kmaq into conflict with inshore fishermen.

Up until about forty to fifty years ago, inshore fishermen caught different kinds of species: ground fish such as cod, hake, and halibut as well as shellfish, such as crabs and lobsters. Today's inshore fishermen tend to fish one species, not several. This change has occurred for two reasons: a change in how fish are caught and marketed and a change in government regulations regarding when fish are caught and how many. These changes began to be made in the 1960s and 1970s, as the region's fishing capacity increased and with it, a jump in the number of landings and the number of species caught. In response, the federal government began restricting the number of commercial fishermen. This was done through a licensing system that placed limits on each fisherman's harvest.[44] The new system did not benefit inshore fishermen. Some stopped catching groundfish and spent more time fishing other species. One of those species was lobster.

Lobster was an appealing catch because from 1962 to 1983 its average price per pound increased almost six-fold.[45] The money was good through the 1970s and 1980s as landings increased and prices rose. But this newfound wealth also came at a cost: dependence on one species made fishermen vulnerable to fluctuations in the stock, to price, and to the intrusion of new players, like the Mi'kmaq.

In 1999 when the Supreme Court released its decision in *R. v. Marshall*, there were few, if any, Mi'kmaw lobster fishermen. This was because when the government began regulating the lobster fishery – much in the same way as they later did groundfish – there were no Mi'kmaq stakeholders and so they didn't receive any licenses. By the 1980s the lack of Mi'kmaw licensees was a problem since the numbers were fixed. If they weren't and a new license was issued every time someone wanted one, the stock would eventually be destroyed. But by the late 1980s and early 1990s, some Mi'kmaw leaders believed their communities' exclusion from the lobster fishery – and the commercial fishery in general – was symptomatic of a government policy which marginalized their peoples' participation in the economy.

The upshot was that prior to the Supreme Court's decision in September 1999, there were simmering tensions between Mi'kmaw and non-Mi'kmaw fishermen. On one side were the professional non-aboriginal fishermen who, in some cases, were indebted to finance their operations. On the other side were the Mi'kmaq who were either unemployed or underemployed and who wanted to catch lobster to make some money.[46]

The 'lobster wars' which resulted from the Supreme Court's Marshall decision in September 1999 and that pitted non-native fishermen against those Mi'kmaq who sought a privileged right to the fishery illuminated different interpretations of Canada's past. The focus was the 1760 treaty, which had formed the basis of the court's ruling. Each side interpreted the treaty differently. To many fishermen, the meaning of the treaty was unambiguous: the Mi'kmaq were subject to federal legislation. If they were no longer fishing, it was because of their profligate ways, not because they had been treated unfairly. To Acadian fishermen, the first European settlers had been a hard working people whose labour had helped to create a land of plenty. The Mi'kmaq had not participated in this grand enterprise but now they wanted to take what had been sown. The Mi'kmaq saw things differently. They viewed themselves as victims whose land was stolen and whose participation in the maritime economy had been marginalized. Forced away from fishing sites, their population had declined and their families had been left to eke out a living on lands lacking the resources available to other Atlantic Canadians. If the Mi'kmaq were no longer part of the fishing community, their leaders said, it was because of a deliberate policy of legal apartheid. While some people might challenge that view, it is a perception that many aboriginal people in Atlantic Canada in the 1990s shared.

That perception did not suddenly emerge in the 1990s but was imbedded in the consciousness of those who had occupied positions of leadership within the Mi'kmaw community from the time the Union of Nova Scotia Indians was formed in 1969. This provincial organization, which was created in the wake of the Trudeau government's ill-fated White Paper, worked closely with Nova Scotia members of the Grand Council in devising the legal and political strategy that would lead to the Supreme Court rulings in Simon (1985) and Marshall (1999). This generation of leaders were, both culturally and politically, tied to Gabriel Sylliboy and to others of his generation.[47] In the pages that follow, I examine the historical roots of these peoples' historical consciousness by analysing the memories of Gabriel Sylliboy and four other men who together formed a critical link with the leaders who later would make the decisions that would lead to the Supreme Court Rulings in Simon (1985) and Marshall (1999).

Doing so presents special challenges. Historians have often used court cases to inquire into social relationships. Since such treatments also focus on cases heard before the superior courts, they give insight into how and why important legal precedents were made, why attempts to do so were rejected by the higher courts, and how public pressure affected juridical decisions.[48] Canadian historians have adopted a similar approach, some of who have written about aboriginal people.[49] Shelagh Grant, for instance, in her examination of an Inuit man from Baffin Island charged with a 1921 murder, uses the resulting court case to illustrate the social and legal relationships within Inuit society and their relationship with outsiders, including the Canadian government.[50]

These studies, however, are only possible because the cases produced an extensive documentation. The same is not true for Sylliboy. There are no court transcripts and there is little press commentary. Moreover, since the magistrate's decision was only appealed to the County Court, the case did not produce much additional commentary. Since Sylliboy was charged with a summary offence, his prosecution also did not initiate much investigation or testimony and the magistrate court records only include testimony of the prosecution's witnesses.[51] The appeal notes are also brief and do not include either an oral summary of the lawyer's arguments or a printed copy of their factums. Besides a typed copy of the decision, the appeal file contains a series of historical documents, which the defence lawyers entered as evidence. These include a treaty signed with the Abenaki in 1727, the 1752 treaty, the Royal Proclamation of 1763, excerpts from Thomas Akin's 1869 history of Halifax City, and minutes from various meetings of the Nova Scotia Council, the eighteenth-century Crown-appointed body that ruled the colony. Although useful for situating the lawyers' use of historical evidence, this documentation does not explain what occurred in Judge Patterson's courtroom. The appeal packet, however, does contain one additional piece of evidence: Judge Patterson's summary of six Mi'kmaw men's testimony about their understanding of the 1752 Treaty. These five pages of testimony offer a unique insight into the men's lives and into their collected memory about the treaty.[52]

This small compendium of documents from Sylliboy's conviction and appeal is the frame that holds this book together. I use the men's testimony as a reference point. Although my main purpose is to understand the historical evolution of the community's understanding of the eighteenth-century treaties, I have organized the book around one question: why was Sylliboy's conviction appealed. The men would not have had the opportunity to testify unless a series of intersecting events occurred. In the book, I group the issues that propelled the case forward into three separate themes.

In Part One, I examine how and why Sylliboy's actions from the 31 October to 4 November 1927 led to his subsequent appearance before a magistrate in mid-November and then before Judge Patterson of the County Court on 2 July 1928. This section of the book assumes that the law may make an act criminal but that only people working within the justice system criminalize a person's actions. I argue that the appeal could only have occurred because of decisions made at the local, regional, provincial, and national levels. In addressing this issue I analyse the motivations of the individuals connected to the events that led to Sylliboy's appearance in magistrate court on 19 November 1927 and that would eventually lead to the appeal. This includes Alex Gillis, the man who spotted Sylliboy camping on his property, Malcolm MacKinnon, the local forest ranger who obtained a warrant to search Sylliboy's tent, and Otto Schierbeck, the province's Chief Forest Ranger, who chose to prosecute Sylliboy. The appeal was also dependent on the defendant's, and the lawyers', willingness to contest the magistrate's decision. In other words, they all must have believed that Sylliboy was innocent. Therefore this section of the book also focuses on the period before 1927 when the Mi'kmaq had claimed a treaty right to hunt and to fish irrespective of government legislation. I also analyse the federal government's motives since it was their decision to pay for Sylliboy's defence lawyers that made the appeal possible.

As the men's appeal testimony shows, their understanding of the treaty was based on the memory of what their parents and grandparents had told them and helps to understand why the appeal was made. In the second section of the book, I therefore trace the historical evolution of how Mi'kmaw leaders understood the treaty from the late 1700s to the late 1800s. These years coincide with the time period when the men as well as their great-grandparents, grandparents, and parents were born and so understanding these years provides an important link between the men's court testimony in 1928 and the memories transmitted to them. Analysis shows, I contend, a shift in how successive generations understood the treaty. In Chapter Four, I do so through reference to statements attributed to Mi'kmaw leaders in 1794, 1825, 1849, and 1853. I cannot directly link the men's families with the statements of Mi'kmaw leaders, but I suggest that they would have eventually come to share similar ideas, even though not always at the same time. Chapter Five continues this discussion by examining how the men came to understand the treaties in the way they did, using their testimony and then exploring their lives in the years before 1928. Both of these chapters therefore are focused on the act of remembering, and focus on a period when the community's memory of the treaty changed.

Despite these changes in how the treaty was recalled the men would not have remembered it in the way they did unless their life experiences had demonstrated the need to do so. Thus, in the final section of the book, I examine the men's personal lives that gave voice to their memories. Each of the men lived through a tumultuous period in global history, years that witnessed the mass migration of people from rural to urban areas, from one region to another, and across oceans. These events also affected Nova Scotians and we might see the Mi'kmaq as part of this global pattern. However, their lives were also different from the norm because they were Indians. As Indians, the men were wards of a paternalistic state, which infantilized their actions and saw them as requiring special attention and a firm disciplinary hand. This policy, however, instead of fostering their integration into Nova Scotian society, did the opposite and marginalized their household economies by confining them to reserves.

Part III therefore focuses on the late nineteenth and early twentieth centuries, years which witnessed these tumultuous events. In Chapter Six I focus on 1881 to 1911, years that spanned the men's middle age. This was a time when the men married, had children, and when their children married. These were also years when most had difficulties in making ends meet. Chapter Seven continues this narrative, by examining what happened to families who had moved to Sydney, Cape Breton Island to improve their lives. The resulting attempts by local elites to remove the community exposed the fault lines between a racialized view of aboriginal people and the government's declared intention of assimilating them into Anglo-Canadian society. Together, these chapters illustrate how the Mi'kmaw lived experience differed from other Atlantic Canadians and so helps to understand the conditions that made the act of remembering the treaty possible.

This analysis is based entirely on the documentary record and has not involved interviewing current members of the Mi'kmaw community. The events described here date from 1794 to 1928. Although there are individuals alive today who were born before 1928, they would not have any memory of the Sylliboy trial, except what their parents and grandparents had told them. Since the principal argument advanced here is that memories are framed by an individual's historical experience, the usage of oral interviews would only be useful for understanding Mi'kmaw memories of the treaty after 1928, not before. This, it seems to me, is a separate project and beyond the scope of the present book.

This book is ambitious in terms of time, space, and purpose. My geographical area is all of present-day Nova Scotia, though at times that focus is narrowed to just Cape Breton Island, the multi-fingered land surface that juts out from Nova Scotia's (and Canada's) mainland. My time frame is also ambitious, the century and a half before 1928. Although some might question the viability of covering such a long period,

I would counter, paraphrasing Fernand Braudel, that only in the long time frame can trends become clear. This is important to do when we examine aboriginal communities because we have few angles from which to view them. A longer period of study, however, gives a variety of differently angled shots to project a panoramic view of the landscapes and of the people.

My purpose in all of this is to conceptualize what was inside the men's minds when they testified in Judge Patterson's courtroom. I do not pretend that my conclusions about their consciousness are entirely accurate. Historians can never fully reconstruct a person's mind and understand why they think what they think. I would say, however, that what follows is a reasonable reconstruction and that is as much as any historian can say.

PART ONE

Why the Men Testified

1 Accounting for Alex Gillis's Actions: The Mi'kmaq in Rural Society

When he was accosted in early November 1927, Sylliboy was violating two different provincial statutes: he was trapping muskrat during closed season and he was camping on private land. He had also built a fire, which may not have been illegal but would have elicited a sharp rebuke from the Provincial Forester. For Sylliboy to be charged with violating the Lands and Forest Act, a number of intersecting events had to occur and decisions made about whether further actions were warranted. In this section of the book, I explain why Sylliboy was charged and tried, and why he appealed his conviction.

I am concerned with three issues: first, the local context of rural Nova Scotia that led people to complain about Mi'kmaw hunting out of season and which would eventually lead to Sylliboy's confrontation with a local forest ranger; second, the impetus behind the provincial government's decision to charge and to try Sylliboy; and third why the Mi'kmaq and the Canadian government wanted an appeal made of the magistrate's judgment. Each of these issues helps us to understand why the Sylliboy case came before the courts and how the five men came to testify at the appeal.

This chapter explains why in early November 1927 Alex Gillis of Askilton, a small village just south of the Bras d'Or Lakes of Cape Breton Island, laid a complaint against Gabriel Sylliboy. I cannot state definitively why Gillis did so, but I contend that his decision to travel to West Bay and talk to the local forest ranger reflected a seething resentment against people hunting and trapping out of season. Although rural residents had not always agreed with the game statutes and had resented how the legislation interfered with where, when, and how they could hunt, by the 1920s some had accepted that regulation was necessary and were willing to inform against their neighbours and especially against people from outside the community. Not everyone accepted this credo. But despite the lack of a consensus, most rural residents opposed granting the Mi'kmaq a right that would have privileged their access to game over others. To most rural residents, this did not seem fair and accentuated the differences between them and the Mi'kmaq.

These differences had been accelerating since the advent of the social reform movement the century before. This movement, which attempted to reform labouring peoples' norms of behaviour to make them consistent with middle-class ideas, emphasized that people be able to restrain their physical and emotional impulses. Closely associated with the development of a disciplined industrial work force, this movement stressed the redeeming value of education, which, in British North America, also imparted conceptions of citizenship and of duty to nation and to Empire. The success of this movement was never complete, nor did it proceed at the same pace in every region of the country.

The Mi'kmaq, like other subaltern members of the British world required special attention. The federal Indian Act of 1876, which made 'Indians' wards of the paternalistic state, exemplified the Canadian state's intention of reforming aboriginal peoples' interior lives, although such policies were not always immediately or successively implemented. Industrialization accelerated this trend and so too did the gradual extension of the state's financial and political power in the late nineteenth and early twentieth centuries. These policies represented a new stage in the colonization of Mi'kmaw communities. This process, which had begun in the early 1600s with French settlement and continued afterwards with the signing of treaties with representatives of the British Crown between 1726 and 1779, had resulted in families' diminished access to lands and to resources. Only in the 1850s did this lead to settlement onto reserves, although this was never, as we shall see, complete. From the 1850s colonization began to assume new forms, embarking on a more consistent and pervasive penetration into Mi'kmaw family life. Paralleling similar movements towards the labouring classes, this movement never had the same effect, a result mostly of the social and spatial distances between the Mi'kmaq and others and the racialized underpinnings motivating government policies.

The consequence was to enlarge differences in how aboriginals and non-aboriginals conceptualized their relationships with central authorities. By reformulating peoples' interior lives, the reform movement tempered differences between communities, races, and ethnicities. Changes in how ordinary peoples conceptualized themselves in relation to others were also enhanced by the formation of local historical societies, the writing of local histories, and the celebration of historical events, such as the Champlain tercentenary.[1] The building of a transcontinental railway, which symbolized the triumph of technology over the wilderness, and united, however imperfectly, peoples' identification with ideas of progress and with each other, also created commonalities out of difference.[2] By articulating a common identity, such ideas and events helped create conditions in which rural residents were more likely to accept government justifications for regulation of hunting and trapping than were the Mi'kmaq.

In Nova Scotia, these differences affected how rural Nova Scotians viewed Mi'kmaw claims to be protected by treaty. Because the Mi'kmaq did not share similar attitudes towards the law, some rural residents were angered by actions that contravened wildlife legislation. This in itself may not have been an unusual reaction. After all, there were many poor farmers and labourers who hunted and trapped out of season as well. The response of rural residents to the Mi'kmaq, however, was much harsher. Alex Gillis was a farmer and owned, as he told the magistrate at Sylliboy's summary hearing in November 1927, several hundred acres along the Long Stretch Road. Gabriel Sylliboy was neither. He was neither a farmer nor was he a landowner. Sylliboy was an Indian and it was this identity that defined him. That perception was an important one. When Gillis saw Sylliboy on his property on 31 October, he did not see Sylliboy. He saw an Indian. As he said, 'I made out they were Indians,' a designation that summoned up all the distrust and suspicion that had characterized relationships between the two communities for more than a century and which the reform movement of the late nineteenth and early twentieth centuries had sharpened. The prosecution of Gabriel Sylliboy was not therefore the result of a timely set of circumstances. It occurred because Alex Gillis shared with many other rural Nova Scotians common attitudes about progress and private property and therefore was willing to invoke the power of the law when he found Sylliboy and his companions camping on his property.

Sylliboy and the Jeddores were all from Whycocomagh, a Mi'kmaw reserve on the northwest shore of the Bras d'Or Lakes. Sylliboy later said that he had been hunting muskrat every fall for the previous thrirty-four years and no one had objected during all that time, and so did not understand what the fuss was about now. The man responsible for provincial wildlife enforcement during the early 1920s, J.A. Knight, would have disagreed. In 1922 and again in 1924, Knight had received written complaints that area Mi'kmaq were hunting muskrat during closed season. Knight responded by instructing the local forest ranger to investigate, and although there were signs that someone was trapping illegally, attempts to catch the culprits were unsuccessful.[3] Thus, the events that ended with Sylliboy's apprehension on 4 November 1927 reflected a simmering enmity towards Mi'kmaq who were breaking the law.

Alex Gillis lived at Askilton, a small village between Port Hastings and West Bay. Gillis later testified that he saw two men 'coming up from a Lake' and that Gabriel Sylliboy was carrying 'two muskrats, a gun and some traps.' Gillis told the men they were trespassing on his property and told them to leave. Sylliboy replied that they were not doing any harm but that they would leave that night. But they did not. At that point Gillis could have simply ignored the men and waited until they had left. Instead, he traveled to West Bay and informed the local forest ranger, Malcolm MacKinnon, that Sylliboy and the Jeddores were camping on his land and were trapping muskrats. The latter, MacKinnon would have known, was in violation of the Lands and Forests Act, which forbade the killing of muskrats from 1 February to 15 November. It was on that basis that MacKinnon traveled to Gillis's farm on 3 November to confront the three men. MacKinnon told them to leave. They agreed to do so. However, since the three did not, MacKinnon again traveled to Askilton the next day, this time with a warrant, which allowed him to search Sylliboy's camp. Finding fourteen muskrat skins and one fox skin in his possession, MacKinnon charged Sylliboy and the Jeddores with hunting muskrat during closed season.[4]

The pace of these events suggests the difficulties of enforcing the law in rural areas as well as the independence with which forest rangers operated. MacKinnon's part-time employment may have prevented a more timely intervention. MacKinnon was not a young man, and the job offered a steady wage for not a lot of effort. It is also possible that he was not keen to charge the three men and that he had delayed traveling to Askilton to give them time to depart. The men had already told Gillis that they intended to leave, and perhaps MacKinnon believed that he should give them more time to do so. Moreover, even after MacKinnon had confronted the three men, the necessity of traveling back to West Bay to obtain a warrant gave Sylliboy and the Jeddores another opportunity to escape prosecution. But once MacKinnon had returned and found the muskrat furs, he had no choice but to take action. All of this suggests that MacKinnon may not have been keen to charge Sylliboy and had given him and his companions a chance to decamp.

As Tina Loo has pointed out, before 1945 communities across Canada continued to exercise some control over conservation measures. The Canadian experience, she says, differed from the United States where game legislation led to the creation of a 'national commons.' In Canada, Loo writes, provincial jurisdiction over game did not immediately lead to complete delocalization and rather a central bureaucracy worked in tandem with local 'practical' men who knew the woods and the populace. These men had the skills and the knowledge, which informed central authorities about wildlife populations and could also catch the malefactors.[5] The events surrounding Sylliboy's arrest would seem to accord with Loo's conclusion, and we might suggest that MacKinnon's foot-dragging shows the ways in which local wardens and rangers could influence how and when action was taken.

What this reading of MacKinnon's motives misses, however, is Gillis's involvement. Residents like Alex Gillis initiated many local investigations and prosecutions, either by complaining about illegal hunting to authorities in Halifax or by taking their complaints directly to a local ranger, as Gillis had done. Such actions showed that some rural residents were concerned about illegal hunting and were willing to do something about it. Indeed, 'localization' encompasses a broad array of individuals, including ordinary property owners like Alex Gillis.

Much has been written about how rural residents, including aboriginal people, resisted the new regulatory conventions regarding hunting and fishing.[6] Parenteau and Judd in their overview of game and fish enforcement in the northern New England States and the Maritimes in the late nineteenth century point out the various reasons for rural residents' unhappiness. At times, this resulted in violence or the threat of it and at other times assumed a more muted format. Such resistance continued into the 1920s, writes Tina Loo, citing several examples from Nova Scotia where ordinary people actively opposed the new legislation. During J.A. Knight's tenure as game commissioner between 1907 and 1926, for instance, he faced a plethora of problems. To cite just one example: in the early 1920s, one of Knight's appointees, C.C. Burrell traveled through Queen's and Shelburne counties trying to 'find suitable men to act as game wardens' but found filling the posts difficult. Some men did not want the work because it offered only partial employment. Others feared retaliation. John Robbins of Yarmouth County discovered how his neighbours felt when they burnt his timber.[7] In other places like Port Mouton in Queen's County, everyone was either a poacher 'or in sympathy with them,' making it impossible to find men willing to do the job. And Port Mouton wasn't the only problem. At Barrington Passage, Burrell went to see a Mr Lewis who is 'magistrate for that section, at first I thought I had found a man who could be depended on in game matters, but I found my mistake. I cannot understand these people.'[8] All of this shows that at the time of MacKinnon's confrontation with Sylliboy and the Jeddores, there were many Nova Scotians who were passively or actively refusing to abide by the game statutes.

But Game Commissioner Knight's files also contain letters from a more cooperative group. These residents complained that their neighbours were hunting in closed season or were exceeding bag limits. For Knight, these letters were useful, because every time a complaint was made, he instructed the local warden to investigate. Sometimes this investigation led to catching the culprit, other times not. The important point is that without some rural cooperation, game enforcement could not have had much success. Resistance there continued to be in the 1920s, but acceptance as well.[9]

The question we need to ask is why people whose lives had been affected, sometimes adversely, by the imposition of the new regulations, informed against their neighbours and why they also targeted Mi'kmaw hunters and trappers. This is all the more puzzling given that sportsmen had been influential in framing game legislation in a way that had undermined rural access.

In the Maritimes and the northern New England states, the first legislation that regulated hunting and trapping reflected the growing importance of sports hunting and the attempts made by its proponents to reshape the rural landscape in ways more amenable to sportsmen's interests. This meant criminalizing rural practices, like jacking and snaring, and introducing other measures more conducive to the sportsman's concept of fair play.[10] Although this legislation was also precipitated by concern about how colonization had reduced wildlife populations, sportsmen were instrumental in framing legislation that would preserve fish and wildlife for their use. As Louis Warren points out in his study of the Pennsylvania game laws, 'Now, instead of selling meat or hides, the hunt itself was for sale. Strictly speaking, the game was not for sale; the opportunity to walk the fields with a gun (and fire it) was. The commodity was no longer deer [or other game] but the activity.'[11] The end result was a shift in the relationship between wildlife and people. No longer was this relationship to be based on rural peoples' needs. Rather, the new concept of citizenship meant that wildlife was to be used for non-commercial and non- consumptive purposes.[12] This was an important change and one that would figure in how rural Nova Scotians, including Alex Gillis, would view Gabriel Sylliboy's actions.

In Nova Scotia, the effect of this movement began to be felt in the early 1860s, when the scope of game regulations became more varied and numerous, gradually imposing a stricter regimen on what, when, and how people could hunt. Before 1900, this mainly consisted of limiting trapping and hunting to specific times of the year, with the most severe restrictions placed on moose, caribou, and beaver.[13] From the late 1800s, however, the government also began limiting the hunting of other species and regulating hunting practices as well. By the time Sylliboy was charged in 1927, the moose hunting season was limited to the period from 1 October to 16 November and that for rabbits and hares from 1 November to 1 March. The killing of mink, otter, raccoon and muskrat was forbidden from 1 February to 15 November, while the trapping of beaver, fisher, and marten was banned entirely. As well, hunters were forbidden to use dogs, snares, or artificial lights. They also faced a bag limit on herbivores, were restricted from selling moose meat except for sixteen days from mid-October, and had to pay for hunting moose or deer or for helping those who did. Fees were introduced initially for non-residents and their guides but by the 1920s all hunters had to pay a two-dollar licensing fee.[14] All of this attests to the degree to which government from the late 1800s restricted rural hunting practices and created conditions in which sport hunting could flourish.

Some members of Nova Scotia's House of Assembly were not happy with the new arrangements and let their fellow members know it. As one member, Michael Keefe, told the Assembly in 1902: 'We [are] going back to the days when a man was not permitted to shoot on his own land, while a privileged few could ride over it in pursuit of game and trample down his crops.' It was time, the member added, 'that the legislature should consider the interests of the natives of the soil, and not those coming outside with a game license.' Charles Cooper, a member from Queen's County, was more blunt when arguing against an amendment that would have further restricted the moose hunting season, a move which, in his opinion, privileged the right of the sportsmen over the poor person: 'the legislation the game society sought to introduce was class legislation of the most objectionable kind for the special benefit of sportsmen, who were very few in number.'[15]

The new regulations adversely affected rural areas but did not always have the intended result. So long as their communities were inaccessible to people from away, residents had little to fear and could just as easily ignore the regulations, as they could accept them. However, by the 1920s, there was more acceptance. To be sure, there was still resistance, particularly in those regions where residents combined multiple occupations, and where trapping and hunting was an additional source of food and income. These communities, as Parenteau and Judd point out for the earlier period, were usually in areas of marginal agricultural value and where fishing was important.[16] Although resistance continued, it was more dispersed, more muted, and less strident than before. There were a number of reasons.

One reason was better enforcement. Before and during the First World War, Game Commissioner Knight had encountered financial difficulties in paying for and maintaining a province-wide network of wardens. [17] As he wrote in 1918, 'a decline in revenue means a weaker warden service. We are heavily handicapped in this work by war conditions. The outlook for receipts from the sale of licenses in the season just begun is darker than ever.'[18] The decline in revenues meant fewer wardens and fewer patrols. In 1908, there had been about fifty wardens and six years later, more than seventy. By 1915, there were only forty-seven, a decline attributable to the war. The cumulative effect was that the wardens were less visible between 1914 and 1918, tempting Nova Scotians to hunt whenever and however they wished.[19] By the early 1920s, however, the situation had brightened. Revenues soared and money poured into the commission's coffers. In 1920–21, the commission took in more than $11,000, a jump due to more out-of-province hunters, and so Knight was able to employ more wardens for longer periods. One result was a jump in successful prosecutions. The money paid in fines went through the roof. In 1920–21, $2,548.09 in fines poured in to the commission.[20]

This growth in successful prosecutions, however, was not only due to structural changes in the commission's work. As Knight's replacement, Otto Schierbeck, wrote in 1929, success could only come by convincing urban sportsmen and rural farmers to protect their common interests.[21] There were not enough wardens to thrust a new regulatory scheme on the populace without their support, even if that support was not always consistent. They did so for a number of different reasons.

Social class was one factor. The more prosperous farmers of the Annapolis Valley and central Nova Scotia likely mouthed the rhetoric of conservation more than others. Hunting had never been a full-time occupation, but as wildlife numbers plummeted and as changes in market relations influenced farmers to produce for the expanding urban market, hunting became less significant in the rural economy. These changes made supplementing the family income less necessary and less possible. In time, these more established farmers may have become more willing to accept the new regulations than others, if not always with equanimity, as they also understood how the laws altered rural property relations and preserved a sportsmen's paradise in lieu of 'pushing back' the wilderness.[22]

Others accepted the new regulations for pecuniary reasons, as they benefited from the influx of sportsmen.[23] These new opportunities, which were mainly centred along the South Shore, benefited not only business owners but others as well, including those able and willing to work as guides.[24] By the 1920s, guiding had become a provincially regulated profession. To hunt and to fish, out-of-towners needed to know where to go, what to do, and how to do it. But just in case they decided otherwise, the government legislated that they did not have a choice. As a 1916 government guide noted: 'the game law allows visitors at hotels to fish by the day without being accompanied by licensed guides, but parties staying the woods over night must be accompanied, no guide being permitted to serve more than three persons.'[25] One sportsman who often stayed at Milford House, not far from the town of Annapolis, recalled that 'during the heyday in the early 1920s, there were twenty-eight guides going out there. They brought in guides besides locals from Maitland and a couple of Indians from Milton. The others were locals, from within a radius of five miles, you might say.' In 1927 there were 572 licensed guides.[26] Hotel and sports camp owners also benefited from the new regulations, catering to sportsmen from within the province and outside. In the early 1900s American sportsmen built hunting lodges at Caledonia, South Brookfield, Bangs Falls (Queen's County), and East Kemptville (Yarmouth County), attracting the notice of such luminaries as Henry Ford and Babe Ruth.[27] As privately owned clubs, membership was limited and exclusive. Tourist homes also became more common. Mike Parker writes that by 1930 Nova Scotia had about 400 tourist homes, half of which catered to sportsmen. As these examples illustrate, support for the game laws spread in areas that benefited from out-of-town traffic.

Changes in transportation technologies, which increased travel between rural and urban areas of Nova Scotia and from the American eastern seaboard, also changed peoples' thinking. Up until the early 1900s, much of rural Nova Scotia remained relatively inaccessible, except by

Mi'kmaw guides from Bear River at camp near Weymouth, N.S, ca. 1893 (Nova Scotia Archives: J.A. Irvine NSARM Photo Drawer negative no. 3833)

boat and by horse and wagon, and from 1854, via a limited railway network, which by 1867, totalled only about 145 miles and which operated on a small circuit linking Halifax, Windsor, Truro, and Pictou.[28] Travel was difficult and time-consuming, given the poor quality of the roads and the primitive nature of the technology.[29] As a result, most rural residents would have been able to ignore urban demands for conservation and would have relied on their own understanding about when and where they might hunt. However, the penetration of rural areas by the motorcar and by the railway after 1900 changed the nature of the rural landscape and the numbers who frequented it. This, in combination with a government and private initiative to attract out of province travellers to bask in the Nova Scotia's authentic folk experience, made the countryside a more feasible destination than before. This also meant an increase in sport hunters, and their ability to reach areas that formerly had been the purview of locals or of elite sportsmen. This included Mi'kmaq, like Gabriel Sylliboy and the Jeddore brothers, who owned a motorcar or who had access to one.

Much of this had to do with Henry Ford and other manufacturers who made the motorcar affordable. The Model T was a prime example. In 1908, when the Model T first rolled off the assembly line, it sold for $850. In 1920 that cost had been reduced to $440 and by 1925 to $290.[30] Cars, which once had been the toys of the rich, were no longer. As Donald Davis argues, the larger American automobile manufacturers accelerated motorization in Canada, by forcing Canadian automobile makers to lower their own costs.[31] Motor vehicle ownership in Nova Scotia skyrocketed between 1907 and 1923. In 1907, there were only fifty-five registered vehicles. Sixteen years later, there were 18,103 and by 1930, 36,078. This growth reflected the expansion of motor vehicle ownership across Canada near the end of the First World War and immediately afterward. Although motorization did not occur evenly across Canada, and was dependent on a variety of factors, including rural resistance, road networks, and maintenance issues, the 1920s were a watershed in motor vehicle ownership and in the expansion of provincial roads.[32] These data are summarized in Tables 1.1. and 1.2.

While the motorcar made rural areas accessible to urban Nova Scotians and to Americans, the railway and steamship made the province more accessible to sportsmen from away. In the 1920s, the tourist trade ballooned, as Maritime governments sought to lure tourists east, where they might enjoy an '"authentic experience" by mingling with the folk.'[33] Families were the mainstay of this trade, but the region's game and fish

Table 1.1
Registered Motor Vehicles in Nova Scotia by County, 1907–1914

County	1907	1911	1914
Mainland			
Annapolis	5	34	57
Antigonish	0	5	15
Colchester	3	13	67
Cumberland	12	89	201
Digby	0	21	45
Guysborough	0	2	4
Halifax Region	7	133	283
Halifax Co.	0	4	7
Hants	1	24	45
King's	12	37	94
Lunenburg	0	10	34
Pictou	4	15	90
Queen's	0	9	20
Shelburne	0	2	7
Yarmouth	10	76	149
Cape Breton Island			
Cape Breton	4	34	121
Inverness	0	1	5
Richmond	0	0	4
Victoria	0	0	0
Total	58	509	1,248

Source: Provincial Secretary's Report for the Year Ended 30th September 1911, *Journals and Proceedings of the House of Assembly in the Province of Nova Scotia, Session 1912*, Appendix 12 (Halifax, 1912), i–xxi; and Session 1915, Appendix 12, 1–21.

also attracted hunters and anglers. Nova Scotia, like New Brunswick, was blessed with both. Such bounty appealed to sportsmen from the northeastern United States. New Brunswick was especially adept at attracting Americans, an ability, however, which was premised on leasing river rights to private sportsmen's clubs.[34] As their game commissioner told Knight, 514 Americans had trooped through the province in 1920, contributing a healthy proportion of the total revenue garnered from the sale of licenses yet accounting for only one-seventh of the game killed.[35] Knight and others did their best to attract a similar clientele to Nova Scotia. Nova Scotia was never as successful as New Brunswick in attracting out-of-province hunters, but Knight cheerfully noted in 1921 that

Table 1.2
Motor Vehicle Registrations in Nova Scotia 1914–1924

Year	New Registrations	Total	Increase (%)
1914	546	1,710	
1915	970	2,300	590 (34.5)
1916	1,725	3,050	750 (32.6)
1917	2,581	5,100	2,050 (67.2)
1918	2,816	8,150	3,050 (59.8)
1919	2,486	10,030	1,880 (23.1)
1920	3,203	12,450	2,420 (24.1)
1921	2,785	14,050	1,600 (12.9)
1922	3,135	15,884	1,834 (13.1)
1923	3,652	18,103	2,219 (14.0)
1924	349	20,569	2,466 (13.6)

Source: Provincial Secretary's Report, *Journals and Proceedings of the House of Assembly of the Province of Nova Scotia, Session 1925*, Appendix 12 (Halifax, 1925), 10.

124 American hunters had visited in 1920, 'a considerable increase over the previous year.'[36]

As motor vehicles became more common, as more money was poured into upgrading roads, and as government and businesses promoted railroad travel, rural areas were beset by town folk on weekends and on holidays, some to hunt. In 1921 a Mount Uniacke businessman complained of the 'fishing and shooting carried on by parties who come out of town on Saturday evening train and by auto on Sundays.'[37] This led to calls for a better regulation of city hunters. As one South Rawdon resident told Knight, the people there wanted the government to appoint a game warden to stop all the strangers who come out of town on the railway 'fishing and shooting.'[38] Similar requests came from other parts of the province.[39] Otto Schierbeck, who was responsible for game enforcement between 1926 and 1933, expressed the problem aptly: 'The era of the motor car has made it possible for the moose hunter to get around in much higher degree than in the olden days of the horse and buggy, and shank's mare.'[40] This was especially true for those central mainland communities, like Mount Uniacke and South Rawdon, which were easily accessible from Halifax and Truro, and it was also true for other areas where car ownership had skyrocketed during the war and afterwards, such as Annapolis, Cumberland, King's, and Yarmouth counties as well as the industrial heartland of Cape Breton Island. Whycocomagh's town newspaper noticed the change. 'On Labour Day,' the 15 September 1928 edition of the *Inverness County Bulletin* remarked, 'a great many tourists passed through the village. While many of the cars were Nova Scotian, there were a number of American cars among them. Tourist trade in Whycocomagh was probably better this season than ever before.'[41] Such developments, while offering opportunity, also limited peoples' ability to control the pace of change, making them more willing to accept regulation than they might otherwise have been. This was also true for Alex Gillis, as Gabriel Sylliboy's presence on his land demonstrated.

Thus, in each region of the province, there were some rural residents who, for various reasons, were willing to inform against others. It was this willingness that Game Commissioner Knight and his successor, Otto Schierbeck, cultivated so as to police a population that otherwise would have been impossible to do. One of their targets was Mi'kmaw trappers and hunters.

Between 1921 and 1926, Knight's office received twelve complaints regarding Mi'kmaw hunting. Eight complaints were received in 1922, two in 1926, and one each in 1921 and 1924. The complaints received in 1922 came from all over the province: from Inverness, (in Cape Breton Island), Annapolis, Antigonish, Colchester, Guysborough, and Yarmouth counties. We would also suppose that other people complained to their local warden or ranger directly, much like Alex Gillis did. As well, Knight's wardens charged an unknown number of Mi'kmaq with hunting and trapping during closed season or selling meat without a license.[42]

All the letters sang a similar refrain: local Mi'kmaq were hunting and trapping out of season. J.W. Hattie's letter from Caledonia in Guysborough County was typical. 'Game protection at Sunny Brae is no more than a farce. On Dec. 26th at or near Rodie Sutherlands the Indian Peter Wilmot the one I informed you about some time ago killed a moose and is blowing about it and telling everyone he meets. If he cannot be stopped peaceably he should put where he would not incite others to break the law.'[43] Mr Noble Creelman from Lower Truro was similarly incensed. 'As I am a licensed guide I thought it was no more than right that I should inform you of what I know of Moose being killed last winter and this winter by the Indians at Hilden last winter they made their boast of killing fifteen and this winter Eight moose and seven Deer since Xmas.' Creelman went on to explain that he would not mind if they had done their hunting from September up until Christmas but to do so afterward was just plain wrong. 'After that a moose ain't fit to eat and is only a wast to kill them last winter they killed a cow-moose and took two calves out of her now that [ ] wasnt fit for a Indian to eat or anything but a dog.'[44]

What motivated the men to write? For Creelman, the interest was pecuniary. He was a registered guide and therefore viewed out-of-season hunting as threatening his own livelihood. The same was true of A.H.H. Desbarres of Guysborough County.[45] However, most of the men, like Alex Gillis, were not guides. Parenteau and Judd contend that for most rural people, it was easier to condemn the Mi'kmaq than a non-aboriginal neighbour, an argument that is suggestive, but not fully elaborated.[46] Indeed, such condemnation reflected rural residents' distrust of their Mi'kmaw neighbours. The basis of this distrust was a growing disconnect in how rural residents and Mi'kmaq conceived of their relationships towards central authorities and of their attitudes towards private property.

As a generation of historians have pointed out, from the mid-1800s governments in concert with private groups and agencies introduced various reforms, which reshaped Canadian life. This movement was partly precipitated by economic changes in the North Atlantic world, which had lead to separating work from the household, deskilling labour, and creating structural unemployment. The social convulsions precipitated by these changes led reformers to agitate for new social institutions, which would serve as a moral corrective in a period of social turbulence and would also provide labourers the skills to work in the new political economy. Initially directed at children, criminals, and others whose actions could be corrected through public institutions, by the early 1900s this movement had broadened to include other sectors of society, the intent of which was to reshape peoples' morals, attitudes, sense of identity, and concepts of citizenship so as to make them better workers, better citizens, and fitter soldiers.[47] In the sixty years since the sports lobby had first orchestrated a change in wildlife legislation, this reform movement had also affected rural Nova Scotians in ways that demarcated the differences between themselves and their Mi'kmaw neighbours and also affected Alex Gillis's attitudes when he confronted Gabriel Sylliboy in 1927.

For most rural residents the most visible agent of this movement was the school system. Like the other British North American colonies, Nova Scotia's public school system developed from elite and middle class attitudes regarding education's morally redemptive value. In Upper Canada, where the school movement had been strongest, the political turmoil of the 1837 Rebellions had instilled fears that unless remedies were developed, the colonies would become absorbed into the American orbit. The migration of thousands of Irish, Scots, Welsh, and Americans in the first half of the century, which raised the possibility of future turmoil, reinforced this sense of urgency. Elites were also concerned with falling further behind the United States and pointed to American schools as one of the mainsprings of that nation's economy. By the mid-1800s therefore, elites thought education was a magical elixir, which could solve all the ills that seemed to beset British North America – insurgent republicanism, cultural heterogeneity, and economic listlessness. Education, these promoters argued, would instill British values, ideas, and culture, reinforce identification with Great Britain, and drill into the populace the skills and discipline needed to compete with Yankee ingenuity.[48] Although researchers are unable to come up with a model that would explain why state-controlled educational systems emerged in various jurisdictions in nineteenth-century Europe and North America, there is a consensus that one effect was to forge 'cultural and political union' among heterogeneous groups of people.[49]

The same was true of Nova Scotia, where teachers conveyed Christian moral values, which included, as the 1900 Education Act outlined, 'truth, justice, love of country, loyalty, humanity, sobriety, industry, frugality, chastity, temperance, and all other virtues.'[50] These values were meant to teach children how to become good citizens. In the early 1900s, conflict emerged about the duties and responsibilities of citizenship; however, what was critical was that students develop a love of and loyalty to their country, and that they be willing be serve when needed. By the 1920s, the aftermath of war had illustrated the dangers of rampant nationalism, but nonetheless one of education's goals was for students to 'have a sense of national identity and, better yet, of patriotism, which meant knowing something of their country's history and heritage, of visualizing its geography, of cherishing its culture.'[51] The schools' emphasis on instilling a model of citizenship became more than just a means of teaching literacy and numeracy, but also increased self-regulation, by internalizing prescribed norms of behaviour. Laws, although necessary as a means of deterrence, were never sufficient. Compulsory schooling helped to fill that void, but developed gradually from the mid-1800s as identification with local communities and with established religious institutions continued to be important parameters of cultural identity.[52]

Gabriel Sylliboy and other M'kmaw men of his generation were more insulated from these educational initiatives, and this enlarged the social and cultural distance between them and men like Alex Gillis. Government officials, first in the colony of Nova Scotia and later in the Dominion of Canada, considered education as key for speeding Mi'kmaw integration into Anglo-Canadian society, but schooling never had that effect. This was true for Gabriel Sylliboy and it was also true for four of the other men who testified at his appeal, Andrew Alek, Andrew Bernard, Joe Christmas, and Francis Gould. It was also true of their parents, illustrating each succeeding generation's insulation from the colony's educational system. Instead of fostering closer social and cultural relationships with rural neighbours, education had the opposite effect.

All of the men who testified at Sylliboy's appeal in 1928 were from Cape Breton Island, and five of them had been born in 1875 or before. Andrew Alek, Andrew Bernard and Joe Christmas were all born in 1850, and Francis Gould, four years later. Sylliboy was considerably younger and was born in 1875. We know less about the birthdates of each man's parents, but would suppose that they were born between 1820 and 1835. Gabriel Sylliboy's mother Mary Basque was born in 1830 and Andrew Alek's parents sometime between 1829 and 1832.

For both generations of Mi'kmaq, illiteracy in the English language was the norm. Joe Christmas told Judge Patterson that he could not read. Andrew Bernard was also illiterate in English and so too were most men and women of his generation.[53] This is shown in Tables 1.3, 1.4 and 1.5, which compare illiteracy in English among three age cohorts in 1871 and 1901. These cohorts roughly coincide with the five men's generation and with their parents. Data from the 1871 census shows illiteracy rates for people born between 1822 and 1851 and data from the 1901 census for people born between 1852 and 1881. We might have expected that illiteracy would decline over this period and it does, but only minimally. In the thirty-year span from 1822–31 to 1852–61 and from 1832–41 and 1862–71, illiteracy only decreased marginally and, among some gender-specific cohorts, actually grew. For men and women of these age groups, illiteracy hovered around 80 per cent and was often higher. This is a somewhat surprising discovery, although perhaps not totally unexpected. These figures illustrate that few children from the men's generation or from their parents' attended school, and if they did, only infrequently.

Before 1867, this was because of funding issues. Early legislative enactments were premised on the consent of each school section's ratepayers. Because Mi'kmaw families generally did not own either real or personal property, they would have been disqualified from participating in section meetings and, if they lacked funds to pay for the teacher, from their

Table 1.3.
English Illiteracy Rates, Nova Scotia Mi'kmaq 1871 and 1901

Age Cohort	1871 Census						1901 Census					
	Women		Men		Total		Women		Men		Total	
	n	Rate	n	Rate	N	Rate	n	Rate	n	Rate	N	Rate
20–9	123	.756	94	.787	217	.770	112	.723	113	.628	225	.676
30–9	77	.818	85	.800	162	.809	68	.801	60	.767	128	.789
40–9	55	.909	83	.759	138	.819	45	.889	54	.796	99	.838

Sources: LAC, RG 31, 1871 and 1901 censuses, Nova Scotia.

Table 1.4.
English Illiteracy Rates, Mi'kmaq of Mainland Nova Scotia 1871 and 1901

Age Cohort	1871 Census						1901 Census					
	Women		Men		Total		Women		Men		Total	
	n	Rate	n	Rate	N	Rate	n	Rate	n	Rate	N	Rate
20–9	75	.760	66	.773	141	.766	74	.689	64	.703	138	.696
30–9	58	.826	60	.833	118	.831	50	.780	43	.791	93	.785
40–9	45	.840	59	.729	104	.817	31	.839	37	.784	68	.809

Sources: LAC, RG 31, 1871 and 1901 censuses, Nova Scotia.

Table 1.5
English Illiteracy Rates, Mi'kmaq of Cape Breton Island 1871 and 1901

Age Cohort	1871 Census						1901 Census					
	Women		Men		Total		Women		Men		Total	
	n	Rate	n	Rate	N	Rate	n	Rate	n	Rate	N	Rate
20–9	48	.735	28	.821	76	.776	38	.789	49	.531	87	.644
30–9	19	.789	25	.720	44	.750	18	.889	17	.706	35	.800
40–9	10	.800	24	.833	34	.824	18	1.00	17	.824	35	.914

Sources: LAC, RG 31, 1871 and 1901 censuses, Nova Scotia.

children attending schools where monies were raised through voluntary subscription. An 1842 statute passed by the House of Assembly tried to force by law what had not been accomplished in practice. However, such attempts at bonhomie were easier said than done. Joseph Howe's efforts to encourage Mi'kmaw attendance met resistance in many quarters: the local school sections who resisted the presence of the poorly clothed children, House of Assembly members who balked at voting funds to pay for the children's education, and Mi'kmaw parents who thought that the white man's school would alienate children from them.[54] Although the assembly did allot funds 'in educating children in different parts of the Province and at St. Mary's Seminary' it is probable the affected numbers were small.[55] The exception may have been those communities that were more stable and where local priests mediated the difficult issues of race and social class that in other areas probably prevented Mi'kmaw children from entering classrooms. On Cape Breton, the situation was similar.

This led to suggestions that the children be educated separately, and from the late 1850s and early 1860s more Mi'kmaw communities were requesting assistance to build schools.[56] However, no schools were built, mostly for financial reasons but also because officials believed that most Mi'kmaw families lived itinerant lives. Immediately after Confederation, for instance, the Roman Catholic Bishop of Cape Breton told former Commissioner for Indian Affairs Samuel Fairbanks that the only community where the Mi'kmaq might attend school was Eskasoni but that 'the long unsettled habits of others would make it very difficult to get a School in operation.'[57] The consequence was that before 1867 few Mi'kmaw children would have attended school, accounting for the fact that Bernard and Christmas were illiterate and probably Alek and Gould as well.

After 1867 and the federal government's assumption of responsibility for Indian Affairs, more efforts were made. This was done in two ways: the integration of school children into the public system and the creation of schools on reserves. As in other parts of Canada, the latter were called day schools. Day schools were only built on the larger reserves, and this meant that children who lived on a small reserve or who lived off reserve had fewer opportunities to attend school. Gabriel Sylliboy probably benefited from this development, since he was born in 1875 and a day school was built at Whycocomagh soon after but most men and women of his generation were not as fortunate.

At Confederation, more than half of all Nova Scotia Mi'kmaq lived off reserve and so this meant that most would not have had access to day schools. This included Andrew Bernard's family, who had moved from Wagmatcook to North Sydney in the 1860s. There were other Mi'kmaw families living there. This created difficulties in schooling children, an issue mentioned by Bernard in a petition he and other members of the North Sydney community sent to the Department of Indian Affairs (DIA) in January 1907.[58] The only recourse for these children was to attend the common schools. This was also true for many other Mi'kmaw children before the 1890s, especially on the mainland, where there were fewer reserves on prime agricultural land and where, because of the circumstances in which colonization had evolved, families were more scattered than concentrated. This presented problems in placing children in schools and then getting them to attend regularly.

One problem was determining who would pay for them. Because schools were funded from ratepayers and from provincial grants, trustees were unlikely to welcome Mi'kmaw children unless their parents contributed their share of taxes. Although the Nova Scotia Education Act of 1884 made education of all children between the ages of six and sixteen mandatory and provided for poor families, the federal government's fiscal responsibility for Indian affairs likely induced trustees to insist that the DIA subsidize Mi'kmaw children's education.[59] This was the situation in Cumberland County where, beginning in 1897, the DIA subsidized the education of Mi'kmaw children.[60]

We know from DIA agents' correspondence that children did attend public schools but how many did so and how often is unknown. In most cases, agents wrote about the children who did not attend rather than those who did, and so we lack the same type of statistics as available for the non-Mi'kmaw population. At most what we can do is discuss why some children did not attend. In some cases, the agents reported that parents wanted their children in school but various obstacles prevented them from attending. Sometimes the schools were too far away, a point that probably reflected some families' physical isolation from other communities.[61] In other cases, the children refused to go. As the agent for Queen's County reported in 1890, 'the public schools are within reach, yet the Indian child does not take kindly to such a school; one of the many reasons being the cold reception given him by other children who have better clothes and whiter skins.'[62] The agent for Antigonish County explained that Mi'kmaw children were shy and timid 'in the presence of whites,' and that this discouraged them from attending. This appears to have been the most common problem[63] and we might suppose that the children's spoken language as well as their different attire and skin colour made them objects of ridicule in the schoolyard, convincing them it was better not to attend. But it also likely that the children's different cultural attitudes towards authority made them uncomfortable as well as the subject of a disciplinary code to which they were unfamiliar.

From these anecdotal accounts we can make two conclusions. First, in those areas where day schools were not available, the DIA encouraged children to attend the common schools.[64] This policy was applied to those families who did not live on reserve or who lived on reserve but whose population was too small to justify a day school. Second, since the DIA either could not or would not provide the clothes and other necessities for the children, attendance was inconsistent. As well, local prejudices discouraged children from attending. Similar problems characterized aboriginal children attending common schools in other parts of Canada. As Jean Barman points out in a case study of one British Columbia school, the failure of integration 'became inevitable because of federal parsimony and White prejudice.'[65]

One man who was familiar with the issue was Silas Rand, a Baptist missionary who had spent more than twenty years trying to improve the Mi'kmaw community's socioeconomic status. In 1868, he wrote: 'The Superintendent of Education informs me that the question has several times been raised as to whether the Indians have the right to send their children to the Public Schools, and that he has always decided that they have the right. I was told by the Indians at Shubenacadie that the white people made strong opposition to it when some of the Indian children attempted to go, and that the result was their withdrawal.' Although Rand believed that some Mi'kmaq attended he thought 'the number was not great.'[66] A survey of Mi'kmaw children who would have attended common schools in 1901 confirms Rand's conclusion. According to Martha Walls' examination of the 1901 census, only one of nineteen school-aged children in Antigonish County and six of thirty-three in Queen's County and Shelburne County attended school.[67]

From the late 1800s, the Department of Indian Affairs realized that a better policy was to school the Mi'kmaq separately. This was part of a general change in the DIA's policies, reflecting the failure of the public school system and a belief that by schooling aboriginals in their own environment they would adapt more easily to the educational system.[68] The schools subsequently established were called day schools. They were not unique to Nova Scotia but were also built in the other provinces east of the Manitoba-Ontario border and in the Western provinces, including British Columbia and the Yukon. Day schools were on reserves and were run like common schools. For this reason, they were called day schools in order to distinguish them from residential schools, which also emerged in the same period and were based on the earlier industrial schools of Upper Canada.[69] In Nova Scotia, the number of day schools increased as the reserve population grew. As Table 6.4 shows, between 1871 and 1901 the percentage of families living on reserve grew, on the mainland from 28.7 per cent to 56.8 per cent of the population and on Cape Breton Island from 50.7 per cent to 91.1 per cent. Between 1872 and 1913, the government built schools on fifteen reserves and, with the exception of Cow Bay, Sheet Harbour, and Tuft's Cove, all of these continued to operate into the 1920s.[70] These schools were built incrementally, beginning with the largest reserves. Three schools were built in the 1870s, four in the 1880s, four in the 1890s, and four more in the early 1900s.[71]

The cumulative effect of this building program was to increase enrolments. In 1881 there had been 107 students. Forty years later, there were 240.[72] This growth in absolute numbers also reflected an increase in the percentage of children enrolled. In 1881, only 27 per cent of all Mi'kmaw children between the ages of six and fifteen were registered in day schools (107 of 397). By 1911 this had grown to 53 per cent (240 of 449). There were, however, differences between the mainland and the island. By 1911, virtually all Cape Breton children were registered but only 27 per cent of mainland children (79 of 292), the same percentage there had been thirty years earlier.[73] Thus, while the percentage of Mi'kmaw children registered in day schools increased between 1881 and 1911, the largest growth was on Cape Breton Island. From this it is evident that more than 70 per cent of all Mi'kmaw children on the mainland either did not attend school or attended common schools. This contrasts with Cape Breton where most attended day schools.[74]

The creation of the day schools boosted literacy rates, even though the schools faced a number of problems, in terms of attendance, instructional levels, staffing, and fiscal difficulties.[75] This is suggested in Table 1.4, which shows a decrease in English illiteracy among adults born between 1872 and 1881, who would have benefited from day schools built in the 1870s and 1880s. The most significant shift occurred among Cape Breton men, where illiteracy dropped to 53 per cent from 82 per cent a generation earlier. A reduction also occurred among both men and women on the mainland, although not among Cape Breton women.

The creation of a separate system, while increasing literacy, did not always facilitate integration into rural communities. English was almost always the language of instruction in the schools, but the fact that all students were Mi'kmaq and spoke Mi'kmaq undermined attempts to assimilate them into neighbouring communities. Sylliboy more than likely attended the day school at Whycocomagh, but his chosen language of communication as an adult was Mi'kmaq, as the need to hire a court-appointed translator at his appeal attests. This was also true of the youngest person to testify, Ben Christmas, who was born in 1894 and as a youth would have attended the day school on the King's Road reserve in Sydney. The day school system therefore tended to reinforce cultural identity by creating social situations in which Mi'kmaq was the principal language of communication. The effect was to reinforce, rather than eliminate, social distinctions from their rural neighbours.

The schools also isolated Mi'kmaw children within rural communities. In forcibly bringing children together daily, schools foster social connections among families, and sometimes across racial and class boundaries. This was even more likely to occur in rural communities where neighbourhoods were less segregated and where the smaller population did not make always make it possible to choose childhood friends on a selective basis. In this sense, the creation of a separate school system isolated Mi'kmaw children socially and enlarged the distance between their parents and other rural residents. The physical distances that separated Whycocomagh and Wagmatcook from adjacent rural villages were therefore reinforced. The bifurcated school system cemented social cohesion within existing identity groups and reinforced their social isolation from each other. This occurred at the very time when public schools had become a forum for channeling concepts of moral and civic identities. The result was to foster, and possibly to deepen, distrust between the two communities when points of potential conflict emerged, as was the case when the Mi'kmaq defied wildlife legislation and hunted during closed season. This was less true in mainland communities where there was a greater reliance on the public school system. However, as the Indian agents' reports from the late 1800s and early 1900s suggest, Mi'kmaw children were not always welcome there, or could not attend because of the distance from their homes. So, even though more children attended common schools on the mainland than on the island, non-attendance created similar dynamics in Mi'kmaw relations with rural neighbours.

All of this suggests the difference between Alex Gillis and Gabriel Sylliboy. Gillis had, like other men of his generation, gone to the common school, had mingled with other white children, and had learnt the basic rudiments of reading and writing as well as arithmetic. Gillis also spoke English, and when he testified in court, he did so in a way that the magistrate easily understood, although Gillies may also have spoken Gaelic. In contrast, Gabriel Sylliboy likely attended the day school at Whyco-comagh with other Mi'kmaw children and although he also learnt to read and to write in English, his first language was Mi'kmaq. It was this language that he spoke in Judge Patterson's courtroom. Both Gillis and Sylliboy recognized this cultural difference when they confronted each other on 31 October 1927, and it was also a difference that fueled rural peoples' distrust of the Mi'kmaq.

Also underlying Gillis's distrust was an implicit recognition that the two men did not share a common political space. As Gillis told Magistrate Angus McDougall, 'I made out they were Indians. I think the Indian tribe of Cape Breton are Mic-macs. I learned they came from Whycomagh. I heard the Indians are claiming the right to hunt & fish under a treaty.' In other words, Gillis recognized the political distance between himself and Sylliboy. Sylliboy was an Indian and as an Indian his political status made him different. One of those differences was that Sylliboy lived on reserve and there were other differences as well. As Gillis told the magistrate, the Mi'kmaq claimed certain privileges that others did not enjoy. Gillis likely did not understand exactly how Indians were defined in law, but he, like many other rural residents of early twentieth century Cape Breton, would have known that one critical difference was that the Mi'kmaq neither paid taxes, nor voted in muncipal, provincial, or federal elections.

Like other aboriginal people the Mi'kmaq had their own system of governance and it was this system that Gillis explicitly recognized when he called Gabriel Sylliboy 'chief' in Magistrate McDougall's courtroom. Before 1899 and a federal Order-In-Council which mandated the creation of band councils, the community's governing body had been the Grand Council. Although the council's origins are unclear it was, from at least the mid-1800s, if not before, an important political body within the Mi'kmaq community. At least three of the men who testified at Sylliboy's appeal were associated with the Grand Council, including Sylliboy, who was known as the Grand Chief and who worked with various other community leaders, often called captains.

The Grand Council oversaw the election of chiefs for each of the Cape Breton reserves and also influenced elections on the mainland. For instance, after the death of the Sydney Reserve chief in 1904, Grand Chief John Denny, his captains, and other Mi'kmaq appointed the new chief.[76] The council's relationship with the mainland reserves is less clear, because there is little documentation. We know, however, that the Grand

Chief visited the mainland and was involved in the election of reserve chiefs and councilors. Gabriel Sylliboy, who became Grand Chief in 1918 after John Denny's death, was present at the election of the chief of the 'Antigonish band of Mi'kmaqs' in November 1920 and was also instrumental in convincing the Millbrook people that they should elect a chief to represent their interests to the Indian agent.[77]

The Grand Chief's relationship with the reserve chiefs is unclear. The evidence on this matter is limited, but we would suppose that, with the increase of on-reserve populations in the late nineteenth century, different political structures emerged than had existed earlier in the century when more people had lived off reserve and when representation in the council was determined according to district, not according to reserve. This led some reserves, particularly on the mainland, to push for the election of individuals who could represent them and who would also be able to solicit federal and provincial assistance, especially as communities became more dependent on government and the wage labour economy. This meant adopting the prescribed rules of election set out in an Order-in-Council in 1899, which outlined Canadian models of representation and election.[78] That the council continued, however, to influence the form in which elections occurred is suggested by C.W. Vernon's remark that at the annual meeting at Chapel Island in 1903, the Grand Chief was 'assisted by captains, one elected for each reservation.'[79] These chiefs also represented broader geographical regions that may have corresponded to earlier council districts. This is suggested in a 1912 memo written by the curator of the Nova Scotia Museum, Henry Piers. According to Piers, the chief of Shubenacadie had jurisdiction over 'Halifax, Lunenburg, King's, Hants, Colchester and Cumberland Counties, the chief at Bear River had jurisdiction over Annapolis, Digby, Yarmouth, Shelburne, and Queens counties, the chief of Pictou over Pictou county, the chief at Pomquet over Antigonish and Guysbourgh counties, and the chief at Eskasoni governs the whole of Cape Breton Island.'[80] On Cape Breton, reserve chiefs were the main spokesmen for their community but consulted with the Grand Chief and with the council. As one agent noted in 1902, the Sydney Mi'kmaq considered John Denny to be 'Head Chief of all the Micmacs, and every Micmac admits his claim and tribal traditions and customs carry great weight with the Indians.'[81] It is probable that this relationship was stronger on Cape Breton than on the mainland, where distance and a dissimilar history had created a different political relationship between the council and reserve communities.

This separate political and juridical system reinforced rural residents' suspicions about their Mi'kmaw neighbours. In the same way as education socializes people in a shared understanding of what is normal and what is not, participation in government, either directly in voting for it, or indirectly, in paying taxes used in the 'public interest,' helps to create a shared feeling of citizenship. Though people may not always agree with taxation or with government policies, the act of paying taxes and by voting for governments unites them and makes possible discussions across social, ethnic, gender, and religious divides. Generally, aboriginal people were not part of a reform of the political system, which between the 1820s and the 1920s, gradually expanded Nova Scotia's tax system and electoral lists. Though in the 1840s, the Mi'kmaq briefly were able to influence the political process, they were soon after disenfranchised, a process that was repeated at the federal level between 1885 and 1898.[82] The community's absence from the main centres of civic assemblage reinforced a separate sense of identity, both within their community, and outside of it.

All of this fuelled the belief of rural residents like Alex Gillis that the Mi'kmaq could not be trusted to adapt to the new laws. People knew that the Mi'kmaq operated according to a different set of rules and lived differently from everyone else. The reserves at Chapel Island, Sydney, Wagmatcook and Whycocomagh, each of which lay adjacent to non-Mi'kmaw communities, testified to this difference. The reserves' borders were more than just physical barriers; they were social ones as well, which were given an added force by differences in language and race. Alex Gillis knew this difference when he saw Gabriel Sylliboy and the Jeddores on his property on 31 October 1927. Alex Gillis did not know Sylliboy or the Jeddore brothers by name when he saw them on his farm but later said he 'made out they were Indians.'[83] Perhaps Gillis was able to identify Sylliboy by the colour of his skin. However, the difference between the two men was more than a matter of colour. Gillis also would have known Sylliboy to be an 'Indian' because of the clothes he wore, the syntax and phonology of the English he spoke, his use of Mi'kmaq when speaking to the Jeddores, even by the manner he related to Gillis. As Mark Weiner has argued, a shared sense of citizenship consists of more than adherence to the law but also to a common set of cultural practices that publicly announces an individual's identification with the 'nation.'[84] Sylliboy's personal characteristics marked him as an 'outsider,' as someone unlikely to share 'Canadian' values and attitudes. Both men recognized and accepted this difference as part of their everyday lives. When Gillis saw Sylliboy and the Jeddores on 31 October, he knew that they did not share similar values about the sanctity of private property or about the obedience to the law.

It is always troubling when making such a conclusion about ordinary peoples' consciousness, especially given the dearth of evidence about how they felt and acted. It is even more tenuous when we conclude this for one individual. Just what Alex Gillis knew about Gabriel Sylliboy is unclear. As he told the magistrate he knew that Sylliboy was an Indian and so he must also have known that he was governed by a different set of laws than the rest of the population. This seems to be a reasonable conclusion to make, since Gillis's understanding would have principally come from gossip he had heard. This information might have come from individuals who had some direct relationship with the community at Whycocomagh, such as Indian agents, medical doctors, day school teachers, and storeowners. Even if Gillis did not know someone who had such knowledge, he would have heard from others who did. This gossip was complemented by local and regional newspapers, which, for instance, published copies of the 1752 treaty and also conveyed other tidbits of information about the Whycocomagh reserve.

Gillis could not trust Sylliboy, a fact that was reinforced when Sylliboy said he would leave but didn't. Gillis felt therefore that he had no choice but to travel to West Bay to see the local forest ranger. In doing so, Gillis accepted that laws regulating hunting and trapping of wildlife were necessary, if only because it would mean that outsiders could not interfere with what he may have considered to be his customary right to harvest muskrat coming onto his property. Regardless of Gillis's specific motives, he was also a man who had, for whatever reason, come to accept the law as a regulating force in society and that he had a right to use it to protect his property. This is what helped define Alex Gillis and what also distinguished him from Gabriel Sylliboy. Alex Gillis's journey into West Bay therefore was not happenstance but rather reflected more broadly on the social and political differences that had come to separate the Mi'kmaq from their Nova Scotian neighbours in the 1920s and which had helped to shape attitudes towards the Indians' illegal hunting and trapping. Unlike the Mi'kmaq, their neighbours were less insulated from the reform movement of the late nineteenth and early twentieth centuries and this helped to trigger their anger. That some men from rural Nova Scotia were willing to characterize hunting or tapping as an illegal activity shows that some people had come to accept regulation. As well, rural Nova Scotian men were more likely to consider themselves to be members of a broader political spectrum, which encompassed Nova Scotia and Canada. They paid taxes and voted in municipal, provincial, and federal elections. Mi'kmaw absence from both tax rolls and electoral lists, coupled with the separate character of their governing institutions, would have suggested to men like Gillis that Sylliboy conceptualized his relationship to authorities differently. This made Gillis's next actions likely, although never inevitable, as for each Alex Gillis there were other men who would have turned the other way, after a friendly warning.

By November 1927, however, rural communities like Askilton were split between those who accepted regulation and those who did not and between those who were tolerant of the Mi'kmaq and other rural poor and those who were not. The creation of this division is the important point, because once entrenched it made possible the prosecution and persecution of those who still considered game to be an open commons. And since men like Gabriel Sylliboy adhered to the concept of an open commons, this division within Inverness County created the possibility that he, or other members of his community, would one day stand in front of a magistrate charged with trapping out of season. The only question needing explication therefore is not that it happened, but that it happened in November 1927.

2 Why Nova Scotia Prosecuted Gabriel Sylliboy

After Malcolm MacKinnon had seized the fox and muskrat skins he had found in Gabriel Sylliboy's possession on 4 November 1927, he returned to West Bay and informed the region's chief forest ranger, Charles Portus, of what had happened. Portus, after a discussion with MacKinnon, wrote to the Province's Chief Forester, Otto Schierbeck, asking for instructions. Portus wanted to know if he should charge Sylliboy and the Jeddores. In his letter, Portus wrote that 'I have yesterday seized from a party of three Indians out camping on Inverness County 14 Rat-skins and one fox skin. The party consisted of an Indian Chief and two others. Kindly advice if further action is desired also instructions in regards disposal of skins seized.' Schierbeck's assistant, J.H. Congdon replied a few days later. 'You are to take action against the three Indians who held the fourteen rat skins and the one fox skin. You are to employ Daniel McLellan, K.C. of Port Hood to act for you.'[1]

Sylliboy's infraction should not have warranted such special attention because he was contravening a law, where the Crown only had to show that he had committed the offence. In most criminal matters the prosecution has to prove two things: that the accused brought about the criminal act and that this resulted from his rational will. This latter principle is called mens rea (Latin for 'guilty mind') and is often explained through reference to Sir Edward Coke's pronouncement in 1623 that 'an act does not make [the doer of it] guilty, unless the mind be guilty: that is unless the intention be criminal.' According to Coke, 'the intent and the act must both concur to constitute the crime.'[2] Proving intent is not always possible or desirable; the common law also recognizes that not everyone has the capacity to form the intent to commit a criminal act. As Justice Oliver Wendell Holmes, Jr. of the U.S. Supreme Court once observed 'even a dog knows the difference between being stumbled over, and be-ing kicked.'[3]

In some cases the prosecution does not need to prove intent, only that the individual brought about the criminal act. As Phil Harris ex-plains, with industrialization, governments introduced regulatory of-fences whose purpose was 'the establishment of standards which must be continuously observed in certain kinds of social and economic activity.' This might include 'purity and hygiene in the preparation of foodstuffs and other edible goods, and honest and fair dealing in matters such as the provision of professional services and commercial transactions with the consuming public.'[4] Wildlife legislation comes under this rubric, be-cause the intent is to conserve wildlife and to protect access to it. Sylliboy and the Jeddores had been caught with fourteen green muskrat skins in their possession, and therefore the only question that the magistrate needed to determine was who was responsible for killing the muskrats. Portus, however, decided to tread carefully, an action he probably took because of Sylliboy's claim to be protected by treaty. This would suggest Portus's knowledge that Sylliboy would be contesting any prosecution. Schierbeck, however, instructed Portus in a reply dated 10 November 1927 to proceed with the matter.

In this chapter, I explain Schierbeck's decision by placing Sylliboy's actions within the context of the reorganization of the province's for-est management, which had been implemented the year before Portus's letter. Schierbeck's decision to charge Sylliboy was partly motivated by the fact that the three men were camping on private land and had cut timber for their personal use. Their action, in Schierbeck's view, con-travened government attempts to restrict rural residents' access to the forest commons. Such restrictions, the government believed, were neces-sary to protect timber for export and to encourage investment in pulp and paper production. However, if Sylliboy had been the only Mi'kmaw person to contravene these government guidelines, then Schierbeck might have counselled Portus differently. But Sylliboy's trespass was only one of many occasions where the Nova Scotia Mi'kmaq had used and occupied off-reserve forest resources. Put in this context Schierbeck's decision to charge Sylliboy illustrates how actions taken at the provincial level pushed the case forward.

Scholars have stressed how Mi'kmaw hunting and trapping ran afoul of game legislation in the late nineteenth and early twentieth centuries, but these analyses have not placed such actions within the context of the Mi'kmaw household economy. [5]Hunting was only one instance of

Mi'kmaw use of off-reserve resources. Families also travelled off reserve to fish, and to harvest wild fruits and plants, to fish, to gather wood for fuel, and to collect materials to make baskets and other wood products. Schierbeck's decision to initiate a criminal prosecution against Sylliboy therefore had much larger consequences, because the intent was to undermine Mi'kmaw use of off-reserve lands, a policy of dispossession that had begun more than a century before.

These actions formed a new phase in the colonization of Mi'kmaw lands and through it a further change in peoples' interior lives. By the 1920s plans to reorganize the management of provincial forested lands reflected changes in the region's political economy and was the result of a compendium of factors, including the aftershocks of a globalized war. Although removed physically from the war's brutal realities, Canada entered the 1920s a different country than it had been before 1914. In the Maritimes, the years after 1918 were marked by special hardships, as demand for lumber, pulpwood, coal, and steel plummeted and resulted in falling employment, outmigration, and labour unrest.[6] Adding to the region's problems, government expenses were increasing while families and communities were attempting to reintegrate returning soldiers into the labour market as well as coping with the war's emotional and physical scars. These developments intensified business and government interest in the commercial exploitation of the province's woodlands. The 1920s therefore represented a new conjuncture in contestation between those, such as Mi'kmaw families and other poor rural residents, who had historically used common forested lands to supplement their income and those who owned forested lands, such as lumber companies, woodlot owners, and farmers. The intersection of these factors helps to explain why Sylliboy's prosecution occurred in 1927 and not before.

From the late nineteenth century the same impetus that had propelled state and provincial governments to regulate wildlife also influenced attitudes towards forested lands. In the United States, this movement was led by the enigmatic Gifford Pinchot, the scion of a wealthy Pennsylvania family who was appointed to head the United States Forestry Service in 1898 and who, during Theodore Roosevelt's administration from 1901 to 1909, was instrumental in extending the use of scientific techniques in managing the nation's forested lands. Pinchot, like his later counterparts in Canada, did not advocate the preservation of the forest, but its conservation so that it would continue to yield its bounty.[7]

These changes in how the professional middle classes, businessmen,

Mi'kmaw man, child, and woman with woodsplints (Nova Scotia Museum, Halifax: P113; N-7436)

and politicians viewed forested lands were also felt in Canada. As H.V. Nelles points out, even up until the late 1800s, many people thought of the forest as a non-renewable resource. By the early 1900s, attitudes had changed and governments had integrated the newer scientific thinking that conceptualized the forest 'as a permanent renewable resource.' Its continued availability was dependent on using professionally trained men to assist in developing scientific, but also economical methods of conservation. This entailed applying new surveying techniques and developing new practices, such as imposing no-fire policies, combating insect infestations, promoting reforestation, and introducing better harvesting methods. In most Canadian provinces, such policies were more easily implemented than in the United States, because the provinces had retained control over their forested lands.[8] Nova Scotia did not have as much Crown land as other provinces, and this may have been one factor precipitating Premier E. N. Rhodes's decision to reorganize the department responsible for forested lands and to appoint a professional forester as its administrator.

Rhodes's choice was the Danish expatriate, Otto Schierbeck.[9] Schierbeck was a former employee of Frank Barnjum, whose interests at one time had included timber leases for over 200,000 acres of Crown land in Cape Breton Island. Barnjum was an important figure in Nova Scotia's lumber industry in the 1920s and a confidant of provincial Conservatives and federal Liberals.[10] Schierbeck had one other notable qualification: he was a professionally trained forester and was part of a new university-trained elite who influenced government policies in the first half of the twentieth century.[11]

The new government also reorganized how the province's forested lands were to be managed. This began with legislation in March 1926, which centralized the work of rangers and their subordinates into a new government department, the Department of Lands and Forests, whose operational head was to be the chief forester. This legislation provided for the hiring of ten permanent chief rangers, as well as sixty-two sub-rangers who were to work six months of the year and thirty other sub-rangers who were to be hired for two months to bolster game enforcement.[12] The act made the chief forester responsible for many of the same duties J.A. Knight had had as game and forest commissioner, and it also added to Schierbeck's workload by making him responsible for all Crown lands and for reforestation and scientific enquiry.[13]

In Schierbeck's estimation, the new system was an improvement to the more decentralized model he had inherited from Knight when the government had depended on part-time employees. In a February 1926 memo, Schierbeck explained the consequences of such a system when responding to forest fires.

> Let us suppose that something really went wrong, that a big forest fire got out of hand through negligence and destroyed a lot of property. What would happen? The newspapers would start a hue and cry. The Attorney General would demand an explanation of the Commissioner of Forests and Game who immediately would point out that he had no say in the matter and put the whole blame on the Chief Forest Ranger. The Chief Forest Ranger would reply that he was only getting a salary of $200.00 a year and had his private business to look after and that he could not jeopardize his livelihood by chasing fires all over the Country for a mere pittance. He would politely inform the Commissioner of Forests and Game that he, with pleasure, could have his resignation, but at the same time he would put in a strong kick through to the Member for the County if his resignation was accepted. He would further blame his sub-ranger. When the sub-ranger was appealed to he would immediately use the same argument. He is perhaps only getting $15.00 a year for his work and he would further point out that the fires should have been looked after by the neighbouring fire ranger. This gentleman would apply the same argument, and pass the buck to somebody else. In short, the whole thing would peter out in the sand with no security for the future assured.

Schierbeck added: 'The above description of the happenings after such a fire is not fiction. I have experienced it during my work as a private forester.'[14]

The intended changes were meant to improve the department's efficiency. Because the ten chief forest rangers were to get full time pay, the new chief forester could now demand their full-time attention. In future, the forest rangers could not say they were indisposed or could not respond to a fire because of their private business. The new pay guidelines would help avoid this situation and it was hoped would undermine communities' influence over local rangers. Schierbeck could also demand that the men be qualified. To weed out patronage appointees, the act detailed that all chief forest rangers should hold a certificate as a provincial land surveyor as well as have 'experience in the woods as surveyor, cruiser or scaler.'[15]

The 1926 Lands and Forests Act also consolidated jurisdiction over the province's forested lands into one government department. The Attorney General was nominally responsible for this new department, but its day-to-day management and direction was entrusted to Schierbeck. Significantly, the act named the operational head of the new depart-ment the *Chief Forester*, and not the *Game and Forest Commissioner* as had been the case during Knight's tenure. The change in name represented a shift in attitudes toward forest management. Henceforth, the govern-ment strove to implement a new management plan, whose purpose was to extract as much profit as possible from the province's forested lands. Although the creation of the new department did in theory, at least, translate into the use of new scientific management plans, the net effect of such moves was to broaden private interests.[16]

The government's emphasis on forest management reflected an in-terest in encouraging capital investment in the province's woodlands at a time when other sectors of the economy were in decline.[17] Dur-ing the 1925 election campaign, the Conservatives had made much ado about one of their candidates, Frank J.D. Barnjum, who had 'promised a 200-ton-per-day paper mill on the Mersey River' and which in his opin-ion would help to expand the province's economy. The mill, Barnjum argued, would bring money into the province and create new jobs, by more fully exploiting the province's rich forested lands, instead of con-tinuing to ship pulpwood to be processed elsewhere.[18]

From the late nineteenth century, American newspaper companies had come to rely on Canadian pulpwood, including from Nova Scotia. In 1927 Schierbeck estimated that American pulp and paper companies owned two million acres, or about 20 per cent of the province's freehold woodland. As well, pulpwood exports to the United States had increased, most of it cut and sold by farmers and small woodlot holders.[19] However, this had not translated into attracting investment in a paper mill because most of the province's woodlands were privately owned. As Clancy and Sandberg point out, by the early 1920s 'small woodlot owners possessed 43 per cent of all forest lands, corporations held slightly over 40 per cent,' and the remaining 17 per cent was vested in the Crown.[20] The small percentage of Crown lands presented a nettlesome problem be-cause to attract pulp and paper investors, the province needed to assure them long-term access to prime woodlands. In 1899, the Nova Scotia government had attempted to do so by leasing one company the prov-ince's largest contiguous Crown land, which was then in Inverness and Victoria counties.[21] The planned pulp and paper mill, however, never materialized.

By 1926, discussions about building a pulp and paper plant finally bore fruit. The impetus behind the plans was Izaak Killam, who told the provincial government he was willing to arrange financing if the province would build a hydroelectric dam on the Mersey River, near the town of Liverpool. Killam also demanded, and received assurances, that the government would issue the new company timber licenses to cut on Crown land, most of it in Cape Breton. In the meantime, the Montreal-based entrepreneur purchased woodlands in Halifax, Queen's, and Shelburne counties. Construction began in June 1928. Seventeen months later, the mill opened. The new company did not use much timber from its Cape Breton leases; however, the effect of the 'million cord agreement,' as it was called, was to demonstrate the government's intention of policing its properties, as they now had a legal and political obligation to protect the company's access to Crown timber.[22]

One effect of the government's emphasis on developing and managing the forests was to restrict rural residents' right of access to the 'forest commons.' Sandberg and Clancy write that for much of Nova Scotia's history, rural residents used the 'forest commons.' 'By forest commons we mean those forest lands, public or private, which by virtue of being either abandoned or unsupervised, were used in common for a variety of purposes by rural dwellers.'[23] Before 1926 such property included unregulated Crown land as well as private lands owners had abandoned and no longer used. One such 'commons' was near Little Dover in Guysborough County. Edmund Conway said the land had belonged to Edward Bourds. However, since his death twenty years ago, Conway wrote in 1929, the land 'has been unoccupied and is a commons without a fence.'[24] As Conway's letter suggests local residents often knew when such lands were unoccupied.

People using the 'commons' ran afoul of Schierbeck's attempts to restrict their access. Rural residents used them for various purposes. They were there to hunt, to set traps, to cut wood for fuel, to pick berries, and to fish. But from Schierbeck's perspective, unlimited access meant an unregulated use of timber. It also increased the danger of forest fires, especially as rural residents used fire to replenish soil nutrients and to encourage secondary growth. Farmers burned their fields, blueberry pickers burned the barrens, and hunters burned the woods to attract deer and moose. They also allowed fires to burn out of control by failing to extinguish them.[25] For Schierbeck, changing the way rural residents used forested lands would minimize the risk of potentially larger conflagrations.[26]

Efforts to restrict usage of the forest commons assumed two forms: the government, by expanding the duties and responsibilities of chief forest rangers and large private landholders by policing the woods.[27] As one agent for two companies reported in 1934, the new land regime was not entirely successful. 'The situation regarding trespassing is better than it has been in the past, but is still a drain on the timber supply. They keep off the land while we are in that vicinity but [return] as soon as our back is turned. It is impossible to get an honest native to watch the land as they are all related, and will not act to the betterment of the company's interest. There is not sufficient wood on the land to warrant a full-time man watching it.'[28] The effect of both measures was to gradually enclose the forest commons.

This then is the broader context for understanding Schierbeck's decision to proceed with charges against Sylliboy in November 1927. Although his crime was hunting muskrats, he was also using unfenced lands. When accosted, Sylliboy and the Jeddore brothers had been camping on Alex Gillis's land for five days and had cut wood for their personal use. As another resident of Inverness County informed officials in early November 1927: 'There are roving bands of Indians in this County who trespass on farmers' lands, killing game out of season and otherwise defying the laws that apply to residents of this place. They claim that they have full privilege to camp, cut trees, etc. on these properties.'[29] The culprits had to be stopped, as much to appease Alex Gillis and his neighbours as to punish those Mi'kmaq who continued to harvest wood on Crown and private land.

Sylliboy's action in cutting wood on Alex Gillis's property was not an isolated infraction but was part of a general pattern of Mi'kmaw use of the forest commons in the 1920s and before. Mi'kmaw families harvested wood for two purposes: for firewood and for making various wood products for sale. From the early to mid-nineteenth century, families had turned to wood working to supplement their income. In 1914, eighteen of the province's nineteen agencies reported that families made wood products for sale. Some of these products were intended for the household, such as baskets, axe handles, and butter pails. Other items were for water travel, such as paddles, oars, mast hoops, and jib hanks. Such work, which was sold to merchants, shipowners, and to farmers, was also done by other aboriginals in other parts of the Maritimes, and represented an adaptation to the changing economy.[30]

Both men and women made these items, although women also worked alone, making baskets, moccasins, and necklaces for sale.[31] The women were renowned for their basketwork, a trade, which emerged in the early 1800s as the immigrant population surged and as farmers and town folk came to appreciate the baskets' versatility. In the early 1830s, Catherine

Parr Traill explained how Upper Canadians used Indian made baskets and birch bark containers.

> We find their birch-bark baskets very convenient for a number of purposes. My breadbasket, knife-tray, sugar-basket, are all of this humble material. When ornamented and wrought in patterns with dyed quills, I can assure you, they are by no means inelegant. They manufacture vessels of birch-bark so well, that they will serve for many useful household purposes, such as holding water, milk, broth or any other liquids. Some baskets, of a coarse kind, are made use of for gathering up potatoes, Indian corn, or turnips, the settlers finding them very good substitutes for the osier basket used for such purposes in the old country.[32]

Richard Uniacke wrote in the 1850s that Mi'kmaw baskets 'were made of the smooth inner bark of the birch tree, with an inner lining of thin pinewood. The outside is generally covered with a variety of pretty mathematical figures, worked with the quills of the porcupine, which are dyed of the most brilliant colours for this purpose.'[33] The gendered nature of the baskets also likely appealed to farm women, and not only because of their functional use, but also because of the colour they added to the household.[34]

Baskets were a mainstay of Mi'kmaw craft in the nineteenth and early twentieth centuries, but other items they made responded to the changing vagaries of their customers. One new product was the hockey stick, which the Mi'kmaq became so adept at making that the Dartmouth-based Starr Manufacturing Company named their sticks, the *Micmac*.[35] This stick, read a November 1909 advertisement in the *Toronto Globe*, is 'made of second growth Yellow Birch. The natural grain of the wood runs with the curve of the blade. This makes the "MICMAC" far superior to sticks made of steam-bent wood. MICMAC hockey sticks are light and strong – will not fray at the bottom of the blade – and are always correct in design and weight.'[36] As the Department of Indian Affairs reported in 1922: 'A profitable employment among Indians in a few sections of Nova Scotia is the manufacture of hockey sticks, and they appear to be experts at the business.'[37] Families from Millbrook, Shubenacadie, and Halifax County did so, and as the agent for Hants County reported in 1903, this employment was 'becoming every year a more permanent industry among those who are not prominent in agriculture.'[38]

Just how much money could a family earn selling baskets, hockey sticks, and other assorted house wares? On this score, there is little documentation, although the depositions made in the 1908 divorce proceedings between Thomas and Mary Jane Newall of Enfield provide some suggestion. In her reply to Thomas's suit, Mary Jane said her husband owned one-third of an Enfield farm and also made hockey sticks and other items. From this work, she said, Thomas made about five hundred dollars a year, an estimate the court seems to have accepted since as part of the divorce proceedings, the judge ordered Newall to pay Mary Ann, $2.50 per week or $130 a year.[39] We might estimate that Thomas earned one-third of his total income from the farm and two-thirds from his woodwork. This would place an approximate value of $330 for his coopering work. Such estimates, of course, are fraught with difficulties as most families likely bartered a portion of their wares for goods and so estimating a cash value for their products is difficult. The agent for Antigonish County indicated this in 1882 when he wrote that 'it was impossible to form any accurate estimate of the proceeds of their coopering and basket work, as they barter these away in most cases in small lots for the necessaries of life.'[40] Martha Walls suggests that families at the turn of the century may have made 40 per cent of their income from making and selling crafts, although she admits that these figures, garnered from the annual DIA data, are problematic.[41]

Where families sold their wares depended mainly on where they lived. Families near towns and cities went door to door or set up camp alongside busy roadways and in open-air markets.[42] They also sold merchandise to local merchants. The Yarmouth Mi'kmaq sold axe handles to the storeowner nearest the reserve while Truro families sold dash churns, butter tubs and baskets to merchants, who then resold them to their Halifax connections.[43] People in Cumberland, Pictou, and Cape Breton counties sold pickaxe and shovel handles to miners[44] while those from Annapolis, Yarmouth, and Lunenburg counties sold mast hoops and jib hanks to shipbuilders. And by the early twentieth century, some families were also benefiting from a growing tourist industry, offering their crafts at such places as the Pines, near Digby, and at Baddeck on Cape Breton Island.[45]

We can estimate the number of families who made most of their income from coopering by reference to the 1881 and 1911 censuses, which give occupations for each head of household as well as for dependent male adults.[46] Comparison between the two censuses shows a decline in coopering and basket-making and, as we will see in Chapter Seven, a greater reliance on wage labour. The 1881 census shows 142 of 357 people on the mainland and 81 of 119 on the island who declared coopering or basket-making as their principal source of their income. By 1911, this proportion had declined to 59 of 309 on the mainland and 31 of 179 on the island. However, the 1911 census also shows that few, if any, men who declared that they made most of their income from wage-labour jobs worked year round, suggesting that they did other types of work as well. No doubt, some fished, but many more likely also made baskets, hockey sticks, and other wood products for sale.[47] Women's work in this regard also likely continued, because it could be done at home while caring for young children and would have become more necessary as men worked in wage-labour jobs where the work was not always steady and dependable.

In the years before Sylliboy's arrest, the federal Department of Indian affairs had received several complaints about families trespassing on private woodlots. Such complaints were not new. From the late 1800s, Indian agents had reported that families routinely cut wood on private and Crown lands. 'They locate themselves where wood is most plentiful,' the agent for Pictou County wrote in 1897, 'and claim the right of taking whatever they require.'[48]

These problems with private landholders intensified in the early twentieth century as the Mi'kmaq had more difficulties acquiring the wood they needed. To make some items, they needed special types of wood. Ash and poplar trees were used to make baskets. These trees were felled, peeled, and the trunk split into thin layers that were then spliced into strips for weaving.[49] Ash trees were also used to make pick and axe handles and fir trees to make butter tubs.[50] Difficulties in finding a dependable wood supply intensified as more families turned to coopering and as the rural population grew. Some families were able to satisfy their needs from timber on the reserve, but others were not.[51] Families from Yarmouth County had 'to go 30 miles to get the wood for making baskets.'[52] Families from Millbrook did the same in the early 1900s. As one Stewiacke resident wrote in 1929, 'until a few years ago, Indians from the Reserve at Truro came every year to spend a few weeks in the [Stewiacke] Valley. They encamped on the Ridge near a spring. The women sat before the wigwams making baskets while the men tramped the forest in aimless fashion or sat smoking beneath the trees.'[53] By the late nineteenth and early twentieth centuries, wood supply was becoming a problem but the Mi'kmaq found their efforts stymied by private landholders, who cut wood for export, and at a rate that exceeded pre-1900 levels.

Most complaints came from Colchester and Halifax counties. In some cases, the Mi'kmaq were squatting on private lands; in other cases they

were cutting timber from private woodlots. In both instances, the owners demanded compensation for their losses.[54] In Halifax County, the
majority of Mi'kmaq lived off reserve, and some woodlot owners thought
they constituted an unseemly menace. Although the government had
established reserves in the county, by the early 1900s most families had
voted with their feet and were living closer to Halifax. Why they did so
is unclear, but there may have been a number of reasons, including the
importance of Halifax as a market for Mi'kmaw products, easier access
to the railway, and until 1915, the city's immunity from the Temperance
Act.[55]

Louis and Maria Newall and their five children are just one of many
examples we might use to illustrate this migration. Originally, the Newalls had lived at Cow Bay, a reserve which the federal government had
created in 1880 on the outskirts of Cole Harbour, a village adjacent
to Dartmouth. The family later moved to Windsor Junction, near the
Bedford Basin.[56] Both Louis and Maria must have believed that their
new home was better situated because it was close to the railroad and
so afforded easy access to Halifax and to other employment opportunities. For the Newalls, such access was important, as both were basket-
makers. As court records from January 1902 show, Louis was well known
to the men who worked on the Halifax railroad. When he was arrested
for mistakenly taking a package not his own, Newall had travelled into
Halifax that morning, probably to sell some baskets. While there, he had
also bought some pork, sugar, and tobacco.[57] Louis may also have been
drinking, or at least a magistrate who was also a passenger thought so.
However, the testimony may also indicate a common Haligonian perception that any Indian in town was there in search of liquor.

The Newalls were one of seventeen families living on the outskirts of
the city early in the century. Sixteen other families lived in the Sackville
area, near Fall River, Hammonds Plains, Wellington Junction, and Windsor Junction.[58] Not all of the land they occupied was fertile and so families relied on piecework and wage labour to make up the difference. The
families at Windsor Junction lived on a small piece of land, 'consisting
for the most part of rock.'[59] Other families were in Elmsdale and Enfield
– both about 40 kilometres inland from Halifax – and Sheet Harbour, a
small fishing village on the Eastern Shore, about one hundred kilometres up the coast.[60]

In the late 1700s and early 1800s, rural Nova Scotians had coexisted
with this population, if not always with equanimity. Often times, Mi'kmaw
families squatted on unfenced private lands, forming friendships

with the landholders. From this, customary relationships emerged, which were passed down to subsequent generations. The Mi'kmaw encampment on the Langille property at Martin's River is one such example.

Martin's River is in Lunenburg County and today can be reached via Highway 3, a winding road that skirts the coastline from Mahone Bay to Halifax. In 1918, the community became embroiled in a civil trial involving members of the Langille family. The case concerned a disputed property, which the Langille children claimed had been left to them by their father. This was the 'oak woods,' which the son, J.W., claimed to be his own. His sisters, however, thought not. At trial, one of the sisters' husbands, Alpheus Millet, recalled visiting the disputed property with his wife and her parents in the summer of 1913. Asked about the purpose of the trip, Millet replied: 'They wanted to see the oak woods there, there were Indians at the time.' Millet's wife also testified about that day. The place they visited, she said, 'was called the Indian camp. That is the place that my father and my mother and myself went to.' As J.W. said, the Indians had camped in the oak woods for a long time and had been 'all through it.' Significantly, none of the siblings contested the Mi'kmaq's presence. Indeed, in 1918, the plaintiff and the defendants referred to this part of the disputed property as the 'Indian camp,' as did the surveyor who drew a map for the court. All of this suggests that the Langille and Mi'kmaw families – who remain unnamed throughout the trial – had enjoyed an amicable relationship that had spanned at least two generations.[61]

Such interactions had been part of customary friendships from generation to generation, emerging first during the early years of British settlement when immigrants had relied on neighbouring Mi'kmaq for fresh meat and fish and which had assumed other forms as the Nova Scotian population grew. By the mid to late nineteenth century, some continued to honour the relationship they had inherited from their parents, although perhaps now the Mi'kmaq worked on the farm, cutting firewood, mending fences, baling hay, or doing other odd jobs in exchange for flour, sugar, tobacco, and other items. The important point is that these relationships were informal, were family-based, and were part of a customary pattern of interaction originating in the earliest days of European settlement. Implied, although perhaps never stated, was that the Mi'kmaq and the settlers had once lived side by side, each using the land and its resources. However, as the European population grew, Mi'kmaw use and access declined.

Susanna Moodie's description of her relationship with the Anishinabeg of southern Ontario illustrates how such relationships first emerged. As is well known, Moodie and her husband moved to Upper Canada from England in the early 1830s, eventually settling northeast of Toronto. The Anishinabeg were Moodie's constant, and sometimes, only companions. Their presence, however, was not happenstance, because the Moodies lived adjacent to the sugar bush. Moodie explains:

> A dry cedar swamp, not far from the house, by the lakeshore, had been their usual place of encampment for many years. The whole block of land was almost entirely covered with maple trees, and had originally been an Indian sugar bush. Although the favorite spot had now passed into the hands of strangers, they still frequented the place, to make canoes and baskets, to fish and shoot, and occasionally to follow their occupation. Scarcely a week passed away without my being visited by the dark strangers; and, as my husband never allowed them to eat with the servants (who viewed them with the same horror that Mrs. — did black Mollineux), but brought them to his own table, they soon grew friendly and communicative, and would point to every object that attracted their attention, asking a thousand questions as to its use, the material of which it was made, and if we were inclined to exchange it for commodities?[62]

But Nova Scotia in the early 1900s was not Peterborough in the early 1830s. By this time a new dynamic had creeped into relationships between the Mi'kmaq and rural residents, reflecting the scarcity of hardwood and the growth of a commercial pulpwood export market. The land had always been exploited for lumber, but the early 1900s represented a shift with the growth of demand south of the border for pulpwood to feed the growing newspaper market. For the Mi'kmaq who had come to rely on easy access to hardwood stands, the growth of this export market brought them into conflict with landowners and eventually with the Department of Indian Affairs. George Musgrave's run-in with some Mi'kmaq camping on his land is one example.

Musgrave owned the Musgrave Lumber Company, and among its holdings was an 800-acre woodlot on Grand Lake, about 20 kilometres inland from Halifax. In 1916 a group of eight Mi'kmaw families settled there, likely because it was adjacent to the Intercolonial Railway.[63] Although the families only stayed on Musgrave's land for part of the year, by November 1917 they had cut a substantial quantity of maple and ash trees. H.J.

Bury, the Department of Indian Affairs (DIA) timber inspector, 'found evidence of large numbers of young hardwood trees having been cut and the best portions of the straight grained wood being split for the purpose of making axe-handles, hockey sticks and basket wood.'[64] Musgrave initially demanded $250 in compensation but later advised the DIA that the total would be $400 if the families stayed another winter.[65] The department balked at the request, realizing the other complaints they would receive if Musgrave's demands were met. But officials also believed that Musgrave's grievances were legitimate, because some of his most valuable timber had been cut. Bury, the DIA's timber inspector, proposed a compromise: instead of accepting liability for the damage done, the department would pay Musgrave $250 rent for the two years the families had lived on his land.[66] Ottawa agreed and Musgrave accepted, even though he did not get the $400 he had originally demanded.

The cutting at other Grand Lake properties, however, did not stop. As one Indian agent explained, property owners were 'accustomed to having a certain amount of timber stolen and destroyed each year and had agreed to continue to do so for at least some time longer.' R.W. MacKenzie and William J. King, however, decided that they too had had enough and pressed their claims. The department investigated the allegations and found that 185 ash trees had been destroyed, probably to make splint baskets. Mi'kmaq from Wellington Station admitted to being on both the MacKenzie and the King properties, but the department refused the men compensation and urged the two to prosecute. This, in the department's view, was a much better policy because the threat of action might deter other Mi'kmaq. But MacKenzie knew he would not get any money if he did prosecute. The guilty parties might end up in jail, but that was it. What then was he to do? MacKenzie did the only thing he could: send the department a bill. MacKenzie and King only wanted what was fair and knew that only a few years before Ottawa had 'allowed an extremely generous settlement for damage claimed on land' owned by George Musgrave at King's Siding, also on Grand Lake.[67] These appeals failed to elicit the expected response.

Halifax County was not the only place where such problems occurred. Families trespassed on woodlots elsewhere in the province as well. Annapolis County landowners grumbled about Mi'kmaq from Lequille, a small village within walking distance of the old British fort at Annapolis Royal.[68] At Sheet Harbour, the agent moaned about families who had 'done a large amount of cutting and damage' to his property 'by peeling birch trees for torches, cutting spruce for oars and timber for boats, houses, axe handles and firewood.'[69] From Cumberland County, a woman wrote in 1901 that her 100-acre property 'is now occupied and being stripped of its timber by Indians who are wards of the Government. This land I consider to be purchased by the Government and appropriated to the use of the Indians and by this means settle all damages claimed by me. I am unable to sell the land by reason of the said damages and I think the Government should be responsible.'[70] And from Guysborough County, a magistrate complained about Indians who 'go upon private property and cuts wood, poles and other trees when he wishes when forbidden by the owner.'[71]

All of the examples cited above stemmed from families living off reserve, but officials also received complaints about reserve residents. H. Smith's letter to the agent for Colchester County in 1923 was typical. Smith owned 200 acres adjacent to the Millbrook Reserve near Truro, which was 'covered with maple, birch and poplar, the largest stand of such wood for miles around. Smith grumbled that over the past two winters, Mi'kmaq had cut trees on his property, bringing teams of horses into the woods to haul the timber out. Smith had posted *No Trespassing* signs and had threatened the offenders with jail, but his words had had little effect. To the contrary: the men had said they would very much like to spend some time in jail where they could be warm while the government could feed their families.[72]

The litany of complaints goaded federal officials to move Halifax County families onto reserves.[73] This was done in the hope that they would be better off and would be able to combine farming with some off-reserve work.[74] The Millbrook Reserve on the outskirts of Truro was one alternative, although officials favoured Indian Brook, near Shubenacadie, because it was in a rural area and large enough to accommodate new residents.[75]

These efforts had a mixed success. The department was able to convince five families from Windsor Junction to move to Millbrook[76] but had less success in Elmsdale, perhaps because the families had lived there for some time and because their principal spokesman, Jerry Lone Cloud, had a personal relationship with the curator of the Nova Scotia Museum, Harry Piers. From 1916 to 1933, the community resisted relocation and proposed alternatives that would have allowed them to remain where they were. Indian Affairs denied these requests, believing the Mi'kmaq should live on reserves and not among the general population.[77] In sum, by 1927, the department's efforts to relocate Halifax County's off-reserve population had only limited success. Seven families numbering sixty-two people had been moved but an equal number had not.[78]

The reorganization of the Nova Scotia's Department of Lands and Forests and the government's efforts to better manage the province's woodlands unfolded in the midst of this conflict. The reorganization meant that Mi'kmaw families would be less able to do as they pleased, because Schierbeck's plan entailed hiring qualified men who would work under his direction. This meant more man-hours scouring the woods in search of malefactors and other derelicts.

A couple of examples show how the Mi'kmaq were affected. In August and September every year, from fifty to a hundred Mi'kmaq picked blueberries on the barrens between Oxford and Amherst. For years this had been a welcome source of income.[79] Their presence for such an extended period meant they were doing more than picking blueberries. Their presence did not sit well with Schierbeck, who in 1926 approved the cost of patrolling the area.[80] The Pictou County Mi'kmaq also came under Schierbeck's telescope for allegedly starting a fire near Alma. According to the local ranger, the fire started from an 'Indian camp fire.' The guilty parties were duly visited, and although they denied any wrongdoing, were warned of future prosecution if they continued to be so careless. In all about five or six acres of coniferous growth were burned.[81]

These changes in regulating forested lands developed as government and businesses were trying to attract capital investment in the province's forest industry. Jobs were at stake, and so government was willing to intervene to create them. Officials believed they had the responsibility to protect the province's natural resources and equated that protection with the 'public interest.' Part of the rhetoric was to protect existing jobs and to create new ones. For the Nova Scotia government, the declining value of coal exacerbated the situation. The volume of coal exports declined in the 1920s, as markets secured during the war were lost, as industry began switching to oil and gas to fire their engines, and as labour unrest interfered with production.[82] This, in combination with the decline in lumber exports, helped to precipitate a crisis in the government's finances. The provincial government's efforts, therefore, to expand the use of the province's woodlands were part of a strategy to improve the province's economy at a time when its most important tax-generating industries were in decline. But changes in how woodlands would be used also meant the loss of livelihood for those who depended on using the forest commons to make their living.

The Sylliboy case therefore was not only about protecting muskrat or about enforcing game laws. The case was also about curtailing Mi'kmaw access to off-reserve lands and was part of a government effort to better manage the province's timber reserves. The Mi'kmaq were not the only culprits. Other rural Nova Scotians were as well. The difference was the legal basis on which the Mi'kmaq justified their actions. They said they had a treaty that the British King had signed with them 160 years before.

When Charles Portus, the chief forest ranger for Inverness County and the man who would ultimately be responsible for laying charges against Gabriel Sylliboy and the two Jeddore men, wrote to Chief Provincial Forester Otto Schierbeck, he did so in the midst of an ongoing struggle between the government and rural inhabitants about the use of the forest commons. By the 1920s, Mi'kmaw households were less dependent on coopering and basket-making than they had been forty years before, but such work was still an important source of income for families when wage employment was less readily available. This would have been especially true immediately after the First World War when demand for Maritime lumber plummeted, resulting in fewer Mi'kmaw men working in the woods. This would have made reliance on handcrafted items more prevalent than during the war, or immediately before. While the growth of mass-produced goods and motor boats undermined the market for some handmade Mi'kmaw items, the development of Nova Scotia's tourist trade in the 1920s and the search for replicas of authentic Indian culture created new markets for baskets and other touristy items. The Mi'kmaq also frequented off-reserve areas for other reasons, all of which brought them into conflict with forestry officials. Therefore, when Schierbeck recommended that Portus proceed against Sylliboy, he did so knowing that toleration would encourage more violations.

Schierbeck could have chosen leniency. Not more than a decade before, this is what Duncan Campbell Scott, the Superintendent General of Indian Affairs, had counselled Nova Scotia officials when deciding whether or not to prosecute Mi'kmaq hunting out of season. The return of the peace in 1918, however, brought a reassertion of competition for jobs and capital. The 1920s were not kind to Nova Scotians, and this set off a decade of consternation and hand-wringing. The emergence of a protest party, like the Farmer-Labour coalition, although not unique in a postwar period that witnessed the fracturing of the nation's polity, was the most tangible example of the decade's social and political instability.[83]

This struggle to develop Nova Scotia's economy limited Schierbeck's choices in a way that had not been true a generation or even a decade before. Here, we find the limits at which even the most empathetic bureau-crat is able to negotiate alternative solutions when faced with personally unpalatable choices. I am not suggesting that Schierbeck hesitated when he received Charles Portus's letter. Nor am I suggesting that Schierbeck sympathized with either Sylliboy or with other Mi'kmaq. What I am suggesting is that by the 1920s men like Otto Schierbeck had less flexibility in making choices than they had a generation before, and this is what made Sylliboy's appearance before a magistrate in Port Hood probable once he had decided to confront Malcolm MacKinnon in early November 1927.

3 Moving to Appeal: Mi'kmaw and DIA Motivations

The Sylliboy case would not have transpired the way it did if not for two additional actions taken. First, Gabriel Sylliboy hired a lawyer to represent him in magistrate's court and then, when he was found guilty, appealed the decision. Sylliboy's actions suggest that when Alex Gillis confronted him, he and other members of the Grand Council had decided to place the 'treaty' at the centre of the dispute. Second, Sylliboy was only able to appeal his conviction because of funds from the federal Department of Indian Affairs. Even though the department had initially refused requests to pay Sylliboy's legal fees, they later reconsidered that decision. In this chapter, I explore the reasons behind Mi'kmaw and government motivations and argue that both believed that the courts offered an alterative solution to resolving their disagreements. That decision would have important implications for the Mi'kmaq, by forcing them to adapt their political strategies to the vagaries of a text-driven, common-law system.

When Malcolm MacKinnon arrived in Askilton with a warrant to search Sylliboy's tent on 4 November 1927, four days had passed since Alex Gillis had first seen the three men camping on his property. The three men had told Gillis that they would leave that night but did not. Then when MacKinnon confronted the men on 3 November, they repeated their intention of quitting Gillis's property. The three men's foot dragging would suggest that they wanted to be to be charged and had waited while Gillis contacted MacKinnon and then MacKinnon had obtained the requisite legal documents. This scenario seems all the more plausible because within days Sylliboy had retained a lawyer, who had traveled from Sydney to represent his clients. Indeed, from the first moments of the confrontation between MacKinnon and the three Mi'kmaw men, Sylliboy had placed the 'treaty' at the centre of the dispute. When MacKinnon moved to seize the fourteen muskrat skins, Sylliboy had replied that 'he had law from the King to catch fur at any time which the English laws did not provide.'[1] Later at the appeal, Sylliboy gave his account of this conversation: 'When officer took pelts I told him I had treaty. He sd he knew nothing about that. I sd let me go and I'll show you copy of treaty. I sd if I wanted to I cd prevent him taking furs but as he didn't know about Treaty I wd let him take furs.'[2] Sylliboy's response suggests that he and other members of the Grand Council had already considered the possibility of challenging the government's attempts to restrict Mi'kmaw access to off-reserve resources.

This was not the first time that the Mi'kmaq had claimed that a treaty signed with the British overrode provincial and federal legislation. Since the Nova Scotia government had first introduced more stringent game laws in the late 1800s, the Mi'kmaq had been talking about a 'treaty,' as had other Mi'kmaq and Wustukwiuk people.[3] Indian Affairs officials first heard mention of a Nova Scotia treaty in June 1894 when Abram Toney from the Bear River Reserve in southwest Nova Scotia was jailed for hunting moose in closed season. The Indian agent, Freeman McDormand, wrote to the Deputy Superintendent General of Indian Affairs, Hayter Reed, asking whether or not 'an Indian under the existing treaties and arrangements [can] be prohibited at any time from hunting, fishing etc.,' presumably in response to Toney's statements. Over the following years, Mi'kmaq in other parts of Nova Scotia made similar claims. Initially, they tried to get the laws modified.[4] Later, the tone of the letters changed. The Shubenacadie Mi'kmaq, who lived on a 1700-acre reserve about halfway between Halifax and Truro, illustrate this shift. In February 1903 their chief, John Noel, told the local teacher that the 'Indians were free to kill animals at any time, that they could not be fined or imprisoned for shooting game in close season the same as a white man could.'[5] Three years later a similar statement was made in a petition and forwarded to Ottawa by the agent for King's County. This petition, sent from Lequille, a small village south of the town of Annapolis Royal, was signed by fifteen Mi'kmaw men, including Chief Paul, who identified himself by his 'old name' Bainweet, or Penminiwick. Unlike other petitions and letters sent in the name of Mi'kmaw leaders, the men wrote themselves:

Then two men of generals. Indian and white man. Mead thaire grementes by old tready. And therefore We would like for you to give us Better under-

stand. a format. Old law. Hunting and fishing. Then our Wood. If we have
free will. Let or not. At all. And give us Better comperhand. If g leave. Free
Will. By Selling Moose meat. At any present time. For my living. Because
our Familys is to live as ever.[6]

In forwarding the petition to Ottawa, the agent wrote that the Lequille
Mi'kmaq wanted a better understanding of the law as it was their view
that a treaty their ancestors had signed 'over two hundred years ago'
meant they could cut wood and hunt and fish whenever they wanted[7]
and added that he could not convince them that the treaty was no longer
valid.

Between 1908 and 1921, no similar complaints landed in either Ottawa or Halifax. The hiatus was probably because game wardens were
less aggressive than before. This was certainly the case between 1914 and
1918 when Deputy Superintendent General of Indian Affairs Duncan
Campbell Scott counselled the Nova Scotia government to be more flexible in their attitudes towards illegal hunting and trapping. This was necessary, said Scott, because of declining fur prices; he urged Nova Scotia
to allow trappers to make up the shortfall. Although the legislation was
not changed, Game Commissioner Knight perhaps instructed wardens
to be more understanding of the special situation of the Mi'kmaq.[8]

The end of war brought a rise in fur prices and a reassertion of the
wardens' authority, which led to more complaints. In May 1921 the chief
of the Pictou Landing Mi'kmaq, Matthew Francis, wrote to Ottawa that a
treaty made with the British in 1752 had given his people the privilege of
getting their livelihood at all times of the year. Francis was not claiming
an unrestricted right to hunt and fish but wanted people to be able to
hunt when in need. This is what three men had been doing at Cariboo
Island when stopped by the game warden. As Francis explained to Scott,
some people were having a hard time and, as they did not enjoy the
same government support as their white neighbours, the government
should be more flexible.[9] Later that same year, Francis and Chief William Paul of the Shubenacadie Reserve jointly wrote to the department,
arguing that the treaty provided the Mi'kmaq with special rights and so
they should be exempted from paying licensing fees.[10]

William Paul also addressed a letter to King George V in the name of
all Nova Scotia Mi'kmaq.

They have taken the treaty from us altogether. What we want to know is if
our Treaty stands good today as it rests as the sun and moon shall never

see an end. Oh Crown Protect us. They have taken our rights away and we have not got what we ought to have. We are not like the white man, go to the town and get work. White man don't look at Indians and what we would like to have is the protection of our treaty of 169 years ago. We protected the forests until 59 years ago and they have gradually taken all away from us and have put the same law on the Indians that they have on the white man and strangers that comes into this country. England never made a treaty to be broken don't let this one be broken.[11]

Soon afterward, a delegation of chiefs traveled to Halifax. Peter Paul from Truro represented the Nova Scotia Mi'kmaq, Isaac Peters the Prince Edward Island Mi'kmaq, and John Augustine the Mi'kmaq of Northumberland County, New Brunswick. The three came, wrote a local reporter, to 'interview the provincial government' regarding the applicability of the Lands and Forests Act of Nova Scotia. Chief Peters had a copy of an 'ancient treaty' with him.[12]

These petitions, remonstrances, and delegations were part of a broader agitation to pressure the provincial government to incorporate the treaties into wildlife legislation. Earlier efforts to ameliorate the effects of the new restrictions, by either extending the hunting season or by easing the rules, had sometimes worked. By the early 1920s, provincial government officials were less flexible, a policy shift related to the issues discussed in Chapters One and Two. This resulted in more complaints about Mi'kmaq hunting out of season and more efforts to catch the malefactors. This spurred a more publicly visible and aggressive Mi'kmaw attempt to convince the provincial government to recognize the community's special status.[13]

The Grand Council's role in this agitation is suggestive, rather than definitive. The principal evidence comes from the council's reference to the treaties in guiding relationships with non-Mi'kmaw peoples. C.W. Vernon, who attended St Anne's day celebrations at Chapel Island in the early 1900s, later wrote that 'during their stay in the island the chief, assisted by the captains, holds a court in one of the larger tents for the settlement of any disputes that may have arisen. The treaties made in early days with other tribes and the laws which govern their own, are exhibited.'[14] Clara Dennis's notes from interviewing Gabriel Sylliboy and Andrew Alek in the early 1930s provide more details. According to Dennis, the Mi'kmaq maintained their relationships with other people through the treaties they had signed with them. Sylliboy and Alek, she said, referred to two treaties in particular. One treaty was with the Mohawk, which at some indeterminate time had ended the conflict between the two tribes and which was woven unto a wampum belt. According to Alek, this 'Wampum belt made of Leather w white & black beads / It was made in Quebec/purple green & blue beads is 69 years old purple long, black long; Mohawks in Quebec have one. They come here next week Micmacs go to Mission in July in Quebec and they [Mohawks] come here in July to St. Peter's.' This treaty was part of a compact made with the Houdenosaunee and other peoples in the early 1700s, which had evolved from a common alliance with the French Crown.[15]After the fall of New France, this relationship changed, and although the Mi'kmaq upheld relations with the Houdnenosaunee, as shown by references to wampum belts and Alek's discussions with Dennis,[16] the exact form that this assumed is unclear.

In their conversations with Dennis, the two men also discussed the 'English treaty.' According to Sylliboy, the English treaty was the foundation of how the council adjudicated relationships with the non-native population. He told Dennis that we 'talke the English treaty. We got it from the [ ] king long long ago to keep and honor it honor it and serve it and follow it. If a [ ] person run against it we give him to go on English law. If he do anything to white man or stole from White man, we agree to give him English law and punish the last day before we leave.' According to Dennis, Sylliboy showed her 'the old parchment treaty,' which she said, was 'read and talked of at the council.'[17]

The Grand Council's understandings of the treaty focused primarily on the relationship between the Mi'kmaq and the British. Sylliboy spoke of a relationship that the Mi'kmaq were bound to follow. At the appeal trial, Joe Christmas, Francis Gould, and Sylliboy elaborated on how this relationship worked. Joe Christmas, who was 74 years old in 1928, told Judge Patterson: 'Remember hearing that goods were given blankets under Treaty. (Objected to) About 65 years. In the fall before Christmas. Big coats. And old-fashioned guns & powder horns also And some hide to make moccasins. And some food. In the spring potatoes & beans and corn for seed. Tobacco too. And some spears for spearing eels. Where people had little farms they got oats. These good distributed every six months.' Sylliboy said much the same thing: 'Under Treaty get from Gov't blankets and flour and some shoe & long coats. Still get them. From Mr. Boyd Indian Superintendent River Bourgoise. In Spring get seeds. Gov't put & maintain schools on every reservation. Putting up Home at Shubenacadie. All by virtue of Treaty. In Treaty promised to teach us.' Gould, who came from Eskasoni, said 'Remember my grandfather going to Sydney & getting blankets long coat corn (3 bushels) gun powder flour sometimes seed corn beads for moccasins, He told me he got these from the King. Under the Treaty. We promised to keep Treaty & got these things in return. That is what my grandfather told me.' In other words, the treaty bound the Mi'kmaq to obey certain laws. The men did not discuss these laws, but they did say that there was a correlation between adherence to the treaty and government aid. This mainly consisted of financial assistance, but it also included building schools.[18]

The men also contended that the treaty gave the Mi'kmaq certain positive rights. Joe Christmas said, 'Heard that according to treaty we had right to hunt & fish at any time.' Sylliboy said that 'since I was boy heard that Indians got from King free hunting and fishing at all times. Still believe Treaty good.' And Andrew Bernard, originally from Wagmatcook, told Judge Patterson that 'Micmacs can fish or shoot any thing they want all year round. Father told me that. Got right from King.'[19] The Mi'kmaq recognized that this right was not open-ended, but was subject to the community's rules and customs. Joe Christmas discussed this in his testimony, in a transparent attempt by Sylliboy's lawyer, Colin MacKenzie, to show that the Mi'kmaq were as concerned with conservation as everyone else was. Christmas told Judge Patterson that 'While I was chief made rules for people not to disturb other peoples' rights. Told them they must not hunt when fur not fit, but that they could at any other times. For example, when muskrats had little ones, must not kill them. When fur was fit, they cd. Dry and sell it, they could hunt.'[20]

At no time during their testimony, however, did the men refer to a treaty text. Nor did they refer to the 1752 treaty. Because the lawyers' questions are not included in Judge Patterson's notes, it is possible they asked about the 1752 treaty. This seems unlikely, however, for two reasons. First, as defence counsel, the lawyers needed to make a connection between the treaty and the right claimed. This could best be done, by directing the court's attention to specific treaty articles where the British had recognized Mi'kmaw hunting rights. Because the 1752 treaty includes a passage where the British conceded that the 'said tribe of Indians shall not be hindered from, but shall have free liberty of Hunting and Fishing as usual,' the lawyers' failure to question the men about this article would have been a curious omission.[21] Second, the lawyers only introduced a copy of the treaty after the five men had finished their testimony and just before Ben Christmas's testimony began. The timing of the treaty's introduction as evidence would show that none of the previous witnesses referred to it, as witnesses do not refer to documents unless copies have also been formally given to the judge and marked as exhibits. The only logical conclusion therefore is that the men's testimony was based on their oral memories of the treaty and not upon a reading of an English text.

This is also suggested by the tone of the men's testimony, which indicates that the lawyers focused on the men's oral memories about what they had heard from their parents and grandparents or referred them to their how the government's actions confirmed the treaty's centrality in the community's relations with outside forces. Christmas said that as chief his job was to instruct his people in the community's 'traditional rules,' and this included understanding the Mi'kmaw treaty relationship. Christmas said that he *heard* the Mi'kmaq had a right to hunt and fish. Andrew Bernard referred to a conversation with his father, while Francis Gould said that his knowledge of the treaty came from his grandfather. After establishing where their understanding of the treaty had originated, the two lawyers then asked each of the five men how they knew that the government still recognized the 'treaty' to be valid. In each case, the men referred to their own life experiences, which they believed illustrated the treaty's continuing validity. However, in none of this testimony did they mention the 1752 treaty.

The men's limited understanding of English also would have restricted their knowledge of the treaty's text. All relied on John Gould to translate their words from Mi'kmaw. The men's uneasiness in speaking English would have made discussion of the text difficult. As explained in Chapter One, most men of this generation were unable to write in English and, even though the younger Gabriel Sylliboy likely had a better facility than the others, his skills were probably also limited and certainly would not have included deciphering historical texts. Moreover, his conversation with Clara Dennis in the early 1930s shows that he thought about the treaty as a relationship, which could not be reduced easily to a written text. To therefore ask the men to interpret the English copy of the 1752 treaty would have been a frustrating and potentially damaging exercise.

Sylliboy's actions in 1927 and 1928 therefore should be interpreted by understanding how he and four other men spoke about the treaty. Sylliboy and the Jeddores may have simply gone hunting for muskrats as Sylliboy said he had done every autumn for the past 34 years. However, the manner in which the men dallied when given the opportunity to leave, and then hired a Sydney lawyer to represent them in Magistrate's Court would suggest that a decision had already been made to challenge the government's legislative authority. This decision was probably made because of the council's understanding of the treaty. Just how and why the men thought about this issue, I will examine in later chapters. The important point is that government efforts to restrict Mi'kmaw use of wildlife shaped the council's memory of the treaty. This memory stressed that the treaty was embedded in a relationship, which governed the community's interactions with non-Mi'kmaw peoples and that included a guarantee that people would have access to fish and to wildlife. The government's actions from the late 1890s therefore, acted as a catalyst in recalling this memory but also in shaping how the men thought about it, a point I will analyse more fully in Chapter Five.

The federal government's decision to fund Sylliboy's appeal was not made for similar altruistic reasons. To the contrary: the Department of Indian Affairs believed the appeal would probably fail and therefore believed Sylliboy's prosecution was an opportunity to establish a precedent in the case law. The DIA also viewed the courts as a less controversial method of dealing with areas of provincial-federal overlap, one that had the added benefit of removing the issue from departmental purview.

Officially, the Department of Indian Affairs discouraged aboriginal people from hiring lawyers. Faced with a restive aboriginal population in the postwar era, Parliament in 1927 had passed an amendment to the Indian Act that had made it more difficult for Indians and Indian communities to hire lawyers independent of the department's approval. Although this measure was supposedly to protect communities from unscrupulous lawyers, the government was mainly concerned with legal actions that would interfere with departmental policies and objectives.[22] It was on this basis that the Sydney lawyer, Colin MacKenzie, had first contacted the DIA about a week before Sylliboy's appearance in magistrate's court, outlining the charges and requesting financial assistance.[23] Assistant Deputy J.D. McLean replied on 21 November that the 'department considers Indians subject to Provincial game laws and does not undertake defense of Indians prosecuted thereunder.'[24]

McLean's response was consistent with how the department had answered earlier claims that the Mi'kmaq were protected by treaty. In 1894 in response to Freeman McDormand's request regarding Abram Toney's conviction for killing moose out of season, Deputy-Superintendent General Hayter Reed had replied that 'Indians are libel [sic] to punishment the same as other men if they violate the law for the protection of game.'[25] Three years later, Reed told the Bear River Mi'kmaq that they benefited as much as 'any other section of the community' because the game laws were intended to conserve game, not destroy it.[26] Later officials adopted the same policy. J.D. McLean wrote in March 1906 that like other Indian communities who had signed treaties, the Mi'kmaq did not enjoy any special privileges. The courts had upheld this position, said McLean, and so 'the department would not assist those charged with breaking the law.'[27]

When the Mi'kmaq began appealing to the 1752 treaty as the basis of their claims, however, the federal and provincial governments were forced to adopt another tack. Other judicial decisions and Department of Justice opinions had already ruled on the inter-relationship between provincial wildlife legislation and treaties, but those treaties dated either from after 1867 or from immediately before. The Mi'kmaw treaties, however, were of a different character as they were made before Legislative Assemblies had been elected and were treaties of peace and friendship and not of surrender.

The initial salvo came in 1922 from Nova Scotia's Game Commissioner J.A. Knight:

> Indians the same as other people are subject to the Laws relating to hunting, fishing, and trapping. They claim to be entitled to certain privileges by Treaty, but I cannot find anything to sustain such a claim. Several Treaties were made with the Indians, the last one being that made at Halifax with the Micmacs in 1760. This was a renewal of a Treaty made originally in 1726 with the addition of some provisions relating to trade with the Indians and the prices to be paid for pelts. The only Treaty that I have been able to find any record of which refers to rights of hunting and fishing is one negotiated in 1752 or 1753 with some Indians representing themselves as acting for the tribes. The Indians afterwards repudiated this Treaty generally, whom neither observed nor recognized it. With the exception of the Treaty last mentioned, which related particularly to the tribes in the Eastern part of the Province and which was repudiated by the Indians, I can find in none of the Treaties any reference to the right of hunting, fishing, camping or taking wood. Whatever license, constructive or otherwise, the Indians may have enjoyed in the matter of fishing and camping over public lands, there seems to be nothing in the records on which to base any claim on the part of the Indians to enjoy greater privileges than the general public on privately owned lands.

Knight was willing to make one concession: 'owing to their poverty' the Mi'kmaq did not have to buy a big-game hunting permit. But this was the only concession the provincial government was willing to make. In all other matters, the Mi'kmaq were to be treated the same as other Nova Scotians.[28] The federal Department of Indian affairs adopted a similar view and its negative response to MacKenzie's initial request to fund Sylliboy's defence in 1927 was consistent with that position.[29] The department continued to maintain this opinion during the winter of 1927–28 as MacKenzie renewed efforts to obtain funding.

Surprisingly, in March 1928 the DIA reversed its earlier decision. The about face was made even though officials believed the 1752 treaty did not confer any rights. DIA Superintendent General Duncan Campbell Scott did not explain the reasons for the change, but it is possible that the Department of Justice thought that the government's case against Sylliboy had a good chance of success and that the resulting decision would serve as an important precedent in Maritime case law. This opinion was likely based on the fact that MacKenzie would have to overcome several legal hurdles. We can divide these problems into two groups. The first area of contention was how the treaty should be interpreted and the second was whether the treaty had any standing in common law.

There were two main interpretive problems. First, because Sylliboy was from Cape Breton he either had to demonstrate a connection between the treaty and Cape Breton or had to show that people from Whycocomagh had signed the treaty. Neither of these propositions was likely to be proved in court as the English copy of the treaty showed that the principal individual who signed the treaty, Jean Baptiste Cope, had identified himself as the chief of the Shubenacadie Mi'kmaq. Three other men had also signed, but their places of residence were not given. In the absence of evidence, this seemed to undermine Mi'kmaw claims. Second, at the time the treaty was signed, Cape Breton was under French suzerainty and would not be formally become a British colony until 1763. Because Sylliboy was from Cape Breton, the question therefore was whether Mi'kmaq living on the island in 1752 were included in the agreement. In other words, could the treaty be retrospectively extended to Cape Breton Island after 1763 or could this only have been done by amendment?

Sylliboy's lawyers also had to address the treaty's legal standing. The first problem concerned the effect of later hostilities. Soon after the treaty was signed in November 1752, hostilities between the Mi'kmaq and the British flared and some documentation showed that the Mi'kmaq had been responsible.[30] This would suggest that they had not recognized the treaty's validity. J.A. Knight had hinted at this problem in his 1922 letter when he wrote to A.J.W. Desbarres that 'This Treaty was afterwards repudiated by the Indians generally, who neither observed nor recognized it.' The implication was that the Mi'kmaq had not upheld the promises they had made and for this reason, the treaty did not have any legal standing because 'consideration' had not been executed. As James Oldham points out, consideration was an integral part of eighteenth-century contract law and to be enforceable the parties signing an agreement had to fulfil the promises they had made to each other. Otherwise the contract was void.[31]

Even if Sylliboy was successful in overcoming these legal hurdles, he still had to satisfy the court that a treaty signed a century and a half before was legally binding, despite the changes in government that had occurred since. His principal problem was convincing the court that the treaties overrode government legislation. To do this, his defence counsel had to provide a plausible theory concerning the treaty's legal standing that would not undermine the government's legislative authority. Were the treaties parts of the common law? Or were the treaties the equivalent of constitutional guarantees? And if this was the contention, then how could this be reconciled with the changes that had occurred in Nova Scotia after the treaty was signed? This was the most difficult question that Sylliboy's two lawyers had to address, because by claiming a treaty right to hunt the Mi'kmaq were arguing that their right superseded Parliamentary democracy.

Ideas of Parliamentary democracy are central to both the history of Great Britain and to the colonies it established in North America. As is well known, the years before 1689 witnessed an upheaval in English politics, as Parliament undercut the king's power. This involved the execution of Charles I in 1649, the deposition of James II in 1689, and the succession of a distant Hanoverian in lieu of a Stuart claimant in 1714.[32] When the 1752 Treaty was signed, King George II exercised an uneasy rule through his ministers, who were now members of, and beholden to, Parliament. Although the king remained the most powerful and influential member of the British government, by the mid-eighteenth century his power and authority had been eclipsed.[33]

The relationship between king and Parliament and the colonial assemblies was also fraught with tension, which would reach its apogee with the American Rebellion of the 1770s. The colonial assemblies claimed the right to rule and to pass laws independent of Britain, and pointed darkly to the ways in which the Imperial Parliament and the King in Council had undermined the colonists' freedoms and liberties. One area of contention was the king's relationship with aboriginal people. Much of this dissent centred on the Royal Proclamation of 1763; the basis of the colonists' vitriol was a belief that they had established in common law a right to occupy aboriginal lands, and therefore the Crown did not have the power to arbitrarily alter the legal standing on which settler occupation was based. By establishing authority over how lands west of the Appalachians could be purchased from the Indians, the Crown had overstepped its prerogative. This animus, however, was also directed at how the British government's efforts to reduce a mounting national debt entailed a more liberal policy towards heterogeneous groups of communities that included aboriginals, blacks, German Protestants, and others.[34]

Similar problems between the Crown's prerogative and Parliamentary democracy bedevilled the legal basis of the Mi'kmaw treaties. Although the 1752 Treaty was signed six years before the election of Nova Scotia's first assembly, the ascendancy of parliamentary rule in the years afterward undermined political and legal support for it. As in the New England colonies, by the 1780s the Nova Scotia House of Assembly assumed that the treaties were part of the common law or as Peter Hoffer argues, 'law at the edge of Empire.' Treaties, says Hoffer, were an adaptation to the practical problems of enforcing the common law on aboriginal people in areas where government exercised little force and was unable to exert its power continuously. And so treaties became a diplomatic strategy for negotiating the terms in which the common law would be extended, but were temporary agreements that were broken and then renegotiated as English settlement rolled westward. As settlers surrounded aboriginal communities, negotiating the terms of how the common law would mediate relations became redundant and each community thereafter became subject to the same law and statutory oversight.[35]

We might argue that Nova Scotia's elected representatives understood the Mi'kmaw treaties in similar ways. Perhaps no clearer indication of this is that after 1779, they ignored Mi'kmaw complaints regarding the violations of the king's treaty promises and passed laws and granted lands as though those promises had no legal standing.[36] The formation of the Dominion of Canada out of the former British colonies, however, subtly changed the tenure of these relationships and would eventually spark controversy between provincial and federal officials over their respective legal responsibilities toward aboriginal people.

Sir John A. Macdonald, one of the principal architects of the British North America Act, assumed that the act gave the Dominion the right to centralize power at the expense of the provinces. While subsequent conflicts showed the difficulty of welding together colonies with different statutory histories and the tensions implicit in the negotiations leading up to Confederation, they also reflected different conceptions of federalism. Partisanship spurred the squabbles and so too did regional interests, with Ontario pushing the hardest to protect a vision of the union which would safeguard that province's autonomy. Disputes focused either on areas of responsibilities not explicitly mentioned in the BNA Act or on areas where there were overlapping jurisdictions, with the provinces adopting a more flexible interpretation than Ottawa. As the political rhetoric escalated, both parties resorted to the courts when they failed to resolve their disagreements.[37]

The provinces never questioned the federal government's ultimate responsibility for 'Indians and Lands reserved for the Indians,' but the fact that aboriginal people lived in areas under provincial jurisdiction meant that determining when federal responsibility ended and provincial responsibility began was not always clear.[38] For instance, in 1870 members of the Nova Scotia House of Assembly wondered whether townships remained liable to assist 'Indian paupers' as they had been before 1867. As one member pointed out 'formerly the overseers of the poor took some charge of this class and the accounts for their care and attendance were sent to the government to be paid, one half by the treasury and one half by the townships. The overseers considered that since Confederation they had no right to take charge of the Indians and, in some cases where they had furnished assistance from motives of humanity they were informed, on applying for re-imbursement, that the Indian Commissioner had no funds. Two years ago he had handed a bill to that officer, but it was unpaid to this day.' On the other hand, the province's Attorney General had threatened to indict one township 'if they failed to relieve the Indians,' a position that the minister later confirmed. As the AG told the House of Assembly, he had recently 'had occasion to call upon the Dartmouth overseers to render such relief to save some Indians from starvation.'[39] As this example illustrates, although the BNA Act may have made the federal government responsible for Indian affairs, their charges often lived off reserve, where they continued to depend financially on provincial and municipal governments. They also used resources over which provincial authorities exercised jurisdiction and which therefore came into conflict with federal authority. One of those areas of conflict was wildlife.

By the early 1900s, most provinces had passed legislation regulating hunting and trapping.[40] The curtailment of aboriginal hunting did not always sit easily with federal officials who believed that the legislation interfered with Ottawa's responsibility toward aboriginal people. Although agreeing that Indian hunting should be limited, officials feared how different provincial laws would affect an area of federal responsibility, particularly when the result would undercut family economies and increase the department's financial responsibility. This went against the spirit in which the federal union had been created. In a series of court cases and Department of Justice opinions in the late nineteenth and early twentieth centuries, federal officials argued that provincial game laws were *ultra vires*, or outside provincial authority, an argument Ottawa had made before and often with less than stellar results. As one Department of Justice lawyer pointed out in a 1910 opinion regarding an aboriginal who had been convicted of violating the Ontario Game Act. 'I think, in case you decide to instruct counsel to appear for your department, the point that the Ontario enactment under which the magistrate proceeded is ultra vires, should be very carefully argued in addition to the point that arises by reason of the treaty rights of the Indians.'[41] In making this argument, some officials believed the federal government, as both the inheritor of the Crown's responsibility toward aboriginal people and as the principal party to treaties signed after 1867, was the only authority able to balance the rights of settlers with the rights of aboriginals.

This was not the first time the provinces and the federal government had squabbled about aboriginal peoples' legal status. The *St Catharines Milling* case, which came before the Judicial Committee of the Privy Council (JCPC) in 1888, had also addressed the issue. The case was not directly concerned with Indian title, but both parties were forced to deal with that question. On one side was the federal government, which claimed that aboriginal people had held a perfect title to their lands prior to contact. The British Crown, said Ottawa's lawyers, had confirmed this through the Royal Proclamation of 1763 and had reserved lands west of the headwaters flowing into the Atlantic Ocean as the Indians' hunting grounds. After 1871, various aboriginal communities inhabiting the Northwest had surrendered title to the federal government, and therefore only it had a right to determine how those lands should be used. The Ontario government disagreed and argued that before contact, aboriginals had been a primitive warlike people, who had lived without laws and therefore had no concept of ownership. They had an imperfect title to their lands and at most only occupied them. It followed therefore that the Royal Proclamation and the later treaties were agreements of convenience and did not convey to the federal government control over the lands surrendered and that Ontario, as the successor to the previous colonial government of Upper Canada., retained the underlying title.[42] While the JCPC's decision did not directly address the issue of land title, it indirectly accepted the Ontario government's contention that treaties were agreements of convenience and therefore did not have the same legal status as those signed between independent nations.

The federal government's position towards treaties in 1928 reflected the ambiguous legal status that it had inherited from previous colonial governments. Although pecuniary interests drove the federal government's position, it was also influenced by their legal responsibilities. The issues raised by the Sylliboy case therefore were fraught with legal and political implications, and some officials believed a court hearing on the Maritime treaties was one way of dealing with the problem of determining the legal status of these early treaties. As Duncan Campbell Scott explained to a group of visiting Maritime chiefs, the treaty's constitutional validity was a legal question, not a political one, and therefore it could only be decided by the courts. In one sense, Scott was absolutely right: there was nothing the federal government could do because the provinces retained control over natural resources, including wildlife, forests, and the inland fishery. However, Scott also believed that where aboriginals depended on hunting and where settlement was limited provincial governments could do more by accommodating their needs.[43] As he wrote to Premier Rhodes of Nova Scotia, 'the delegation informed me that the Indians have never been interfered with in taking game until recently, and it has occurred to me that possibly this prosecution is due to the fact that some of the recently appointed game wardens may not be aware of the privileges that the Indians have always enjoyed under this Treaty.'[44] If Scott was correct, then this would have confirmed the appeal's importance, since any decision would resolve the political inconsistencies in the statutes' enforcement. As we have seen, local and provincial politicians had been unable to settle the issue. A court decision would resolve the matter, either by forcing the provincial government to make some allowances or by forcing the Mi'kmaq to adhere to the law. For all of these reasons, Scott now informed MacKenzie that the case 'would be an opportune occasion to have the legality of this treaty decided.'[45] The Department of Indian Affairs asked for and received approval from the Department of Justice.[46]

That decision now set the stage for the appeal, which was heard in the county court house in Port Hood on 2 July 1928. After years of claiming a treaty right to hunt and to fish irrespective of provincial and federal legislation, the Mi'kmaq would finally have a chance to state their views in a forum that circumvented the political process. Their leaders had at first sought a political solution to the disagreement, but those efforts had failed and the courts now appeared to be the only other way to force the provincial government to modify its position. Sylliboy's delay in vacating Gillis's property therefore may have been deliberate, meant to provoke a court battle, which would allow the Grand Council to voice its own understanding of the treaty. The game laws of the early twentieth century which criminalized Mi'kmaq hunting made this possible and, as government restrictions intensified, the council seized the opportunity, although as I will argue later, never with equanimity. For the federal government the appeal also offered a solution to what had become a political and legal problem. Superintendent General of Indian Affairs Duncan Campbell Scott believed the provincial government should have been more accommodating, but he also understood that determining the treaty's legal status would have a beneficial result. Department of Justice officials likely only agreed with this direction, however, because they had already concluded that the legal problems posed by the 1752 treaty would be too difficult for Sylliboy's lawyers to overcome and therefore any appeal would almost certainly fail.

Because of the prickly legal questions raised by Sylliboy's defence, the appeal focused on whether the 1752 treaty superseded provincial legislation. This type of defence called for something more than just the normal list of witnesses. Sylliboy's appeal lawyers, Colin MacKenzie and Joseph MacDonald introduced two different types of evidence: primary and secondary materials relating to the early history of Nova Scotia and the oral evidence of six Mi'kmaq men. In the following four chapters, I will focus my attention on five of these men.

What all this means is that Sylliboy's appearance before Judge Patterson in Nova Scotia's Inverness County Court in July 1928 was historically contingent. It resulted from a series of intersecting developments that had occurred over a long period. Sylliboy did not *have* to hire a lawyer, nor did he *have* to contest the provincial government's right to legislate when he could hunt muskrat. In the same vein, Alex Gillis, Malcolm MacKinnon, and Otto Schierbeck did not *have* to take actions that resulted in Sylliboy's prosecution. At each moment there were opportunities for individuals to make different choices, and that would have resulted in different outcomes. The Sylliboy case was one such moment when individuals and governments might have chosen a different path. Colonialism does not project a certain sequence of events and so ordinary people retain an ability to influence how those events will unfold.

One question that requires further explication is why the Mi'kmaq believed in the treaty's validity. In the pages that follow I focus on the development of the Mi'kmaw community's belief in its 'treaty rights' and that led to Sylliboy's decision to contest his conviction.

PART TWO

How the Men Remembered

4 Parents, Grandparents, and Great-Grandparents, 1794–1853

In this section, and the next, I place the men's testimony about the 'treaty' within the historical frame in which their memories about it were formed and were later recalled. This entails examining the time when they were born, matured, married, and were appointed as community leaders and members of the Grand Council. Because four of the men were born between 1850 and 1854, and the fifth, Gabriel Sylliboy, in 1875, in this section I focus on the history of Nova Scotia between 1850 and the early 1920s.

The men also spoke about their parents and grandparents' memories, and I therefore examine the years before 1850 as well. Previous generations had transmitted a memory of the treaty to the men. This was also true for their parents and grandparents. This memory of the treaty can be found in documentation dating from 1794 to 1853, when the men's parents, grandparents, and great-grandparents had been born and had matured, forming a link between the men's memories and the memories of previous generations.

Remembering is not an objective process. The brain is not a perfect repository of information from which the individual can instantly recall events exactly as they happened. To the contrary: remembering is a subjective exercise in which individuals selectively recall past experiences or events. How they do so is influenced by various factors, some of which we can understand and some of which we still do not. To achieve this insight about people of different cultures and of different historical epochs is difficult. Recent research, combining the disciplines of psychology and neuroscience, with its emphasis on neural functions, can help to evaluate the transmission of memories by peoples of different cultures and of different time periods. To be sure, biases remain that we cannot overcome. Nonetheless, this research provides clues to the complexity of human memories, how they are created, how they are remembered, and how they are later recalled.

This research shows that memory is an active exercise, which begins when events are encoded with information that later allows for their recall. This event thereafter becomes a memory. When we do this, we create a memory trace, or *engram*. An engram is built by 'associating it with knowledge that already exists in memory.' In analysing this process, Daniel Schacter uses the example of how we remember telephone numbers. If we simply try and remember a number by memorizing it, we will have more difficulty than if we encode the number with information that is meaningful to us, and that is built on our pre-existing knowledge. As a historian, I am sometimes able to encode certain telephone numbers with historical events, such as 1713, 1763, 1812, 1867, and 1982. For a historian of Canada, these numbers have meaning. The same is true for establishing what Schacter calls durable memories. These memories are built on pre-existing knowledge. Because we cannot remember everything exactly, our memory system selects what to remember and what not to remember. 'What we already know,' the Harvard psychologist writes, 'shapes what we select and encode: things that are meaningful to us spontaneously elicit the kind of elaboration that promotes later recall. Our memory systems are built so that we are likely to remember what is most important to us.' This has implications in terms of what people remember and how they remember it.

Our pre-existing systems of memory may also distort the past. To illustrate this point, Schacter shows how our memory helps us to go about our daily lives. When we enter a movie theatre or restaurant, we expect a certain sequence of events to follow. This knowledge of what should happen, however, may distort what does happen. All of this suggests that remembering is an active process, not a neutral one. In remembering, we create a new emergent entity, which, however, intersects with pre-existing memories and knowledge.[1]

For evaluating how the Mi'kmaq transmitted information from one generation to the next, this understanding of how people remember has important implications. If people remember things differently based on pre-existing knowledge and memory, then how people remember between generations is also influenced by what they know and by what they already remember. Systems of knowledge and memory are never the same for two succeeding generations, and therefore how people remember information must also differ. The core of the memory will remain, particularly when the event is constantly recalled, but the details may change or be modified.

In this section and the next, I use this analytical framework to understand how memories of the treaty changed over succeeding generations. In this chapter, I examine the 1790s to the 1850s, years that roughly correspond to when the men's parents and grandparents were born and matured. In the next chapter I consider the period from the 1850s to the 1880s, the years when the men were born and matured.

As Schacter's research suggests, context is important for understanding and for evaluating the transmission of memories between generations. Thus, we must situate the men's memories and those of their parents and grandparents within the context of the British world and of the Canadian federal structure, of which Nova Scotia was at different times a part. This means documenting how the Mi'kmaq did or did not become integrated into the economic and political fabric of colonial and provincial life. It also means understanding how their position within colonial society tempered the cultural context in which their thoughts were interpreted and written.[2]

The 1790s to the 1880s were years of change for Mi'kmaw communities and also for the men's parents, grandparents, and great-grandparents. In 1794, Nova Scotia, although nominally part of the British Empire, was thinly populated by New England Planters, American Loyalists, Highland Scots, English and German Protestants, Acadian Catholics, former African-American slaves, as well as the Mi'kmaq. This heterogeneous group of women and men were not so much English as subjects of His Brittanic Majesty, and as the events of the 1770s had demonstrated, their loyalty was not always certain. The Loyalists had forestalled any further slippage of loyalty but the poor soils and tenuous nature of British dominion remained an indelible facet of late eighteenth-century life in Nova Scotia.

By the 1820s this instability had been tempered, reflecting the growth of British immigration worldwide and a robust rate of natural increase by white settler populations. That change infected both colonizers and the colonized, setting each against the other and against the Mi'kmaq in competing for lands and resources and in creating a shared language of loyalty, which became, by the 1820s, a competing site of struggle.

By the late 1840s and 1850s, Nova Scotia's position had changed once again and so had the Mi'kmaw community's place within it. Like other indigenous people in Canada, Australia, New Zealand, and South Africa, the Mi'kmaq had become by the 1830s subject to Imperial inquiries, an outgrowth of a humanitarian impulse, which stressed integrating aboriginal people into mainstream colonial economies. This impulse was part of a pragmatic attempt to reduce the costs of empire and to create a free market of goods and labour. Like other indigenous people, the Mi'kmaq formed an unseemly impediment to development and so some provision had to be made for them. The result was the creation of reserves, which had begun earlier in Upper Canada but which now spread belatedly to Nova Scotia. In this new political economy of private property, the Mi'kmaq were no longer competing for land, but had become dependent on the colonial state in making the transition to a more settled and productive life as farmers and wage-earners. However, their success was undermined by the infertility of the lands they occupied and the pressures exerted on them by a growing settler population.

This trajectory of forced dependence continued with the creation of the Dominion of Canada in 1867. On the one hand, the transfer of responsibility for 'Indians and Lands reserved for the Indians' to the federal government provided the Mi'kmaq with an attentive bureaucracy more willing and able to support families financially. But this assistance was accompanied by federal officials using their power to reshape and to reform community life. Although it was never fully successful, this intervention, coupled with declining standards of living, created new dynamics, and cultural perceptions became frozen with a more rigid racial typology that viewed the Mi'kmaq as biologically inferior to the superior northern European races.

This transformation in Mi'kmaw community life, from living independently of the colonial state to dependence on it, reshaped how people remembered the past and the treaties that their ancestors had made. In charting Mi'kmaw memories from one generation to the next, the following chapters examine these nuances. The focus, however, is less on central or imperial authorities than on how their policies, or lack of them, impacted Mi'kmaw communities. This often means understanding the financial basis of household economies and charting how those economies faltered from the 1790s to the 1920s. As the following analysis shows, examining these changes is important for evaluating the documents that convey Mi'kmaw memories of the treaty.

The documents that convey these memories assume two different forms. In this chapter I rely on four Mi'kmaw petitions from between 1794 and 1853, which purport to convey inter-generational Mi'kmaw memories but were written by Englishmen for the Mi'kmaq. The first dates from 1794 and was written by Commissioner of Indian Affairs George Henry Monk, who had been sent southwards from Halifax to

investigate rumblings of discontent among His Majesty's Mi'kmaw subjects. The other three petitions are from 1825, 1849, and 1853, and were
all penned by reform-minded middle-class professionals, Walter Bromley, Abraham Gesner, and Silas Rand.

Illiteracy in English was the norm for most Mi'kmaq in the mid-1800s,
and we would therefore assume that each of these men influenced how
and what the Mi'kmaq said. For instance, the men would have used words
they would normally use in educated circles. They would have also employed phrases that London officials would have expected to read from
subservient subjects expressing their undying loyalty and obedience. For
these reasons, we might suspect that petitions do not accurately convey
what the Mi'kmaq thought. However, there are also reasons to conclude
that the petitions do reflect Mi'kmaw concerns and ideas. First, all of
these men had had a long association with the Mi'kmaq, and this would
have facilitated the formation of trust and also rendered the translations
more accurate. As well, each wrote for a larger array of communities.
The 1794 petition was written on behalf of the 'Mickmack Indians,' but
we would suspect, based on Monk's journals, that his main contact was
with communities living in the triangular area bordered by Yarmouth,
Digby, and Windsor. The other petitions were written in the name of
specific individuals. The 1825 petition was signed by James Meuse, otherwise known as Adelah, 'Indian Chief of the Micmac Tribe' but whose
home community was along the Annapolis Basin; the 1849 petition by
ten individuals, who are identified as the 'Chiefs and Captains of the
Micmac Indians,' but whose last names are associated with the southern
mainland; and the 1853 petition by Francis Paul, who was named the
'Head Chief.' Finally, each of the petitions refers to an oral memory of
the treaty. This mention of a treaty at a time when Nova Scotian and British officials had done their best to forget that a treaty had ever existed
suggests that the core of the statements reflected the petitioners' intent.

In the next chapter, I rely on the men's memories about the treaty as
they recounted them at Sylliboy's appeal in July 1928. This testimony is,
like any historical document, a creation of its intended function. In this
case, Sylliboy's lawyers tried to make a link between the treaty and the
right claimed. This meant showing that the government had always recognized the treaty's legal validity, thereby demonstrating the federal government's own belief that the treaty superseded provincial legislation.
The lawyers also tried to show Mi'kmaw beliefs that the treaty protected
their hunting rights. Issues that were not germane to these two matters
were not discussed. For this reason, the testimony gives an incomplete

picture of the men's memories. However, with the exception of Clara Dennis's conversations with Andrew Alek and Gabriel Sylliboy in the early 1930s, this is the only information regarding how Mi'kmaw leaders in the early 1900s understood the treaty. It is therefore valuable, even if incomplete. Its value lies principally in Judge Patterson's careful note taking, which rendered the men's testimony in their own words, albeit through an interpreter.

In both chapters I situate memories about the treaties within the context of nineteenth-century Nova Scotia and argue that this context shaped what was remembered. The process of reconstruction is a tortuous one. This is true when I link the men's parents, grandparents, and great-grandparents with the petitions of 1794, 1825, 1849, and 1853. As far as I know, none of the men's relatives were involved in the discussions that preceded these written appeals. They may have been but such is the nature of nineteenth-century documentation that linking individuals with historical events is fraught with uncertainties and unknowns. This is always true when we analyse the life histories of ordinary aboriginal people. In the absence of such records, I have concluded that colonization created a commonality of memory even though there were differences in the form and timing. However, those differences were overridden by the similarities of experience. Although my analysis does not always mention either the men's parents or grandparents, I have assumed that their lives were similarly affected by the events I describe and that they would also have remembered the treaties in ways similar to the ideas expressed in the four petitions in 1794, 1825, 1849 and 1853.

Although we know little about the men's grandparents, we can probably say that they were born between 1790 and 1805. We know this based on what we can glean about the men's parents and then counting backward. For example, we know that the men's parents were born between 1820 and 1835. This was true even of Gabriel Sylliboy, whose mother, Mary Basque, was born in 1830. It was also true of Andrew Alek, whose parents Thomas Alec and Mary Wilmot, were probably born between 1829 and 1832 and of Joe Christmas, whose parents Michael and Suttee, were born in 1833 and 1837.[3] From these dates we can assume the men's parents' birthdates to have been twenty to thirty years before, between about 1790 and 1805. None of this is exact, as various factors influence the average age at first marriage, as well as the interval between births. However, in the absence of firm evidence, these dates are reasonable approximations, given that in natural fertility regimes women are more likely to have children in their twenties and early thirties.

We also do not know much about where the men's parents and grandparents were born. Although each of the men was born in Cape Breton, their parents were sometimes not. Suttee Christmas, for instance, was from Prince Edward Island and Andrew Alek's mother, Mary Wilmot, from the mainland. Thus, they were linked through their extended families to other regions of Nova Scotia and of the Maritimes, and this was likely even more true when we factor in their grandparents' heritage. In the absence of direct evidence, we can reasonably assume that the five men had relatives in various communities, on both the mainland and Cape Breton Island, as well as in other Maritime communities.

The men's parents and grandparents lived through a tumultuous time in Mi'kmaw history, when families who had used and occupied large swaths of territory discovered that their abilities to garner a livelihood were becoming more constrained. This occurred as the size of the white settler population grew. This growth happened first on the southern mainland and at other strategic points where land was fertile and easily accessible. It was within this context of a growing settler population and Mi'kmaw families declining access to land that leaders first began referring to the treaties their parents and grandparents had made with the British a generation before.

The first such reference was in January 1794 in a letter that George Henry Monk wrote to Nova Scotia Lieutenant-Governor John Wentworth. Monk, who had briefly served as the colony's Superintendent of Indian Affairs ten years before, had been dispatched by Wentworth to placate a troublesome group of Mi'kmaq who were camping near Windsor, a small farming community on the edge of the Annapolis Valley. As the war with Republican France in Europe had spread, Wentworth had become concerned that colonials previously evincing Francophile tendencies would rekindle their sympathies. As the Mi'kmaq were former allies of the French King and only recently brought under the Crown's protection, Wentworth knew that caution was needed and so appointed Monk to investigate the white settlers' complaints.

What Monk found could not have assuaged Wentworth's fears. Instead of a quiet peaceable people, Monk found a disaffected community. Part of the problem, Monk discovered was that families were unable to support themselves over the winter months. Some Mi'kmaq blamed their predicament on the government, which had allowed immigrants to settle along the rivers and streams that flowed into the sea. Their unfettered access to these lands became, over time, disastrous for Mi'kmaw families who had historically lived in coastal areas and had depended on the fisheries for food and income.

At the root of the problem was that after 1763, the British colonial government had not reserved land for Mi'kmaw use and had not restricted immigrants' movements. This contrasted to Lower Canada, where Catholic Indian missions had been created and to Upper Canada where the Crown had reserved lands west of the Ottawa River for the Indians' use. The effect of these measures was that by the 1830s, both Lower and Upper Canada had provided some security for their aboriginal populations, which, although imperfect and limited, did mean that they retained the ability to provide for their families, despite declining off-reserve resources.[4] In Nova Scotia, however, European settlers dispossessed families without the Crown attempting to protect the Mi'kmaq or to extinguish their title.

Why no provision was made for the Mi'kmaq is somewhat curious since in the neighbouring northern New England states, settlers had often purchased land before settling on it. This policy, which by the nineteenth century had become integral to British and American policy, was not entirely for altruistic reasons but reflected a pragmatic assessment that it was cheaper to buy the land than to conquer it. And often, such efforts at bonhomie disguise the ruthless manner in which such land transactions were completed.[5] Evaluating Nova Scotia in the light of this policy is complicated by the British-French conflict, which led to the British conquest of mainland Nova Scotia in 1710 and of Cape Breton in 1758. The treaties were made in the shadow of these conflicts and were intended to neutralize the Mi'kmaq as military adjuncts to French forces in an area the British coveted for its strategic value. As J.M. Bumsted has argued Nova Scotia's value lay not in its timber and fish, but in its location.[6] Before 1749 British authorities had exhibited little real interest in Nova Scotia. However, as rivalry with France escalated administrators took the unusual step in June 1749 of using public money to fund the creation of Halifax. Henceforth, Halifax and its harbour would serve as the base for the British fleet in the northwest Atlantic, acting as a counterweight to French warships anchored at Louisburg, and securing shipping lanes between the southern colonies and Great Britain. In the final apocalyptic war of the 1750s and 1760s, Halifax earned its fare well, serving as the marshalling ground to launch the triumphant campaigns against Louisbourg (1758) and Quebec (1759), which together would secure British economic interests on the northern mainland. Although there was certainly an intent after the expulsion of the Acadians in 1755 to expand white settlement, the British did not seek to purchase Mi'kmaw lands but to accommodate them under the umbrella of the Crown's protection and friendship, a policy that continued in the 1760s and 1770s, when both the Mi'kmaq and settlers maintained a semblance of co-existence. This relationship was undermined by the American Revolution, catapulting the Mi'kmaq into conflict with the settler population.[7] As Loyalists flooded Nova Scotia's coastlines, the government tried to placate Mi'kmaw disquiet by reserving some lands for their use. This policy foundered, however, because of the unilateral nature of the action, the shifting nature of the Mi'kmaw economy and government inattention in protecting the Mi'kmaw interest.[8]

In his sometimes magisterial overview of eighteenth- and nineteenth-century government policy towards the Mi'kmaq, L.F.S. Upton views the dispossession that had begun with the Loyalists and had accelerated in the years afterwards to be the result of Imperial inattention and colonial neglect. The inattention, he argues, was because the Mi'kmaq had never been allies of the Crown, as had other aboriginal communities who had fought alongside British troops. Implicitly, Upton suggests that a more attentive and capable Imperial administration would have intervened.[9] British inattention, however, was not solely due to animus but reflected the nature of European and colonial expansion. Colonialism is not a benign process, and those regions of the world which stood in its path, as did Nova Scotia and other parts of British North America in the late eighteenth and early nineteenth centuries, became subject to its insatiable appetites. Although Nova Scotia was not an attractive destination for immigrants before 1780, it became so afterwards as the crisis created by the American Revolution forced Great Britain to seek alternative lands on which to settle their Loyalist supporters. Nova Scotia fitted the Empire's needs well, even though not all those who came, stayed. The Loyalists, however, were only the first of a wave of immigrants who would come to Nova Scotia in the years afterwards, as the reorganization of land and capital in the British Isles wreaked havoc for ordinary people, leading some families to seek better opportunities across the Atlantic.

The resulting expansion that began with the Loyalist immigration undermined the Mi'kmaw household economy. Families had occasionally faced times of scarcity, and such occasions often resulted from unexpected shifts in weather. But by the late 1700s white settlement had begun to affect wildlife and fish populations and to change their patterns of movement. And on the southern mainland, the settlers' presence along river and estuarine systems, along with an intensified commercial fishery, meant that families who had formerly depended on the fishery were less able to do so, forcing them to adopt other ways of making their living. This led to more consistent and longer periods of scarcity.[10]

The human consequences of this policy were expressed in Monk's letter, which accompanied the 1794 petition to Lieutenant-Governor Wentworth.

It is certain and obvious that the Indians in this province are extremely wretched & exposed without having it in their power to relieve themselves. This arises from their particular situation. NS is a peninsula with many inlets and Rivers running far into the Country to sources not distant from each other: the whole coast of the Peninsula and all the Rivers are nearly everywhere settled by the English; Those settlements are extended many miles into the Country; roads have been made thru the most interior parts of the province and settlements formed on those Roads; the Inhabitants almost everywhere hunt the game in their neighbourbood & the Fisheries are entirely engrossed by them. Thus the Indians lose their usual means of subsistence without having as in other colonies on the main any Country or hunting ground to which they can retire, and from the same cause their suffering & complainings must inevitably increase with the Settlement & population of the province.[11]

One of the best-documented cases illustrating these problems concerns the plight of the Alexey family from Cape Sable, who were among the people Monk encountered soon after his appointment in October 1793. Acadians had first settled the Alexey family's lands in the 1630s and after their expulsion in 1757, by Massachusetts fishers and Loyalist and British immigrants. As the numbers grew, so too did the Alexey family's complaints. By 1823, family members had been forced to move four times. In a petition addressed to the Lieutenant-Governor in that year, Jean Bartlett Alexey recounted what had happened.[12]

Your petitioners were formerly settled at Eel Brook in this [Argyle] Township and was drove off by the Lands being granted and since that they have settled on three different tracts of Land and have also been removed in the same manner at Last Your petitioners settled on a Tract of land up the Tusket River twenty miles from Salt Water the last season we built on House and a number of Hutts and raised one hundred Bushel of potatoes, Some Indian Corn and considerable garden Stuff last [Fall] three men came on the Land with the intention of taking possession your petitioners having been so often removed, beg Your Excellency will take the [case] into your consideration and grant them the Land they now occupy or such other Lands as you Your Excellency may think proper.[13]

The Alexey family's problems had begun soon after Mi'kmaw leaders had negotiated a treaty with Lieutenant-Governor Belcher in June 1761. Ten years later, one of Jean-Baptiste's forbears, Francis Alexey, had written to the Nova Scotia Council complaining about interference with his family's fishery on the Tusket River, located north of present-day Yarmouth. The council assured him that the Mi'kmaq had a common right to the fishery, although not an exclusive one. 'I do grant unto you the said Francis Alexis,' the council's edict read, 'leave to Fish Hunt and Improve lands under the Usual Instructions, particularly in the Creek, called Ell Creak without hindering or Molesting any other Subjects who may choose to Fish there also.'[14]

The council's directions stemmed from their understanding of the English common law, which recognized tidal waterways as public waters.[15] Although landowners whose property abutted the river had a privileged access to the fishery, they could not set nets entirely across since this would mean infringing on the rights of upriver inhabitants.[16] Circumstances varied from county to county, and so the Halifax-based council left legislating and enforcing regulations to each county's Court of Quarter Sessions, a municipal-based body composed of Crown-appointed justices of the peace.[17] In 1791 the King's County sessions, for instance, ordered that nets could only be used in the Annapolis River three days in every week and could 'not extend more than one half across.'[18] The sessions for Yarmouth and Argyle enacted similar regulations for the Tusket River, legislating that nets should not extend more than one-third the distance across and not be placed within one hundred yards of each other.[19] This provision would have provided landowners a portion of the migrating fish.

This application of the common law, which emerged out of the particular historical context of a land tenure system, was antithetical to the Mi'kmaw economy. First, Mi'kmaw families worked cooperatively, but the English common law system was based on protecting individual rights, not collective ones. This presumed that some people would harvest more than others, depending on their location. Second, access was gradually limited as settlers acquired property adjacent to the river's edge. For the Mi'kmaq this meant they would have to secure rights to property if they wanted access to the fish.

By the early 1790s, this extension of common law principles had begun to adversely affect Mi'kmaw families in southwestern Nova Scotia and was one factor that precipitated a crisis in the colonial government's relationship with them. The government's concerns, however, were mainly driven by security issues and less by anxieties about the law's inequities. When Lieutenant-Governor Wentworth received information in October 1793 that Mi'kmaq near Windsor had stolen some sheep and had refused to surrender them, his orders to Monk were to use force if necessary. 'You are,' Wentworth wrote, 'to apprehend and confine in Fort Edward as many men, women and children as you may think necessary' and also disarm them. However, Wentworth also urged caution and preferred that such drastic actions would be unnecessary, as he hoped to secure Mi'kmaw assistance in any future conflict. 'If you can attach them to our cause in such a manner that the peace of our scattered inhabitants may not be disturbed by them and also that they will join us, in case of an invasion, you may promise they shall have some provisions and clothing for themselves and children and the men who join us be fed, as English men are.' After a month's investigation, Monk was able to assuage Wentworth's fears and to report that the 'depredations they were charged with having committed, were not on enquiry, found to be such as to make it necessary to disarm them or to require Hostages.' However, Monk's enquiries did reveal some unsettling intelligence that Wentworth did not care to hear: that many families were wretched, starving and destitute and that if some relief was not provided, they might take by force what they needed.[20] As Daniel Hammill, who was in charge of the stores at Windsor's Fort Edward, wrote to Monk 'if it is in your power to afford them any relief, I hope you will do it as well as for the sake of the inhabitants whose property is exposed, and will be certainly be plundered as in compassion to the poor distressed wretches whom necessity may compel them to commit depredations, for want of other means of relief.'[21] Such warnings goaded Wentworth to provide the needed provisions which over the next several months, Monk distributed.

From mid-November 1793 to early January 1794, Monk parceled out the parsimonious goods and rations Wentworth had provided to Mi'kmaw families who visited his lodgings in Windsor. What he discovered were rumours about meetings and councils, which portended a conspiracy afoot. Monk was unable to gauge the truth of such rumours, but his suspicions remained, borne from his separation from the men he encountered, who did not often speak English and conversed with each other in 'Indian.'[22]

Monk's suspicions centred on one member of the Alexey family, Charles whose family relationships reflected the heterogeneous character of the Empire's subjects in the late eighteenth century. From Cape Sable, Alexey's community lived close to French-speaking Acadian families. The two communities' proximity to each other and similar household economies had created a myriad number of interconnecting webs, including marriages. As the Acadian population on the Bay of Fundy grew, these relationships became fractured and intermarriages less common. However, the expulsions of 1755 and 1757 led some Acadians to seek refuge with the Mi'kmaq, and among these was the family of Anthony Hébert, who Monk later described as 'one of the late Acadians who it seems was an active man at the time of the Removal.' British actions drove the Acadians and Mi'kmaq together, and from this emerged new familial relationships. Among these was the marriage of Charles Alexey to Anthony's Hebert's daughter.

The marriage created a toxic mix, combining the savage nature of the Mi'kmaq with the Acadians' Gallic slothfulness – or so some English officials might have thought. More troubling was that the couple was Catholic and Anglophobic.[23] The result was not the amelioration of enmity but the reinforcement of dangerous sentiments, cultural values and attitudes, sympathies, and loyalties. Monk's recitation of Alexis's marriage to Wentworth therefore was not an idle observation but was deliberately made to underline the potentially treasonous character of Charles Alexey's complaints.

In his conversations with Monk, Alexey stressed that his own family had been sorely hurt by white settlers, an issue, he intimated, was also true for other Mi'kmaq. 'This man, Charles Lexi, complains the French people and some English have taken away the land that he had cleared and made a Garden of – that he, on a former complaint to Governor Parr received a promise that the land should be restored to him but he was deceived.' While Monk may have been concerned by these complaints, he was also unsettled by Alexey's other comments. Alexey told Monk that the Indians wished Wentworth to 'be made acquainted with their situation and with the treatment they have received since the English came among them at first giving them everything they asked for and continuing to give them supplies till all their Land Rivers Hunting Places were taken up and Settled in Townships and then Stopping all Supplies and leaving them deprived and destitute of every means of Subsistence.' One of Alexey's sons, who spoke broken English, added to Monk's uneasiness when he said that 'the Indians regret having peaceably suffered the English to possess the whole country before they were made secure of a continuance of supplies.' According to Monk, the younger Alexey repeatedly asked, 'what country was left for the Indians now the English give no more provisions or Cloaths what must the Indians do?'[24] This talk suggested that some families were desperate and might take what they needed from white settlers and might also band together with outside forces to unseat the British.

Monk's disquiet deepened after meeting with James Paul's family. Paul was angered by Monk's economy and told him that the governor had always given them more. Monk replied that the 'Governor gave what the King ordered and that I was his Servant to do what he told me, not to tell him what he must do.' After Louis Anthony translated these words into Mi'kmaw, James Paul's son, John, 'immediately said in english that if King George was so poor that he could give no more to Indians, the Indians better take nothing.' Monk was incensed and noted in his letterbook that he had an 'inclination' to take back what he had already given the men. However, they hastily picked up their packs and left, but not without a parting shot. John Paul's father, James, turned as he exited and said 'I won't trouble you again, the Indians must take care of themselves.' Monk replied that such 'young, stout men as he was were well able to take care of themselves and ought to learn how to behave themselves' as well. Monk's reply could not have elicited a friendly response, as his comments were meant to insult the men, claiming that they were lazy no-goods who by their selfish actions were taking food away from those more in need.[25]

For Monk and Wentworth, the men's anger and Alexey's warnings suggested the unsteady nature of British dominion and the potential damage on outlying white settlements that this disquiet could unleash. Wentworth's ability to punish disloyal Mi'kmaq, however, was limited, not because he lacked the military force but because his actions might spark a more general uprising by other Mi'kmaq. Without a sufficient military and colonial presence to cow the recalcitrant, Monk had few options other than use the King's stores to maintain a semblance of loyalty among these, His Majesty's unruly subjects.

In the midst of these discussions between Monk and disgruntled families, Mi'kmaw leaders referred to the treaty made a generation before in a petition forwarded by Monk to Lieutenant-Governor John Wentworth. The petition mentioned the problems the Mi'kmaq faced and lamented that families' access to favoured fishing and hunting sites was limited. The English, the petitioners said, 'have taken all the Coast & rivers and make Roads & settlements through the Woods every where & leave no place for the Indians to hunt in.' The result, they feared, was that 'they & their wives & Children must in a few years all perish with cold & hunger' unless the government granted them some relief. In previous years, the government had done so but insisted that the Mi'kmaq desist from bothering the settlers. The Mi'kmaq had agreed, even though the settlers had encroached on their hunting grounds. This had occurred immediately after the end of the American rebellion, when the size of the British population had grown. 'That nine years ago when the Superintendent [Monk] was settling English Towns he told the Indians they must live as Brothers to the English who came to settle where the Indians used to hunt, and that they would always be taken care of – treated kindly as they had been before and Gov Parr told the Indians they should always be taken care of and have relief when they were in distress.' These promises, they said, had first been made in the years after the Mi'kmaq had made peace with the English, at which time 'there was Country enough in NS for all the English French & Indians in the province.' Yet since that time, white settlers had continued to intrude onto Mi'kmaw lands and the government had done nothing to uphold their side of the agreement.

The men's words as recorded by Monk illustrate how the historical context of the late eighteenth century influenced how the Mi'kmaq remembered the treaty. In 1794, some community members would have still been able to recall when the treaty with the British governor was made and the words that had been spoken, but these memories were also shaped by the circumstances in which they were recalled.[26] For the Mi'kmaq those conditions centred on the rising tide of Loyalists who had flooded southwestern Nova Scotia in the late 1770s and early 1780s and which had led to a hasty conference with Governor Parr. Grievances then and ten years later centred on how to reconcile the treaty with this new population, whose presence was the result of the metropole's political and economic needs and heralded a reconfiguration in how loyalty would be constructed. At that moment the British still needed Mi'kmaw friendship and Monk and Wentworth knew it.[27] The men's reference to the 'peace, which had been made' therefore was a blunt reminder that the Mi'kmaq posed a potent threat to British settlers. How the men encoded information about the 1760 treaty reflected that pragmatic evaluation. The peace that had been made a generation before could also be broken, and it became part of a strategy to demand that promises made be honoured.

Monk and Wentworth understood the limits of their own power and that dominion the British might have, but control of the population they did not. When the Mi'kmaq voiced their discontent in ways which suggested that they might rebel, Monk did not use military force but threatened to withhold provisions. Although Wentworth had not ruled out military action and had instructed Monk to take children and women hostage, he knew, and Monk recognized, that such actions would expose the limits in protecting those under the Crown's stretched umbrella. All of this suggests the 'thin red line' that held the British world together in Nova Scotia in the late eighteenth and early nineteenth centuries.[28]

The threatened rebellion never happened, however, reflecting the Mi'kmaq's own tenuous situation and how by the 1790s, ideas of loyalty towards the Crown had permeated their consciousness. While Monk's petition may be read to show Mi'kmaw agency, it also shows how the British presence had affected Mi'kmaw family and community life. Monk's admonitions and distribution of the king's stores helped to bind the Mi'kmaq to the Crown by creating a shared concept of loyalty. Mercy and majesty, to borrow Douglas Hay's paradigm, formed a substantive, if still incomplete, 'structure of reference and feeling' that would, over time, bind families to the British Crown: mercy by showing the king's benevolence towards his wretched and destitute subjects, and majesty, by demonstrating the power of his person and those of his servants who served him in Nova Scotia. Lieutenant-Governor Wentworth reinforced these messages in his personal audiences with Charles Alexey and others, which, we would assume, were intended to demonstrate the omnipotence of the king and his mercy towards even the most lowly and distant subjects. Neither of these messages were lost on the Mi'kmaw families Monk encountered, who understood the consequences of rebellion, if only obliquely, and the benefits of loyalty.[29]

The flexibility implicit in these discussions evaporated over the next generation, and the pragmatic limits of British power were replaced by a new context, which underlined Mi'kmaw subservience to larger economic and political forces they could no longer affect. These new patterns did not emerge overnight but incrementally from the early 1800s, as the settler community grew. The flood of new immigrants and the competition for land from the next generation of native-born Nova Scotians propelled a reconfiguration in loyalty and exposed differences between the Mi'kmaq and others. This difference in how loyalty was defined would widen over the next half-century, as the white settler population's identification with Britain's unique global mission to spread ideas of English liberty and progress assumed importance in defining peoples' social and political place within Nova Scotia.[30] This redefinition also assumed a more racialized tone and was part of a general trend in Imperial relations with indigenous inhabitants, which valorized the actions of British soldiery in a positive light and informed differences between whites and non-whites.[31]

This change is again illustrated by the Alexey family's plight, an experience that shaped an 1825 reference to the treaty. This appeal, however, was framed differently than in 1794; it resulted from the growth of the non-aboriginal population and a more forceful and assertive British imperial presence. It also portended a shift in sentiment within the metropole, in terms of how Englishmen perceived the colonies. This change, which emerged out of the evangelical movement of the late 1700s and which stressed the redemption of the human spirit, began to focus its attention on subject peoples and their capacity to be redeemed through Christianity and labour.[32] This movement also found its way into Nova Scotia and became an avenue through which the Mi'kmaq, now beset by the violent vicissitudes of colonization, again referred to the treaties. The Alexey's family's problems illustrate this dynamic, and helps to situate the context of the 1825 petition sent to the British Colonial Office in the name of James Meuse.

The problems that the Alexey family had in accessing the fishery continued after 1794. In 1800 and again in 1803 they complained to the Court of General Sessions but did not receive a satisfactory answer. After petitioning the court in April 1800, for instance, the magistrates ruled that Alexey 'with the other Indians have a privilege in common with the white people of Fishing in all streams in this district.'[33] Three years later the family's problems were again the subject of discussion after Alexey had appealed to the lieutenant-governor. Wentworth instructed the members of the court to investigate whether the settlers' 'nets [were] entirely across the Brooks and small rivers, which entirely prevent any Fish running up the Streams and of course deprive the upper residents of any share.'[34] The magistrates were non-plussed and said that 'so far from the complaints of the Indians being well founded, that they have ever enjoyed and exercised as great if not a greater share of the privilege claimed, than any of His Majesty's natural born Subjects resident in the district.'[35] The effect of these rulings barred the Alexeys from accessing the fishery. In theory they had a common right, as the English common law said they should and as the lieutenant-governor confirmed in his 1803 message to the court. The reality, though, was that the settlement of landowners along the county's shoreline meant that fewer fish moved upstream and that the Alexey family lacked a shoreline site from where they could set their nets.

This was because the family did not own land. One place they had historically fished was at Ouikmakagan.[36] However, the Crown had never translated the family's occupation there into a grant of the land in fee simple, perhaps because the Alexeys had not petitioned for it or because the Crown had failed to recognize their presence. The upshot was that unless they had directly petitioned for, and received a land grant they were excluded from legally occupying Ouikmakagan. Unable to settle there, the Alexeys moved. This was what they appeared to have done in the 1770s, when the immigrant population was still small and so there were still choice spots to be had. As the settler population swelled, however, so too did their occupation of lands adjacent to the region's major river systems, which would have gradually restricted Mi'kmaw families' access. Indeed, the escalation of conflict from the 1780s suggests that a hierarchy had emerged between those who held property rights to lands abutting the most lucrative river fisheries and those, like the Alexey family, who did not.

If the Alexeys were no longer able to live along the Tusket River, where were they to go? How were they to support their families? We do not know what they did and can only surmise that they moved elsewhere and settled in a less-contested area. Here, they once again cleared the land and planted some potatoes. However, they did not live there year round but moved to the coast or to the interior as the seasons and their needs changed. They could not do otherwise, because they lacked the capital, the knowledge, and the friendly assistance of neighbours to turn their lands into something more than a garden plot. The effect of this peripatetic lifestyle made the lands they had improved vulnerable to dispossession by settlers who could claim the Alexeys had left. The more this population grew the more this sort of thing occurred. By the 1820s, two generations of immigrant children had reached maturity, and they too needed land to farm and fish to harvest. And like most families before them, parents wanted their children nearby. Unless the Alexey family was willing to use force to press their claims or to sue the malefactors before the Court of General Session – and assume any costs if they lost – attempts to reclaim land would have been futile. The effect of the Court of General Session's rulings, coupled with the shifting character of the Alexey family's movements, meant that they were forced to move four times between 1771 and 1823.

There is likely more to this story, however, than is suggested in Jean Baptiste Alexey's 1823 petition. His petition only says that his relatives had been forced to flee their lands on four separate occasions. How did the white settlers force them to flee? Did they simply ask the Mi'kmaq to leave, whereupon they left? Or had the Mi'kmaq left for a few weeks and when they returned, some family had settled upon their lands? What happened then? Were there angry words? Confrontations? Or worse?

In an 1819 publication, Walter Bromley gives another way of thinking about relationships with white settlers when such conflicts emerged. 'In Chedabucto Bay,' Bromley wrote, 'where the Indians have been in the constant habit of fishing, and supplying the white fishermen with their manufactures, peltry, &c for several years, they have been expelled in the brutal manner from that fishing ground by the white people who entered their camps, defiled their women, abused and beat the men, and, in fact, conducted themselves in such a manner as to prevent the possibility of their remaining any longer.'[37] A similar sequence of events may have also befallen the Alexey family in 1807. Four years before they had complained to the Court of General Sessions but they did not lodge another complaint; the reason may been that the white settlers had taken matters into their hands and settled by force what the courts had tried to settle by law.

Like much else that concerns the Mi'kmaq, evidence regarding this is not extensive, and so we have to imagine the sequence of events rather than to know them absolutely. What is clear is that in October 1807 Bartlett Alexis (Alexey), another member of the Alexey family, told justices of the sessions that Miner VanderHorn of Tusket Village had assaulted 'the body of Jane Alexis' (Alexey). The records do not tell us more about Jane Alexis, and so we can only assume that she was Bartlett's wife, daughter, or close relative. Nor does the court's summary explain the allegations. We might suspect, however, there was more to the incident, and that VanderHorn or his son had raped or had tried to rape Jane Alexey.

In the early 1800s, the common law only recognized a rape had occurred if a man had forced a woman to have sex with him against her will. This meant that he had penetrated her body or as Sharon Block explains, 'partial intercourse, or other sexual acts that did not involve both a penis and vagina were not the criminal act of rape.'[38] In some English cases, a man must also have ejaculated within the woman though, as Constance Backhouse points out, proof of emission was not always necessary.[39] In early nineteenth century Nova Scotia rape was a capital offence and was tried by the superior courts. Sexual assaults were less serious and so were administered by the Courts of General Session.[40] The sheriff, to whom the complaint had been made, appears to have had no evidence to support a charge of rape as the case was tried before the Court of General Sessions in the Yarmouth and Argyle District in October of 1807. However, the case may have been more serious than the records show. Jane Alexey was Mi'kmaq, not white and therefore a woman who could be trifled with. What jury would believe the word of a 'savage' and a woman who could barely speak English? Regardless, the men admitted their culpability and were freed after paying a fine of six pence plus costs.

Even though there is no direct evidence linking Mi'kmaw complaints regarding the fishery and the later assault, the tensions probably boiled over into attacks on the Mi'kmaw community, and especially on women, such as Jane Alexey.[41] As others have shown assaults on women is commonly used to terrorize a population.[42] Bromley's comment that the men of the Guysborough shore had 'defiled' Mi'kmaw women leading to their families' flight provides vivid testimony of how violence might have been used to goad families away from contested areas. And although there is little documentation regarding such incidents, there are reasons why they were not reported.[43]

It was during this period that in 1825 the Mi'kmaq again appealed to the treaty, but this time in a petition addressed to Lord Bathurst of the Colonial Office. Written in the name of James Meuse, a Mi'kmaw chief from the southern mainland, the petition shows a change in how the next generation of leaders remembered the treaty. In 1794, the Mi'kmaq had only obliquely mentioned the treaty in the context of discussing the peace that they had made. In 1825 Meuse referred to the 1760 treaty and enclosed a copy of it in his letter to the Colonial Secretary. While this shift from the *discussion of a relationship* to the reference to a *treaty text* shows the increased importance of non-Mi'kmaw peoples in mediating relations with British colonial officials, it also illustrates how colonization altered memories of the treaty.

Meuse's ultimate purpose was to protect his people, and the most effective way of doing so was to obtain a Crown grant of land in fee simple. To obtain the colonial government's approval, he felt that the best strategy was to show that his people were loyal subjects of His Majesty. This he did by pointing to the community's continued adherence to the treaty, an interpretation that differed from 1794 when Charles Alexey and James Paul had emphasized the flexibility of their relationship with the British Crown. By 1825, however, the treaty had become an example of Mi'kmaw submission. We have, Meuse said, continued to obey the law even though settlers had violated the 'sacred rights' of the Mi'kmaq. By attaching a copy of the treaty, Meuse gave a tangible example of that loyalty by showing that, despite being victims of settler violence, the Mi'kmaq had continued to honour the treaty. This showed, he implied, an equal, if not a superior, act of fealty. In not retaliating against the settlers, Meuse was extolling those Mi'kmaw virtues that paralleled the common law's emphasis on fleeing from an assailant and thereby protecting the king's peace.[44] Now, said Meuse, the Mi'kmaq had no other place to flee and appealed to the king's mercy 'to relieve their distress and to save them from ruin.' He requested that 'the Government would appropriate a small portion of the vast Tracts which remain unoccupied by the Whites and unproductive to the use of their Tribe, so long as they shall exist, in such a manner, that neither the Artifice of a White Settler, nor the imprudence of the Indian shall deprive him of it.'

Meuse's appeal was couched in ways similar to those of immigrants whose requests for land were accompanied by proclamations of loyalty. In an 1820 letter asking land for his sons, for instance, John Nichols boasted that he 'was among those loyalists who early forsook their homes and property and joined the British Standard at the American rebellion, and fled to the wilds of Nova Scotia, for conscience sake!!!'[45] Others, although unable to trace their heritage to the American Revolution, discussed their past and continuing loyalty.[46] As Donald Akenson has pointed out regarding similar entreaties made by Irish residents of Upper Canada after 1815, such assertions were used to demonstrate a virtue that should be rewarded. In Nova Scotia, such protestations of loyalty in areas where settlers contested access to land with neighbouring Mi'kmaw communities assumed a more sinister meaning with the settlers implying that because the Mi'kmaq had never fought for the Crown, they were therefore less loyal and so less deserving.[47] Indeed, such sentiments were commonly heard among early nineteenth-century British officials, including Major-General H.C. Darling, the Superintendent of Indians in Canada East who, in a letter to Secretary of State Lord Dalhousie in 1828 wrote of Mi'kmaq who frequented Quebec, 'They are in general a degenerate race,' Darling wrote, 'who have rendered Government but little service in war, and who do not promise ever to become valuable subjects in peace.'[48] Meuse's 1825 appeal tried to deflect such aspersions by focusing on adherence to a treaty his people had made two generations before. The implication was that the Mi'kmaq exercised a privileged right to the king's beneficence because their relationship to him and to Nova Scotia predated that of the white settlers.

The Meuse petition signifies a modification in how the generation after 1794 remembered the treaty. By 1825, the community's situation in Nova Scotia had changed as the colony's non-Mi'kmaw population grew. This later generation spoke not of the *peace that had been made, but of a treaty that had been concluded* and which listed the mutual promises each party was obliged to uphold. In 1825 the treaty had become an avenue to demonstrate Mi'kmaw loyalty and to secure a reward in return. This was a subtle shift from 1794, when leaders had demanded the resumption of an annual supply of provisions. Then, Mi'kmaw leaders had emphasized that the peace created by the treaty might be broken but Meuse, who had heard of the treaty from an earlier generation of leaders, recalled the treaty's meanings in a different context. For Meuse, the Mi'kmaq could no longer demand concessions. Maturing at a time when communities were overwhelmed by settler populations and where violence became a way of resolving conflicts over land and resources, he recalled the treaty as an emblem of loyalty and from a time which preceded the arrival of those settlers who now claimed a privileged right to the soil.

The late 1840s and early 1850s represent a further shift in how the Mi'kmaq remembered the treaty. As a result of agitation by men like Bromley and others, British policy towards aboriginals now stressed integrating them into colonial society so that they might become better farmers and better Christians. In Nova Scotia, this led to a more attentive government, which now finished what they had begun twenty years before by surveying lands set aside for Mi'kmaw use and by imposing penalties on those non-natives who squatted or otherwise used reserve lands without consent.[49] Governments also attempted to integrate Mi'kmaw children into the common school system as well as providing them with medical care.[50] This effort was partly moved by humanitarian concerns and an evangelical movement that stressed that all peoples, including the Mi'kmaq, could be redeemed. This entailed teaching them the value of hard labour, thrift, modesty, and the sanctity of the home but could only accomplished by ensuring that they had land. Otherwise, the family would be forced apart, and the incidence of ragged children frequenting the streets of Halifax would lead to a life of juvenile delinquency, debauchery, and prostitution. People such as the Baptist missionary Silas T. Rand were at the forefront of this movement, and he along with Joseph Howe, who had been appointed Indian commissioner in 1843 and who was replaced by Abraham Gesner, advocated for the Mi'kmaq through the 1840s and 1850s, seeking to create conditions in which they could become productive, if unequal, members of colonial society. Land, however, was not reserved for them in all regions, or if land was reserved not in areas that communities had used.

The families of Pictou County are an example. As James Dawson reported to Joseph Howe in 1842, some Mi'kmaq from the region had grown and harvested potatoes on a plot of land and were 'passionately fond of this lot as it affords them great facilities for the fishery.' However, the land had been granted some years before to officers of the 82nd Regiment, 'but no one claiming it has ever had anything like possession of it.' The owners' absence meant that the Mi'kmaq had continued to use the land as they had always done. This changed when the land was sold. As Dawson recounted, the new owners 'drove the Indians from the clearing where they grew potatoes.' The Mi'kmaq, said Dawson, 'have been driven from one place to another till they have not a foot hold left they can call their own. The very burying grounds have in some instances been desecrated by the plough.'[51] However, not until the 1860s would land be reserved for the Pictou County Mi'kmaq. Similar situations occurred in other areas of the mainland, where reserves were not created until after 1867.

The lack of an extensive land base exacerbated the plight of many families. The 1830s and 1840s were hard years for those living in more populated rural areas. These families confronted a growing settler population who were beset by the economic turmoil precipitated by Great Britain's dismantling of the colonies' preferential commercial ties with the British market.[52] The intensified use of the colony's resources and the lack of reserve land forced most Mi'kmaw families to rely less on fishing and hunting and more on other sources of income. Making baskets and other items to service Nova Scotia's agricultural and shipping industries were not always successful, however, especially as economic turmoil beset the colony, between 1841 and 1843 and again from 1846 to 1849.[53] Without a land base, families wandered from place to place within their home region and became a subject of ridicule and concern. Even those families who had settled on reserve suffered as the potato blight of the late 1840s destroyed their harvests. Despite a more attentive government, problems remained and levels of distress did not abate, as the petitions of 1849 and of 1853 illustrate.

In contrast to Meuse's submissive plaint in 1825, these later petitions adopt a more strident tone and document in more detail the ill effects of white settlement. Like Meuse, the petitioners stressed that the treaty was an important part of Mi'kmaw relations with the British Crown. However, unlike Meuse, this next generation argued that the British had broken the treaty's terms. In 1849, the chiefs wrote: 'Tired of a war that destroyed many of our nation, almost ninety years ago our chiefs made peace and buried the hatchet forever. When that peace was made, the English Governor promised us protection, as much land as we wanted and care of our fisheries and game.' They then described how the white settlers had violated the treaty's terms by limiting Mi'kmaw access to the land. The 1853 petition struck a similar chord. 'When peace was made between the Micmacs and the British, and the sword and the tomahawk were buried by mutual consent, by the terms of the treaty then entered into, which were ratified by all the solemnities of an oath, it was stipulated that we should be left in the quiet and peaceable possession of far the greatest portion of this Peninsula.' This, however, had not happened, and the white man, instead of leaving the land for Mi'kmaw use, had taken most of it. While some lands had been reserved, they were small in number and were not 'in reality the Indians' property. They are not under our control. They cannot therefore be truly said to be ours. At any moment they may be taken from us and we have no means of obtaining redress.' Even though this had led to impoverishment, the Mi'kmaq had never violated the treaty's terms. The white man had, by taking the land without Mi'kmaw consent.

This generation remembered the treaty differently from James Meuse because the context in which they absorbed memories about it differed. The 1820s to the 1840s were years of intense unease as the next wave of immigration rendered Mi'kmaw families' dependence on fishing and hunting untenable. In their petitions of 1849 and 1853, this generation therefore stressed how the British had broken the promises they had made and dispossessed the Mi'kmaq of their land. In part, this changed emphasis also reflected the different political context in which the Mi'kmaq addressed British officials. By the early 1840s, the colonial government had taken some tentative measures to provide relief to the Mi'kmaq. For this generation therefore, their principal purpose was not on securing protection from unruly settlers, as had been Meuse's intention, but on acquiring additional assistance. This included enlarging the number of reserves and obtaining other aid that would allow families to make the transition to their new status within the colony.

No doubt the letter writers also influenced how the petitioners' framed their appeals. Abraham Gesner penned the 1849 petition and Silas Rand the one four years later.[54] Both men were conversant with the Mi'kmaq and each had visited their communities, Gesner in his office as commissioner of Indian Affairs, Rand as a missionary to them. This affected

Silas Rand with two Mi'kmaw boys (Nova Scotia Museum, Halifax: P113/90-645; N-18,013)

how the petitions were written and, although Rand later said that he had transposed the words of the Mi'kmaq line by line, his own beliefs must have influenced how he chose to phrase and to translate their words.[55] Both men were committed to improving the community's economic status, but in ways that illustrated their own cultural blinders. The Mi'kmaq were, in these men's estimation, like children and needed the firm but benevolent guiding hand of their Anglo-Saxon betters, whose race had improved the world by bringing parliamentary democracy to its colonies and by creating bounty from the wilderness. As the world's greatest imperial power, Great Britain had a Christian responsibility towards subject peoples like the Mi'kmaq, to guide them on the road to progress and enlightenment. Just in the same way as Great Britain had advocated for black slaves, they should now do the same for other races, including the Mi'kmaq. Thus, Gesner and Rand likely pushed the Mi'kmaq to demand more assistance from colonial officials so that they too could make the transition to a civilized British life.

The petitions also reflect the community's perception of how settlement had undermined their access to land and to its resources, an issue that had been part of the 1794 and 1825 petitions. Thus, part of each petition reflects the community's disquiet about the white settlers' appropriation of land. In emphasizing this history of white settlement, the Mi'kmaq demonstrated their own understanding of the colonial state and ideas about the sanctity of private property. In doing so, they also underlined the fault lines of the humanitarian crusade, by exposing the hypocrisy of British treatment of subject peoples.

One of the hallmarks of humanitarianism was the redeeming value of education, which would reform individuals and inculcate civilized norms of behaviour. This included not only the three Rs, but also proper ways of speaking, writing, and behaving within the home and outside of it. It also stressed the values which it was thought had fueled Great Britain's industrial progress, such as the sanctity of private property. Ownership was correlated with prosperity as well as the possibility of upward social mobility.[56] This idea, however, conflicted with Mi'kmaw accusations that their land had been taken from them. Mi'kmaw appeals therefore that they exercised a prior right to the land were based on an understanding of human societies which emphasized the sanctity of prior ownership and that such notions were grounded on rights of equal access, regardless of race or status.

The 1849 and 1853 petitions implicitly recognized this contradiction and stressed the law as an arbiter to mediate relations with subject peoples. This perception reflected the evolution of the common law in the post-1800 period, with its own rules and practices and which theoretically treated every subject equally. The petitioners played on this belief, attempting to broaden the common law's application to indigenous peoples. This sense of distinctiveness became the basis of a new legal conjucture, one which, however, made its appeal to the king's law. From this time forward, the Crown in Mi'kmaw memories would be a 'Protector and an Omnipotent Lord' from a historic law that civil authorities no longer recognized. Thus, while the demise of the humanitarian movement in the 1840s and 1850s resulted in the refusal of civil authorities to deal with Mi'kmaw complaints, the Mi'kmaq now used their allies to launch a legally based appeal. This change was an important one and would become the basis through which Andrew Alek, Andrew Bernard, Joe Christmas and Francis Gould, would filter memories of the treaty.

We cannot document the relationship of the men's parents, grandparents, and great-grandparents to these ideas, but we can link them, if only indirectly, to the events which shaped the memories of the men who had met with Monk, Bromley, Gesner, and Rand. Like those men, the men's parents, grandparents, and great-grandparents had been dispossessed of their lands, which had resulted in a fracturing of their community and family life. As Andrew Parnaby has pointed out, for Cape Breton Mi'kmaw communities the 1830s to the 1850s were years of adjustment. This change, which paralleled earlier events on the mainland, meant a diminished access to hunting and fishing sites and to a greater reliance on wage work and to making finished goods for the Nova Scotian economy. It was also a time when agriculture became integrated into the household economy. Although families continued to engage in an eclectic usage of resources, the reserve became, by mid-century, a focus of community life, including for each of the men's families.[57]

The men's families were insulated from some of the worst abuses to which southern mainland communities were exposed and to which the petitions of 1794 and 1825 had referred. This was mainly because the island's mountainous ranges and poor soils made the area a less attractive destination than points south and west. When immigrants did arrive, they came later and in fewer numbers, and this affected how much and what land was reserved for Mi'kmaw use. On Cape Breton, reserves were set aside in the early 1820s and 1830s when the non-aboriginal population was still small. This meant that more land was reserved, and that it was of a better quality than if the government had acted later when the island population was higher.

The Cape Breton reserves were all still occupied in 1928. This included the five different reserves where the men who testified at Sylliboy's appeal were born. These are perched on or near Lake Bras d'Or, which, as Nova Scotia travel writer Clara Dennis wrote in 1942, forms 'a great saltwater inland sea, seventy miles long and from ten to twenty wide,' and borders on each of the island's four counties, Cape Breton, Inverness, Richmond, and Victoria.[58] Three of these reserves, Whycocomagh, Wagmatcook, and Malagawatch, are on the lake's northwest shoreline and not far from each other. In the 1830s, the largest of the three was Wagmatcook, with more than 4,000 acres; the smallest was Malagatwatch, at 600 acres. The other two reserves are on the other side of the lake. The larger is Eskasoni, on the western side of East Bay, about forty kilometres south of Sydney. The other reserve, Chapel Island, is on the southeast end of the island.

Despite more favourable conditions, the Cape Breton reserves became subject to intimidation by neighbouring farmers in the 1840s and 1850s and this must have become part of how the men's parents understood their relationship with non-Mi'kmaw peoples. The worst abuses occurred at Whycocomagh and Wagmatcook, where the Sylliboy and Bernard families lived in the mid-1800s. The Scots had arrived in the early 1800s, but by the time the last immigrants came ashore the best land had already been taken. Some of the new immigrants settled on reserve lands. This was sometimes unintentional and sometimes not, the problem stemming from the government's failure to clearly mark the reserves' boundaries. This was the claim of some Scottish families who settled at the rear of the Wagmatcook reserve between 1828 and 1832. Donald McRae, one of the region's oldest residents, said the surveyor-general of Cape Breton had given six families permission to live on the reserve's border but it was impossible to know its exact parameters.[59] The immigrants later admitted their mistake, but they claimed that the error was unintentional and so they should not be punished.

The squatters insinuated that the Mi'kmaq were unworthy and therefore less deserving, echoing the predominant European attitidues towards non-Western peoples. As Michael Adas points out, the basis on which non-Western peoples like British North America's aboriginal population were evaluated was different than the standard used to judge English or other European peoples because they were descended from cultures who had been unsuccessful in taming their environments. With industrialization, Europeans had begun stressing the importance of 'scientific and technological accomplishments as proof of the superiority of

Europeans over non-Western peoples.' This had become the measure of success and was viewed as the engine that had fueled the economy and had increased peoples' standard of living. This became clearer with the realization in England that its population was increasing, not contracting as had been thought. Therefore Europeans had a duty to 'expand into and develop regions occupied by less advanced people.'[60] With expansion, Europeans would bring progress and rationality and free the forces of production that otherwise would lay dormant.

Thus, as Ian Radforth points out, aboriginals became the foil to illustrate the progressive development and improvement of the Canadian wilderness that English constitutional liberty had made possible. In an address to the citizens of Toronto on the occasion of the visit of the Prince of Wales in 1860, for instance, the Indians were used to show the city's progress by contrasting the primitive nature of their life with the civilization that had been created since. 'The generation which saw the settler's log house succeeding to the red man's wigwam on the site of Little York,' read the published address, 'has not yet wholly passed away, and yet we venture to hope that Your Royal Highness will look with satisfaction on the evidence which our city presents on our streets, our railways, our private buildings, and our public institutions, of the successful results of industry and enterprise, fostered by constitutional liberty.'[61]

New immigrants played on such sentiments, contrasting their positive contributions to God's purpose and the Mi'kmaq's negative influence. 'We have not the least desire of dispossessing the poor Indians,' wrote three farmers, 'but we are convinced that a less quantity of land would equally do them for generations to come for all.' McRae added that 'there are not many Indian families and the number does not exceed sixteen, that the improvement of the Indians is near the mouth of the River and it is a rare instance for any of them to plant crops or cultivate the soil.'[62] Government officials disagreed and tried to eject the trespassers.[63]

Although there were various options the government might have pursued, in the opinion of the island's two Indian commissioners, Edmund Dodd and H.A. Crawley, nothing could be done. 'That the Micmacs' fathers were sole possessors of these regions is a matter of no weight with the Scottish emigrants,' the two men wrote in 1845. 'They are by no means disposed to leave the aborigines a resting place in the Island of Cape Breton; and it will not be easy for any Commissioner holding a seat in the Provincial Assembly, either for Cape Breton or Inverness, to do justice to the Indians, and to retain the good will of his constituents.'[64] The legislature, said the commissioners, was not the best forum to pursue the matter, as the local representatives would oppose ousting the trespassers. The Mi'kmaq might have used the courts, but Crawley believed that a civil suit would also fail, as a jury would not convict one of their own. Nor would finding a lawyer to represent Mi'kmaw interests be easy.[65] The government might have chosen to prosecute the offenders using the 1842 statute forbidding trespassing on Indian reserves as the basis but no such action was taken.

At Whycocomagh, similar events unfolded. There, as the number of Scottish immigrants swelled and a new generation sought lands for their children, life became difficult for reserve residents. Peter Googoo wrote to Crawley in November 1850 that 'they threaten us every day [and] since last May our wifes can hardly walk the highway without been annoyed.' People feared what the trespassers might do. 'This Philip McDonald took his pistol and was going to shoot Steven Googie's children, saying that the children was stealing their potatoes.' The result was that reserve residents allowed Morrison, McDonald, and others to do what they wanted, which included interfering with the community's common lands.[66]

We cannot know exactly how these events affected the men's families, but we do know that the squatters' actions convinced the government that it was better to accommodate them than the Mi'kmaq. In the 1860s, the government decided that the squatters should be allowed to purchase the land they occupied. As the commissioner investigating the situation at Wagmatcook wrote in 1861, the number of Mi'kmaq living there had dwindled considerably since the early 1800s and 'it is certain therefore that they do not require as much land as they did in 1810, particularly when it is remembered that the reserve is useless to them for hunting, fishing or lumbering.' He added: 'I fail to perceive any good that would result from their eviction, but rather the reverse, as it would stir up a feeling of hostility towards the Indians that heretofore has not existed and might cause serious results.'[67] In other words, reserve land had to be sold, since the alternative might incite violence. And politicians such as Charles Tupper were willing to accommodate the settlers at the expense of the Mi'kmaq; he, like many others, feared that too many Nova Scotians would continue to leave the colony, as many had done since the 1840s.[68]

The sale, however, limited farming income and the Mi'kmaw community's expansion. The Andrew Bernard family's emigration in the 1860s illustrates how troubles with neighbouring farmers sparked dispersal in the years afterward. All of this suggests that the nature of colonization may have varied from region to region but that its effects were similar. This is perhaps best encapsulated by how each successive generation of Mi'kmaw leaders since the 1790s conceptualized their community's status before the white settlers had arrived.

Each of the petitioners in 1794, 1825, 1849, and 1853 shared a common historical understanding of how white settlement had led to Mi'kmaw impoverishment. This, the writers lamented, had occurred because British farmers and fishermen had occupied more and more of Nova Scotia. The result was that Mi'kmaw families were deprived of their hunting and fishing grounds as well as their village sites. The 1849 petition described this turn of events, which was repeated in different forms in the three other petitions:

> You have taken from us our lands and trees, and have destroyed our game. The moose yards of our fathers where are they? Now whitemen kill the moose and leave their flesh in the woods. Your have put ships and steam boats upon the waters and they scare away the fish. You have made dams across the rivers, so that the salmon cannot go up and your laws will not let us spear them. Upon our old camping places you have built towns. And the graves of our fathers have been broken by the plow and the harrow. Even the Ash and the maple are growing scarce, and we are told to cut no trees upon the farmers' grounds. The lands you have given us are every year taken away. Now the small pox, measles and fevers destroy our people. The rum sold to them makes them drunk and they perish. They learn wickedness.

This situation was contrasted to Mi'kmaw community life before European arrival. In 1825, Meuse had written that before the white men had come, the Mi'kmaq 'could procure without difficulty abundance of Fish from the Lakes and Rivers, and Game from the Forest.' In 1849, the chiefs and captains made similar statements. 'We had plenty of wild roots, plenty of fish and plenty of corn. The skins of the moose, carriboo and beaver were warm to our bodies, we had plenty of good land.' In other words, before contact, the Mi'kmaq had been happy and their communities prosperous.

The white settlers' expansion had led to the deterioration of Mi'kmaw communities. In 1794, the petitioners complained that many had died, and in 1825 Meuse expressed a serious 'alarm for the safety of their Wives and Children, lest they should perish in their sight.' By the late 1840s a new generation of leaders was expressing the same concerns, although their penury was exacerbated by two successive years of potato blight. 'Our Nation is like a withering leaf on a summer's day,' the chiefs wrote. The prognosis of community leaders four years later was bleaker still. 'We are often reduced to the greatest straits,' they said. 'Our children suffer from cold and hunger, and we are compelled to witness their sufferings and hear their cries without the means of alleviating them and all this has befallen us because our means of obtaining food and clothing have been wrested from us.'

Mainland and Cape Breton communities likely came to share similar views regarding the effect of colonization, but the timing when this occurred differed. In Cape Breton, that difference meant that Mi'kmaw communities there were less directly exposed to settlers' violence, were effected by changes in wildlife and fish populations at a later date, and were able to settle on lands they had historically occupied and used. Did this also translate into differences in how community leaders and members thought about the treaty? There is little doubt that it did and that in the years immediately after the treaty had been signed, some communities began to form a different understanding than others. For instance, Charles Alexey and James Paul in the early 1790s probably voiced a more aggressive view of the treaty than the Cape Breton Mi'kmaq, who at this early date had yet to be exposed to the vicissitudes of white settlement. Similarly, in 1825 Meuse's reference to the treaty as a species of loyalty would not have resembled how Cape Breton leaders thought about the treaty. Such differences, however, which had animated discussions of Mi'kmaw councils in the late eighteenth and early nineteenth centuries, became less fulsome by the 1840s and 1850s, as differences among communities were flattened. This is illustrated by the paralleled experiences of mainland and Cape Breton communities, which by mid-century were surrounded by white settler populations whose presence interfered with their fishing and their hunting and which had forced an adaptation in how families made their living. Some Mi'kmaw families lived on reserve but, as we will see in the next chapter, most did not, forcing them to adopt alternative strategies. And even in those instances where families farmed reserve plots, they discovered, as did the Cape Breton Mi'kmaq, that this did not protect them from settler violence. From this emerged a more publicly visible Mi'kmaw leadership, a situation that the creation of reserves aided by fostering the conditions in which leadership could be more easily exercised. These conditions led to the formation of a more cohesive community than had existed before, when the fractured nature of both the colonial state and Mi'kmaw communities had created differences. The men and their parents were part of this new dynamic in Mi'kmaw social and political life and it is for this reason that the men's memories of the treaties were created.

This common understanding was also reinforced by the social and political inter-relationships between mainland and Cape Breton communities. These relationships date back to at least the early 1600s and had formed the foundation on which the eighteenth-century treaties had been made with British officials. Such relationships continued into the following century, although they were sometimes fractured. We get some sense of these relationships from the annual gatherings on St Anne's Day near Chapel Island, which were from at least the mid-1800s a point of social and political assemblage for Mi'kmaq from both the mainland and Cape Breton. This and the kinship ties created by marriage were points from which the treaties became part of inter-community discussions. This assisted, we would suppose, in the emergence of common ways of conceptualizing the community's history and the eighteenth-century treaties.

By the time the men who testified at Sylliboy's appeal were born, Mi'kmaw perceptions of the treaty had changed from how it had been understood generations before. This understanding, which in the 1790s had complained of encroachment on hunting and fishing grounds, had become by the time of the men's birth a story of hopelessness and poverty and of British indifference and cruelty. The treaty's place within this story had also changed. In 1794, the Mi'kmaq had referred to the peace that had been made and the promises made afterward by Governors Parr and Wentworth. Thirty years later, the treaty had assumed a more specific meaning and was invoked as an example of Mi'kmaw loyalty. By the 1850s the treaty assumed more importance still, recalling the Crown's commitments and its failure to live up to them. In making these appeals Mi'kmaw leaders began to attach meanings to the treaties in ways they had not done previously. The most important difference was how they spoke about land. In 1794, peaceful co-existence had been at the heart of the treaty but by the 1850s leaders said that the British had agreed to protect land for Mi'kmaw use. These meanings were not necessarily contradictory but do reflect that, as the Mi'kmaq struggled to support their families, they searched for ways to ameliorate their situation.

The assistance given to the Mi'kmaq in penning appeals to metropolitan officials, by Walter Bromley in 1825, Abraham Gesner in 1849, and Silas Rand in 1853, influenced how some leaders thought about their history. Bromley, Gesner, and Rand were familiar with the 1760 treaty but they differed on the legality of British occupation and aboriginal dispossession.[69] Although Bromley and Gesner bemoaned the injustices and inequities, they never maintained, as Rand did, that Mi'kmaq fishers and hunters had a perfect title to the land.[70] Rand's radical stance may have influenced how he translated Mi'kmaw words. Gesner, Rand, and others may also have helped Mi'kmaw leaders think about the treaties differently by explaining the political nature of imperial government. For the Mi'kmaq in the 1840s and 1850s, the treaty offered a strategy of inviting the Colonial Office's intervention by underlining the Crown's responsibility at a time when Great Britain was reducing its management, interest, and financial responsibility in its North American colonies. To provoke the Crown's assistance the Mi'kmaq needed to do more than just outline their grievances: they also had to detail the promises that the Crown had made. Although Meuse's 1825 letter had included a copy of the 1760 treaty, that agreement did not on its own include specific references to the Crown's obligations. In 1849 and again in 1853, the Mi'kmaq provided the details. While this interpretation resembled the earlier references of 1794 and 1825, it also inserted new ones, which stressed how the British had agreed to leave the Mi'kmaq in the greater possession of their land and to protect access to their fisheries and to their hunting grounds. This strategy was based on a realistic assessment that some British politicians continued to worry about the Crown's responsibility towards aboriginal peoples, as the 1857 House of Commons Select Committee on the Hudson's Bay Company suggested.[71] The petitions played on this sentiment, but unsuccessfully.

The men's parents and grandparents would have understood these issues in comparable ways. Although the Cape Breton Mi'kmaq were insulated from the worst abuses to which mainland families had been exposed, the growth of the settler population underlined the gradual deterioration of their lifestyle. This issue was emphasized by the demographic imbalance between the two communities, by how neighbouring farmers intruded on reserve lands and harassed Mi'kmaw residents, and by how the Nova Scotia government urged the surrender of disputed lands. Such actions fueled resentment towards the government and invoked memories of the treaty, which had promised the Crown's protection. This understanding was at the centre of their generation's oral memory of the treaty.

This interpretation, which had evolved as settlers dispossessed the Mi'kmaq of their lands, was set in a narrative that stressed their community's increasing impoverishment. The government, however, had recognized the wrongs that the white men had committed and had dispatched agents to Cape Breton to assist the Mi'kmaq and to help them make the transition to reserve life. In their testimony at Sylliboy's appeal, the men mentioned these agents by name. The first agent, in their memory, was Dodd. Joe Christmas said that when he was a youth 'at that time only one Indian agent in Cape Breton. Old Judge Dodd's father.' Andrew Bernard and Francis Gould said the same. Bernard added: 'After his death, the Dr. Cameron at Christmas Island was the agent.' Their assistance had taken a number of different forms but mainly consisted of clothing, seed potatoes, and powder for guns. Christmas said 'Dodds told people goods came from Government.' Government assistance also included building schools and came from appeals made by Christmas's grandfather. 'My grandfather got word from Halifax 62 or 63 years ago and his brother. They and another man went to Halifax. One Campbell was member and sent for us. Looking to get school for Micmac children. After two years got school. They were representing Cape Breton Micmacs.'[72]

What this suggests is that Mi'kmaw understanding of the treaty had changed by the 1850s and 1860s. The context in which memories were recalled was different. By the 1850s, the Mi'kmaq had come to consider the treaty as the basis of a relationship that would steer the community's relationship with outside forces. It was both a protective barrier and a political tool. This change had come about from the intercession of men like Gesner and Rand but also from the Grand Council's discussions with other aboriginal communities in Canada, and particularly at Kahnewake, which had become by the 1850s, a central meeting place for eastern aboriginal peoples. We lack transcripts of these meetings, but we can assume that the Mi'kmaq would have learned of the Mohawk's struggle to maintain sovereignty over their reserve and the intercession of the Legislative Assembly to protect them.[73] They must also have come to know about the ongoing disputes between the Six Nations and squatters in the 1840s on the Grand River and of agitation by the Anishinabeg of central and northern Ontario against mining speculators later in the decade.[74] All of this prodded Mi'kmaw leaders to re-conceptualize the treaty's meanings and to view it as a source of rights, in the same way that other aboriginal people were beginning to use the law to maintain political space in opposition to settler societies. This was part of a mid-century flowering in aboriginal politics, which swept the eastern colonies of British North America and which would later factor into why the men who framed the BNA Act made the 'Indians and Lands reserved for the Indians,' a federal, as opposed to a provincial reponsiblity.

The next generation of Mi'kmaw men, including Gabriel Sylliboy, would live in a very different polticial world than their parents and their grandparents. They would live in Canada and they would live on reserve. In this new world, they would have less freedom and less flexibility. That constriction of social and political space would lead to a subtle shift in how they remembered their peoples' treaty relationship with the British Crown.

5 Reserve Life, 1850–1881: Remembering the Treaty

Soon after 1867, the Canadian government completed the great task of nation building by signing treaties with the aboriginal peoples of northern and western Canada.[1] The treaties are part of our national heritage and, regardless of how they might be interpreted, represent a crucial juncture that transformed Canada into a continental power. The treaties also were transformative for Plains aboriginal communities, turning migrant buffalo and deer hunters into farmers.

As is so often the case, the past is more complicated than this scenario suggests. Not all communities signed the treaties, not all moved immediately onto reserves, not all families made the transition to a farming life, and not all 'Indians' were easily identified and distinguished from others. Rather, for most people who were aboriginal, life changed gradually and, as the 1885 Rebellion attests, was marked by periods of resistance to the federal government's imposition of a new legal, political, and economic order.[2]

The same was true of Nova Scotia. Each man who testified at Sylliboy's appeal was born on reserve and, as Joe Christmas did, worked alongside his parents, planting and harvesting garden crops, cutting and raking hay, and performing other farm-related work. Yet Christmas and the other men did not spend all their time on reserve, nor did they spend most of their days doing farm work. Rather they and their families also lived and worked off reserve. They had to, because their farms did not produce enough food or income to support their households. Although sometimes such employment included working for wages, most families made up the difference between what they were able to make through farming and what they needed to feed their households, by fishing, hunting, gathering berries, and making baskets and various wood products for sale. This often entailed living off reserve.

This movement on and off reserve became part of how the men came to remember the treaty. Like their parents, the men inscribed their personal life histories onto the treaty and so interpreted their families' and their communities' usage of off-reserve resources as part of this relationship. This memory of the treaty was a subtle change from that of the generation before. The men's parents had come to see government support as compensation for the land that had been taken from them. The next generation built upon this memory and interpreted the treaty as a source of rights that others did not enjoy. At the appeal, Sylliboy told Judge Patterson 'When officer took pelts, I told him I had treaty. He sd he knew nothing about that. I sd let me go and I'll show you copy of treaty. I sd If I wanted to I cd prevent him taking furs but as he didn't know about Treaty I wd let him take furs.'[3] As was true for their parents' and grandparents' generations, the way the men remembered the treaty in 1928 was conditioned by the context in which they had heard about the treaty and formed a memory about it.

In this chapter, I examine Mi'kmaw household economies in the 1870s and 1880s. This period roughly coincides with the years when Alek, Bernard, Christmas, and Gould were young adults and when Gabriel Sylliboy was a youth. I am interested in one question: where did people live? The question may seem innocuous. And perhaps it is. But the answer is not easily given. The Mi'kmaq, like other aboriginal people of late nineteenth-century Canada, did not always live on reserve and they did not always live in one place. Rather, their tenuous existence forced them to adopt a more eclectic lifestyle than their neighbours. Although other historians have outlined how declining access to fishing and hunting led to changes in the Mi'kmaw economy, they have not explored how household residency was affected.[4] Indeed, the implicit assumption is that most Mi'kmaq lived on reserve or off reserve. More recently in his study of mid-nineteenth-century Cape Breton communities, Andrew Parnaby has suggested that families moved and worked in neighbouring towns and villages, and that as transportation improvements were made, the range of these movements increased.[5] In this chapter, I explore these themes in more detail and suggest that from the mid to the late nineteenth century, the division between on- and off-reserve populations was more malleable and more flexible than it would later become. Since the men were children of a generation who had only recently been dispossessed of their land and who continued to think of it as a resource to use as needed, this cultural understanding was transmitted to the men's generation and formed the context in which they would remember the treaty in Judge Patterson's courtroom in July of 1928.

By the early 1870s, more Mi'kmaw families lived on reserve than had done so thirty years before. In part, this was because there were more reserves in 1871 than in 1841. But it was also because from the early 1840s the Nova Scotia government had created, for the first time, a permanent bureaucracy to assist their transition to farming. We see this change in how the men who testified at Sylliboy's appeal mentioned receiving aid from the government in the 1850s and 1860s. After 1867, and the federal government's assumption of responsibility for Indian affairs, the Mi'kmaq continued to receive aid, and in many different forms, including medical care, educational assistance, and material support, although this transition did not occur smoothly.[6]

Indian agents noted that some families were adapting to reserve life, but they also complained that some families roamed the woods, fishing, hunting, and harvesting wood. Some agents thought this was because the Mi'kmaq were not suited to farming. William Chisholm, the agent for Antigonish County, believed they had an irrational impulse to roam. 'The same love for roving about in bands from place to place,' Chisholm wrote in 1883, 'the same aversion to a settled life and the cultivation of the soil, which characterized the Indians of former days, still continues in a greater or lesser degree to actuate their descendants.'[7] The Bear River agent shared Chisholm's pessimism, explaining that the community's lack of success at farming was because they were 'never intended for a systematic farmer.'[8] Others believed that the Mi'kmaq lacked ambition and intelligence and this explained their inattention to farm work.

These comments mask the complexity of the Mi'kmaw economy of the late nineteenth century. Government policy was to move the Mi'kmaq onto reserves and to encourage them to farm so that they would one day assimilate into Anglo-Canadian society. However, the historical legacy of not reserving enough arable land created difficulties in making this policy work. Like other farmers who either lived on marginal lands or had not yet cleared sufficient acreage to sustain their households, reserve residents had to find other means to supplement their income. As in neighbouring New Brunswick, families did so in a variety of ways.[9]

The 1871 census helps us to understand the strategies families employed. Taken in April and May of 1871, the census was the first enumeration of the Canadian population and so provides the first substantive demographic portrait of the Mi'kmaw community in the late nineteenth century, the general timeframe when the five men were born and grew to maturity. In contrast to earlier attempts, the 1871 census was a crowning achievement. There were problems in how questions were asked, answered, reported and then tabulated, but the final result was a more reliable portrait than previous censuses completed by the individual colonies. One important innovation was to count people according to their legal (de jure) place of residence, rather than according to their de facto location on the day the census was taken.[10] The census also included additional questions that had not been part of earlier censuses and were incorporated into supplementary schedules. Unlike the later censuses from 1881 to 1911, these schedules were preserved and so can also be used to analyse household economies.

Counting aboriginal people presented special hurdles because many people worked and lived off reserve. This is not, however, what makes their situation unique. Many non-aboriginal people worked away from their legal place of residence as well. As Peter Baskerville and Eric Sager tell us, the late nineteenth-century labour market was volatile, forcing workers to constantly search for work, and often away from home. This was also true for urban workers in mid-nineteenth-century Halifax and Hamilton.[11] However, determining the residence of these rural residents presented fewer problems. Non-aboriginals generally lived in log or frame houses, and so enumerators would have had an easier time establishing if an entire family had moved, or just the male or female head of household had. Mi'kmaw families' situations were different as many lived permanently or temporarily in birch bark camps. How were these people to be counted? According to their location on the day the census was taken or according to their principal place of residence? How was that to be determined? By the place where they lived longest? There was no easy solution to these problems, but as far as we know the enumerators were told to record 'Indians' living in birch bark camps according to their location on the day the census was taken. This was spelled out in the enumerators' manual. 'Persons having no family abode and no fixed domicile of any kind,' the manual read, 'are to be registered wherever met with, whether on board ship, in shanties, public institutions, or private houses.'[12] The census therefore reflects the location of Mi'kmaw families in April and May of 1871 but does not show their residency at other times. We should keep this issue in mind when evaluating the data presented below.

According to the census, less than 50 per cent of all Mi'kmaq enumerated for Nova Scotia lived on reserve. On Cape Breton Island, however, the opposite was true but there were variations according to region. For instance, in Cape Breton County, the centre of the island's coal-mining district, 78 per cent of all Mi'kmaq lived off reserve. In the other three counties, more people lived on reserve than off. In Victoria County all Mi'kmaq lived on reserve, while in Richmond County only 25 per cent lived off reserve (66 of 78).[13]

On the mainland, the off-reserve proportion was higher (65% or 837 of 1191). As on the island, some counties had more off-reserve residents than others. This was because the government had not set aside reserve land in every region, and so some Mi'kmaw families in the early 1800s had petitioned for, and received, land grants. Others squatted on private or Crown lands. This was true of Annapolis, Yarmouth, Shelburne, Guysborough, and Colchester counties.[14] There were also more people who had married out of their communities, and so there were a number of mixed-blood families. Such communities were small and often only consisted of two or three families.

Mi'kmaw families lived in three different types of dwellings: frame or log houses, birch bark camps, or shanties. J.P. Gilpin described one frame house he visited on the Bear River reserve in 1877. 'The houses were small frame ones, with glazed windows, shingled, and each with a porch. Inside they had good floors, chimney, cook-stove, table, but few chairs, and walls not plastered, although some were papered with the *Illustrated London News*. A porch and single room formed the lower floor, but there was an upper loft, approached by a ladder which formed sleeping apartments.'[15] Other families lived in wigwams. At Whycocomagh in the 1870s, the American novelist Charles Warner saw a 'permanent encampment of the Micmac Indians, – a dozen wigwams in the pinewoods. Though lumber is plenty, they refuse to live in houses.' The wigwams, said Warner, were 'built up conically of poles, with a hole in the top for the smoke to escape, and often set up a little from the ground on a timber foundation.' The poles were usually covered with birch bark because it contained a resin that made the exterior waterproof. By the early 1890s when birch bark was not so readily available, families used tarpaper and furs instead.[16] Other families lived in small shanties, and although we do not have any descriptions of these dwellings, we would assume they were simple board structures, without foundations and with one room, and little more.[17]

Census enumerators classified each family's dwelling according to the instructions they had been given. Column Two of Schedule One was to be used to designate 'all dwellings of a temporary character, only in-

Wigwams in Tufts Cove, Dartmouth, 1871 (Nova Scotia Museum, Halifax: P113/N-9922)

habited for a part of the year, such as lumbering shanties, Public Works shanties, fishermen's huts, Indian wigwams, &c'; these were grouped under the more general term 'shanties.' Shanties, the census instructions outlined, was a word 'borrowed from the French Canadians by the early English settlers, [and] means a hut or cheap dwelling put up on a new settlement or temporary abiding place.' These places were differentiated from 'dwelling-houses,' which enumerators used to describe permanent dwellings.[18] Most of the time the enumerators followed their instructions. A few did not. Sometimes, they wrote 'wig' or a similar acronym in the 'shanties' column despite being told not to include such idiosyncrasies. Other times, they also made additional notes in the right-hand column of their schedules. For instance, the enumerator for Little Bras d'Or wrote that the forty-nine Mi'kmaq who lived there 'own no Houses. They live in Wigwams.'[19] Most enumerators, however, were more attentive to their instructions and checked the appropriate box to show that a family was living in a 'shanty' or in a 'permanent dwelling' and made no further comment which might add to, confuse, or obscure the census's purposeful ordering of Canadian society.

In all, enumerators noted seventy of the island's ninety-one Mi'kmaw households living in 'shanties' (76.9%) while the remainder occupied 'frame or log houses.'[20] In some areas, all families lived in 'shanties.' On the Chapel Island reserve in Richmond Country all fourteen households did so.[21] At Wagmatcook in Victoria County this was true for ten of fourteen families and in Inverness County, twenty-four of twenty-six households. As the agent for the Wagmatcook reserve wrote in 1881, the people there 'have a decided preference for camp life.'[22] In contrast, Christmas Island and Eskasoni had a higher percentage of permanent dwellings. At Christmas Island, nine of thirteen households were living in frame houses while at Eskasoni, five of seven households did so.

A similar proportion of mainland Mi'kmaw families also lived in shanties. There, 175 of 244 households lived in 'shanties' (71.7%). Areas where Protestant missionaries had been most active, at Bear River in Digby County and at Falmouth in Hants County, had the highest percentage of permanent dwellings. Together, these two communities accounted for almost half (32 of 69) of all frame and log houses. These communities, however, were the exception, not the norm.

Just what the enumerators saw when they placed a check in column four showing that a household occupied a 'shanty' is ambiguous. We might assume that they saw exactly what the word 'shanty' suggests, buildings of boards and nothing more. However, I think this was not always true and that more often families said to be living in shanties inhabited a structure made of birch bark. I say this for two reasons. First, there are a number of travelers' accounts of encountering families living in wigwams in both summer and winter and in various regions of the province.[23] As well, there is no clear understanding for how enumerators defined shanties, except that the word encompassed a variety of structures that were considered to be less permanent than frame or log houses. The different ways in which the word was used from the mid-1800s illustrates this diversity. Early settlers of Upper Canada, for instance, often lived in shanties, which were built in just a few days. 'Logs were left in the round and were cross-notched at the corners, the floor was usually dirt, the chimney, if built at all, was usually made of small green rounds chinked with clay, and the roof usually had but a single slope.'[24] However, the word could also be used when referring to habitations occupied by aboriginal people. The 1858 commissioners' report on Indian Affairs for Canada East and Canada West refers to 'bark Shanties or Wigwams' to describe the dwellings of a peripatetic band living near Point Pelee in southwestern Ontario.[25] As these examples illustrate, for some enumerators, the word shanty and wigwam might be used interchangeably, and so there may not have been a contradiction between what they saw and what they marked on their schedules.

Regardless of what might be concluded from this, there was not a strict separation between those living in birch bark camps and those who did not. Some families probably lived in a log or frame house, or even in a 'shanty' when on reserve and in a more temporary structure when off reserve. J.L. Gilpin said as much in 1877 when he wrote that 'they all now have permanent winter houses' but 'their summer camps are still as of old.'[26] As late as 1899, the agent for Whycocomagh reported that 'when the Micmac goes abroad for a short time, to make and sell his wares for better advantage, he builds a wigwam as a temporary shelter for himself and his family.'[27] So, we might interpret the enumerators' tabulations literally: when they said that families lived in shanties, they meant just that. However, even if we accept this interpretation – and there are reasons why we might not – we should not conclude that families lived in these shanties year-round. Indeed, the very usage of the term – regardless of its actual character – meant that Mi'kmaw families were living in dwellings that European observers considered to be less permanent and less solid than those other residents occupied.

The men's living situation is not mentioned in other documentation, and the census helps to understand something more about their lives than we might otherwise have known. Sylliboy was not born until 1875, so the 1871 census is only useful for tracing the four who were born between 1850 and 1854. Of the four, only Andrew Alek and Joe Christmas appear on the 1871 census. In both cases, the enumerators recorded that the men's families lived in temporary dwellings. In Christmas's case, this was identified as a shanty, whereas Bernard's family lived in a wigwam. The 1881 census shows similar living circumstances for both men, and also lists Andrew Alek's family who the enumerator for the Chapel Island reserve said lived in a 'shanty.' In sum, the two censuses show that at least three of the four men were still living in 'shanties' in 1881, when they would have been in their late twenties and early thirties. This also suggests that, like other Mi'kmaq of their generation, their residency on reserve was less permanent than their enumeration there would suggest.

For those living on reserve, the main reason that their residency was unstable was the limited income derived from farming.[28] This was also true for the men's families. Their precarious situation is illustrated through an analysis of agricultural data contained in the 1871 census. This data can be used to determine each household's ability to meet its annual caloric needs.[29] Bitterman, MacKinnon, and Wynn use this method in their analysis of the Cape Breton community of Middle River. In making these calculations, the authors provide average caloric totals for wheat, barley, potatoes, beef, and other assorted farm products. They also give an average daily caloric requirement for each household member: 3,500 calories for men, 2,500 for women, and 1,500 for children ten years of age and younger.[30] Although the census does not report the number of livestock slaughtered, I have used Bitterman, MacKinnon, and Wynn's method, which supposes that householders would kill 0.72 cows per year for every cow owned and 1.25 swine for every pig owned.

There are three main provisos about using this method. First, it entails calculating a standard output of milk per cow. The amount of milk a cow produces is dependent on a number of factors, including its breed and age, and the quality and quantity of its daily food. A cow browsing in a pasture full of weeds will not give as much milk if it had fed on better grasses.[31] Milk production thus varies from cow to cow and from region to region. In the late 1800s, experts recommended that Ontario cows giving less than 6,000 lbs. per annum be sold. Quebec cows, however, produced from 2,500 per 3,000 lbs. Bitterman, MacKinnon, and Wynn's estimated annual yield of 2,000 lbs. therefore is a reasonable average given Cape Breton's shorter growing season and less fertile soils. Applying this average to cows owned by the Mi'kmaw may be too generous. The feeding and caring of milch cows requires considerable knowledge and experimentation in how to feed, calve, and care for them and to grow and harvest the hay needed for winter feed.[32] Cape Breton Mi'kmaw families only began raising cattle sometime in the 1840s,[33] so that by 1871 livestock farming was still relatively new. We should not suppose therefore that their cows yielded as much milk as their Scottish neighbours who had more experience, both in Nova Scotia and in Scotland, on which to draw.[34] For this reason, the average annual production of 2,000 lbs per cow used here may overestimate the actual yield. A second problem is the assumption each household would consume everything it produced. As Bitterman and his co-authors recognize, this was never the case; families sold what they produced to purchase what they did not.[35] One item they likely sold was butter. In his analysis of Charles MacLean's business at North River Bridge in Victoria County, Robert MacKinnon found that between 1885 and 1890 'butter accounted for over one-quarter of payments on account' between a farmer and a local merchant and was a dependable source of income for many Nova Scotia families.[36] Such transactions may have increased farmers' 'income' by converting farm products into a higher caloric value than if they had been consumed within the home, although the inverse may also have been true.[37] Finally, these daily caloric averages probably err, as they do not fit every situation. This is only common sense as the food people require to maintain their body weight is influenced by age, height, body mass, and daily physical activity. Lacking a sophisticated mathematical model that would take all these variables into consideration, we should assume that the averages used for each household's caloric output and needs err, although the margin is unlikely to make a significant difference.

These calculations help to evaluate the viability of farming on Cape Breton reserves. Forty-two of ninety-one households reported growing garden and field crops and keeping livestock in 1870–71. These households were located on four of the island's five reserves. Not every Mi'kmaw household is included in these totals because some families did not report growing garden or field crops. This was true in both reserve and non-reserve communities. For instance, five Wagmatcook households and seven Chapel Island households neither grew any garden or field crops nor had cleared land either for cultivation or for pasture. Other communities were in more urban environments, and for this reason did not grow any crops or own any livestock as far as we know, although many non-aboriginal urban families in the same period did.[38] Andrew Bernard's family was among those living in urban areas, and so did not report growing garden or field crops or owning any livestock.

The figures show that only two households produced enough food to support themselves. Thirty-four households produced less than 40 per cent of their needs: seven households produced less than 10 per cent, seven between 11 and 19 per cent, eleven between 20 and 29 per cent, and nine others between 30 and 39 per cent. Significantly, the only two households which produced more than 100 per cent of their needs were at Christmas Island, which is part of the Eskasoni reserve.

A more detailed analysis shows differences among communities. Farming was not an important part of the Chapel Island economy, with only six of thirteen households reporting farm produce. Only two of these declared farming as a principal occupation while the remaining four planted crops but made most of their income from coopering, basket-making, and fishing. Whycocomagh, Wagmatcook, and Eskasoni only fared slightly better. At Whycocomagh, seven of eight households produced between 22 per cent and 41 per cent of their needs. The most successful farmer was John Sylliboy whose farm met 90 per cent of his household's requirements. Nine of fourteen Wagmatcook households harvested field crops, but none relied on farming to meet many of their needs. Indeed, three households generated less than 10 per cent of their annual requirements, and four others between 20 and 30 per cent. Eskasoni was much the same. Two of seven households produced less than 20 per cent, two others between 20 and 30 per cent, and the remainder between 32 and 42 per cent.

Christmas Island farms were more prosperous. Five of thirteen farming households generated more than 75 per cent of their caloric needs. Their success was mainly attributable to livestock. Collectively, the thirteen households owned nine milch cows, twenty-two horned cattle, forty-five sheep, and fifteen swine. This was four times as much livestock as any other community. Significantly, the Christmas clan were the community's most successful farmers, and although Joseph Christmas's family produced only 12 per cent of their household food, his father likely farmed land in common with his father and brother.

As the Christmas Island example illustrates, cows were an important part of a family's income. As in eighteenth-century England, milch cows could mean the difference between feast and famine, especially when crop yields plummeted or when natural disaster struck.[39] 'The value of the cow,' writes Jeannette Neeson, 'lay in her calves and in the milk she gave. In season between spring and autumn in each year, she would give anything from under one to three gallons of milk a day.'[40] Nineteenth-century cows may have produced more, even though their yields varied according to feed and climate. One Massachusetts farmer in the mid-1870s wrote that his three-year old Alderney cow 'weighing somewhat over seven hundred pounds' yielded between twelve to sixteen quarts daily but in the hot summer months only gave three quarts.[41] In a three-year period, the cow also calved three times, providing the farmer with additional income, even though he had to pay for the services of a bull. Calves could be sold, while milk could either be consumed or be turned into butter and sold. Before the First World War, most butter was made on the farm, not in the factory, and so it is likely that Mi'kmaw families who had a cow did so as well.[42] The 1871 census gives amounts churned but these figures are not always reliable because some enumerators filled in the relevant information by calculating how much butter one cow might produce.[43] Finally, cows produced manure. As one Quebec agricultural brochure from the 1890s pointed out, 'a cow of average weight kept in the stable all the time, produces about 20,000 lbs. of dung per annum and about 8000 lbs of liquid manure' and was essential for enriching a farmer's fields.[44] All of these products contributed to a household, either directly by providing milk or income or indirectly by producing fertilizer. For these reasons, cows were an important aspect of the late nineteenth-century Cape Breton economy and so too for the Mi'kmaq.[45]

In comparison to their neighbours, Mi'kmaw farmers owned proportionally fewer cows. At Christmas Island, thirteen households owned eight cows. Proportionally, their neighbours had four times as many, with 83 households owning 207 milch cows. In other communities, the disproportion was more pronounced. At Eskasoni, for instance, seven households owned only four milch cows, while 184 neighbouring households owned 518.[46] The relative scarcity of Mi'kmaw livestock only compounded Mi'kmaw families' penury.

This synopsis might suggest that the Indian agents' assessments were correct: the Mi'kmaq were lazy and just were not meant to be farmers. While this may have been true of some, there were two factors which made Mi'kmaw farms unstable. First, some reserves had little fertile land. On the mainland, the Bear River reserve was one such place, which the local Indian agent once described as 'very rough, almost covered with granite.'[47] The Cape Breton reserve at Eskasoni was another. Although Eskasoni had 2,200 acres, less than a third of it was 'fit for cultivation, the remainder being rocky mountains.'[48] As Commissioner of Indian

Affairs William Chearnley wrote in 1854, the reserves had 'not been selected with due caution by those appointed to perform that duty. They
are chiefly barren, and spots removed from the sea coast.'[49] Second, the
reserves were too small to accommodate the population, a problem that
became acute after 1870 as reserve populations grew. The agent for Antigonish County wrote that the Afton reserve 'is small, and the individual
allotments are so limited that the lots will hardly yield a sufficient means
of subsistence.'[50] This was also true in the Annapolis Valley, the centre of
the province's farmland but where less than a hundred acres had been
reserved.[51] As Agent Beckwith recounted in 1881, by the mid-1800s all
the land in King's County had been sold or granted. In the 1860s, there
still had been some ungranted land, but the government decided to sell
it to timber speculators.[52] In the case of Wagmatcook and Whycocomagh,
the lack of land by 1871 was also because of the government's decision to
allow squatters to buy reserve lands they had illegally occupied. By 1867,
408 acres of the Whycocomagh reserve and 2,491 acres of the Waga-
matcook reserve had been sold.[53] In 1919 H.J. Bury, an inspector with
the Department of Indian Affairs, summarized the Nova Scotia situation
when he wrote that only three reserves, Millbrook, Shubenacadie, and
Whycocomagh, 'had a certain amount of land fit for agriculture.' The
rest did not have enough. Five years later, Bury observed that the total
harvest from all the reserves equaled 'the produce that might reasonably be expected from a fairly large farm.' He concluded that the situation would not improve until families were moved onto better and larger
lands.[54]

The lack of suitable or sufficient land is evident from the 1871 census.
The Cape Breton Mi'kmaq lagged behind their white counterparts in
the amount of acreage occupied and improved. On average, Mi'kmaw
farms had 45 per cent less land than their white neighbours (73 acres
as opposed to 134 acres). Households also had less improved acreage.
Improved land was 'that portion of land on which some work of meas-
urable importance has been done, such as underbrushing or chopping
trees, or breaking up marshes, meadows, pastures or plains.'[55] On average, Mi'kmaw farms had 55 per cent less improved acreage than their
neighbours (17.1 acres as opposed to 38 acres).

These 'averages' disguise the differences among the four communities. Eskasoni and Wagmatcook landholdings were smaller. On average
the seven Eskasoni families occupied only 17.6 acres of land or about
one-seventh as much as their white neighbours. Put another way, a white
landholder of East Bay used, on average, seven times the amount of

land an Eskasoni resident did. In total, families occupied only 123 of the reserve's 2,800 acres.[56] Wagmatcook landholdings were also small but mostly because there was not enough land. Nine families occupied 397 acres or about two thirds of the reserve's 600 acres, a total which was likely incomplete as the enumerator did not record the landholdings of five households. Wagmatcook's limited land surface meant that individual holdings averaged about one quarter the size of adjacent white farms (44.1 to 169.1 acres). This also meant less improved land, averaging 4.3 acres as opposed to 30.5 acres among neighbouring white farmers.

Whycocomagh families faced similar difficulties, but for different reasons. Families occupied much of the reserve land, 1,200 of 1,500 acres or 80 per cent of the total land surface, but farmed more, averaging 150 acres per household. This was 15 acres more than their neighbours' average landholding. Although Mi'kmaw farmers had not improved as much land, the difference was not large (35.8 acres as opposed to 41.1 acres).[57] However, the average acreage per family may have been less than the census shows. As Bruce Curtis has pointed out, the 1871 census enforced a static, homogenous model, which did not always reflect the population's local character and peculiarities.[58] The Mi'kmaq were one of those 'local particularities' which did not fit easily into enumerators' instructions and schedules. Enumerators normally recorded families living in birch bark camps according to their place of residence on the day the census was taken. But some families living on reserve in summer were absent at the time of the enumerator's visit, which would have inflated the size of each family's landholdings. We might suppose, for instance, that a unilingual enumerator might mistake land farmed by two or three families to be the property of a single household. This may have been true of Whycocomagh and would account for the relatively large average size of individual landholdings.

Among Christmas Island families, landholdings were on average larger, something that should not be surprising since most harvested a higher percentage of their annual needs than other island families. But here too, individual landholdings were smaller than those of the neighbouring population, averaging about 70 per cent the size of other farms (75.4 acres as opposed to 106 acres). Individual landholdings also had fewer improved acres and averaged about 50 per cent of the size of neighbouring farms (16.3 acres opposed to 32.7 acres).

In sum, the small size of Mi'kmaw landholdings, either because reserve land was not suitable for agriculture or because the reserve was not large enough to accommodate the actual population, meant that most families were not full-time farmers. As Bitterman, MacKinnon, and Wynn have showed, this was also true for about 50 per cent of non-aboriginal farming families living at Middle River in 1871, suggesting that this pattern of poor soils and poor farming returns was the norm among Cape Breton farmers.

There is little doubt that nineteenth-century Nova Scotia farms were less productive than those in points westward, a situation mainly attributable to the relatively poor quality of the soils and the expansion of the farming frontier into areas ill suited to agriculture.[59] This forced many farmers, including those at Middle River, to depend more on additional income sources than was true of farmers elsewhere. This more than ever illustrates the tenuous nature of Mi'kmaw agriculture.

Of the two men who appear in the 1871 census, there is only agricultural data for Joe Christmas because Andrew Bernard was living and working at North Sydney. Christmas's family situation was probably the norm, as his parents were only able to meet about 12 per cent of their family's needs from farming, although they likely also farmed in common with their relatives and so this figure may not accurately reflect the amount of the family's farming income. Even if the percentage were higher, household members still would have had to find other sources of income.

In their analysis of Middle River, Bitterman, MacKinnon, and Wynn, show that most farmers made up the deficit between what they produced and what they needed by working for other farmers or by working in lumbering, shipbuilding, or mining. Some Mi'kmaw families probably did the same. However, such employment was likely less accessible and less appealing to most families, and they appear to have made up the difference by harvesting on-reserve and off-reserve resources. Although from the 1840s families had turned to wage labour, harvesting off-reserve resources remained an important part of the household economy, particularly in rural areas where the rise in population and emigration would have led local employers to hire fewer Mi'kmaq rather than more. Thus, the relative importance of wage employment as a part of families' income fluctuated according to time and place. Recent analysis therefore suggesting that a break in the household division of labour had already occurred by the late 1860s reflects a developing trend among a limited number of households and was not the norm in the early 1870s. This trend would only become more pronounced later in the century as more Mi'kmaw families moved into urban areas and their children began attending schools more regularly.[60]

Mi'kmaw families made up part of the household deficit by fishing.

Often this meant working off reserve because few reserves were on or near the coast or fresh water. In some cases, the entire household moved, in others, not. For instance, men from the Bear River reserve on the southern mainland spent periods of the summer hunting porpoise on the Bay of Fundy, leaving their wives and children behind, adopting a pattern of work much like other Digby County fishermen.[61] In other areas entire families moved to live along rivers, lakes, or coastlines. The Lunenburg County agent wrote in September 1880 that eight to ten families were fishing along the LaHave River, while the agent for Guysborough County reported a similar scenario there in 1872. There were two or three families, he said, who 'fish every summer at Cape Canso and camp every winter near the town of Guysboro and live by coopering and making baskets.'[62] And in 1880 the Antigonish County agent noted that even though a number of families had built frame houses on the Pomquet reserve they only lived in them 'a part of the year' as the owners 'go away in fishing season.'[63] Generally, the Cape Breton Mi'kmaq had more opportunities to fish, as reserves were adjacent to the Bras d'Or Lakes; this is illustrated by Andrew Alek's comment that Chapel Island families caught 'all kinds of fish.' This would suggest fishing to be common for people living there, and this was also true for Whycocomagh, Malagawatch, Wagmatcook, and Eskasoni, all of which border the lake. As Joe Christmas told Judge Patterson, 'when I was a boy used to fish around shore.'[64]

This difference between mainland and island Mi'kmaw families is shown by the figures tabulated from the occupational descriptions enumerators recorded as they went from door to door. On the mainland, 21 of 224 men declaring an occupation said they made a significant portion of their income from fishing and so either described themselves as fishermen or said that fishing was one of their two principal sources of income.[65] Most of these men were living off reserve. The only reserve residents to declare fishing as an occupation came from Bear River, where men hunted porpoise, and from Shubenacadie, not far from the Shubenacadie River. The other fishing households were in off-reserve areas.[66] In contrast, a higher proportion of Cape Breton households declared fishing as one of their primary occupations (22 of 94), fourteen from Wagmatcook and six from Chapel Island.[67] This difference between island and mainland householders would confirm the importance of Lake Bras d'Or to island communities.

These numbers, however, only concern householders declaring fishing as one of their primary occupations and do not include those who fished but described their work differently. Many more families fished than said the man of the household was a fisherman. An examination of Schedule Eight, which reports each household's declaration of fishing done over the past year, shows an additional fifty families fishing. Even this total is likely incomplete, as we would expect that others caught fish but did not report it. Nonetheless, combining the totals taken from Schedule Eight with the occupational descriptions in Schedule One shows a minimum of ninety-four Mi'kmaw fishing households in all of Nova Scotia (from a total of 316) or about 30 per cent of the total. Although fishing need not have entailed a family's movement off-reserve, it sometimes did.

Families also made income from hunting and trapping. This was the case with Gabriel Sylliboy and the Jeddore brothers who were trapping muskrat on Alex Gillis's land from 30 October until they were arrested on November 4. Sylliboy said in 1928: 'start to go trapping on Halloween. For last 34 years. Get few muskrats then.'[68] Muskrats were also trapped in the early spring, as suggested by some Cape Bretoners' complaints in the early 1920s that the 'Indians' had set some traps in and around Iona, a small village near Whycocomagh.[69] In the late 1800s, island Mi'kmaw families mainly hunted for fur-bearing animals, because the moose population was at that time relatively small if not non-existent. In contrast, mainland Mi'kmaw families hunted moose. In 1895 the Bear River agent wrote that 'The Indians were very fortunate in hunting the last fall and winter, having killed a great many moose, which helped them to live through the winter very comfortably.'[70] In the 1920s, Louis Luxey, then 74 years old, told Clara Dennis 'One day when I was a young man I killed 6 [moose] – that's the highest I killed. We smoked them to have it dry. Meat will keep one year after it get dry.'[71] As both these examples illustrate, moose was a mainstay for some families in the southern half of the province, providing food for the winter. On Cape Breton where moose were less abundant, families trapped, as Gabriel Sylliboy was doing in 1927.

Among mainland households, 89 of 257 men declared hunting as one of their main occupations. Among Cape Breton households, only one of 94 did so. Those declaring hunting as a principal source of income were primarily from Annapolis, Digby, Queen's, Lunenburg and Halifax Counties where 56 of 108 men said they hunted. The high proportion of hunters from southwest Nova Scotia reflects the importance of game as a source of food and income, work that would have included guiding urban sportsmen.[72]

More men hunted than said they were hunters. In the 1901 census, an enumerator described Gabriel Sylliboy as a farmer, a description that disguises his annual trapping forays. Schedule Five of the 1871 census shows another forty-three mainland men and thirty-seven islanders who said they had hunted or trapped over the past twelve months. To cite a couple of examples from Cape Breton: eight Whycocomagh households reported taking 423 muskrats, 53 minks, three martens, and 280 other pelts. Similarly, five of fourteen households at Christmas Island declared they had trapped 533 muskrats, even though all five had said that farming and coopering were their main occupations. In sum, 129 of 318 households trapped and hunted wildlife.[73] The actual proportion was probably higher. The Indian agent for Cumberland County, for instance, reported in 1905 that nearly all families hunted, 'more or less.'[74] Location was a factor. Rural families hunted more, urban families less. Joe Christmas, who spent most of his adult years in Sydney, said in 1915 that he did not hunt in the winter.[75] As well, moose and caribou were more plentiful in remote areas, like Cumberland, Guysborough, Queen's, and Shelburne counties than the populated coastal areas of Halifax County or the richer agricultural counties of Annapolis, Hants, and King's.[76]At the very least, therefore, about 40 per cent of all households hunted or trapped.

Just where did men hunt? During his travels through Nova Scotia in the early twentieth century, the American anthropologist, Frank Speck, found that Mi'kmaw communities had divided adjacent woodlands into hunting territories. Speck believed these territories dated back to at least the 1600s, if not before. Significantly, most were grouped around reserves, and this may suggest that families used reserves as bases for hunting and trapping.[77]

For most families of the late 1800s, coopering and basket-making were probably the most important source of supplementing household incomes. This is evident from the 1871 census, which shows that 270 men and women made all or part of their income from either coopering or basket-making. This represents 70 per cent of the total number of people declaring an occupation (270 of 385). Woodworking was especially important in the Cape Breton communities, where 144 of the 159 individuals declaring occupations said they made wood products. This represents 86 of 90 island households. Of the on-reserve population, at least one member of every household said they made a major part of their income by fashioning wood products.

As explained in Chapter Two, both women and men worked with wood, although enumerators normally reported men to be coopers and women to be basket-makers, wicker makers, or quill makers.[78] This was the case in Cape Breton, where enumerators noted a higher percentage of women basket-makers than on the mainland. Whether this reflected a difference between mainland and island households or that Cape Breton enumerators were more likely to note a woman's occupation than their mainland counterparts is unknown. What is known is that basket-making was an integral part of the household economy in the late nineteenth and early twentieth centuries. As one Indian agent noted, while other Mi'kmaw products may not always been in demand, baskets were. Both Andrew Bernard and Joe Christmas worked with wood. In the 1881 census, Bernard was identified as a wicker-maker, and so, too, was his wife, while Christmas told Judge Patterson that he did 'Indian work, making baskets & handles tubs etc.'[79] Like many men and women who said they were coopers or basket-makers, Christmas made a variety of items.

To work with wood, however, families needed an adequate supply of it, and this could mean traveling or living off reserve. 'As they live at a distance from the wood,' wrote the agent for Bear River in 1883, 'and have no teams of their own, it is exceedingly difficult when the storm rages and the snow is deep, to obtain fuel sufficient to keep them warm.'[80] Eskasoni and Christmas Island households faced similar problems in the 1880s as the agent for these two communities reported that 'the wood required for Indian work – coopering – is becoming every year more and more difficult to procure so much so that in a few years it will be entirely exhausted.'[81] William Chisholm, the agent for Antigonish County, wrote in 1880 that once the reserve wood was gone, families had begun camping in the woods 'where they can more easily procure materials for coopering and basket works.'[82] Often, women hauled the wood long distances. 'The Indians settled near Kentville [in King's County],' wrote J.E. Beckwith in 1881, 'having to travel some fifteen miles to procure the more valuable kinds and even the young maples from which the females make their baskets and fancy work, are cut and drawn, or in many instances lugged home on their backs a distance of from three to five miles.'[83] By 1891, Eskasoni families were attributing their frequent aliments to carrying wood long distances.[84] From such reports, we would conclude that families had more and more difficulties in getting wood and this required more energy and time to procure it, adding to the itinerant nature of their lives.

As well, families traveled to neighbouring towns and villages to sell their wares. For the Kentville Mi'kmaq, this meant a journey of ten to fourteen kilometres and for the Wagmatcook Mi'kmaq a twenty-kilometre trek to Baddeck. Some families spent several days in town, selling their goods in the streets or markets or going from door to door.[85] Eskasoni families became such a fixture in Sydney that in 1878 the federal government decided to purchase a piece of land there for their use, resulting in visiting families staying there longer. This is what happened with Joe Christmas, who eventually decided to move his entire family to Sydney.[86]

All of this shows the eclectic nature of the Mi'kmaw household economy in the late nineteenth century. To survive, families did many things. Those who had a plot of land farmed. But they also made baskets, fished, trapped, hunted, gathered berries, wildflowers, and worked for wages. In some ways, this economy was not that different from that of other rural households whose farms were too small, or where the labour of every able-bodied male and female was not needed year round. As Larry McCann has pointed out, residents in such areas often had several jobs: men fished in the spring, summer, and fall and worked in the woods and did other jobs as well while women worked in various capacities. The same was true of many Cape Breton farmers, especially those who lived on less-fertile land.[87]

There were, however, three crucial differences between the Mi'kmaq and their neighbours. First, proportionately fewer Mi'kmaq worked for wages. Rather, we might characterize most families at this time as small independent producers, making various goods for sale to farmers, miners, merchants, shipbuilders, and lumber operators. Second, many rural Nova Scotians had familial, social, and political connections that made finding wage employment easier. This was less true of the Mi'kmaq, and the lack of such linkages made it more difficult for families to find gainful employment when other sources of income failed. Third, even if work was not available nearby, non-aboriginal families whose men worked away from home would have stayed where they were. This was true of Cape Bretoners from Mira and Grand Narrows who worked summers at Reserve Mines in the 1880s or of others who laboured in the lobster canneries.[88] This was less true of the Mi'kmaq where the movement off reserve generally included all members of the household, not just some of them.

The Alek, Bernard, and Christmas families illustrate the sometimes, tenuous nature of Mi'kmaw families' rootedness and reflect how this generation understood their relationship to the land. All three families lived in some form of dwelling that census enumerators described as 'shanties.' Such temporary dwellings suggest that these families did not think of their presence on reserve as permanent and the investment they made in establishing a residence reflected that understanding. The reserve, although it had become part of the Mi'kmaw economy nonetheless remained a less politically and socially defined area than it would later become. This partly reflected government's previous and continuing inattention to protecting reserve lands. However, it also suggested that reserves in the 1870s and 1880s were still a relatively new phenomenon, and families only gradually adjusted to seeing them as permanent places of residence. This change in perception could only occur once the reserves became economically sustainable. In the 1870s and 1880s, this was not the case, and the reserves were just one aspect of a multisite Mi'kmaw economy that included off-reserve areas used for fishing, trapping, and gathering wood.

This transiency, however, did not sit well with federal officials, an attitude reflected in Indian agents' reports in the late nineteenth century regarding some Mi'kmaw families 'love of roaming.' Such remarks illustrated federal insistence that the Mi'kmaq, like other aboriginal people, should become civilized, and this meant learning the value of hard labour, thrift, and private property. Movements off reserve therefore raised concerns that these lessons had not been sufficiently inculcated into Mi'kmaw family life. For federal officials, the reserve was a great social engineering project where aboriginal people would shed their Indian other and become members of the British Dominion, with the rights and obligations that entailed. This included a restricted right to vote and an obligation to obey the law. The generation of Mi'kmaw men who matured in the late nineteenth century came to understand this relationship differently, partly because the reserves were not economically sustainable and families were therefore forced to move off reserve. This affected how they remembered the treaty.

The five men who testified at Sylliboy's appeal matured at a time when the majority of Mi'kmaq lived a more itinerant life than in 1928. This is especially true for the four oldest men, Andrew Alek, Andrew Bernard, Joseph Christmas, and Francis Gould. The 1871 census tells us that throughout Nova Scotia, more than half of all Mi'kmaq lived off reserve but that on Cape Breton Island, this proportion was higher. These statements, however, are only partly true because they disguise the complexity of household movements. Like most censuses, the 1871 census reflects a static view of Mi'kmaw communities and so only tells us where families were living at the time the census was taken. Regardless of what the census actually says it is certain that the four men as well as Gabriel Sylliboy spent periods of their childhood and teenage years on reserve and periods off reserve. The timing of these movements varied according to each family's situation. For instance, in Cumberland County, the agent there wrote on 10 November 1893 that 'at this time there are none residing on reserve. During the summer there are usually several families on the Reserve but when cold weather approaches they generally move out.'[89] When off reserve, the men's families fished, trapped, hunted, gathered wood, sold their wares, and worked for wages. The men also spent periods living in temporary dwellings. While on reserve, they may have lived in a wooden structure, which enumerators called a 'shanty' even if most families probably did not. When off reserve they lived in birch bark camps. Thus, even though the men were born on reserve, they spent parts of their early lives elsewhere.

As the men had spent their youth and young adult years camping off reserve and harvesting off-reserve resources without interference, they came to identify these activities as integral parts of their community life. Each man spoke about this in his testimony. Joe Christmas said: 'From my earliest recollections no one ever interfered with our rights to hunt and fish at any time.' Gabriel Sylliboy said that he had been trapping muskrats for the past 34 years and had never been 'interfered with in my hunting before.' Andrew Bernard said that 'Micmacs can fish or shoot any thing they want all year round.' Andrew Alek, from Chapel Island, told Judge Patterson that 'Micmacs had right to fish all they cd eat or sell at all seasons of year.' From this it is evident that the men interpreted their lived experience as reflecting their community's treaty relationship.

This emphasis on fishing and hunting was a subtle difference from that of their parents' generation. Then the treaty had been employed to provoke the Crown's intervention by demonstrating how immigrants had violated the treaty by occupying land to the exclusion of its use by the Mi'kmaq. This earlier generation had been born and had matured when reserves were still new and the Mi'kmaq were integrating the reserve more fully into their household economies. In contrast, the men who testified at Sylliboy's appeal were part of the generation born on reserve. Joe Christmas's work as a cooper reflected this change. He said that he was not a hunter but 'did Indian work making baskets & handles tubs etc.' Although the other men did not make similar qualifications, Christmas's candor illustrates a shift in Mi'kmaw society in the late nineteenth century.

For the men, the treaty had become about defining the parameters in which families living on reserve could access *off-reserve resources*. This was different from their parents' generation. Then, the treaty had symbolized Mi'kmaw dispossession. For the men of Sylliboy's generation, however, the treaty was not *about protecting their fishing and hunting grounds*, but about *protecting their access*. While this might be construed as an adjustment to the realities of early twentieth century life, it also reflects how the men transposed memories of the treaty into the narrative they had created about their own lives.

The men had been born and had grown to maturity at a time when the borders separating the reserve from life outside of it were still flexible. In 1927, Alex Gillis and Malcolm MacKinnon had no trouble in saying that Sylliboy was from Whycocomagh. Gillis's and MacKinnon's parents and grandparents would have had more difficulty in making such a statement because then Mi'kmaw families did not live solely on reserve and so identifying a person from Whycocomagh would not have been easily done. This permability was the world the five men knew, and that memory was fixed in their minds when they testified in July 1928. They transposed that memory onto the treaty, and recalled conversations when their parents and grandparents had told them that the king had given the Mi'kmaq the right to hunt and to fish whenever and wherever they wanted. *It is unlikely that these words were ever spoken in the way the men said.* What is more likely is that their parents had said that the king had promised to protect fishing and hunting grounds for Mi'kmaw use. The men transposed those words into their memories and recalled them in ways which fitted their own life experiences but also reflected how the lawyers cued their memories. In this way, the memory of the treaty was modified and assumed a different emphasis than it had a generation before.

PART THREE

Why the Men Remembered

6 The Demography of Mi'kmaw Communities, 1871–1911

If we remembered everything that had ever happened to us, then we would be unable to make sense of our lives. As Daniel Schacter points out, we would be so overwhelmed with memories that we would be unable to conceptualize our lives and would be incapable of constructing a narrative that would explain our lives to others. Instead of remembering everything that happens each day, our minds selectively create trace memories or engrams for certain events. We actively engage in this process every day and mainly during sleep when the mind chooses those events that have meaning to us and discards the rest.[1] Placed in this perspective, the fact that the men created a memory trace and encoded information about the treaty assumes more significance; it suggests that at the time when they first heard about the treaty, it already had some meaning for them.

It is also significant that the men were able to retrieve the memories in 1928. Schacter contends that the way we retrieve a memory is complex; he compares the process of recalling memories to assembling a large jigsaw puzzle. Once retrieval has been made and is repeated at regular intervals, it becomes consolidated and is lodged in the brain's medial temporal lobes from whence it is more easily recalled than when the various components of the memory were scattered in the brain's other parts.[2]

Schacter's explanation helps to evaluate the men's memories. The men's ability to recall their memories of the treaty in 1928 suggests that the same memories had been retrieved on previous occasions and thereafter had become consolidated. Remembering the treaty in Judge Patterson's courtroom was a continuation of a process that had begun years before. This act of remembering, however, did not occur in a vacuum.

To understand why the men's memories persisted, we need to analyse the social and economic forces that created the conditions of what they would remember.

In this chapter and the following one, I explore two ways to approach this context. In this chapter, I examine the demography of Mi'kmaw communities from 1871 to 1911. This analysis shows a shift in household economies, the effect of which was to lower the average life expectancy. One factor contributing to this change was the expansion of on-reserve populations. Some families adjusted by moving to urban areas. Thus, in the following chapter, I examine what happened to Mi'kmaq who had moved to Sydney and North Sydney in the late nineteenth and early twentieth centuries.

These two chapters place the persistence of memories about the treaty within the larger context of late nineteenth-century and early twentieth-century Cape Breton. My purpose is to show that the persistence of memory is more likely to occur where there is a reason for its retrieval. For the men who testified at Sylliboy's appeal, their experience of living in a community which had a lower life expectancy than other Nova Scotians and whose efforts to adapt to the urban wage labour economy were met with hostility, illustrated the difference between themselves and others. These developments reinforced their belief that they occupied a unique position within Nova Scotia's political economy and underlined the importance of the treaty in defining their status. The memory of the treaty therefore remained a part of the men's lives, but only because social realities created the conditions in which it would be remembered.

In 1928 all five men were living on reserve. Gabriel Sylliboy and Andrew Bernard were living at Whycocomagh, Joe Christmas at Sydney, Andrew Alek at Chapel Island, and Francis Gould at Eskasoni. That all five men lived on reserve in 1928 reflected a general pattern among the island's Mi'kmaw population. In 1925, about 1,500 of the province's 2,040 Mi'kmaq lived permanently on reserve but the percentages were much higher on Cape Breton.[3] This movement onto reserve occurred from a series of upheavals in Nova Scotia's economy. These developments, which were tied to global changes in population and production, accelerated in the last decades of the nineteenth century. One result was that Mi'kmaw families had less access to off-reserve resources. This led them to search for work and sometimes to migrate to the province's growing urban areas, where they might find wage employment and a market for their goods.

The men's personal histories illustrate these changes. Andrew Alek, Andrew Bernard, Joe Christmas, and Francis Gould were all born on reserve but thereafter their lives diverged. Alek told Judge Patterson in 1928 that he 'Live[d] on Indian Reserve near St. Peters. Born there & lived there all my life. I am 78 years old.'[4] Francis Gould was also born on reserve. Andrew Bernard's life story, however, was very different. As he told Judge Patterson: 'Am 78 years of age. Born at Nyanza [Wagmat-cook], Victoria Co. on Indian Reservation.' But when he was a teenager his family had moved to Little Bras d'Or, a small village west of Sydney . It was here that he married and raised his children, working first in the coal mines and later, with his wife, making baskets and other domestic wares.[5] Joe Christmas's life story was similar. Born at Christmas Island on the Eskasoni Reserve, Christmas had moved to the Sydney area when he was a young man. Over the next twenty-five years, Christmas and his family traveled between Sydney and Eskasoni but only moved permanently to Sydney in the 1890s.

The birthplace and life story of Gabriel Sylliboy is less certain, so it is difficult to know exactly when and where he lived. Sylliboy did not talk about his life at the appeal, so we must try to reconstruct his movements through other sources. Unfortunately, these are not always helpful. Sylliboy was from Inverness County but just where he was born is unclear. His mother was Mary Basque, who was widowed when she was young and later remarried. Gabriel was the product of this second marriage and was born on 16 August 1875. Nothing is known about Gabriel's early life; his name does not appear in the census until 1901, when he was living at Whycocomagh with his mother, his two siblings, and his grandmother, Mary Ann Gould.[6] This would suggest that before 1901 he spent time off reserve, like many other families of his generation. From at least 1901, however, Sylliboy lived more permanently at Whycocogmagh, as his enumeration in the 1901 and in 1911 censuses shows.

The five men's personal histories tell us something about Mi'kmaw residency in the late nineteenth and early twentieth centuries. Some people were born on reserve and lived there all their lives. Others moved. Andrew Alek, Andrew Bernard, Joe Christmas, and possibly Francis Gould were all born on reserve. Two of the four were closely identified with the reserve life they had been born into, so that enumerators consistently recorded their families living there in each of the federal censuses taken between 1871 and 1911. Although the men continued to live and work off reserve, the reserve gradually became their family's principal residence. The other two men's movements, however, integrated the island's coal mining belt as part of a constellation of work sites. Neither Bernard nor Christmas initially lived permanently in the Sydney area, but by the 1890s and early 1900s, they both had established permanent roots there. In contrast, Sylliboy spent much of his youth off reserve, or so it would seem, as his name does not appear in either the 1881 or the 1891 census. Yet by 1901 he was living at Whycocomagh and would still be living there in 1928. All of this suggests an incremental change in families' residency in the late nineteenth and early twentieth centuries: a gradual expansion into the province's growing urban centres and a more permanent presence on reserves.

While many scholars have analysed the changes that occurred in aboriginal communities across Canada in the late nineteenth and early twentieth centuries, most of these studies have focused either on documenting the implementation of, and resistance to, government policies or on analysing how settlement and industrial development undermined indigenous economies. There has been less work done on documenting how these changes affected their population. As a generation of scholars has shown the late nineteenth and early twentieth centuries were an important transitional point for the Canadian population, which led to changes in fertility, average life expectancy, household composition, ethnicity, work, and residency.[7] Similar analyses of aboriginal communities are few. In part, this dearth of research is the result of incomplete census and parish registers. This seems to be especially true for western Canada and for northern Ontario and Quebec.

In this chapter, I discuss the changing demography of Mi'kmaw communities through reference to the 1871, 1881, 1901, and 1911 censuses. This analysis suggests manifold changes in community life. The censuses, when combined with data compiled by the federal Department of Indian Affairs (DIA) shows a drop in the population from 1881 to 1911. There are many possible explanations for this decrease, including changes in fertility and out-migration. An equally important explanation was a drop in the average life expectancy, resulting mainly from increased mortality among infants and young children. This decline resulted from several intersecting factors, including decreased access to off-reserve resources and the growth in on-reserve populations. The dual effect was to lower nutrition levels, spiking death rates. The men who testified at Sylliboy's appeal lived through this time and may well have been directly affected.

It was during this period of turmoil and personal anguish that the treaty became a public memory and a clarion call for citizenship among those claiming Mi'kmaw ancestry. This occurred at a time when other Canadians were stressing duty to Empire and to nation. In the same way as other aboriginal people used public celebrations to invoke an alternative perspective of the 'nation's' history, so too did the Mi'kmaw leadership turn to the treaty to establish their own stake in the nation. This call, however, did not occur without reason, and only by giving a context to the parameters of reserve life in late nineteenth and early twentieth century Nova Scotia is this possible. One might refer exclusively to Indian Affairs files to paint such a portrait, but these files tend to provide a skewed overview by the haphazard method in which the correspondence was created. Although valuable, these files only give an occasional glimpse into the crises that afflicted communities. Thus, such files must be complemented with a demographic analysis of Mi'kmaw families.

In the late nineteenth and early twentieth centuries, millions of people were on the move. Much of this movement began in rural Europe where families picked up their belongings and left. Some went to the nearest town or city. Others moved to Argentina, Australia, Brazil, Canada, New Zealand, and South Africa. Many more went to the United States. How and why this occurred, and to so many people at the same time is something of a riddle. Generally, historians believe that two interconnected processes triggered this migration: changes in population and changes in the world economy.

From the mid-seventeenth century, the average life expectancy in parts of Western Europe rose. This meant that more girls were surviving childhood and that more and more of them were bearing children. Various factors contributed to this change, including better nutrition and a better understanding of infectious diseases.[8] In earlier times, when a population exceeded the economy's capacity to feed it, mortality rates increased. That did not happen this time and so the population grew.

Historians believe the population continued to grow because of transformations occurring in Europe's economy. This is generally associated with industrialization and the period immediately preceding it. As is well known, this era witnessed a revolution in how goods were produced, how food was grown and sold, how non-European lands and people were exploited, and by the mid- to late 1800s in how goods and people were transported. These changes affected rural labourers and small landowners the most, for two reasons. First, with declining mortality there were more people to feed and more sons to settle on the land than before. Second, changes in production and consumption had a ripple effect on the countryside's poorest residents, who were vulnerable to minor changes in the local economy, such as the loss of access to pastures and to forests, the loss of piecework done over the winter months, and a drop in grain prices. With the development of urban factories, some families and young people, no longer able or willing to live tenuously from year to year, moved to the nearest town or city where they believed that their lives would be better. Others left for North and South America and later to Southern Africa and Oceania.[9]

These changes occurred first in the United Kingdom and later in Central and Eastern Europe. But by the time the economies of Central, Southern, and Eastern Europe were experiencing these changes, new modes of transportation had developed which had not existed in the late 1700s and early 1800s.[10] The railroad and the steamship were the most notable innovations. Their introduction lowered the costs of transporting food from North America to Europe. The steamship affected people in other ways as well, facilitating their movement across the Atlantic in much larger numbers than ever before.[11]

Nova Scotia was affected by similar changes to its rural economy, precipitating movement within the province and outside of it. Patricia Thornton has calculated that about 114,000 Nova Scotians left between the 1870s and the 1890s, with about 95,000 departing in the 1880s and 1890s. Out-migration continued in the early 1900s, although just how many people left is unknown. Thornton believes that migration declined in the first decade of the new century and then picked up again afterward.[12] Most people went to the United States, many to the Boston area. A smaller percentage moved to Moncton and to Saint John. Some went to work in the British Columbia coalfields, others to work on Prairie farms.[13]

There was also movement within the province, mainly from rural to urban areas. In 1871, 17 per cent of all Nova Scotians lived in towns of 1,000 or more. Fifty years later, this had ballooned to 42.6 per cent. The number of rural residents declined from a high of 359,129 in 1881 to 311,842 in 1911 and 294,596 ten years later. In some counties, urban growth was spectacular. This was true of Cape Breton County, where the number and size of towns increased with the expansion of the coal and steel industry. In 1871, the county had about the same urban/rural split as the rest of Nova Scotia. By 1921 town dwellers accounted for 85 per cent of its population. The number of rural residents had also shrunk from a high of 25,218 in 1881 to 12,777 forty years later. This decline was steepest between 1911 and 1921, when the countryside lost 9,800 residents.[14] As one of the county's wardens reported in 1921, 'The sections are losing their inhabitants day after day, and if the migration to the industrial centres continues a number of our Districts will largely be deserted in a short while. Our assessments will naturally decrease and arrears of taxes are already shown on the different Rate Rolls on account of deserted homes.'[15]

The population of other counties declined as well. The most pronounced changes occurred where agricultural lands were marginal and where a large percentage of landowners had worked for others to make ends meet. Antigonish lost 35.88 per cent of its people between 1881 and 1921 and Victoria County, 29.32 per cent. The populations of Annapolis, Guysborough, Hants and Richmond counties also fell, by between 12 and 16 per cent.[16]

Most migrants were between twenty and thirty years of age,[17] and their departure had two important effects on those who stayed behind. First, fewer young people meant a decline in fecundity. This had a negative effect on population growth because out-migration of the young means fewer children in the future. Second, the average age rose.[18] As we shall see, the anxiety created by out-migration affected communities' interactions with the Mi'kmaq, as couples eager to keep their children nearby searched for additional land to keep them there.

The reasons for this migration are unclear. As Thornton points out, most explanations attribute out-migration to the undeveloped nature of the Maritime economy. This, she says, was not always the case, as many left in the 1880s when Nova Scotia's economy was outstripping growth rates in other regions of Canada.[19] For Cape Breton, Stephen Hornsby is of another mind; he argues that many left because the rural population had expanded beyond the capacity of the land to support it. To accommodate these growing numbers, farmers needed additional land. Some put new fields into production. This strategy brought little relief because the best land was already used and the new acreage was of poor quality. Others subdivided their farms. Adding to young peoples' troubles was the mechanization of agriculture. As Hornsby says, a horse-drawn mower took four hours to cut the same amount of hay a man could cut in twenty-one hours.[20] The number of farm jobs plummeted as did wages,[21] exacerbating the difficulties of young people finding work. Hearing from other relatives, friends, or neighbours that work was to be had elsewhere, many left, sometimes returning, but more often not.[22]

Alan Brookes's micro-study of Canning, an Annapolis Valley community not far from Wolfville, supports Hornsby's conclusions. Brookes contends that by the 1870s, Canning's population had grown because of a high fertility rate and, one would presume, a rise in the average life expectancy. Young people had fewer economic prospects than their parents had. The land was fully settled and this coupled with the economic downturn of the 1870s precipitated at the local level by the termination in 1866 of the Reciprocity Treaty led to out-migration.[23]

Similar economic and social pressures affected the Mi'kmaq, and in response many moved. Like other people of their generation, they emigrated because of internal and external factors, which are not always discernible or subject to statistical analysis.[24] One factor was population growth. This began in the middle decades of the nineteenth century and continued until the 1880s. In 1847 Abraham Gesner reported 1,461 Mi'kmaq, 961 on the mainland and another 500 on the island.[25] After 1847 these numbers grew: in 1861 there were 1,407 people, in 1871, 1,664, and ten years later, 1,870.[26] Table 6.1 summarizes the Nova Scotia Mi'kmaq and total populations.

The increase from 1847 to 1881 can be attributed to several factors. In explaining population change, demographers stress the inter-relationship between birth and death. Europe's population grew initially from a rise in average life expectancy. Fertility rates, however, remained the same, so that in any given year there were more births than deaths. As the average life expectancy rose, the disparity between births and deaths widened, leading to a steady population growth. This continued so long as the economy expanded.[27] Sometimes, this growth was accelerated by a decrease in the average age at first marriage, which would have increased the number of children a woman would bear. Eventually, the size of this difference between births and deaths declined as families realized their children were less likely to die than before, and so consciously reduced conception. This occurred during the transition from an agricultural-based to a machine-based economy. Both rural and urban populations were affected, although not always at the same time and at the same pace. Generally, the transition to lower fertility occurred first in towns and cities and later in the countryside. This was not always true, however, as fertility also declined in rural areas where there were fewer opportunities for young people to acquire land or to find work.[28] As we will see below, this was true of farming communities of the Annapolis Valley.

These general concepts are useful to explain demographic changes among peoples of European ancestry before and during industrializa-

Table 6.1
Mi'kmaw and Total Nova Scotia Population, 1871–1921

Year	Census	Mi'kmaq	Change (%)	Nova Scotia	Change (%)
1871	Federal	1,664		387,800	
	DIA	n/a			
1881	Federal	1,870	+12.4	440,472	+13.6
	DIA	2,219			
1891	Federal			450,398	+2.3
	DIA				
1901	Federal	1,629	−12.8	459,574	+2.0
	DIA	2,020	−9.0		
1911	Federal	1,758	+7.3	492,338	+7.1
	DIA	2,026	+4.3		
1921	Federal	2,048	+16.5	523,837	+6.4
	DIA				
1871–1911	Federal		+5.6		+35.1
	DIA				
1881–1911	Federal		−6.0		+18.9
	DIA		−8.7		

Federal = federal census; DIA = Department of Indian Affairs census
n/a: not available
Sources: LAC, RG 31, 1871, 1881, 1901, 1911, 1921 Census; 'Census of Indians, 31 December 1881,' Sessional Papers, no. 6 (1882), 220; Census Returns, 30 June 1901, Sessional Papers, no. 27 (1902), 156; 'Census of Indians, 31 March 1911,' Sessional Papers, no. 27 (1912), 30.

tion, but they are less helpful for understanding the Mi'kmaq. This is because they were neither farmers nor factory workers. Rather they were originally fishers and hunters, and thus their experience differed from other Nova Scotians. The colonization of their lands in the early 1800s undermined families' abilities to support themselves solely by using the commons to harvest fish, wildlife, and other resources. As a result of both their own efforts and government initiatives, families began using reserves as their principal location from which to support their households. Cape Breton families were more successful in doing so, largely because of differences in topography and in the history of colonization. While on reserve, families integrated gardening and farming into their household economies. They also turned to other cottage industries, besides fishing and hunting, to supplement their income. From the mid-1800s, coopering and basket-making became the mainstays of a burgeoning cottage industry. This difference in how Mi'kmaw communities lived and worked meant that their fertility and death rates differed from other Nova Scotians.

Before 1850, Mi'kmaw fertility was lower than Western European norms. This was for three reasons. First, as various anthropologists have argued, an itinerant lifestyle tends to suppress fertility by increasing the interval between births.[29] Based on his observations of the Mi'kmaq, the Nova Scotia judge and historian, Thomas Chandler Haliburton, wrote in 1823 that 'Among wandering tribes who depend upon hunting and fishing for subsistence the mother cannot attempt to rear a second child, until the first has attained such a degree of vigour as to be in some measure independent of her care. From this motive, it is the universal practice of the women to suckle their children during several years, and as they seldom marry early, the period of their fertility is over before they can finish the long but necessary attendance upon two or three children.'[30] In other words, because of their itinerant lifestyle, women nursed their children longer than the norm, which suppressed fertility. Second, harsh living conditions reduced fertility by delaying the age of menarche, impeding conception, and inducing miscarriages.[31] Poor nutrition may also have intensified pre-menstrual cramps, further limiting conception. The extreme form of this condition, pre-menstrual syndrome (PMS), is a condition that mainly strikes women in their thirties and forties and incapacitates some women for as much as two weeks before the beginning of their menstrual cycle. One factor affecting PMS is nutrition as well as physical and emotional stress. We might suppose therefore that increasing mobility and declining nutrition would have adversely affected the fertility of Mi'kmaw women, by reducing their libido.[32] Finally, the probability of regular sex makes conception possible, and the opposite is also true. As for most populations, we do not know how often Mi'kmaw women and men had sex. What we do know is that there is a short window in every woman's ovulation cycle when conception is more likely to occur.[33] In a society where movement in search of resources is common, and where the separation between men and women also occurs on a regular basis, we would expect that fertility rates would be lower than in societies where there this does not happen. Although Mi'kmaw families generally stayed together during the year, there were also periods when men traveled and worked alone, often in tandem with other males. This was more likely to occur during periods of scarcity. Colonization also affected couples' relationships, as from the early 1700s the intercession of conflict and the creation of permanent Catholic missions, lengthened the separation between couples.[34] All of these factors meant that

Mi'kmaw women's fertility was lower than the rates for European women of the same period; how much these ratios differed is not known.

Many of these same conditions likely characterized Mi'kmaw and Euro-Nova Scotia women before the 1780s, but such differences widened in the late eighteenth and early nineteenth centuries as the immigrant and native-born non-Mi'kmaw population skyrocketed. As we have seen in Chapter Four, when non-aboriginals interfered with Mi'kmaw farming, fishing, and hunting, families were forced to move. This reduced women's consumption of food and nutrients. Increasing mobility, declining nutrition, and nursing practices would have further suppressed fertility among married women by lengthening the average interval between births, reducing the probabilities of conception, and retarding the menarche of young girls. Thus, we would expect that after 1780, fertility rates declined further, exacerbating the differences between Mi'kmaw and Euro-Nova Scotia population rates.

The other major difference was that Mi'kmaw life expectancy was lower. Like other aboriginal people, the Mi'kmaq were susceptible to European-borne diseases, such as smallpox, measles, and whooping cough. This was especially true in the late 1500s and early 1600s. Although we would expect that the average life expectancy increased in later centuries, there is evidence that the Mi'kmaq continued to be adversely effected by European-borne diseases in the early 1800s, a situation exacerbated by declining nutrition. Virginia Miller, for instance, argues that from the early 1500s until the 1840s the Mi'kmaw population declined, mainly from a reduction in the average life expectancy.[35]

One consequence of lower life expectancy was that fewer women reached maturity. This translated into fewer children in the period when European fertility and fecundity were rising. Moreover, since the size of Mi'kmaw communities was relatively small, increased death rates distorted sex and age ratios. Skewed ratios may have led some young people to move to other communities or to marry into non-aboriginal families.

Of course, these are general comments and do not provide a nuanced portrait. Cape Breton Mi'kmaw communities were more insulated and less effected by the onrush of European settlers after 1760, creating a different demographic regime there than on the mainland. This may explain why the island's Mi'kmaw population increased relative to the mainland during the first half of the nineteenth century. This growth, we would suppose, was mainly the result of a higher life expectancy among island families.

After 1850 two factors led to population growth. First, fertility increased. As well, the average life expectancy rose as infant and child mortality decreased. One factor contributing to this change was that more families lived on reserve or established a more permanent presence in one location, a move that was influenced by the constriction of off-reserve resources and by the intercession of the federal government as the principal architect of Indian policy. The change in fertility and in average life expectancy also reflected a shift in Nova Scotia's political economy and Mi'kmaw participation within it. As certain sectors of Nova Scotia's economy grew in the 1850s through 1870s, Mi'kmaw families' involvement in cottage-like industries, such as making items for the shipbuilding, coal mining, and lumbering industries, expanded. This may have led to couples marrying younger, a pattern of behaviour probably related to the new opportunities which coopering offered to young people in ways similar to those in which the buffalo-robe trade affected Métis young people in the same period.[36]

Child/woman ratios calculated using the federal censuses for 1871 and 1881 illustrate these changes (Table 6.2). Modern demographers calculate fertility rates by dividing the number of live births in one calendar year by the number of women of reproductive age, usually between the ages of fifteen and forty-nine. This calculation is only possible to make when there are consistent birth records and this only begins in Nova Scotia in 1912.[37] Because of similar problems among other populations, researchers have devised an alternative method to measure fertility, which entails using census data to calculate the ratio of the number of children under the age of five to the number of married women of reproductive age (15–49).

This method has advantages and problems. First, it allows the analysis of fertility differences within populations, such as how class, ethnicity, education, and fluctuations in the economy may have influenced birthrates. Second, it also allows the micro-analysis of differences among women of different age cohorts.[38] But this method is not foolproof either. First, it only measures ratios among married women. Second, the ratio does not include children who died before their fifth birthday. Their deaths meant that they were not alive when the census was taken and therefore their names were not recorded. Thus, the ratios do not give an exact measure of fertility, as they do not include all children born in the five years before the census was taken.[39]

Among the Mi'kmaq, child/woman ratios increased between 1871 and 1881 for several reasons. One factor was that some families moved

Table 6.2
Child/Woman Ratios, Nova Scotia Mi'kmaq, 1871–1911

Age Cohort	1871 Ratio	1871 Married women (n)	1881 Ratio	1881 Married women (n)	1901 Ratio	1901 Married women (n)	1911 Ratio	1911 Married women (n)
15–19	0.27	22	0.45	29	0.36	22	0.91	11
20–4	1.07	54	1.15	54	1.16	32	1.13	40
25–9	1.02	60	1.31	58	0.96	56	1.31	45
30–4	1.09	46	1.06	53	0.70	40	0.95	44
35–9	0.93	28	1.11	37	0.73	30	0.90	40
40–4	0.50	26	0.47	32	0.76	21	0.50	30
45–9	0.30	23	0.36	22	0.29	17	0.25	32
All Women 15–49	0.853		0.954		0.776		0.884	
All Women 20–49	0.911		1.008		0.823		0.883	
Total Women		259		285		218		242
Standardized rates ages 20–49	0.84		0.93		0.76		0.85	

Note: Ratios have been expressed as decimal fractions. To put the ratio into the format used by Hareven & Vinovksis, multiply by 1,000. Using this method, the overall (non-standardized) rate for 1881 of 1.008 would be $1.008 \times 1,000 = 1,008$ children under the age of five for every 1,000 women, aged 20–49. To make these figures comparable to the Mi'kmaq entails counting only women 20–49 years old and recalculating Mi'kmaw child/woman ratios to fit a standardized age structure, an equation the authors use to minimize the affect of differential sizes among age cohorts. They used the equation $Y = 0.10X_{20-4} + 0.17X_{25-9} + 0.21X_{30-4} + 0.22X_{35-9} + 0.17X_{40-4} + 0.13X_{45-9}$, where Y = 'the age-standardized fertility ratio per 1,000 women aged 20–49 to be calculated' and X_{20-4} is 'the number of children under 5 per 1,000 married women aged 20–4,' etc. (Hareven and Vinovskis, 'Patterns of Childbearing,' 93).
Source: LAC, RG 31, 1871, 1881, 1901, and 1911 Censuses.

onto reserve. A more sedentary lifestyle shortened the average interval between births, increasing the number of children born. As Warrick explains in his study of the pre-contact Huron-Petun population of southwestern Ontario, 'an increase in fertility after the adoption of agriculture can be attributed to increased maternal health, as a result of a more reliable food base and decreased birth spacing caused by reduced breastfeeding and suckling of infants by mothers who had become sedentary and who supplemented infant diets with cereal porridges.'[40] This was also characteristic of differences between on- and off-reserve populations of nineteenth-century Upper Canada.[41] Settlement onto reserves led to an improvement in families' nutrition. Earlier in the century nutrition levels had declined as families were forced away from coastal fishing areas and from hunting grounds. With the settlement onto reserves, agriculture was integrated into the household economy, providing an additional source of food, and especially of milk. This likely led to a drop in infant and child mortality. Both factors, a reduced interval between births and a decline in infant and child mortality, increased child/woman ratios between 1871 and 1881.

We can test this hypothesis by comparing child/woman ratios between on- and off-reserve women. Although this division is somewhat arbitrary the analysis confirms that married women living on, or resorting to, reserves had more surviving children than married women living off reserve.[42] In 1871 among non-reserve families, the child/woman ratio was 0.813 and among reserve families, 0.953.

While families living on reserve had more surviving children than those families who did not, Table 6.2 also shows that in 1881, on average, women, regardless of their residence, had more surviving children than they had done ten years earlier. Put another way, between 1876 and 1881 married women had more children than married women had had ten years earlier. We can quantify these figures. In 1871, a woman twenty years of age who continued to live with her husband until the age of forty-nine could expect to have 4.91 surviving children. In 1881, a twenty-year old woman could expect to have 5.46 children.[43] This suggests that the rise in child/woman ratios occurred among all women regardless of where they lived.

This growth before 1881 contrasts with the period afterward. Table 6.2 also summarizes the child/woman ratios in 1901 and 1911. The table shows a decline from 1881 to 1901 and an increase from 1901 to 1911. If we confine our analysis to women between the ages of twenty to forty-nine and use the standardized rates developed by Hareven and Vinovksis, these observations would be the same.[44]

A family of Mi'kmaq on Cape Breton Island, ca. 1900 (Nova Scotia Museum, Halifax; Jack Woolner Collection)

Fertility rates decreased across Canada between 1861 and 1891, and we might therefore think what was happening to Mi'kmaw families was not unique.[45] As researchers have pointed out, wage labour was one factor that contributed to a drop in fertility as the separation of work from the household made families less dependent on children as a source of labour. Urban living costs were another. Over time, these factors led to a reduction in fertility.[46] We might suppose that similar changes affected Mi'kmaw families; they too were drawn into the wage labour economy in the late 1800s. Their participation, we might say, was part of a broader change in Nova Scotia's economy, as new innovations in shipping and transportation and the expansion of continental markets intensified the exploitation of timber, coal, and fish. Some families moved to Halifax, Pictou, Sydney, Truro, and Yarmouth with the hope of tapping into this new-found wealth. As the Mi'kmaq merged into urban life, family size shrank.

This explanation will not do for two reasons. First, the majority of Mi'kmaw families lived in rural areas, where we would expect child/woman ratios to exceed urban norms. Second, families living in the city had more children than those who did not.[47] There are several explanations for this apparent anomaly. As Peter Gossage explains in his study of Saint Hyacinthe, Quebec, fertility sometimes remained high because of working class families' short- and long-term needs. Children still contributed to some families' incomes, cared for younger siblings, and performed other essential tasks. Children were also valued because of the support they could provide for parents in their senior years.[48] All of these factors influenced couples' decisions. Even though there were many reasons why urbanization would spark a decline in fertility, this trend was not true of every family. The same seems to have been true for the Mi'kmaq, all the more so because they remained on the margins of the urban economy and so children were a source of labour and of support for elderly parents. This is reflected in both the 1901 and the 1911 censuses, which show that Sydney Mi'kmaw families were larger than the norm.[49] Changes in where people lived or how they earned their living therefore were not important factors contributing to the decline.

Alternatively, we might speculate that the drop paralleled similar decreases in rural Nova Scotia. In other words what was happening to the Mi'kmaq was also happening to other rural Nova Scotians. To test this hypothesis we need to compare Mi'kmaw and non-Mi'kmaw ratios. Making such a comparison, however, is not possible as we cannot compile figures for the entire province. I have therefore focused my attention on three

Table 6.3
Overview: Child/Woman Ratios in Five Non-Mi'kmaq Communities, 1871–1911

Community	1871			1881			1901			1911		
	Ratio	Std	*n*	Ratio	Std	*n*	Ratio	Std	*n*	Ratio	Std	*n*
Centreville	1.04	1.08	392	0.92	0.99	251	0.96	1.00	110	0.93	0.93	131
River Hebert[a]	1.19	1.17	221	1.02	1.13	244	0.99	1.00	117	1.09	1.16	491
Sheet Harbour	1.05	1.10	116	1.07	1.06	134	1.28	1.31	157	1.06	1.14	107
St Peter's	1.09	1.11	92	1.19	1.16	131	0.90	1.01	97	0.90	1.02	107
Whycocomagh	1.31	1.30	185	1.48	1.29	119	0.97	1.05	134	0.81	1.00	110

Legend: *n* = married women
        Std = Standardized ratio
[a] For 1911, three new electoral districts were created out of the River Hebert District. In
  order that the figures measure the same geographical area, the 1911 figures include
  these three newly created census districts: Joggins, Lower Cove, and Shulee.
Source: LAC, RG 31, 1871, 1881, 1901, and 1911 Censuses: Centreville, King's County;
River Hebert, Cumberland County; Sheet Harbour, Halifax County; St Peters, Richmond
County; Whycocomagh, Inverness County.

mainland and two Cape Breton communities. The three communities
on the mainland are Centreville, a predominantly farming area in the
Annapolis Valley, Sheet Harbour, a fishing community about a hundred
kilometres east of Halifax, and River Hebert, which is in Cumberland
County and which had a mixed labour force of farmers, lumberman,
miners, and mariners. These three communities represent different aspects of Nova Scotia's rural economy. The two Cape Breton communities, on the other hand, have been selected because of their proximity to
reserves: Whycocomagh, a village east and west of the reserve of the same
name, and St Peter's, which is adjacent to the Chapel Island reserve.
Data for these five communities appear in Table 6.3.[50]
    Comparison of Mi'kmaw and non-Mi'kmaw ratios illustrates various
differences. First, with the exception of the 1911 listing for Whycocomagh, the non-aboriginal ratios are generally higher. This is a telling
reminder of the demographic imbalance between the two communities.
In 1881 a woman twenty years of age living at Whycocomagh (in the non-
aboriginal community) could expect to have 7.41 surviving children and
a woman from River Hebert, 6.04. This contrasts with a Mi'kmaw average of 5.46. In 1901, this difference persisted. While ratios declined in
all communities, the non-aboriginal ratios remained higher. Even if we

were to assume that the average life expectancy was similar for both the Mi'kmaq and non-Mi'kmaq, the differential meant that the non-aboriginal population was increasing faster.

These average figures disguise differences between mainland and island Mi'kmaw communities. For this reason, we need to examine averages for each region separately. The differences between Mi'kmaw and non-Mi'kmaw communities were greater on the mainland. While in 1901 the mainland Mi'kmaw communities had a combined child/women ratio of 0.745, the non-Mi'kmaw ratios ranged from Centreville's 0.96 to Sheet Harbour's 1.28. In other words, child/woman ratios among mainland Mi'kmaw women were between 28.9 per cent and 71.8 per cent lower than those of non-Mi'kmaq women. In contrast, differences between the two communities on the Cape Breton Island were considerably less, with the Mi'kmaw ratios ranging between 10 per cent and 18.6 per cent lower. What can conclude from all this? First, while child/woman ratios declined among all Mi'kmaq between 1881 and 1901, the drop was greater on the mainland than on the island.

Regardless of the differences between Cape Breton and the mainland, child/woman ratios dropped between 1881 and 1901. The most important factor was the changes in Nova Scotia's rural economy. This was a period when more than 100,000 Nova Scotians left the province because there was not enough land or work to support them. The Mi'kmaq were similarly affected. Because they were dependent on harvesting timber, fish, and wildlife to supplement farming incomes, they also suffered as the rural population expanded and as governments assumed more control over natural resources. Their families' situation paralleled the experience of the Mi'kmaw and Maliseet populations of neighbouring New Brunswick, as new restrictions limited access to fish and game.[51] For the Mi'kmaq of Nova Scotia, this situation was exacerbated by a growth in population. Nutritional levels dropped and, as families had to provide for more children on less income, the average life expectancy declined. As well, the average age at first marriage may have increased, as young couples delayed marriage because of economic uncertainty.

This crisis of the late 1800s impacted Mi'kmaw families in several ways. First, the crisis precipitated by the out-migration of young Nova Scotians led some non-aboriginal farmers to increase the size of their landholdings and to appropriate common lands for their own use. Mi'kmaq living off reserve were particularly vulnerable, because they generally did not own the land on which they lived. At times, this led to physical confrontations reminiscent of incidents earlier in the century. This is what happened in 1884 to two Annapolis Valley families. In 1884, the agent for the Annapolis region filed the following report: 'Some six weeks since I received information of an outrage committed upon two peaceable, inoffensive families, by two drunken roughs breaking into their camp in the night, beating the men, the women fleeing into the woods in their fright, for safety. They then set fire to their camp, after breaking and destroying everything valuable. I immediately wrote to a prominent magistrate in that neighbourhood, asking him to take notice of the affair and bring the offenders to justice. I have since learned that with the help of Father Holden they have compromised the affair with money; but it should have been a criminal matter.' Others facing similar threats fled.[52]

Reserve Mi'kmaw populations were also effected by the rural crisis as the dearth of arable land led some farmers to appropriate reserve lands for their own use.[53] On the mainland, some ignored reserve boundaries. Farmers next to the Shubenacadie Reserve, for instance, let their cattle graze freely on the Indian meadows, a low-lying area near the reserve's entrance.[54] Although agents tried to curtail such abuses, their efforts often failed because of local resistance.[55]

The events at Whycocomagh involving Donald McLean illustrate how local attitudes undermined efforts to protect reserve lands. In 1879, the Indian agent, Donald McIsaac, reported that McLean had planted, harvested, and enclosed a portion of the Whycocomagh Reserve. McIsaac authorized members of the 'Indian Board of the County of Inverness to enter onto the lands claimed [by McLean] and cut and carry away the hay growing there.' In 1882, McIssac went one step further and had Mclean and his son arrested. They were tried before a stipendiary magistrate, found guilty of occupying reserve land, fined, and jailed after failing to pay the fine.[56] After his release, McLean sued McIsaac, claiming that the agent did not have the authority either to lay a complaint or to seize the hay. Contrary to the judge's advice, the jury decided in McLean's favour. The agent appealed to the Nova Scotia Supreme Court, which set aside the verdict and confirmed McIsaac's authority to arrest McLean.[57] However, the jury's rejection of the judge's admonition suggested that future efforts to protect reserve land would face opposition. Even though the law protected the Mi'kmaq from white interlopers, the McLean case illustrates how citizens banded together to protect their own interpretation of the law, in the courtroom, and outside of it. The result was that white farmers steadily chipped away at the borders of reserve lands.

In other cases, local residents pressured the DIA to surrender lands. In 1879, for instance, residents of Inverness County petitioned the government to force the surrender of the Malagawatch Reserve, which they claimed had been 'not occupied nor settled by Indians for several years with the exception of an occasional residence of one Indian family.'[58] In the case of Wagmatcook such pressures led to the DIA seeking the surrender of reserve land, without the unanimous consent of the Mi'kmaq. In this case, the object of the white community's efforts was a group of islands in the Middle River, which the Wagmatcook Mi'kmaq had rented to neighbouring farmers but which was also used to supply hay for reserve cattle. The consequence of the Indian agents' actions undermined the band's economic welfare, as the islands were sold for less than market value and deprived the community of a source of cattle feed and income.[59]

The second factor affecting Mi'kmaw households was that game populations plummeted, depriving families of a much-needed source of winter food and income.[60] The Mi'kmaq attributed the decline to white hunters and cited examples, such as in 1849 when Guysborough County hunters had killed two to three hundred moose in one season.[61] Such rapacious hunting practices had a long-term impact on the herd, by reducing its reproductive capacity. Mi'kmaq in other regions voiced similar concerns. In 1844 some Annapolis County families complained that if their white neighbours continued to hunt moose in February and March, the population would not survive. As the petitioners explained, at this time of year 'the female is heavy with young and becomes an easy prey, the hard Crust on the deep Snow rendering it impossible for her to escape, that consequently a great number of the females also are killed.'[62] Over-hunting contributed to the decline, but white settlement was also a factor. As communities expanded, wildlife feeding areas were restricted, decreasing fertility and lowering average life expectancies. A similar scenario had affected caribou herds on the southern mainland earlier in the century when one of their principal foods, white reindeer moss, was destroyed.[63]

From the 1880s, some agents reported that the scarcity of game was hurting families.[64] The agent for Eskasoni wrote in 1883 'game, such as the moose and caribou, which in former years almost exclusively constituted their daily food, are now nowhere to be found.'[65] The same was true on the southern mainland, in Annapolis, Queen's, Shelburne, and Yarmouth counties.[66] In the early 1920s Louis Luxey, a 74-year old resident of the Yarmouth reserve, summed up the decline when he told Clara Dennis that 'no animals now, 2 or 3 maybe but that's nothing. When I was a boy couldn't travel ¼ mile of a mile without seeing a bear, moose, or wild cat.'[67]

   The third factor was that Mi'kmaw families had more trouble fishing. On the mainland, where most lived on landlocked reserves, some families were still able to fish on inland rivers and streams. Such practices became more difficult in the late 1800s as the rural population swelled, new lands were cleared, mills were built, and rivers were used to float lumber to the coast.[68] The expansion of the lumber industry, resulting from demand south of the border, had a negative effect on river systems, as mills were built on most of the province's major rivers. As the agent for Annapolis County wrote in 1886, 'owing to the fact that the millers are not prevented from throwing sawdust and other matter into the water, and that there is no proper conveyance for fish to pass up and down,' fish were quickly becoming extinct.[69] Other counties faced similar difficulties, even though new laws forced millers to build ladders, which would allow salmon and other anadromous fish to move upriver.[70] On the mainland, the Bear River Mi'kmaq noted that 'the waters of the Bear River which were formerly well stocked with fish and furnished a considerable income to the people of this Reserve have been depleted of such fish as Salmon and others by neglect of mill owners to furnish means by which such fish ascend.'[71] Lumbering and land clearing also contributed to the decline either directly by dumping logs and brush into riverbeds or indirectly by increasing erosion. As the fishery overseer for Cape Breton wrote in 1881, 'some of the rivers best suited for salmon are almost ruined by the masses of brush, &c in their beds.'[72] By 1891, some Pictou County families had abandoned fishing because 'it is so uncertain on the coast.' This was an abrupt change from ten years earlier when fishing had been a mainstay of their local economy.[73] This was not true in all regions, however, as Mi'kmaq living in Queen's County continued to harvest large quantities of salmon into the 1880s.[74]

   The growth of the commercial fishery in the late nineteenth century was an additional factor that limited access. In the late 1800s, the commercial fishery expanded with the adoption of new preservation methods and with the emergence of new urban markets in the northeastern United States. Canning was one such innovation, providing merchants an alternative means to ship fish, and with fewer anxieties that it would spoil enroute. In the 1870s Nova Scotia companies began canning lobster for export. In 1881, these plants spewed out 813,552 cans.[75] Antigonish and Guysborough counties were the centre of this new industry; other factories also operated in Inverness, Lunenburg, and Richmond counties. Ten years later, the annual production skyrocketed to 6.323 million cans, and production extended to most communities fronting the sea.[76] Production had declined by about a million cans in 1900, but the opening of a live lobster market, in England and in the United States compensated for the shortfall. In terms of value, lobster was Nova Scotia's second most important fishery in 1900.[77] The trade had expanded to such a degree by 1884 that one packer complained that the supply had dropped off by about 50 per cent as a result of over-fishing.[78] The expansion must have affected Mi'kmaw families as the rise of a new commercial inshore fishery led lobster fishermen to claim a customary right to the areas where they placed their traps. This reduced families' access to the inshore fishery and to the local lobster market. Significantly, accounts from before the 1870s describing Mi'kmaw canoes coming ashore with fresh lobster to sell at market do not recur later in the century.[79]

Lobster was only one of a number of species fished for export. Gaspereau, herring, oysters, and salmon were also shipped southward and in greater numbers as the urban population of the eastern United States exploded in the late nineteenth and early twentieth centuries. The Mi'kmaq also engaged in this trade, including Gabriel Sylliboy and other families from Whycocomagh.[80] As the size of this export market grew, however, fishermen interfered more often with the Mi'kmaw fishery, ultimately forcing families to be less reliant on fishing as a source of income and food.[81]

Fourth, in the last decades of the nineteenth century, Mi'kmaw families' access to fish and game was gradually restricted by government fiat. As we have seen in Chapter One, plummeting wildlife numbers and the rise of the sport lobby spurred the provincial legislature to impose limits on hunting and trapping. This led to changes in when and where families hunted. To cite two examples: in 1875 Game Society wardens from Antigonish County seized a moose carcass from a Mi'kmaw family, after receiving a tip from some local inhabitants,[82] while in 1889, the wardens had three Mi'kmaq tried and convicted for hunting illegally. Some members of the society believed the Mi'kmaq to be the greatest obstacle 'there is to contend with in carrying out the Game laws.'[83] Although the new restrictions were not always applied, Mi'kmaw hunters were easier to prosecute because they lacked familial and community relationships with local enforcement officers.[84] Mi'kmaq in southwestern Nova Scotia were a favourite target, as the area was favoured by out of province hunters who brought tourist dollars to the region.

After 1867, federal legislation also restricted Mi'kmaw access to the fisheries, enforcing a common standard of when and how salmon and other anadromous fish could be caught.[85] In 1891 fishery courts were created on Cape Breton Island to prosecute fishermen accused of violating the Fishery Act. The effect, in terms of the law and the methods used to enforce it, restricted Mi'kmaw families' access to the fishery in a way that had not been true before.[86]

Finally, Mi'kmaw families were also affected by structural changes in Nova Scotia's economy. As we have seen, most families made wood products for sale. With new technological innovations, some of these items became superfluous. To cite one example: some families made mast parts for sailing vessels. With the emergence of the steamship in the late 1800s, demand for mast hoops and jib hanks decreased. As well the development of standard and interchangable machine parts and the growth of mass woodworking industries paved the way for assembly-line production, reducing the demand for some products the Mi'kmaq had once made. Other craft industries also declined, as mass-produced items penetrated the Maritime economy.[87] In 1915, Joe Christmas said of the Mi'kmaw community living in Sydney that 'We used to make pick handles for the mines but not now. We cannot sell Indian work now, it is all manufactured in factories.' This had forced people to find other work. 'The people are working at day's work now.' Christmas himself was personally affected by technological changes. As he told Justice Audette of the Exchequer Court, 'I can't sell my oars now. The gasoline boats spoilt me altogether.'[88] These changes in production may have been one factor that forced Bear Reserve residents to wander further and further from their reserve in the mid-1880s. According to the local agent, many left their homes in early spring and summer in order to sell their products, 'having overstocked the market for miles around the reserve.'[89]

Like other people of their generation whose world had been transformed by changes in populations and economies, the Mi'kmaq tried to find new ways to support their families, by using other types of wood to make their products, by altering what they made, and by finding additional sources of income. They also moved, some onto reserves or making their residence more permanent there than they had before. Other families moved from one reserve to another. In some cases, this led to a more itinerant lifestyle, as people searched for work and resources. In other cases, this led to the physical separation of married couples, with men working in town or in the bush and women selling baskets. All of this illustrates the transient nature of Mi'kmaw family life in the late nineteenth century, a pattern of life that was also true of other Maritimers, and had also characterized other workers in other urban and rural settings.[90] What made Mi'kmaw experiences different were their more limited options in where they lived and how they could make their living.

Some people moved onto reserve or spent more time there they had before. This led to overcrowding. As we have seen in previous chapters, the reserves were too small and too infertile to support the populations as they existed in 1871. With the growth of the on-reserve population from 1881, the average farming income per family declined. The result was a drop in income and therefore nutrition.

Data regarding on- and off-reserve populations between 1871 and 1911 are summarized in Table 6.4. The table includes census and DIA data. As pointed out in Chapter Five, in 1871 30.0 per cent of the mainland and 50.7 per cent of the Cape Breton population lived on reserve. Over the next ten years, these percentages increased only marginally, but the number of people on reserve grew. By 1881, 41.0 per cent of all Mi'kmaq lived on reserve (767 of 1,870). The most dramatic changes occurred on the island, with 66.2 per cent now living on reserve (354 of 535), and less so on the mainland, where the percentages increased more slowly.

After 1881, this movement accelerated. There are discrepancies between the census and departmental figures, but both data sets show a shift onto reserves. By 1901, 70 per cent of all Mi'kmaq in Nova Scotia lived on reserve. The most significant change was on the mainland where 56 per cent were now living on reserve, a striking shift from twenty years earlier when only about one in four persons did so. The percentages remained more or less the same over the next ten years. On Cape Breton, the population became even more concentrated, and by 1911 only seven people lived off reserve. In contrast, about 28 per cent of all mainland Mi'kmaq lived off reserve.[91]

In some cases, this migration led to a sharp rise in the population of the reserves. The major changes occurred on the island. Chapel's Island's population doubled, while Eskasoni's and Whycocomagh's numbers tripled, even though Cape Breton's total Mi'kmaw population did not. Such increases contrast with the major mainland reserves, where growth was more modest – Bear River's population declined from 153 in 1871 to 94 in 1911. Information about reserve populations is summarized in Table 6.5. Although we should not interpret these figures to mean that people lived on reserve twelve months of the year, the totals do show a larger and more permanent on-reserve population than in 1871.

People moved onto reserve and made their residence more permanent because they believed their lives would be better there. There were two reasons they thought so. First, the transfer of Indian Affairs to federal control had translated into more government assistance to reserve

Table 6.4
On- and Off-Reserve Mi'kmaw Population of Nova Scotia, 1871–1911[a]

	1871	1881	Change (%)	1901	Change (%)	DIA/1901	1911	Change (%)	DIA/1911
Cape Breton	473	535	+12.7	539		633	664		625
On reserve	240	354	+47.1	491	+39.1	574	657	+33.8	625
Off reserve	233	181	−18.5	48	−63.2	59	7	−83.3	0
% on reserve	50.7	66.2		91.1		90.7	99.0		100
Mainland	1,191	1,335	+12.2	1,003		1,387	1,094		1,401
On reserve	358	413	+15.4	577	+39.7	816	784	+16.8	776
Off reserve	833	922	+9.2	426	−54.4	517	310	+37.8	625
% on reserve	30.0	30.9		56.8		58.8	28.3		55.4
Total Nova Scotia	1,664[b]	1,870[b]		1,542[c]		2,020	1,758		2,026
On reserve	598	767	+19.4	1,068	+49.0		1,441	+34.9	
Off reserve	1,066	1,103	+3.5	474	−57.5		317	−33.1	
% on reserve	35.94	41.0		69.3		68.8	82.0		69.2

[a] All data come from printed and manuscript copies of the 1871 through 1911 censuses. The census often does not show if people lived on reserve. Therefore, I have compared the census with the known locations of reserves to render a reasonable conclusion as to each family's residency. I have not included the 1921 census since only printed aggregates totals are available and do not provide an accurate portrait of people's residency. For instance, the census shows 175 of 188 people in Halifax County living on reserve. We know from other sources that this cannot be true, as many families lived in Bedford, Elmsdale, Wellington Station, and Windsor, Junction.
[b] These are corrected populations totals from the printed census records based on a reading of the manuscript copy of the 1871 and 1881 censuses. The printed 1871 census says there were 1,666 Mi'kmaq and the 1881 census, 2,125. As explained in the Appendix, these figures do not accord with the manuscript copy of each census.
[c] Does not include people identified as 'half-bloods' in the census.

Source: Columns marked 1871, 1881, 1901, and 1901 come from the Canadian federal censuses. Column marked DIA/1901 comes from Census Returns, 30 June 1901, Sessional Papers, no. 27 (1902), 156; 'Census of Indians, 31 March 1911,' Sessional Papers, no. 27 (1912), 30.

Table 6.5
Population of Main Reserves in Nova Scotia, 1871–1911

Reserve	1871	1881	Change (%)	1901	Change (%)	1911	Change (%)	Change 1871–1911 (%)
Cape Breton								
Chapel Island	66	94		131		139		+106.1
Eskasoni	53	39		109		170		+239.6
Sydney	–	44		66		95		+115.9a
Wagmatcook	69	89		70		94		+36.2
Whycocomagh	52	88		115		159		+205.7
Total Cape Breton	240	354	+47.5	491	+38.7	657	+33.8	+173.8
Mainland								
Bear River	153	68		72		94		–37.3
Boat Harbour	–	109		109		165		+51.4a
Indian Brook	62	6		52		71		+14.5
Millbrook	–	52		111		91		+75*
Total Mainland	215	235	+9.3	344	+46.4	421	+25.3	+95.8

aCalculated for period 1881 to 1911
Source: LAC, RG 31, 1871, 1881, 1901, and 1911 Censuses.

residents than had been true before 1867, and although the effects were not immediately forthcoming, the prospect of receiving assistance likely attracted people to spend more time on reserve than they had before. Second, beginning in the 1870s, DIA began building day schools on reserve and paying for the teachers who taught there, something families had been requesting since mid-century.[92] We would suppose the availability of schools pushed families onto reserve when their ability to make ends meet became more difficult. As well, as discussed in Chapter Two, the DIA pressured families to move onto reserve, a process that was sometimes aided by local inhabitants who objected to the Mi'kmaq attending common schools and living near white communities.[93]

People also adapted to the problems of making ends meet by moving from one reserve to another. Evidence regarding this comes from agents' annual reports but is difficult to quantify. Some agents reported when new families moved onto a reserve, others did not. Nor did an agent always indicate a family's former residence. Despite these problems, we can calculate the level of migration by adding the numbers of people who either left an agency or moved to another one. We should keep in mind, however, that the totals are incomplete because more people moved than agents reported. Data for Cape Breton between 1901 and 1910 are summarized in Table 6.6. No comparable data are available for mainland communities.

These figures help give a better overview of transience than anecdotal accounts. First, the figures suggest a higher level of migration in Cape Breton County than in other counties. This occurred mainly but not exclusively between Eskasoni and the coal mining areas of Sydney, North Sydney, and the neighbouring villages and towns. Second, Chapel Island was more volatile than any other island community. This volatility is measured in the last column of Table 6.6, which gives the ratio of people moving into and out of the agency relative to the average size of the population.

There are two important conclusions to be made from this data. First, most people moved from rural to urban areas. As one agent noted in 1891, many people in his agency 'left the reserve and settle[d] in the vicinity of towns, villages and mines.' He explained that the major reason they did so was because 'they are so far away from market' at which they could sell their handicrafts. 'None of them' he wrote, 'live exclusively by farming, and as they find it almost impossible to ply their trade and continue farming at the same time, many of them forgo the latter, remove to places within easy reach of a ready market.'[94] One of their destina-

Table 6.6
Mi'kmaq Migration in Cape Breton, 1901–1910

	1901	1902	1903	1904	1905	1906	1907	1908	1909	1910	Total 1901–10	Population[a]	Migration/Population (%)
Cape Breton County													
Eskasoni	+7			−5	−20		−9			−19	55	122	45.0
North Sydney	−14	−10					+11			−10	24	38	63.2
Sydney				+6	−20		−9			29	35	86	40.7
Subtotal	21			36	20		20			29	114	252	45.2
Inverness County													
Malagawatch		+8		−2					−8	+2	18		
Whycocomagh			8	2		−14	14		8	+11	27		
Subtotal		8		2			8		8	13	45	168	26.8
Richmond County													
Chapel Island	−10	−4	+5				−27	+17		+1	64	114	56.1
Victoria County													
Wagmatcook	+1	−7									8	96	8.3
Total	21	11	19	43	20	14	47	17	8	43	203		

[a] Average population, 1901–10.

Source: Indian agents reports, Annual Report of the Department of Indian Affairs, Sessional Papers, 1902–1911 (Ottawa, 1903–12).

tions was North Sydney, where Andrew Bernard had lived since the late 1800s and where Mi'kmaw families were living on land owned by the Nova Scotia Steel Company. Some of these families lived there only temporarily during the summer, others year round.[95] The federal government, perhaps inadvertently, encouraged this migration by establishing five new reserves in or near urban areas in the late 1800s. Four reserves were established on the mainland – Pictou Landing in 1874 (Pictou), Cole Harbour in 1880 (Dartmouth), Millbrook in 1886 (Truro), and Yarmouth in 1887 – and another at Sydney in Cape Breton in 1882. Second, most of the migrants to Sydney were from the poorer reserves or from those without a solid farming base, namely Chapel Island, Eskasoni, and Wagmatcook. This suggests that people from these communities had difficulty in making ends meet and moved to other areas, if not always to the Sydney area. Third, although in some cases people were continuing earlier patterns of seeking markets for their wares, they were also searching for waged employment.

All of this suggests the transformation of Mi'kmaw communities in the late nineteenth and early twentieth centuries. The most important triggering factor was a restriction in access to, and use of, off-reserve resources, which when combined with a growth in population forced families to find alternative sources of work and income. Some families moved to urban areas or to other regions of the province, where they were able to use their woodworking skills to make items for the shipbuilding, coalmining, or lumbering industries. Sales of these goods would act as a temporary source of income until waged work could be found or as a supplementary source once employment had been obtained, and as income for the aged. Other families moved onto reserve or made their residency more permanent than before. This intensified movement between communities, from rural to urban areas, and onto reserves. It also led to out-migration as well as to changes in fertility and mortality.

This is suggested by a decline in the population from 1881 to 1911 (Table 6.1). Two sets of data are shown: figures from the decennial federal censuses and information collected by Indian agents. In 1881, federal census enumerators counted 1,870 people of Mi'kmaw ancestry and in 1911, 1,758.[96] These figures vary slightly from DIA data, which show 2,219 people in 1881, 2,020 in 1901 and 2,026 in 1911.[97] If we use the census as our standard, then between 1881 and 1911 the Mi'kmaw population shrunk by 112 people or 6 per cent. DIA figures show a decline of 193 people in the same thirty-year period, an 8.7 per cent reduction. Regardless of which figures we use, therefore, between 1881 and

1911 the population decreased. In contrast, Nova Scotia's population as a whole grew from 440,572 in 1881 to 492,338 thirty years later, an increase of 11.4 per cent, despite the emigration of 100,000 people. If the Mi'kmaq had experienced a similar growth rate, then their population would have been 2,083 if we use the census figures and 2,472 if we use the DIA data.

Why the dip in population? There are five probable explanations. First, low fertility may have been a factor. The data summarized in Tables 6.2 and 6.3 show that between 1871 and 1911 child/woman ratios were lower than for the non-native population, although they compare favourably with other regions in the country. For 1901, Gossage and Gauvreau calculated a child/woman ratio of 1.12 for Quebec and 0.75 for Ontario.[98] While the Mi'kmaw ratio of 0.823 was significantly lower than that for Quebec, it still exceeded the Ontario ratio. So, even though child/woman ratios were lower among the Mi'kmaq than for other Nova Scotians, this lower ratio would not have arrested population increases, but only muted them.

Alternatively, for the Mi'kmaq, as for mid-century Ontarians, the lack of available land may have depressed fertility rates. David Gagan, for instance, in his study of rural farmers in Peel County in the mid- to late 1800s has shown that one factor contributing to lower fertility was the declining availability of cheap fertile land, which led women either not to marry or to marry later than their mothers and grandmothers.[99]The same pattern of late marriage may also have characterized Mi'kmaw couples as their community's fortunes declined. Although this would seem a reasonable response, determining the average age of marriage for Mi'kmaw couples of this generation is not possible because parish registers for Cape Breton are not accessible.[100] In lieu of evidence to the contrary, it is probable that the average age at first marriage increased slightly and so led to a decline in fertility by reducing the average number of children born to married women.

A skewed age pyramid in the 1870s may also have contributed to the decline. Analysis of the 1871 census, however, suggests that there were similar numbers of young people in both the Mi'kmaw and non-Mi'kmaw populations. A comparison of the Cape Breton Mi'kmaq with the non-aboriginal population of the island shows that both populations had almost identical proportions of people under the age of 21: 51.17 per cent among the Mi'kmaq (240 of 469) and 51.28 per cent among the rest of the island population (38,469 of 75,001). This compares favourably to the overall Nova Scotia percentage of 51.41 (lower than the

Canadian average of 54.77 per cent, a rate, however, which was the result of immigration).[101] The comparability between the Nova Scotia and Mi'kmaw populations therefore would discount different age pyramids as the reason for a decline in population.

Out-migration may have been an additional factor. In 1907, New Brunswick reported that 109 'Indians of Nova Scotia and Prince Edward Island' were living in the northeastern section of the province. Three years later agents reported that '150 nomadic Indians of Nova Scotia' were still there.[102] Other Mi'kmaw families went south to Boston and to New York. The agent for Shelburne County reported in 1900 that seven people from his agency were living in the United States, and the next year, eleven.[103] Similarly, in 1887, the agent for Antigonish County commented that 'many of the more ambitious pursue fickle fortune, even as far away as Boston.'[104] Some returned, such as the family who returned to King's County from Massachusetts after an absence of eight years, but just how many left and how many returned is unknown.[105]

Some Mi'kmaw families did move permanently to the United States, but we would suppose that they did not leave at the same rates as other Nova Scotians. Race was one reason. The Mi'kmaq were, as Professor Gates was later to write in his expose on Mi'kmaw blood types, O bloods, and so they were often, but not always, racially distinguishable from others.[106] Skin colour, however, was only one trait that distinguished them. There were other markers as well: language, cultural mannerisms, habits of work and custom, as well as attitudes and beliefs, all of which would have made participation in the American economy difficult. These differences would have inhibited people from moving there and in the same proportions as other young people of their generation. Equally important, Mi'kmaw men and women were often illiterate in English and many had few marketable skills; this in combination with their racial distinctiveness would have made full-time employment difficult to obtain for most. This was in contrast to those Nova Scotians who were able to make the transition from shipbuilding to homebuilding.[107] As well, work was probably jealously guarded by certain ethnic and familial groups, especially during the late nineteenth and early twentieth centuries when urban unemployment was the norm and immigration was increasing.[108] Some Mi'kmaw families therefore may have only left the province temporarily in search of work. This appears to be the case, for instance, for the families who worked in Maine during for the blueberry and potato harvests. Some eventually stayed, although this emigration appears to have occurred after 1911.[109]

Some Mi'kmaq could also have been absorbed into Nova Scotian society and no longer recognized as 'Indian.'[110] The Indian Act of 1876 specified that women who married men who were not considered to be Indian, as defined in the Indian Act, would lose their status and so too would their children.[111] Intermarriage between Mi'kmaw and non-Mi'kmaw communities did occur.[112] The 1881 census records twenty-one marriages where one spouse was Mi'kmaq and the other was not.[113] This included fifteen Mi'kmaw men who married non-aboriginal women and six Mi'kmaw women who married non-aboriginal men. In most cases, federal enumerators identified the children of these marriages with their father's origin, not their mother's. If agents strictly interpreted the Indian Act, the twenty children (thirteen girls and seven boys) born to the six Mi'kmaw women who had married out of the community would be identified as white, not Mi'kmaq. As a result, all the children born to the thirteen girls would be lost, with the exception of those who married back into the community.

Three factors limited the impact of inter-racial marriage. First, Nova Scotia agents did not compile band lists as agents did in Ontario and Western Canada. The difference was that in both of these other regions treaty promises had included annuity payments. This necessitated keeping a strict accounting of band members to ensure that people were paid and that they were only paid once. No similar provision of annuities was made in the Mi'kmaw treaties, and so there was less need to keep band lists. Because there was no compelling financial or legal rationale to keep track of who was and who was not an 'Indian,' agents in Nova Scotia did not strictly enforce the Indian Act, so that many couples living on reserve or off were treated as though they were 'Indian,' even though legally they, or one of a couple, might not be. Second, even though the 1881 census shows that six women from the first generation and thirteen women from the second would have lost their status, this loss of fecundity was compensated by the addition of fifteen non-aboriginal women who had married Mi'kmaw men and whose children were therefore defined as Indian. Finally, the loss through intermarriage was limited by region. In 1881, all twenty-one inter-racial marriages involved couples on the mainland, and most of these were concentrated in the province's central and southern regions. Eleven of the twenty-one mixed couples came from either Lunenburg or Annapolis counties. Significantly, the 1881 census does not show any Cape Breton Mi'kmaw men or women marrying non-aboriginals.

There are also factors that would have limited the ability to identify inter-racial marriages and the children from such unions. First, the children of inter-racial couples living isolated from Mi'kmaw communities were more likely to integrate into non-aboriginal communities than children whose parents did not. Ethnicity and race also made a difference. Indian agents were unlikely to accept as 'Indian' children born from intermarriages with the black community. Children of German ancestry may also have been excluded, not because of their skin colour, but because of their parents' decisions. The 1881 census strongly hints this to be the case as German men or women who married Mi'kmaw spouses often identified their children as 'German,' not Mi'kmaq, suggesting an intention that their children would live and work within the white community. Finally, using census data to compile lists of inter-racial couples probably underestimates their number, because census takers were unlikely to have either the knowledge or inclination to record everyone's ethnicity. The examination, for instance, of contemporaneous parish registers for southwestern Nova Scotia in the late nineteenth century shows a number of inter-racial marriages that were not recorded in the federal censuses.[114]

All these factors affected population, but the single most important factor that limited Mi'kmaw growth between 1881 and 1921 was high death rates. Death rates calculate the number of deaths per 1,000 of population. Because the age structure of a population varies from place to place and from year to year, using this method does not give a standard measure of mortality. For this reason, most demographers evaluate mortality by calculating the average life expectancy at birth. This can only be done, however, when the age of the deceased is known. We lack such data for the Mi'kmaq, however, and are therefore forced to rely on the less dependable and less comparable method of crude death rates to evaluate mortality. Data from 1890 to 1916 are summarized in Table 6.7 and are based on information filed by Indian agents in their annual reports; this the only timeframe in which there was some consistency in reporting deaths.

There are three main problems with the data. First, the information is incomplete.[115] Second, in cases where the agent failed to report deaths, I have not included the agency's population in calculating the crude death rate for that year. This adjustment may inflate the ratios. We could, for instance, interpret an agent's silence as indicating that no deaths had occurred. This, however, seems unlikely, because the department's aggregate death figures published after 1900 show more deaths than noted by the agents in their annual reports. Indeed, after 1900, when the DIA

Table 6.7
Crude Death Rates, Mi'kmaq of Nova Scotia, 1890–1916

Date	An	Ant	CB	Co	Cu	Dig	Hfx	Han	In	K	Pi	Qu	Ri	Sh	Vi	Y	To	Population of Counties with Reported Deaths	Rate/1,000
1890	0	1	14	[a]	6	9	[a]	[a]	[a]	[a]	[a]	[a]	[a]	[a]	[a]	[a]	30	674	44.5
1891	1	3	[a]	[a]	6	10	[a]	[a]	3	[a]	[a]	[a]	[a]	2	[a]	3	28		
1892	2	2	8	[a]	[a]	8	1	[a]	[a]	[a]	[a]	[a]	[a]	2	[a]	3	26	915	28.4
1893	2	7	[a]	[a]	4	5	1	[a]	[a]	[a]	[a]	[a]	[a]	[a]	[a]	2	21	733	28.6
1894	0	8	18	[a]	[a]	7	4	1	[a]	[a]	[a]	[a]	[a]	1	[a]	2	41	1,125	36.4
1895	1	3	15	[a]	[a]	1	1	[a]	[a]	[a]	[a]	[a]	[a]	[a]	[a]	0	21	882	23.8
1896	2	7	10	[a]	5	4	3	[a]	[a]	[a]	[a]	[a]	[a]	[a]	[a]	4	35	1,020	34.3
1897	[a]	3	10	[a]	14	[a]	[a]	[a]	[a]	[a]	9	[a]	[a]	0	[a]	3	30	624	48.1
1898	4	4	[a]	[a]	7	[a]	2	[a]	6	[a]	[a]	[a]	[a]	[a]	[a]	3	25	581	43.0
1899	2	7	12	[a]	10	[a]	[a]	[a]	3	[a]	9	2	0	1	[a]	[a]	39	855	45.6
1900	[a]	8	10	[a]	7	[a]	[a]	[a]	[a]	[a]	3	0	[a]	[a]	[a]	[a]	38	883	43.0
1901	3	7	7	3	6	[a]	[a]	1	[a]	3	3	3	7	[a]	2	[a]	55[b]	2,020	27.2
1902	[a]	13	[a]	0	8	8	[a]	[a]	6	[a]	6	[a]	12	0	[a]	2	53[b]	2,067	25.6
1903	1	6	16	3	7	9	[a]	[a]	6	3	5	[a]	8	3	2	2	81[b]	1,930	42.0
1904	4	7	10	3	6	5	[a]	[a]	6	0	5	[a]	3	[a]	4	3	64[c]	1,930	33.2
1905	[a]	6	[a]	3	[a]	[a]	[a]	[a]	3	[a]	[a]	[a]	3	[a]	[a]	[a]	85[b]	1,993	42.6
1906	[a]	6	[a]	[a]	[a]	10	[a]	[a]	4	4	5	[a]	3	[a]	2	[a]	66[b]	2,148	30.7
1907	[a]	4	[a]	[a]	2	4	[a]	[a]	4	[a]	[a]	11	3	[a]	[a]	[a]	66[b]	2,114	31.2
1908	3	5	[a]	2	3	[a]	[a]	[a]	[a]	[a]	5	[a]	0	[a]	[a]	0	66[b]	2,129	31.0
1909	[a]	9	[a]	5	3	5	[a]	[a]	[a]	1	3	9	[a]	[a]	[a]	[a]	63[b]	2,103	30.0
1910	2	4	9	7	2	8	2	5	4	2	7	9	1	0	7	3	73	2,009	36.3
1911	2	11	11	3	2	10	7	0	5	1	3	9	1	0	2	2	69	2,026	34.1
1912	0	11	5	4	4	11	3	7	5	2	3	5	2	1	3	0	65[c]	1,969	33.0
1913	0	7	3	0	5	0	6	7	1	0	7	7	9	2	1	0	55	2,018	27.3

Table 6.7 (Concluded)

Date	An	Ant	CB	Co	Cu	Dig	Hfx	Han	In	K	Pi	Qu	Ri	Sh	Vi	Y	To	Population of Counties with Reported Deaths	Rate/ 1,000
1914	2	2	9	1	7	0	6	3	4	0	7	2	2	1	2	0	38	2,050	18.5
1915	1	3	7	3	5	0	6	0	6	0	8	0	7	0	4	2	52	2,042	25.5
1916	0	9	7	5	0	2	11	6	3	4	4	3	1	0	4	5	64	2,119	30.2
1917																	65	2,031	32.0

An = Annapolis County; Ant= Antigonish & Guysborough Counties; CB = Cape Breton County; Co = Colchester County; Cu = Cumberland County; Dig = Digby County; Hfx = Halifax County; Han = Hants County; In = Inverness County; K = King's County; Pl = Pictou County; Qu = Queens and Lunenburg Counties; Ri = Richmond County; Sh = Shelburne County; Vi = Victoria County; Y = Yarmouth County.

[a] Agents for these years did not report on either deaths or births in their agency. For this reason, I have not included their populations in calculating death rates.

[b] Totals are taken from aggregate totals in report and do not reflect totals given for each county.

[c] Differs from tabular statements as does not include all information from Indian agents

Note: Before 1893, annual reports ended on 30 June of each year. From 1893 to 1906, Indian affairs reports provide data for the year ending on 30 June. From 1907, reports provide information for the year ending 31 March.

Source: Department of Indian Affairs Annual Reports, Sessional Papers 1891–1917.

began publishing annual tallies, the rates only declined minimally from the rates I have calculated for the years immediately before. This would suggest that rates before 1900 were not very dissimilar from the period afterward. An additional problem is that the incomplete nature of the data precludes comparing communities. To make such comparisons possible I have therefore grouped the data into ten-year cohorts (Table 6.8). This provides a more accurate portrait of long-term trends and minimizes the effect of variable age pyramids. It also allows us to isolate those communities where agents were more consistent in reporting deaths. For the period before 1910, data have only been used where agents reported deaths at least five times in a ten-year period.

Table 6.8 shows six important trends. First, death rates between 1890 and 1916 ranged from 27 to 34 per 1,000. Second, death rates generally did not decrease over time but remained relatively constant. In Antigonish/Guysborough, for instance, the rates rose from 27.1 per 1,000 in 1890–99 to 34.1 in 1900–09, before declining to 32.1 in 1910–16. Third, the Annapolis County and King's County communities had lower death rates than those in other regions. The small size of the two communities may account for the difference, but the region's prosperity and the dispersed Mi'kmaw population may also have been factors. Fourth, death rates were higher on the mainland. This is consistent with the other data, which show lower child/woman ratios among mainland communities than on the Cape Breton; one consequence of lower ratios in a natural fertility regime is a higher incidence of infant and child mortality. Fifth, data regarding Cape Breton are relatively scarce. The only consistent reporting is from Cape Breton County between 1890 and 1899, showing death rates higher than for the non-Mi'kmaq population.Much like the Digby and Cumberland agencies, Cape Breton County has little good arable land and so the restriction of access to off-reserve resources probably reduced Mi'kmaw families' nutritional intake. Indeed, the high death rates in the 1890s may have been one factor influencing families to emigrate to Sydney and elsewhere in the following decades. Finally, the data from Cape Breton suggest that death rates gradually declined over time, so that by the second decade of the twentieth century, rates for three of the four agencies ranged from the mid- to high 20s per 1,000. The only exception was Wagmatcook (Middle River) in Victoria County.

These death rates are considerably higher than those for the non-aboriginal population, although they are not strictly comparable because the data are from after 1912, when the provincial government began keeping track of vital statistics. For 1912–13 the government reported

Table 6.8
Crude Death Rates, Ten-Year Periods for Selected Agencies, 1890–1916

Agencies	1890–99				1900–09				1910–16			
	Deaths	Pop.	Years	Rate	Deaths	Pop.	Years	Rate	Deaths	Pop.	Years	Rate
Mainland												
Annapolis	10	605	8	16.5					7	496	7	14.1
Antigonish & Guysborough	44	1,623	10	27.1	65	1,875	9	34.7	47	1,440	7	32.6
Colchester					16	489	6	32.7	23	698	7	33.0
Cumberland	52	672	7	76.9	42	780	8	53.8	25	621	7	40.3
Digby	44	1,210	7	36.4	41	687	6	59.7	31	678	7	45.7
Halifax	12	824	6	14.6					41	1,596	7	25.7
Hants									28	637	7	44.0
King's					11	374	5	29.4	9	611	7	14.7
Pictou					39	1,228	8	31.8	39	1,129	7	34.5
Queen's & Lunenburg									35	1,021	7	34.3
Shelburne									4	258	7	15.5
Yarmouth	20	603	7	33.2					12	470	7	25.3
Totals, Mainland									301	9,655	7	31.2
Cape Breton Island												
Cape Breton	87	1,609	7	54.1					51	1,825	7	27.9
Inverness					23	855	5	26.9	28	1,203	7	23.3
Richmond					36	788	7	45.7	23	898	7	25.6
Victoria									23	602	7	38.2
Totals, Cape Breton									125	4,528	7	27.6

Pop. = Population of agency over period; Years = Number of years in which deaths were reported; Rate = Death rate per 1,000
Source: Department of Indian Affairs Annual Reports, *Sessional Papers 1891–1917*.

the province's crude death rate as 14.5 per 1,000. In 1913–14, the rate
was 15.1, in 1914–15, 15.3, in 1915–16, 15.9, and in 1916–17, 14.9.[116]
By comparison, the Mi'kmaw death rates were more than twice as high,
with the exception of 1914 when the rate dipped to 18.5 per 1,000. In
other words, the Mi'kmaq were dying at more than twice the rate of the
non-aboriginal population. Although we lack statistics for the non-native
population before 1912, data from other regions of Canada confirm that
death rates for the Mi'kmaq were higher than the norm. In 1921, for
instance, the crude death rate for Canada was 12.9 per 1,000, or between
53 per cent and 60 per cent lower than the Mi'kmaw rates.[117]

These data help to evaluate the child/woman ratios discussed earlier.
One of the most important conclusions made then was that there was a
decline in child/woman ratios between 1881 and 1911. There are several
possible reasons for this, including decreasing levels of nutrition, which
would have reduced the likelihood of conception and also led to the
increased incidence of miscarriages. However, because the child/woman
ratios do not include children who both were born and died in the five
years preceding the census, we might also suppose that high infant and
child mortality was an additional, if not the most important, factor contributing to the drop.

Evaluating this last proposition is difficult because there are no data to
determine infant and child mortality rates.[118] We can, however, use the
1911 census in tandem with DIA reports from 1906 to 1911, which report
the births for each agency. Using these two sources, we can calculate the
number of children who might have died before 1911 by totaling the
number of children the agents said had been born between 1 April 1906
and 31 March 1911 and then comparing these totals with the 1911 census. The main problem with this method is the assumption that children
born in this five-year period were still in Nova Scotia when the census was
taken. In the absence of other evidence, however, it is the most reliable
method to evaluate infant and child mortality. This information is summarized in Table 6.9.

Table 6.9 suggests a high incidence of infant and child mortality. DIA
figures show that between 1 April 1906 and 31 March 1911 a total of 389
children were born to Mi'kmaw families. The census, however, shows
only 264 children still living with their families in 1911. To this total we
would add 33 children, recognizing that the federal census undercount-
ed the Mi'kmaq and that the DIA census, showing 268 more people,
might reflect the actual population.[119] This would give us 297 children,
92 fewer than there should have been. Although some of these children

Table 6.9
Children Born between 1 April 1906 and 31 March 1911, According to Agents' Reports and 1911 Census

County	1 April 1906 to 31 March 1907 DIA	Fed	1 April 1907 to 31 March 1908 DIA	Fed	1 April 1908 to 31 March 1909 DIA	Fed	1 April 1908 to 31 March 1910 DIA	Fed	1 April 1910 to 31 March 1911 DIA	Fed	Totals DIA	Fed
Mainland												
Annapolis	n/a	0	n/a	3	n/a	3	2	3	2	3		12
Antigonish	n/a	6		2		5	7	3	13	5		21
Colchester		4		2		3	4	5	2	1		15
Cumberland		2		1		0	5	0	6	3		6
Digby		2		3		4	4	5	5	3		17
Guysborough		3		3		1	a	1	a	2		10
Halifax		1		4		5	5	4	5	0		14
Hants		2		1		1	0	3	6	1		8
Kings		4		3		5	2	1	2	4		17
Lunenburg		0		0		0	4	0	4	0		0
Pictou		9		3		4	5	2	3	7		25
Queen's & Shelburne		2		3		3	4	1	4	1		10
Yarmouth		3		2		1	1	0	2	3		9
Totals, Mainland		38		30		35	43	28	54	33		164
Cape Breton												
Cape Breton		8		7		5	7	9	14	12		41
Inverness		4		3		3	6	7	13	9		26
Richmond		4		5		2	2	4	2	5		20
Victoria		3		3		3	5	4	4	0		13
Total, Cape Breton		19		18		13	20	24	33	26		100
Totals, Nova Scotia	79	57	88	48	72	48	63[b]	52	87	59	389	264

DIA = Department of Indian Affairs; Fed. = Federal Census of 1911; n/a = not available
[a] DIA figures combine Antigonish & Guysborough Counties
[b] DIA gives a total of 64 but is an error in addition.
Source: Indian agents reports, Annual Report of the Department of Indian Affairs, *Sessional Papers, 1906–1911* (Ottawa, 1907–12); LAC, RG 31, 1911 census.

may have left the province with their families, we can assume that the majority died sometime between their birth and May 1911 when the census was taken. In other words, almost one in four children died before their fifth birthday (23.6%). We cannot quantify it, but the figures for 1910 and 1911 – when we have numbers for each agency – suggest that mortality was higher among mainland families. This conclusion is consistent with our earlier finding that crude death rates were higher on the mainland than on Cape Breton. Moreover, it is probable that these figures were lower than in the late 1800s.

Why did the average life expectancy decline? There are two probable explanations. On Cape Breton Island, the number of people living on reserve grew sharply in the late 1800s and early 1900s. As Table 6.7 shows the size of some island reserves doubled and tripled. This exacerbated a situation that most Indian agents already recognized: the reserves were not large enough. The colonial government had never envisioned the reserves as anything more than either a graveyard for a dying race or a place of transition where the better sort would learn to become 'white.' Canadian federal policy after 1867 was predicated on similar assumptions. One purpose of the 1876 Indian Act was to create a statutory framework to compel aboriginal people to become contributing members of society.[120] This plan might have worked in southern Ontario, which was the centre of the country's burgeoning economy and where there was enough arable land, but not in Nova Scotia. The migration onto reserve after 1881 led to a decline of per capita farm production. Because this surge occurred at the same time as the rural population increased beyond the economy's capacity to support it, the effect was to deepen a crisis within Mi'kmaw communities, as families scrambled to find new sources of income and food. On the mainland, the situation was different. There, though the numbers of on-reserve residents increased, many people still lived off reserve. In this situation, families had more difficulties in making ends meet. This would have led to a greater dependence on government assistance, particularly during the winter months.

One result was lower household nutrition levels. This made the population more susceptible to infections and to those diseases that had historically devastated the Mi'kmaw community, such as smallpox, whooping cough, and measles. From the 1880s, agents reported the increasing incidence of disease, and especially tuberculosis, which in 1903, the Chief Medical Officer for Cape Breton County, described as the 'great scourge of our county as of our province.'[121]

Tuberculosis is a bacterial infection that frequently affects the lungs. It also affects other parts of the body, including the kidney, brain, glands, lymph nodes, bones, and joints. The disease is spread by droplets excreted through sneezing and coughing, but this is less likely to occur outdoors, as the sun's ultraviolet rays can kill the bacteria. Indoors, transmission is less likely to take place in buildings that are well ventilated.[122]

Crowded conditions on reserve probably facilitated the spread of the bacterium once it had taken root, a situation that was also more likely to happen as more Mi'kmaw men worked as day labourers and as women and their children sold wares door to door. Transmission was also probably facilitated by the residents' small frame houses, which usually had one or two rooms and which became overcrowded as the population on reserve grew.[123] As in western Canada, the transition from airy lodges to more constrained quarters likely facilitated the spread of the bacterium.[124] It was unlikely that those infected could be isolated from the rest of the household, as was usual practice in North America and Europe to prevent infection.

From the 1870s, families had begun establishing a more permanent presence on reserve. As explained in Chapter Five, in 1871 a majority lived in some type of temporary dwelling. Between 1871 and 1881 more families built frame houses. In 1871, 90 of 356 households lived in frame houses, about five in twenty. Ten years later, 137 of 345 households did so, about eight in twenty (Table 6.10).[125] The trend towards permanent dwellings continued after 1881, although it is not possible to quantify because the later censuses did not make a distinction among householders living in frame houses and those living in shanties or birchbark camps. However, anecdotal testimony would suggest this trend towards more permanent houses continued.[126] By the early 1900s, the majority of families lived in frame houses. This transformation in Mi'kmaw housing, coupled with a surging reserve population, likely facilitated the spread of tuberculosis. The effect was to reduce the average life expectancy to levels that it had been before the 1880s. After 1911, however, the population began to grow, a change that reflected changes in the region's economy precipitated by the war as well as the delayed effects of an increased presence of the Department of Indian Affairs, which led to better medical care.

Five of the men who testified at Sylliboy's appeal were born between 1850 and 1875. This period coincides with the general time frame when the Mi'kmaw population increased. They were members of a genera-

Table 6.10
Housing of Mi'kmaw Households, 1871 and 1881 Censuses

County	1871				1881			
	Dwellings (%)	Shanties	Total	Population (Household size)	Dwellings (%)	Shanties	Total	Population (Household size)
Cape Breton Island								
Cape Breton	15	19	34	188	19	21	40	241
Inverness	2	24	26	138	12	5	17	98
Richmond	0	17	17	78	3	17	20	107
Victoria	4	10	14	69	4	12	16	89
Totals, Cape Breton	21 (23.0)	70	91	473 (5.2)	38 (40.9)	55	93	535 (5.75)
Mainland								
Annapolis	4	8	12	63	9	4	13	63
Antigonish	0	17	17	89	9	23	32	171
Colchester	0	8	8	31	1	18	19	89
Cumberland	0	12	12	44	4	16	20	101
Digby	25	26	51	224	5	23	28	136
Guysborough	2	11	13	48	1	16	17	94
Halifax	4	18	22	115	2	12	14	69
Hants	20	15	35	168	19	4	23	99
Kings	4	9	13	61	14	5	19	97
Lunenburg	1	6	7	50	7	8	15	50
Pictou	2	21	23	125	2	38	40	190
Queens	6	16	22	110	21	1	22	90
Shelburne	0	2	2	15	2	7	9	41
Yarmouth	1	6	7	35	3	6	9	45
Totals, Mainland	69 (28.3)	175	244	1,178 (4.83)	94 (34.8)	176	270	1,335 (4.94)
Totals, Nova Scotia	90	265	355	1,651 (4.65)	137	236	363	1,870 (5.15)

Legend: Dw: Dwelling; HH: Household; NS: Nova Scotia

Source: LAC, RG 31, 1871 and 1881 Censuses.

[a] I have used 1,651 as the population because the manuscript copy of the census is only available for this number of people. In earlier tables I used the figure 1,664.

tion who were better off than their parents had been. The men were also part of a generation whose parents had gradually adapted to living on reserve by growing garden and field crops and by producing items for the agricultural and industrial sectors. As the men matured, however, their ability to earn a living declined, forcing them to make choices they had probably never envisioned. We do not know why the Bernard and Christmas families moved to the Sydney area but we would suppose that their decision had to do with the financial difficulties they would have faced had they remained where they were and was likely induced by the fact that farm work only provided a fraction of the family's income. For Bernard and Christmas, farming was never the centre of the household because the land was too infertile and the reserves too small. But in nineteenth-century rural communities, land ownership was the hallmark of success, a means for young men and young women to establish themselves. As Darroch and Soltow conclude in their study of mid- to late nineteenth-century rural Ontario, the 'chances were quite good that a property less farmer would become a landowner' and that as he grew older his chances of owning land would increase.[127] Nineteenth-century Nova Scotia, of course, was not Ontario, and Bitterman's study of Middle River shows that by the 1870s, the lack of good available land would have made prospects bleak for some farmers' sons. Nonetheless, elder sons could expect to inherit the family farm and those with the best land, to support their families. For four of the men born between 1850 and 1854, there was little chance of having sufficient land to support their families, as the analysis of the 1871 census shows, and so they joined other young Nova Scotians in searching for new opportunities away from where they had been born. Bernard and Christmas were part of this exodus. Although Bernard initially trimmed coal, he later made baskets. Christmas also combined waged work with coopering and making various handicrafts for sale.

In contrast, Andrew Alek, Francis Gould, and Gabriel Sylliboy did not move, but continued to live in the Cape Breton countryside. They were no less affected, however, by the changes of the late nineteenth century. These changes transformed how families made their living and where they lived. As access to, and use of, off-reserve land and resources declined, Mi'kmaw families were pushed, both by their economic circumstances and by government pressure, to move onto reserve or to establish a more permanent presence there. Other factors, such as access to education, medical aid, and financial assistance, would also have influenced them to move. However, the growth in the population of reserves facilitated the spread of tuberculosis and other infectious diseases, lowering the average life expectancy. And it likely also influenced people to move away, to New Brunswick and to the Boston area. Still others, when given the opportunity, married into the white community and thereafter abandoned their Mi'kmaw heritage.

Like other Nova Scotians of the late nineteenth and early twentieth centuries, the lives of the five men who testified at Sylliboy's appeal changed irrevocably. This was the time when Nova Scotia, like other regions of North America, slowly became 'modern.' It was a period when thousands of young people left their community, their province, their region, their country. The Mi'kmaq, however, lived this experience differently. For them, life did not generally include a bold new world of new vistas and new opportunities. Some Mi'kmaq did travel south and west but they were the exceptions, not the norm. The more common experience was for families to move onto reserve. A move there, however, did not bring a better life but ill health and a greater expectation of an early death for their young children.

It was this lived experience which affected the men who testified at Sylliboy's appeal. This experience reinforced a perception of their community's distinctiveness within Nova Scotian society. What they probably understood was a disparity between their own lives and those of their neighbours. Although such disparities had always been apparent, they now became sharper as the concentration of people onto reserve created the conditions in which political discussion and action could be formulated in ways that had not been true before. Recalling the treaty was part of this process, as C.W. Vernon's 1903 comment regarding the ceremonies at Chapel Island on St Anne's Day illustrate. As Vernon later remembered, discussion about the treaty was an important social and political event and one that would have reinforced each man's memories about it.[128]

In this way, changes in the Mi'kmaw economy in the late nineteenth and early twentieth centuries both undermined and strengthened the community. Sylliboy and the other men who testified at the appeal were products of this dual process and would, over the succeeding years, become more vocal in criticizing government policies. Indeed, by the early 1900s, the Grand Council would become involved in the discussions surrounding the relocation of Mi'kmaw families who had migrated to Sydney in the late 1800s. Joe Christmas and his family were among them. That experience would, like the period before, demonstrate to the Grand Council the disparity in how governments treated the Mi'kmaq and lead them to search for an alternative space where Mi'kmaw people could live and flourish.

Indeed, the experience of their adult lives had been that there were few spaces where the Mi'kmaq could live and that if things continued, that in the future there would fewer and fewer Mi'kmaw children. This was not only because more Mi'kmaw children died but because when given the opportunity, people chose life over death; that is, they chose to move away, to Boston, or women chose to marry non-Mi'kmaw men. In both circumstances, men and women perhaps saw a future that would be better, and one that would promise a future for their children. For the men of Sylliboy's generation, such an eventuality would represent a future where the Mi'kmaq as distinctive people would cease to exist. In such a situation, they perhaps felt they had few other choices, than to resist and to use whatever tools or opportunities they could. The treaty was one such tool and the decision to prosecute Gabriel Sylliboy one such opportunity.

7 Moving into the City: The King's Road Reserve and the Politics of Relocation

Both Joe Christmas and Andrew Bernard moved to the Sydney area in the late 1800s. Bernard moved to North Sydney and Christmas to the neighbouring town of Sydney, about thirty kilometres away. Both made their livings doing various jobs. For the first few years after he was married, Bernard and his wife worked together, making baskets and other assorted items, which they probably sold to merchants and to mine workers. Later, he worked in the coalmines, and he and his family lived on property owned by the Nova Scotia Steel Company. Joe Christmas, in contrast, never worked in the coalmines, but like Bernard combined coopering with wage employment. At the appeal trial, he told Judge Patterson that he did 'Indian work, making baskets and handles tubs etc.' Thirteen years before, he had told another Judge that 'my jobs are mostly making oars, but not this year.' But he also said that he did odd jobs around town: 'I get jobs in town, when I finish I get my pay.'[1]

Both men were part of a wave of Mi'kmaq who immigrated from rural communities to the coal-mining towns of northern Cape Breton. In the late 1870s, the government decided to establish a reserve in Sydney along King's Road to accommodate these families. The government, however, did not make similar provisions for the North Sydney people. Despite this, the Bernards and others stayed where they were. Christmas, on the other hand, eventually settled on the King's Road Reserve, which was a twenty-minute walk from Sydney's centre. By the early 1900s, both communities had become a source of anxiety for town councils and business people, who argued that the Mi'kmaq were an unseemly presence, threatening the towns' moral sensibilities, retarding their economic development, and posing a potential threat of contagion. These protests eventually led to the relocation of both communities.

Efforts to remove the Mi'kmaq were part of a broader attempt to reform and to remodel urban areas in the early 1900s and to make them fit for human habitation, by creating an infrastructure that would ameliorate the affect of disease and other physical contagions.[2] These efforts, which had their genesis in the social reform movement in the century before and were also meant to produce healthy males capable of defending the Empire, were principally aimed at urban working-class neighbourhoods. These, in the popular parlance of the day, were dens of iniquity, vice, sexual turpitude, and disease. Unless they were sanitized, the city would become perennial places of physical and social diseases. Efforts to clean up such neighbourhoods were directed both by private organizations and by state agencies, which included the police. People who were not part of the Anglo-Canadian cultural tradition were special targets because they were considered to be less able to restrain their sexual and emotional impulses.[3] Such stereotypes had long characterized European perceptions of the Mi'kmaq, and so it is not surprising that their presence in the growing industrial centres of Cape Breton should have elicited a negative response from both of the towns' business and political elites and from neighbouring residents.

Joe Christmas and Andrew Bernard, through their association with the Grand Council, were at the centre of this dispute. They represented a generation of men and women who had moved to the city in the late 1800s. The families' subsequent removal and relocation, however, arrested their integration into the urban economy, stunting their economic growth and the development of a working-class consciousness that would supersede or undermine peoples' cultural and political identification with other Mi'kmaq. The lesson for Bernard, Christmas, and the other men who testified at Sylliboy's appeal was that city elites did not view them as an integral part of the city's social and economic future. These actions fuelled the men's understanding that their community was not part of the Canadian nation and created the need to identify their place within Canada differently. While the Indian Act legally defined the Mi'kmaq, its frame of reference was their eventual absorption into Anglo-Canadian society. However, the theory and the practice of assimilation did not correlate, as families who had immigrated to Sydney and to other urban areas of Nova Scotia in the late 1800s and early 1900s gradually understood. The treaty therefore became part of an oppositional understanding of the Mi'kmaw community's legal standing within Canadian Confederation. The events at Sydney in the early 1900s helped to cement this sense of community and of difference by demonstrating

government and urban hostility to the Mi'kmaw presence. They also reinforced the men's memory of the treaty and enlarged the influence of
political organizations, like the Grand Council, as the only protector of
the community's long-term interests.

Little has been written about the Mi'kmaq of early twentieth century Nova Scotia. Their history during this period has been told not by
university-based academics but by policy analysts and claims researchers. The King's Road surrender is an example. Although the subject of
a long-standing dispute between the federal government and the Cape
Breton Mi'kmaq, it remains relatively unknown within the academic
community. In this sense, therefore, this chapter breaks 'new' ground.
Yet, in another sense, it only retells what is well known among those, like
Gillian Allen, James Youngblood Henderson, Don Julian, Jim Michael,
and many others, who have at various times researched these issues and
accumulated a knowledge and an expertise that does not always filter
into academia.

In another way, however, this chapter does add to our understanding of industrial Cape Breton. Over the past thirty or more years, scholars have examined the region's industrial history, focusing on the years
when coal and steel were king. Principally centred on understanding
the region's social history, this research has studied the industry's work-
force. Because the Mi'kmaq did not generally work below the ground
or in the furnaces, their presence in the city is not mentioned.[4] As this
chapter shows, the number of Mi'kmaw families living in Sydney during
this period of industrial expansion grew. The silence with which labour
historians have ignored the Mi'kmaq parallels the working class's own
actions of the early twentieth century, which isolated the Mi'kmaq within the city and within the labour movement. Indeed, a more intense examination of the period might suggest that labour's actions to establish
hegemony over the work place, were additional factors which led men
like Ben and Joe Christmas and Andrew Bernard to identify the treaty
as an iconic document in their community's history. While this chapter
therefore builds on the work of other historians, who have examined
the region's early industrial history, it also suggests that future studies of
the area's working class might benefit from a broader perspective, as has
been cultivated by researchers examining the aboriginal labour force in
British Columbia.[5] However, in contradistinction to aboriginal people
there, the Mi'kmaq in Cape Breton were less integrated into the wage-
labour economy, reflecting a different history and pace of colonization.

In the late nineteenth and early twentieth centuries, Sydney was bursting at its seams in more ways than one. In 1871, the city had been home to 2,900 people. By 1901 there were 9,909 residents and ten years later 17,723. Adjacent areas also grew, with the largest expansion occurring on the city's 'south side,' which stretched from the northern tip of Sydney Harbor to Port Morin and encompassed New Waterford, Reserve Mines, Dominion, and Glace Bay. In 1871, this area's combined population was 5,415. By 1901, it was 15,512 and ten years later 26,665. By 1911, the greater Sydney area had 57,623 residents. This was 86.7 per cent of the county's population and 45.3 per cent of the island's.[6]

Journalists, politicians, and businessmen extolled the virtues of the region's growth. Intoned one journalist in 1900:

> In one single year she has outstripped in the race for importance every town in the Maritime Provinces and has emerged from her quiet almost village like existence – awakening, as it were to find herself famous. The citizen to the manor born will recall with conflicting emotions, the deserted thoroughfares, the Sabbath like stillness of the byways, the fresh and verdurous infields, and all these characteristics, which are so charmingly becoming to a resort of rate weary city born. The business streets are no longer silent and the byways are teeming with life, the pastoral scenes in the center of the town have faded away like a pleasant dream, only to become populous with the spirits of industry; and Sydney is known no more as a fashionable watering place but has been transformed into one of the first industrial centers in the continent.[7]

Much of the region's expansion was built on coal and steel. Coal had been mined there since the early 1700s but mining had intensified in the 1820s after the British government leased the rights to Nova Scotia's coalfields to the General Mining Association (GMA).[8] In 1858 the government revoked GMA's monopoly, sparking new interest in the coalfields' potential and beginning a long period of expansion.

Industrialization and the shift from wood to coal precipitated a growth in demand. As Louis Hunter has pointed out, up until 1850 wood met 90 per cent of American heat energy requirements. Fifty years later, wood supplied only 21.1 per cent and coal 71.4 per cent. 'This shift,' says Hunter, 'from wood to coal paralleled, and was closely related to, the changeover from inland waterway to railway transportation and the replacement of waterpower by steam power during the second half of the nineteenth century.'[9]

In 1893–4, with the support of the Nova Scotia government, Boston's Henry Whitney amalgamated a number of operators to form the Dominion Coal Company. Composed mainly of New England, Nova Scotia, and Montreal financial interests, the company was sold in 1901 to Montreal's James Ross. Consolidation facilitated investment and led to improvements in mining techniques and, as demand expanded, to increased production. In 1901 Dominion sold 2.5 million tons of coal, more than double its 893,000 ton output eight years earlier.[10] By 1911, the company was operating twenty collieries in the Sydney area, with plans to open up another four in the next two years.[11]

One reason for increased demand was Dominion's construction of the Sydney steel mill. Construction had begun in 1899, and the first blast furnace had opened in mid-December 1900. With the completion of three other furnaces, the company became one of the largest consumers of the region's coal. In 1913, for instance, the plant used 1.362 million tons.

Federal, provincial, and municipal governments provided financial incentives to keep the steel plant afloat. Ottawa paid a bounty for every ton of pig-iron produced, the provincial government remitted 50 per cent of the royalties it received on coal used by the plant in its first eight years of operation, while Sydney contributed the land on which the steel plant was built, and exempted the company from property taxes.[12]

The island's other major coal company was GMA, whose operations were based at Sydney Mines and to a lesser extent at Lingan.[13] In 1900, the Pictou County-based Nova Scotia Steel and Forge Company had bought GMA's properties, reorganized them into the Nova Scotia Steel and Coal Company and four years later opened its own steel mill in North Sydney. By the early 1900s, the company's Cape Breton properties were producing about 250,000 tons annually or about a tenth of Dominion's output.[14]

Coal and steel provided jobs for workers and revenue for government. In 1921, more than 13,000 people worked in Nova Scotia's coalfields and another 2,000 in its steel mills. Together the two industries employed almost 9 per cent of the province's employed males fifteen years of age and older.[15] No other single industry had so many workers. Although more people worked in the fishery or on farms, their numbers were scattered the width and breadth of the province. In contrast, most of the province's coal and steel workers lived in one of the five Cape Breton communities nestled next to the other in the northeastern corner of the island: Sydney, North Sydney, Glace Bay, New Waterford, and Sydney Mines.[16]

The provincial government benefited financially from levying royalties on each ton of mined coal, and after 1921, from taxing the value of each company's paid-up capital. From 1858 to 1890, the royalty was fixed at seven and one-half cents per ton; it was raised to ten cents per ton in 1891 and to twelve and a half cents in 1894. From the early 1900s to the 1920s, these royalties were the provincial government's single largest source of income.[17] Before then, the other major revenue source was the Dominion government's annual subsidy. As Table 7.1 shows, this subsidy remained the same from 1890 until after the First World War. Royalties from coal mining, however, increased more than 400 per cent between 1890 and 1905, so that its percentage of total revenue increased proportionally. In 1890, mining royalties had been 25.4 per cent of all government revenue while the federal subsidy had been 65.1 per cent of the total. By 1905, mining's percentage had grown to 46.1 per cent while the federal government's contribution had dipped to 32.7 per cent. In addition to paying royalties on each ton of coal mined, after 1919, the coal and steel companies also paid a tax on their paid-up capital. This tax was initially pegged at one-twentieth of 1 per cent and was doubled to one-tenth of 1 per cent in 1921.[18] In 1920, the two companies, Dominion Steel and Nova Scotia Steel, paid $33,487 in taxes. In 1925, the newly created British Empire Steel paid more than three times as much. All of this shows that even though the province's revenue had become more diversified in the 1920s, the health of the provincial government's finances was tied to the coal and steel industry. The rapid expansion of coal and steel from the late 1800s had a salubrious affect; retrenchment had the opposite effect, creating the need to find new sources of revenue, as was the case in 1908 when the government first introduced taxes on financial institutions.[19] Downturns also affected the ruling party's fortunes. Indeed, the Liberal government's defeat in the 1925 election was partly due to the financial difficulties of the coal and steel companies and the attendant financial turmoil this created both for the workers and for the government.[20]

The expansion of the coal and steel industry drew people to the Sydney area, including Joe Christmas. Initially much of this labour was seasonal, spiking during the coal-mining season and dipping in the winter when little coal was mined. Like other Cape Bretoners, Mi'kmaw families came for the work and the financial opportunity that the Sydney area offered. Not everyone welcomed them, however. Perhaps if they had worked in the coalfields or in the blast furnaces or if they had had some specialized skills, then attitudes might have been different. But they did not, and by the late 1800s the Mi'kmaq had become, in the minds of some residents, a menace to the city's public and moral health.

Table 7.1
Mining Royalties and Dominion Subsidy as Proportion of Nova Scotia Government Revenues, 1890–1925[a]

	Coal Royalties ($)	Mining Royalties ($)	Dominion Subsidy ($)	Total Provincial Revenue ($)	MR to PR (%)	DS to PR (%)
1890	129,646	168,644	432,823	664,956	25.4	65.1
1895		251,910	432,811	858,974	29.3	50.4
1899		318,395	432,806	985,681	32.3	43.9
1900		413,383	432,806			
1905	549,639	610,433	432,905	1,324,531	46.1	32.7
1910		614,576	610,460	1,725,914		
1915	673,990	727,223	636,666	3,154,358		
1920	608,364	690,517	636,666	3,801,016	18.2	16.7
1925	307,094	365,391	661,841	4,467,483		

[a] In 1890, the fiscal year ran from 1 January to 31 December. From 1894, the fiscal year was measured from 1 October to 30 September of the following year. Thus, the year 1895 actually refers to the period between 1 October 1894 and 30 September 1895.

Source: Public Accounts, Mines Reports, Journals and Proceedings of the House of Assembly of Nova Scotia, 1891, 1896, 1901, 1906, 1911, 1916, 1921, 1926.

Although the Mi'kmaq had lived near Sydney Harbor long before 1890, the city's growth in the late 1800s spurred families to establish a more permanent presence there. Initially, people came to sell their wares and camped for a few days on the town's outskirts.[21] Sometimes they stayed longer, and some of them eventually began doing odd jobs around town.[22] To accommodate these families, the Department of Indian Affairs (DIA) suggested to the province that the Crown land where families camped be set aside as a reserve. The province agreed and sold the land to the federal government. The property was surveyed in 1877 but was not formally reserved until 1882.[23]

Two and a half acres in size, the King's Road Reserve was next to the Sydney River, about two kilometers from the town's centre.[24] In 1877 John Isaac was the only permanent resident. Two families joined him in 1887. Although each family initially lived in 'birch bark camps,' they afterwards built small frame houses. As the region's coal and steel industries expanded in the late 1800s so, too, did the number of reserve residents.[25]

Joe Christmas came to Sydney in 1875 when he was twenty-one years and two years later, he married.[26] Over the next twenty-five years Christmas moved back and forth between Sydney and Eskasoni, replicating the movement of many other Cape Bretoners and Newfoundlanders who worked in the city when there was work and who returned home when there was not.[27] Sydney was likely the Christmas family's main place of residence during the late spring and summer.[28] It was here, for instance, that enumerators recorded the names of each member of their household in 1881 and again in 1911.[29] It was here also that some of the Christmas children were born. The youngest son, Benjamin, who also testified at Sylliboy's appeal, was born in 1894. The family, however, did not always live on the reserve when in Sydney. As Ben Christmas told the 1915 court hearing regarding the community's relocation, he had been born at Indian Point 'right opposite the situation where the Cement Plant is now; later on we removed to the present reserve where we are now.'[30]

The Christmas family was not alone in making the trek to and from Sydney. Many other Mi'kmaq did the same, especially in the early 1900s when a downturn in the iron and steel works led some to return to Eskasoni and Prince Edward Island. In 1905 twenty people left because of an economic 'depression caused by the strike at the iron and steel works the previous year.'[31] This turbulence was reflected in the reserve's population. In 1904, there were eighty-two residents but the next year only sixty-two. By 1906, the numbers had rebounded to eighty-six but had dipped again to seventy-seven the following year. Over the next two years, the population grew, so that by 1909 there were 112 residents, almost twice the number there had been five years before. In 1915, the year the federal government began formal proceedings to have the population relocated, there were 125 inhabitants, an increase likely resulting from Sydney's booming economy during the war years.[32]

Other Mi'kmaq lived about thirty kilometres distant at North Sydney, an area dominated by the Nova Scotia Steel and Coal Company. Andrew Bernard's family had moved there in the 1850s and by the early 1900s, they and others were living on company land.[33] In 1871, enumerators recorded forty-eight people there, including the 21-year- old Andrew Bernard and his 19- year-old wife, Mabel. Ten years later, there were fifty-two people.[34] As was the case in Sydney, the community's numbers fluctuated. In 1907, few families lived in town permanently but moved between there and Chapel Island, Sydney, Wagmatcook, and Whycocomagh. Indian agent Boyd reported in 1917 that families had 'a camping ground on private property near the town of North Sydney, to which a number, chiefly from Cape Breton Island reserves, resort in summer so as to be near a centre of employment and a good market for Indian wares. At other seasons of the year the place is almost deserted.[35] In 1909, the agent reported a decrease of eleven people, of ten the following year, and, in 1911, an increase of seventeen.[36]

Because North Sydney residents lived on company land they were unable to build permanent homes.[37] Rather, they lived in what census-takers described sometimes as 'wigwams' and other times as 'shanties.' The structures of individual homes varied considerably; some families preferred conical dwellings and others one-room cabins made from wood and tarpaper.[38]

Residents of the reserve in Sydney were much better off. In 1915, there were twenty-three houses, and if the land had been subdivided each family would have been living on land about the size of a town lot. As the reserve was not connected to the sewage line, most houses had an outdoor privy, and for those who did not, the government had built a public lavatory. In the early 1900s, the federal government also built a school.

In 1911, residents of both communities worked mainly as general labourers. This contrasted from thirty years earlier. Then, of the 476 Mi'kmaq from across Nova Scotia who declared an occupation, only twelve said that they worked as labourers, eleven on the mainland and one on the island. Most men had said they were coopers: 142 of 357 on the mainland and 81 of 119 on the island. In 1911, fewer declared coopering as an occupation and more said they worked for wages: on the mainland, 59 of 309 people described themselves as coopers while on the island only 31 of 179 did so. In contrast, the number of 'labourers' increased to 128 on the mainland and to 54 on the island. Labourers now formed 37.2 per cent of the total, reflecting a shift away from piece-work. These changes were especially pronounced in those communities, like Sydney, adjacent to urban areas. Data regarding occupations are summarized in Tables 7.2 and 7.3.

These statistics illustrate the trend towards wage labour. One way to measure this change is to plot age against occupations. In the case of farming communities, evidence suggesting a transition away from farming would mean 'the tendency for greater proportions of younger than older men to be non-farmers.' In the case of rural Ontario farming communities, Darroch and Soltow conclude from an analysis of the 1871 census that there were 'more farmers among the prime aged and older males and more non-farmers among the young.'[39] If the same transition were occurring among the Mi'kmaq, then we would expect to find younger men employed as labourers and other forms of wage-labour.

Men who described themselves as labourers in 1911 did various types of work. Mi'kmaw men most often described their work as doing 'odd jobs.' Others were employed in the lumbering business. Twelve men from the Shubenacadie Reserve, for instance, said they worked in local sawmills, though rarely year-round, while eleven men from the Millbrook Reserve worked in the woods, but only two said they worked more than twenty weeks of the year. Men from the Pictou Landing Reserve, on the other hand, worked for farmers. All of this shows that by 1911 a larger proportion of families' income came from wage employment, although we can assume that they continued to do some piecework, such as making hockey sticks or baskets when they were not employed. The exceptions were the isolated communities in Guysborough and Antigonish counties, where most Mi'kmaq still made most of their income from coopering. On Cape Breton Island, the distinction between rural and urban communities was sharper. In rural communities, the majority combined farming and fishing with making pick handles and baskets.[40] In Sydney, however, the majority worked for wages, not for piecework.

In Sydney, people did various jobs. In 1915 about ten women worked around town cleaning 'lawyers' offices and scrubbing floors,' some part time. Others washed clothes, jobs that were done on an occasional basis, although they usually worked in pairs, rather than singly.[41] Some men worked for the Cape Breton Electric Company, which operated a

Table 7.2
Occupations of Mi'kmaq of Nova Scotia, 1881 Census

Community	B(f)	B(m)	Co	CF	Do	Far	Fi	Gu	Hu	Lab	Lau	Lu	Mi	Tr	O	Total
Mainland																
Annapolis	–	–	4	1	–	–	–	–	3	2	–	–	–	–	–	10
Antigonish	8	–	24	6	–	1	–	–	12	–	–	–	1	–	–	52
Colchester	3	–	14	11	–	–	–	–	6	–	–	–	–	–	–	34
Cumberland	4	5	17	–	–	–	–	–	3	–	–	–	–	–	–	29
Digby																
Bear River	1	–	5	4	–	2	–	–	8	–	–	–	–	–	–	20
Off-reserve	–	–	–	–	–	–	–	–	16	–	–	–	–	–	–	16
Guysborough	–	–	13	–	–	3	1	–	1	–	–	–	–	–	1	19
Halifax	3	1	7	–	–	9	–	–	6	2	–	–	–	–	2	30
Hants	–	2	4	–	–	11	–	–	3	1	–	–	–	–	–	21
Kings	2	4	9	–	–	3	–	–	2	5	–	1	–	–	–	26
Lunenburg	–	–	2	–	–	5	–	–	6	–	–	1	–	–	–	14
Pictou	–	–	36	–	–	–	–	–	1	–	–	–	–	1	–	38
Shelburne/Queens	4	3	7	–	–	3	1	–	16	1	–	1	–	–	–	36
Yarmouth	2	4	–	–	–	1	–	–	4	–	–	–	1	1	1	12
Total Mainland	27	19	142	22	0	38	2	0	87	11	0	3	1	2	3	347
Cape Breton																
Cape Breton County	–	–	44	6	–	–	–	–	–	1	–	–	4	–	–	55
Eskasoni																
Sydney																
Inverness County	–	–	11	–	–	7	–	–	2	–	–	–	–	–	–	20
Malagawatch																
Whycocomagh																
Richmond	–	–	3	15	–	2	–	–	1	–	–	–	–	–	–	21
Victoria	–	–	23	–	–	–	–	–	–	–	–	–	–	–	–	23
Total Cape Breton	0	0	81	21	0	9	0	0	3	1	0	0	4	0	0	119
Total Nova Scotia	27	19	223	43	0	47	2	0	90	12	0	3	5	2	3	476

Note: Occupational descriptions have been simplified to the first named occupation. In many cases, people said they had multiple occupations. For instance, many off-reserve residents of Digby County said they were hunters and fishermen. I have simplified this description for this table to 'hunters.'

Legend: B(f) = Female Basket-maker; B(m) = Male Basket-maker; Co = Cooper; CF = Cooper/Farmer; Do = Domestic Servant; Far = Farmer; Fi = Fishermen; Gu = Guide; Hu = Hunter; Lab = Labourer; Lau = Launderer; Lu = Lumberman; Mi = Miner; Tr = Tradesmen; O = Other

Source: LAC, RG 31, 1881 Census.

Table 7.3
Occupations of Mi'kmaq of Nova Scotia, 1911 Census

Community	B(f)	B(m)	Co	CF	Do	Fa	Fi	Gu	Hu	Lab	Lau	Lu	Mi	Tr	Total
Mainland															
Annapolis	10	4	–	–	–	–	–	1	–	9	–	2	–	2	28
Antigonish	–	1	36	3	–	–	1	–	1	–	–	–	–	1	43
Colchester	–	–	3	–	–	–	–	–	2	9	–	11	–	–	25
Cumberland	–	–	–	–	–	–	–	–	1	1	–	–	–	–	2
Digby	–	–	–	–	–	–	–	–	–	–	–	–	–	–	
Bear River	–	–	2	–	–	–	–	–	–	18	2	–	–	–	22
St Bernard	2	3	–	–	–	–	–	–	–	–	–	–	–	–	5
Guysborough	1	–	10	–	–	–	2	–	–	–	–	–	–	–	13
Halifax	–	–	1	–	–	–	–	–	–	6	–	–	–	–	7
Hants	–	–	5	–	–	4	–	–	–	16	–	–	–	–	25
Kings	3	19	–	–	4	–	–	–	–	3	–	–	–	–	29
Lunenburg	–	–	–	–	–	–	–	–	–	–	–	–	–	–	–
Pictou	–	–	2	–	1	–	–	–	2	44	–	–	–	–	49
Shelburne/Queens	1	1	–	–	–	–	–	–	–	14	–	2	–	–	18
Yarmouth	5	6	–	–	–	–	–	2	2	8	–	–	–	–	23
Total Mainland	22	34	59	3	5	4	3	3	8	128	2	15	0	3	309
Cape Breton															
Cape Breton County															
Eskasoni	20	2	5	–	–	18	–	–	–	4	–	–	–	–	49
Sydney	1	2	2	–	–	–	–	–	–	24	6	–	–	1	36
Inverness County															
Malagawatch	8	–	3	1	–	2	–	–	–	–	–	–	1	–	15
Whycocomagh	–	8	11	3	1	10	–	–	–	3	–	–	–	2	38
Richmond	–	–	10	8	–	1	1	–	–	19	–	–	–	–	39
Victoria	–	–	–	16	–	2	–	–	–	4	–	–	–	–	22
Total Cape Breton	29	12	31	28	1	33	1	0	0	54	6	0	1	3	179
Total Nova Scotia	51	46	90	31	6	37	4	3	8	182	8	15	1	6	488

Legend: B(f) = Female Basket-maker; B(m) = Male Basket-maker; Co = Cooper; CF = Cooper/Farmer; Do = Domestic Servant; Fa = Farmer; Fi = Fishermen; Gu = Guide; Hu = Hunter; Lab = Labourer; Lau = Launderer; Lu = Lumberman; Mi = Miner; Tr = Tradesmen.
Source: LAC, RG 31, 1911 Census.

public tramway between Sydney and Glace Bay, although only two were employed full time while the others were hired as they were needed, particularly to shovel snow from the tracks. Four people, including Ben Christmas, worked at the city hospital. Others did masonry and plastering. Because few people worked full-time, they supplemented their income by making pickaxe handles and baskets, using material from the Caribou Marsh Reserve about four or five miles outside town.[42] All of this suggests that by the first two decades of the twentieth century, Sydney families made most of their income by working for others. This work, however, was casual, not permanent.[43] This trend toward wage employment continued into the 1920s, and not just in Sydney, but in other parts of Nova Scotia as well.[44]

Both Sydney and North Sydney were also places which families and friends from other communities visited, sometimes for extended periods. Such visits were not solely social but for financial reasons as well. Even into the early 1900s many families came to Sydney to sell their wares. One DIA employee, commenting on Eskasoni's economic development, reported in 1902 that 'the rapid development of Sydney affords them a very good market for meat and any agricultural products they have. I found a headman killing a steer to take to Sydney. I saw him the next day and he told me that he had just sold 300 pounds at ten cents a pound.'[45] The agent added that the Mi'kmaq could 'not do without a camping ground in or in the vicinity of Sydney. It is thither they usually go to sell their handicraft, and being unable to return home the same day, and not affording to a boarding house or hotel, they camp on that little Reserve.'[46] The transient character of the reserve's population meant it was a busy place and was sometimes overcrowded. In contrast to the surrounding neighbourbood, it may also have been a noisy place. All of this did not sit well with some of the residents and especially with J.A. Gillies.

J.A. Gillies was not a man to be trifled with. A native Cape Bretoner from humble origins, Gillies had made good. Educated at the Roman Catholic college of Saint Xavier in Antigonish, Gillies had been called to the bar in 1875 and, over the next few years, had filled a number of public posts, including a seven- year stint as Sydney's solicitor. In 1887, he unsuccessfully contested the federal seat in his home constituency of Richmond County, but was successful four years later after joining the Conservative Party. Unseated in 1900, Gillies ran in 1904 and again in 1911, but for naught. In 1900, he returned to Sydney where he resumed his law practice and occasionally did work for the town.[47] He also acted on behalf of various businesses. In 1902 he represented Dominion Chemical Company, which wanted to build a plant in Sydney but only if the city exempted the company from municipal taxes.[48] In 1901 Gillies cemented his influence in regional politics by purchasing the town's major newspaper, the *Sydney Post*.[49]

In December 1877, Gillies had bought land on King's Road. Unbeknownst to him, the adjacent property would be officially deemed a reserve five years later. Just what Gillies knew about this property is unclear. He must have known that it belonged to the Crown. We might suspect he was able to buy his land cheaply and that one of the reasons he was able to do so was because the Mi'kmaq occupied the neighbouring lot. We might also suspect that Gillies, like any person with a little bit of money, bought the land on speculation, hoping that some day his investment would pay off. His subsequent efforts to have the Mi'kmaq removed therefore might have had more to do with protecting his financial interests than anything else.[50]

Gillies's unhappiness first surfaced in 1899 when he was a Member of the House of Commons. Gillies approached Minister of the Interior Clifford Sifton, who was 'sympathetic and anxious to do what he could.'[51] Gillies then wrote to Deputy Minister J.A. Smart: 'They cut down my trees, they break my fences, they milk my cows, and steal everything they can lay their hands upon.' The Mi'kmaq also posed a potential source of disease, as a recent outbreak of diphtheria had demonstrated.[52] Gillies offered to buy another property in exchange for the one they occupied and asked Smart to 'hurry this matter through.'[53]

Gillies's efforts at first seemed to be moving towards a successful conclusion. The DIA attempted to obtain the residents' agreement to surrender the reserve and to obtain a parcel of land elsewhere, but these efforts soon ran into trouble. Initially, they agreed to sell. But after investigating the difficulties in acquiring other land near to the town centre the residents withdrew their consent. The DIA's financial constraints also made a resolution difficult; the department insisted that the new site be financed from the sale of the reserve. Even if this were possible financially, however, acquiring land would be difficult because the council opposed the Mi'kmaq remaining close to the town, making it impossible to comply with the community's request that they be able to remain somewhere nearby.

After months of discussions, the department decided that there was no land that would satisfy both the town and the band. Because the community refused to surrender the land, the department could do nothing 'as under the law they (the Mi'kmaq) have to give their consent before any land can be taken from them.'[54] Gillies was not happy but could do little.

The matter was also complicated by the Mi'kmaq's unusual legal status within the meaning of the Indian Act, the statute that regulated Indians and Indian lands. In Nova Scotia, the Mi'kmaq were considered to be members of one band and therefore had the freedom to move from one reserve to another.[55] This meant that any time the government sought a surrender of reserve land, they had to consult all Mi'kmaw male residents of Nova Scotia twenty-one years of age and older.[56] This was an unusual situation; in the rest of the country, band members were usually associated with one reserve and so surrenders meant obtaining the majority consent of the adult male residents of the reserve in question. This was not true of Nova Scotia. By the early 1900s, the department, on the advice of Department of Justice lawyers, had decided that consulting all adult male Mi'kmaq in Nova Scotia was impractical and that it was enough to consult the members of the agency. In the case of Sydney, this meant the male residents of Cape Breton County, an area that included the Eskasoni and North Sydney communities in addition to the Sydney residents.

C.C. Parker, an inspector of Indian agencies, offered two other solutions. One was that only the current residents of the Sydney reserve be consulted. This was the simplest solution. But he also suggested that since the reserve had been used and occupied by Mi'kmaq from each of the island's reserves, 'negotiations would have to be taken up with the Indians of Inverness, Victoria, Cape Breton and Richmond Counties.' This opinion seems to have been shared by many Mi'kmaq, including Grand Chief John Denny, the principal Mi'kmaq leader who discussed the proposed surrender with DIA officials.[57]

Joe Christmas played an important role in these events, acting as an assistant to Grand Chief Denny in discussions with federal officials. Christmas served as chief of the reserve on several different occasions. In 1909 he was elected to a three-year-term, and within a year after completing his term again assumed the post after John Julien resigned. Christmas was chief, therefore, at a critical time in the negotiations with the federal government,[58] Like Grand Chief Denny, Christmas believed that the King's Road Reserve's location served the community well. As chief, he discussed the issue with other residents. As he later said, relocation 'would never suit his Indians' as they 'do not like to live away from that place. It is handy for their work, and they have a good schoolhouse and everything is complete, and we have good Doctors and good Agents and good teachers and the children go to school every day. I think the children will be alright for a few years more.'

Various alternate locations were mentioned, but Christmas was uneasy about the proposed sites. One such area was on the Lingan road. Christmas had several objections. The land was too rocky and it was too close to the Coke Ovens. The ovens, said Christmas gave off too much gas and 'the children would get hurt. It was also too close to the black neighbourhood. 'There are too many negroes there already. My Indians might get killed there, that is the reason I would not like to go there.' Another proposed location at Cow Bay also did not meet with Christmas's approval; the land there, he said, was hard clay and 'it will never grow anything at all. When a hot day would come in summer, it would be as dry as the floor, no good.' Other parts of the proposed seventy-acre site, said Christmas, were also no good. 'One-half is swampy and the one-half is no good.' As well, the place was four to five miles from town and was too far for the women to get to work. Although Christmas proposed a site on the other side of the Sydney River, he knew that only about half of the residents would choose relocation there. Given the divisiveness such a move would create, he preferred that his people stay where they were. As he said in 1915, 'I tried to help my Indians, and they want to stay there now.' Christmas, however, also realized that the two- to three-acre lot was not big enough to accommodate the growing population. In 1915, he thought that there would be room enough to add another three houses. However, once those houses were built, the community would then face the problem of how to incorporate future population increases. Christmas thought that would not happen for about seventy years yet and so was not worried.[59] His optimism would appear to be ill placed.

At the same time that department officials were pressuring the Sydney Mi'kmaq to move, they were also trying to relocate the North Sydney community. These efforts were less complicated because the families living there were camped on private land. The main problem was how to force their removal. Andrew Bernard was not particularly happy and in 1909 had begun agitating to make their residence permanent. However, the DIA consistently overrode these objections, culminating in a visit by Deputy Superintendent Duncan Campbell Scott which subsequently led to the families' relocation to other reserves. One of those affected was Andrew Bernard and his wife, who decided to move to Whycocomagh.

Bernard's objections were easily ignored because the band lacked legal title to the land they occupied, a situation that did not apply to the King's Road Reserve. There the government faced an apparently insoluble situation, at least until 1911, when the Liberals introduced amendments to the Indian Act meant to hasten the process by which 'surplus' Indian lands were surrendered. As in Sydney, the government was facing difficulty in getting aboriginal communities to surrender lands that were in the way of economic development. Although many of these lands were in the countryside, some were in urban locales.[60] One amendment included provisions to expedite the relocation of reserves in new urban areas. Passed on 19 May 1911, the amendment stipulated that

> In the case of an Indian reserve which adjoins or is situated wholly or partly within an incorporated town or city having a population of not less than eight thousand, and which reserve has not been released or surrendered by the Indians, the Governor in Council may, upon the recommendation of the Superintendent General, refer to the judge of the Exchequer Court of Canada for inquiry and report the question as to whether it is expedient, having regard to the interest of the public and of the Indians of the band for whose use the reserve is held, that the Indians should be removed from the reserve or any part of it.[61]

Comments by Minister of the Interior Frank Oliver suggest that the amendment was a response to the difficulties in persuading 100 Songhee people to surrender land in the town of Victoria, British Columbia. Their presence, said the minister, was a barrier 'to the progress of the city, and therefore, to the welfare of its inhabitants and to the enterprise of the transportation companies.'[62] In an address to the House of Commons, Prime Minister Wilfrid Laurier explained.

> Some forty or fifty years ago, perhaps more, Sir James Douglas made a treaty with the Songhees tribe and he gave them a tract of land on the shore of the ocean. Then it was nothing but the bleak shore, but in the course of time, the city of Victoria grew up around that reserve. It has been for a long time a grievance with the city of Victoria, that they could not improve the Songhees reserve. I need not say to my hon. Friend that the Indians, with their habits, did not at all improve the tract of land, which was in their possession. As this land bordered the ocean it was essential to the development of the city, but the Indians would not surrender their rights and for years it was a constant subject of dispute between the Indians and white men of Victoria.[63]

With Canada's rapid urban development in the late nineteenth and early twentieth centuries, Victoria was only one of many cities where such problems existed, and it is likely that the government was hesitant to point fingers at places where the amendment might be used. Sydney was certainly one of them and, if we can believe Gillies, the city's dispute with the Mi'kmaq contributed to the decision to include an amendment specifically directed at forcing the surrender of reserve lands in urban areas.[64]

Gillies and his friends may have thought that with the amendment's passage, the government would now do something. If they did, then they were to be disappointed. Gillies might also have thought that the election of the Conservatives in the autumn of 1911 would have hastened action, particularly since the new prime minister was himself a Nova Scotia native.[65] Robert Borden and his cabinet, however, did not act for another four years before finally implementing the new provisions of the act.

The government's hesitancy may have had to do with the new prime minister's concerns regarding the government's new draconian powers. Borden had been the opposition leader at the time the amendment was debated and had believed it gave the courts and the superintendent too much power. This unilateral authority, said Borden, would undermine the British Crown's historic relationship with aboriginal people. Speaking in the House of Commons, Borden had pointed out that over the past two hundred years the Crown had entered into various treaty relationships. Since then, the 'Indian has learned to know that he can look forward at all times with confidence to the sacred fulfillment of any treaty he makes with the British Crown.' With the amendment the government was proposing to break these treaties. Although Borden recognized that this action may be justified by the growth of the country, 'especially in the west,' still he was troubled about circumventing Parliament. He suggested an alternative: instead of giving an unelected judge the authority to decide the issue, the government should take no action without first receiving Parliament's approval. The Liberals agreed and so the final draft of the bill was amended to accord with Borden's suggestion.[66]

Perhaps because of Borden's initial concerns, the Conservative government attempted to find a solution that would accommodate the interests of all parties in the Sydney dispute. As before, the stumbling block was finding an acceptable location within walking distance of town. Although the Mi'kmaq suggested a fifteen-acre property about three miles from the city's centre, departmental officials thought that 'within a few years the residential parts of the city would reach there so that the same complaints would likely occur again.'[67] The Borden government was unwilling to refer the issue to the courts, and, according to the statements of the minister in the House of Commons on 1 May 1914, would not do so. 'We have no intention of calling this Act into requisition in order to dispossess them of their land,' said Mr Roche.[68] Sometime between May 1914 and September 1915, however, he changed his mind, a turnabout that may have been occasioned by the outbreak of war, the increased strategic importance of Sydney's coal and steel industries and what this would mean in terms of the city's future expansion.

The hearing before Mr Justice Audette of the Exchequer Court of Canada, held in Sydney in September 1915, was to determine whether it was in the public interest that the Mi'kmaq be relocated. No jury was empanelled but rather Judge Audette was empowered to render a decision.[69] Counsel represented each party to the hearing, with J.A. Gillies representing himself and the City of Sydney, and George A. Rowlings, the Mi'kmaq. Thirty-four witnesses testified. This included medical doctors who discussed conditions on the reserve, local residents who spoke about Mi'kmaw immorality, schoolteachers who had taught on the reserve, town councillors who advocated removal, Indian agents who were familiar with the reserve, and real estate agents who knew the value of the reserve land and its buildings. Only three Mi'kmaw residents testified: the reserve constable, Joe Julien and two of the men who would later testify at Sylliboy's appeal, Joe Christmas, and his son, Ben.

Gillies said that the Mi'kmaq posed a moral and public health hazard. Rowling, who represented the Mi'kmaq, called witnesses who testified either that those then living on King's Road had chosen to live there despite the reserve's presence and therefore others would do the same or that conditions on the reserve were not as bad as others described.

Much of the testimony focused on conditions on the reserve. This evidence was presented by local residents and various professionals, including the parish priest, the Indian agent, and a medical doctor. Although each of these witnesses had different opinions of the Mi'kmaq, they agreed that conditions on the reserve were less than ideal.

Much time was spent discussing the reserve's sewage facilities. The reserve had never been connected to the town's sewage line and so the DIA had built a 'two compartment brick sanitary,' which was connected to the harbour. However, there were continual problems and so the toilets were sometimes not working.[70] In addition, most houses had outdoor privies. These facilities appeared to be inadequate; some neighbours recalled seeing residents relieving themselves out of doors, and especially along the railroad tracks which ran along the back of the reserve parallel to the river.[71]

This description suggested that the reserve's sewage system was sub-standard, but Rowlings got the city's chief medical officer to admit that outdoor toilets were legal in areas where the sewage line did not yet extend. Then on redirect Gillies made the mistake of probing the doctor's opinion. Gillies wanted the doctor to say that the crowded conditions on the reserve were characteristic of the reserve and nowhere else. What Gillies got was more detail than he wanted.

GILLIES: Do you know of any section of the city in which there are 120 people living on a piece of land occupied by 27 buildings and all using that land as privies?

DOCTOR: I think perhaps I do.

GILLIES: Where?

DOCTOR: Down near the steel works. I don't know the number of people in there but I know where there are quite a number of houses owned by the Steel Company.

GILLIES: Near the steel works?

DOCTOR: Yes.

GILLIES: Occupied by foreigners?

DOCTOR: Yes

GILLIES: Poles, Germans, Austrians and Russians?

DOCTOR: Yes

GILLIES: A Foreign element?

DOCTOR: Yes

AUDETTE: And no sewer there?

DOCTOR: No sewer. There are sewers laid for some of the slop water but they have out-houses around.[72]

The chief medical officer's testimony showed that the lack of sewage facilities was because Sydney had failed to connect the reserve to the town system. His evidence also underlined that there were other areas where conditions were similar, yet nobody wanted to relocate those people because they were employees of Dominion Steel and were living on company property. Indeed, the testimony showed a double standard at play, and one that worked against the Mi'kmaq.

More damning was testimony regarding the accumulation of garbage and other odorous items. One local resident said 'I would not call it [the reserve] a very clean or sanitary place. Everybody disposes of their refuse and sewerage by throwing it out, in front of their places or adjacent to the next house, and their natural ditches are full of this sewerage, running across the reservation and the out houses and the dwellings.'[73] John Parker remembered seeing decayed vegetable matter and stagnant water.[74]

This evidence was partially offset by other testimony. First, the reserve physician stated that the refuse problem had improved considerably since 1913 after the department had hired a company to collect the garbage once a week.[75] Second, other witnesses suggested that the problem was not the Mi'kmaq but the crowded conditions in which they lived. One resident explained. 'But all of these houses are crowded together, it is a different matter than if a house occupied a certain portion of land and they threw anything out, there is not enough to make any odor or disturb anybody.'[76] In other words, the problem was not that people threw dishwater and other garbage into their yards. Many other Sydney residents did the same. The problem was that the houses were packed close together and were not parceled out into lots, and that this meant that the soil could not absorb refuse that might normally be compostable.

The implication was that the reserve was overcrowded, and this, coupled with the poor sewage facilities, made the area a public health hazard. Gillies hammered these points home, saying that the Mi'kmaq 'have constantly something wrong with them.'[77] Rowlings countered with Cecil Sparrow, the reserve's physician, who said there had not been any epidemics since he had been appointed to the post in September 1912, even though there had been outbreaks of scarlet fever and diphtheria in the city.[78]

Witnesses called by Gillies also said that the Mi'kmaq morally contaminated the surrounding neighbourhood. Wilfred Winfield said that so long as the Indians remained, nobody would move there. He elaborated: 'I have not discovered anyone who would live there close to them (the Mi'kmaq), for my own part if you built me a house adjoining the reservation I would not live there rent free under any consideration, and anyone [I] am acquainted with would not.'[79]

Another local resident, John McCurdy, said the same thing. 'I don't think there is anybody at all would want to go up there and build any way near the Reservation. I am sure they would not if they [got] a lot of land for nothing.'[80] The implication of this and similar testimony was that so long as the reserve stayed where it was Sydney's southward expansion would be hindered.

Winfield also said that the reserve residents' licentious character posed a moral threat to the surrounding population. Selling liquor to Indians was illegal, but the Mi'kmaq did not have any difficulty in acquiring it and, according to Winfield, were constantly drunk. This resulted, he said, in 'noises and screams coming from the reserve at all times of the day and night.' This posed a problem for his family. 'I have found young men apparently under the influence of liquor skylarking on the road and fighting,' he told Judge Audette. On one occasion Winfield's wife was afraid to pass by them, and only did so after he told her that they would not do any harm.

> They would not be as ordinary drunken people lying down and minding their own business but they are running all over the road hooting and yelling. Their children would run to you as you would go by begging and calling names and it is not very pleasant for pedestrians particularly for a woman. I do not think any woman would be there at nightfall without an escort.[81]

Another witness cast aspersions on the women, particularly those who drank, and claimed that 'they will go with anybody, sleep with them, have sexual intercourse,' a comment suggesting that more was at work here than simply removing the Mi'kmaq for health reasons. There was also concern about the possible 'contamination' of the surrounding population, which by tempting male desire would undermine ideas about white superiority and might also tangibly result in the birth of mixed blood children.[82]

Residents also believed the reserve devalued the land surrounding it. When questioned on this point by Judge Audette, Winfield replied that his property would be worth more if 'they [the Mi'kmaq] were not there.'[83] To buttress this argument, Gillies questioned various realtors. Each of the men said that they would be unable to sell land on King's Road if the Mi'kmaq continued to live there, and gave several examples of people who wanted to buy land but were wary of doing so because of the reserve.

A good deal of prejudice underlay much of this testimony. Occasionally, these sentiments bubbled to the service as happened when the former mayor, W.A. Crowe, testified. A former officer in the Canadian military, Crowe had been mayor of the city in 1900 when the city council had voted to write to the Department of Indian Affairs and request that the reserve be relocated. Crowe clothed his comments in a language that assumed the Mi'kmaq to be inferior. 'They are hardly over the nomad state yet. They are people susceptible to the evils of City life, more than our own people. This is an anomaly in my judgment that in the center of a city which is the size of Sydney that there should be two acres occupied by Indians in that spot.'[84]

Judge Audette's written decision focused on whether the public's interest warranted the removal of the Mi'kmaq to another location. In answering this question, Audette discussed two main issues. First, did the presence of the reserve limit Sydney's expansion and second, did the conditions on the reserve pose a health risk.

In answering the first question, Audette believed that the continued Mi'kmaw presence along King's Road would harm the city.

> Now, this Reserve abuts on King's Road, which is one of the principal arteries of the city, a highway very much traveled and used by the public, and upon which a large number of fine residences are built. No one cares to live in the immediate vicinity of the Indians. The overwhelming weight of the evidence is to the effect that the Reserve retards and is a clog in the development of that part of the city.

In answering the second question, Audette found that the reserve was too small to accommodate the band's growing numbers. 'There are too many buildings upon it, and the band of Indians has become too numerous to be located under the present conditions for sanitation on such a small area. An undesirable and objectionable congestion is the necessary result. Moreover, the band is growing; the young men are marrying and desire to settle there. And while the Reserve is too small for the Indians actually in occupation, we must not overlook that all the Indians of Cape Breton who come to Sydney, reside on the Reserve during the time of their visit. And looking to the future, made wise by looking on the past of this Reserve, it appears that the desirability of a larger Reserve, a matter of expediency now, will become imperative in the near future.' The conclusion was inescapable: the Mi'kmaq had to be relocated. 'I do, therefore, without hesitation, come to the conclusion on this branch of the case, that the removal of the Indians from the Reserve is obviously in the interest of the public.[85]

Despite Judge Audette's decision, the Mi'kmaq stayed where they were for the next nine years, as the department tried to purchase land far away from the local population but close enough to the city. Although Audette's decision may have buttressed the case for removal, it had not resolved the problem of relocating band members to a location that would satisfy the council and ensure that they could still work in the city. As before, the department discovered finding a location that would satisfy everyone was not easy. Their efforts in 1920 were a case in point.

In 1920, the department procured funds to purchase land. Parker recommended a property owned, ironically, by J.A. Gillies, even though much of it had already been destroyed by fire. The big selling point was that the land was within walking distance of the Coke Ovens and of the working class community of Whitney Pier.[86] The plan, however, did not sit well with some residents. In a petition sponsored by the local Member of Parliament, residents made two major objections. First, they pointed out how the Mi'kmaq might be affected by living next to various ethnics, including Poles, Ukrainians, and West Indians. 'It goes without saying,' the petitioners wrote, 'that mixing Indians with this cosmopolitan population will not tend to help out the Indian Problem either morally or from a simple Physical and humanitarian standpoint.' Second, the residents believed the Port's proximity to the proposed reserve would form a dangerous toxic mix. Just what the residents believed would happen was left unstated, but one would presume that alcohol and sex were their major concerns. In total, some 392 people of various professions and occupations, including women, signed the petition.[87]

The Mi'kmaq also were not happy with the proposed location. 'We are quite willing to move,' the new chief Joseph Marshall wrote to the department in November 1920, 'but if we are compelled to do so, we will have to be forced.' The main objection was that the Whitney Pier property was too far away from the water. 'We want to be as close to the shore as possible, because we think it's the greatest protection to our health.'[88]

Despite the opposition of the Mi'kmaw and Whitney Pier communities, in June 1921 the Department of Indian Affairs purchased fifteen and a half acres of the Gillies property.[89] Much to the department's chagrin, the proposed move did not go forward, perhaps because of the uncertainty created by the federal election of 1921 and the town's opposition. As the years of acrimony and litigation had demonstrated, finding a new home for the King's Road residents was beset with tangled and competing interests.

Having abandoned a move to Whitney Pier, the department was, once again, in the search of real estate. In 1924 the department decided on a 65-acre lot and completed the sale in August of the following year.[90] The government's sudden haste was in part attributable to warnings from the city's chief medical officer that conditions on the reserve were deteriorating and that an outbreak of tuberculosis was possible, a fear that was subsequently borne out during the early spring of March 1925 when several cases were reported.[91] Relocation began that year and was completed by June of 1926. Whether the residents of the reserve were satisfied is unclear. Although some may have welcomed the move to a larger property, they must have been embittered by the process, which had revealed tensions with the city's elected officials and with its white Nova Scotian population.

The movement to relocate the King's Road Reserve away from the town's centre may have started with J.A. Gillies and his political cronies, but the force that propelled it forward reflected efforts at reforming the country's urban environment and determining where the Mi'kmaq could live. Although the impetus behind the agitation was to regulate public health, it also illustrated a deep-seated enmity towards the presence of aboriginal people who chose to move to, or to remain in, areas of new urban growth. For business and political elites this posed a troubling series of issues, which they sought to resolve by proposing that the Mi'kmaq be removed to the city's outskirts. In part these problems stemmed from how the white residents of the city received the Mi'kmaq but it also reflected the reforms which governments were attempting to impose on urban areas. The Mi'kmaq did not fit easily into that rubric, according to residents and to the council, as they lacked the moral uprightness that would make them eligible residents. As an official from the Department of Indian Affairs wrote to Andrew Bernard's father in 1881, urging him and other families to move to Eskasoni, relocation would allow families to 'escape the many temptations to which the Indians are always exposed when living in the vicinity of towns or cities.'[92]

This, however, was more than a question of optics. The presence of the reserve near the town's centre presented unique financial and political challenges as well. Unlike the land that surrounded it, the reserve was held in common by the residents, which they parceled out and used according to their dictates and custom. That use conflicted with the interests of nearby neighbours, who were concerned with how the reserve's presence would affect real estate values. The testimony of local residents suggested that because the reserve residents did not own their houses, they also did not care for them in the same manner as other people. The effect was to diminish the appeal of the surrounding neighbourhood and so also its financial worth. Similarly, the city's relationship with the residents posed legal and political questions. Was the city responsible for providing access to sewage lines? And if it was, how was its installation and maintenance to be paid for? Because the Mi'kmaq were not subject to property taxes, then who would bear the costs? Indeed, Nova Scotia town councils had, on previous occasions, expressed concerns regarding the legal status of Mi'kmaw people living within municipal areas and their financial responsibility towards them.[93]

For the men who testified at Sylliboy's appeal in July 1928, the removal of Sydney and North Sydney residents exposed the sharp fault lines between the Mi'kmaq and government and private interests. King's Road and North Sydney had offered people an opportunity to work in an urban environment, where jobs were more easily obtained and where children could learn the skills and make the connections that would make their lives easier. Perhaps the city's working-class residents did not view the Mi'kmaw presence negatively, but the import of Gillies's actions and the subsequent hearing before the Court of the Exchequer in 1915 had revealed a deep antipathy towards them. Although this hostility was mainly led by well-connected business and political leaders, like J. A. Gillies and W.A. Crowe, there is no evidence that working people, or their unions, rallied support for the beleaguered Mi'kmaw community. The effect of the controversy therefore entailed much more than removal; it further deepened the divide between the communities.

Just what each of the men thought is unknown. We might suppose, however, that the controversy illustrated to them the cynicism with which the federal government approached its relationship with aboriginal people. Although advocating the integration of the Mi'kmaq into Anglo-Canadian society, government and private interests conspired to hinder the Mi'kmaq from doing so. Christmas said that his people were happy to stay at King's Road and that there was sufficient land to accommodate their needs for the next seventy years. The Mi'kmaq were not the problem, but the white residents disapproved of their presence, and so the government had decided on removal. The Department of Indian Affairs had initially protected the Mi'kmaq from surrendering title to the reserve, but its efforts were eventually overridden by Parliamentary legislation. This likely suggested to Christmas and to the others that the Mi'kmaq needed their own law to protect them from government actions.

There is no textual evidence to show that Gabriel Sylliboy was involved in the discussions, but his predecessor as Grand Chief, John Denny, was. The DIA's agents and officials had counseled Denny's inclusion in the negotiations, a point that Denny himself underlined in his letters. He was, he said, the head of all the Cape Breton Mi'kmaw communities and the chiefs in each community were his captains. Any discussion, therefore, which involved one community had to involve all of them. In this sense, the King's Road and North Sydney relocations illustrate the important role the Grand Council played during the early 1900s as representing Cape Breton communities in their discussions with federal officials.

The events also illustrate the continuing disconnectedness between the policy of assimilation and its implementation. This disjuncture was evident to Joe Christmas and other members of the King's Road Reserve, and was one further illustration of the difference between the Mi'kmaq and their Nova Scotia neighbours. In this way, the events which eventually led to the King's Road relocation served as a cue to remind the men who testified at Sylliboy's appeal about the narrative which underlay their own understanding of the treaty.

In such moments the treaty assumed an iconic image unifying families and communities by asserting a common identity, borne through a common historical experience. This experience, which had first been set out in the petitions of the nineteenth century spoke to the injustices that had befallen the Mi'kmaq since the time the treaty had been signed, had been sharpened by the demographic calamity that had befallen the community in the late nineteenth century and the political battle over the relocation of the King's Road reserve soon afterwards. In the century and half since the treaty's signing, the Mi'kmaw community had shrunk and so too had the space it occupied. It was the memory of these experiences that Gabriel Sylliboy brought with him when he traveled from Whycocomagh to Alex Gillis's farm in the waning days of October 1927 and which would lead him, whether consciously or not, to confront Gillis, Innis, and MacKinnon on 4 November.

Conclusion

In June 1936, Dr Phillip Smith, a professor of pathology at Dalhousie University traveled to Cape Breton to collect blood samples from the island's Mi'kmaw population. Smith was not particularly concerned with the peoples' health but with the effect of inter-racial marriages on blood types. Research had suggested that aboriginal people had originally been 'O' blood types but as they had intermarried with Europeans their blood groups had become more diversified. R. Ruggles Gates, a professor of genetics at London's King's College was working on this question and had requested Smith's help. Gates wanted to know just how 'Indian' the Mi'kmaq really were. If they only married other aboriginal people, they would all have O blood. If, on the other hand, they did not, their blood types would be mixed. And so Smith had journeyed northward from Halifax to Whycocogmagh and later traveled around Lake Bras d'Or to Chapel Island. At both places, Smith had taken blood samples and had noted the eye and hair colour and skin pigmentation of each tested individual. Smith also took photographs.

Gabriel Sylliboy agreed to be part of Smith's experiment, to have his blood drawn, and to have his personal characteristics noted. He also told Smith about his immediate family, his brothers and sisters, and his grandchildren. And each of them in turn, consented to Smith's bloody experiment. This is why we know a lot about the Sylliboy family's blood types and that we also have a picture of Gabriel Sylliboy as he appeared at the time of Smith's visit.

Gates published his findings in the *Journal of the Royal Anthropological Institute of Great Britain and Ireland* in 1938. He based his conclusions on Smith's fieldwork, on samples taken from adults near Middleton, a small community in the Annapolis Valley, and on samples from 100 children attending the residential school at Shubenacadie. As Gates pointed out, the children originated from different communities throughout the Maritimes and so their blood types were probably a good representative sample.

Gates found that 62 per cent of all tested Mi'kmaq had the '*O*' blood type. For Gates, this high percentage showed that the Mi'kmaq, like most other aboriginals, had been originally '*O*' blood. But intermarriage with Europeans had resulted in '*A*' blood types as well. In 1936, people with '*A*' blood totaled about 33 per cent of all tested individuals. Significantly, the Nova Scotia Mi'kmaq had a higher percentage of '*A*' blood types than 500 aboriginal people from British Columbia, who had been tested in an earlier experiment. Gates wrote that this was 'a natural result of the much longer contact with European settlers' and concluded that it was 'highly improbable that any pure-blooded Micmacs remain.'

In a marked departure from an otherwise technical explanation of blood types, Gates indirectly commented on questions of identity. To Gates, many Mi'kmaq were racially indistinguishable from their white counterparts. 'Many of the segregates [the Mi'kmaq] could pass for whites without any difficulty if they so desired,' he wrote, illustrating his comments by describing a family living at Middleton: 'The Francis sisters are both "*A*," with pale brown eyes and a trace of skin colour; but they differ in that one has hair nearly black and slightly wavy while in the other the hair is light brown and very wavy and the features entirely "white."' Gates believed such racial characteristics would one day lead to the assimilation of the Middleton Mi'kmaq. 'Although these families live in a group of houses segregated from the rest of the population, yet it is clear that they are in a rather advanced stage of amalgamation, and in another two or three generations will probably disappear as a separate entity.'

In contrast, the Whycocomagh Mi'kmaq were more 'Indian' than 'white.' Gabriel Sylliboy's extended family was an example. The Sylliboys, said Gates, were not full-blooded Indians. Although Sylliboy himself was an '*O*' type, his brother had '*A*' blood as did their sister. Even though all of Sylliboy's children were '*O*' types, his eldest daughter had married a man with '*A*' blood. Their children's blood was therefore mixed, four having '*A*' blood and three type '*O*.' In sum, Gates' tests showed the extent of mixed bloods, even in rural villages like Whycocogmagh. Sylliboy himself was an '*O*' blood, but some members of his family were not, including four of his grandchildren.[1]

For Gates, racial similarity made assimilation possible, the more so since Mi'kmaw blood had been mingled with the superior Anglo-Cana-

Andrew Alek, 1930 (Nova Scotia Museum, Halifax: 1930, P113/73.180.626;N-14, 746)

dian blood. But here was the rub: '"Treaty money" and Government care prevents them from doing so.' In other words, many Mi'kmaq would assimilate into Canadian society if not for the federal government's assistance. The government, said Gates, treated Mi'kmaq differently, reinforcing isolation that would not have continued if they had been left to fend for themselves. The result was that the Mi'kmaq, like other aboriginal people in Canada, had evolved into a separate caste, living within the Canadian nation, but not part of it.

Although Gates was correct that government assistance retarded Mi'kmaw integration into Anglo-Canadian society, this was only one of many factors that separated them from the larger population. Alex Gillis did not know Sylliboy or the Jeddore brothers by name when he saw them on his farm in late October 1927 but later said he 'made out they were Indians.'[2] For Gillis, this meant more than that Sylliboy's skin tone was darker. It also meant that Sylliboy had different conceptions of citizenship.

Gabriel Sylliboy believed he was doing nothing wrong in camping on Alex Gillis's land or in trapping muskrats during closed season. He believed that as a Mi'kmaw person, he had a right that superseded government fiats about where, when, and how people could fish and hunt. He believed that this right stemmed from a treaty his ancestors had signed more than a century and a half before. And when Malcolm MacKinnon attempted to take the furs, Sylliboy told him that he had a right to the furs. This suggests that the Gabriel Sylliboy that Phillip Smith met at Whycocomagh in June 1936 differed from Nova Scotians more than the Dalhousie professor and Russel Gates thought. The root of this difference was more than misguided government policies; it was a different understanding of a shared history.

At the appeal in July 1928, Sylliboy's lawyers questioned five elders from the community, including Gabriel Sylliboy. Each man said that the community's hunting rights stemmed from the treaty. They also said that this understanding came from private and collected memories that had been transmitted to them from their grandparents and parents.

In these pages, I have placed the men's private and collected memories into an historical perspective. The men's understanding of the treaty should be understood as part of a historical trajectory of which they, their parents, their grandparents, and great-grandparents were all part. How the men remembered the treaty was different than their parents had done so, and how their grandparents understood it was different from the generation before. This was because each generation lived in different historical epochs, and their life experiences were dissimilar.

First, there was a change in names. As Alfred Young has pointed out the names that are attached to historical events change. Some become part of the public memory and some do not; those that do are sometimes named differently than they once had been. The dumping of tea into Boston Harbour is one example. As Young says the term 'Boston Tea Party' did not have resonance in the city's history until 1831, when the city's social and economic elite renamed it for their own ideological purposes.[3] In the same way, the terminology the Mi'kmaq used to describe the agreement they made with the British also changed, although not all at once. In 1794, the Mi'kmaq referred to the agreement as 'the peace they had made.' Beginning in 1825, the Mi'kmaq began to refer to the agreement as a 'treaty' and enclosed a copy of the 1760 Treaty in a petition sent to the Colonial Office. This change in how the agreement was identified signified a shift in the community's position within Nova Scotia. It also reflected the enhanced stature of Great Britain's industrial power, the strength of its empire, and the intercession of colonial interlocutors as mediators between indigenous peoples and metropolitain officials. The change also represented a modification in how Mi'kmaw leaders thought about the past. No longer a military threat to white settlement as they had been in 1794, the Mi'kmaq began to view the agreement as a legal text that set out each party's legal obligations. This was different from the 1790s, when they had discussed the agreement as a peace, suggesting that they could also be enemies. This was an important change and one that demonstrated the Mi'kmaw community's reduced importance within the British Empire and the beginnings of their absorption into it.

Mi'kmaw leaders also modified the treaty's meanings. In 1825, Muise referred to the treaty as testimony to Mi'kmaw loyalty and used it to request that the King act favourably towards his subjects. By the 1850s Mi'kmaw leaders had inserted additional meanings, this time stressing how the British had agreed to leave the Mi'kmaq a greater part of Nova Scotia so that they might continue to live by fishing and hunting.

These later petitions underline the persistence of oral memories. A literal reading of the 1760 text, which Muise had enclosed in his 1825 petition, might suggest that the British had promised little and that the Mi'kmaq had agreed to submit unconditionally to His Majesty and to abide by the laws created by him. Indeed, this is the interpretation that lawyers representing the Canadian government made before the Supreme Court of Canada in R. v. Marshall (1999) and it has also been the persistent theme in Stephen Patterson's analysis of the treaty's legal implications.[4] We would not expect nineteenth-century commentators to have thought any differently. The later Mi'kmaw petitions of 1849 and 1853, although referring to the treaty, discuss its terms differently. This would suggest that from this date the community had created a memory of the treaty. Although some of the people who had signed the treaty or had been present at the ceremonials in 1760 and 1761 were still alive in the early 1800s, they were not by mid-century. Their private memories of the treaty, however, were transmitted to later generations, as the petitions of 1849 and 1853 show.

These memories were passed on to the generation of men who testified at Sylliboy's appeal. Like their parents their memories did not always accord with previous interpretations. There were two important differences. First, with the exception of the much younger Ben Christmas, each of the men stressed that the treaty protected the community's right to fish and hunt whenever and wherever they chose, subject only to the restrictions that each community placed on their people. This statement differed from earlier generations, who had talked of how the British had violated the agreement by failing to leave the Mi'kmaq in quiet possession of their lands. The men who testified at Sylliboy's appeal, however, focused on how the treaty protected the Mi'kmaw community's right to hunt. In other words, the treaty had become a source of rights for Mi'kmaq *living on reserve*, rather than a source of title for Mi'kmaq who had been *forced onto reserve*. This change in emphasis reflected the men's experience of growing up on reserve and in harvesting off-reserve resources. This was in contrast to their parents' generation who had spent a smaller part of their lives on reserve. The men's parent's generation represented *the age of dispossession*, while the men's generation represented the *age of reserve life*.

The second important change was the men's emphasis on the 1752 Treaty. In 1825, the Mi'kmaq had referred exclusively to the 1760 Treaty. The men of Sylliboy's generation, however, referred to the earlier treaty. Why they did so is unclear. A careful reading of the five men's testimony shows that none referred to the 1752 Treaty. Their 'reading' therefore was not based on a text but on an oral memory that had been part of their parents' heritage and that had become part of theirs as well. Indeed, the divergence between the men's testimony and the 1752 Treaty would suggest that the decision to rely on that treaty had been made by the necessity of linking a treaty with the right Sylliboy claimed. The 1752 Treaty fit the common law's needs. On the one hand, a printed copy of the treaty was easily accessible as the text had been published in community newspapers and was also available in a collection published in 1869 by the provincial archivist, Thomas Akins. Although the lawyers were aware that the Mi'kmaq had signed other agreements those treaties were less well known and copies were less readily available.[5] Thus, the decision to use the 1752 Treaty as the basis of Sylliboy's defence may have been a matter of convenience, providing an easy link between the Mi'kmaw community's memory of the treaty and a written English text, which the lawyers required and which the Court demanded.

However, once the 1752 Treaty became the focus for the defence, the treaty came under the court's scrutiny. Sylliboy's lawyers had to address two principal issues. They first had to make a link between the treaty and the right claimed. This was easily done, because the 1752 Treaty included an article in which the British had promised that the Mi'kmaq 'would not be hindered from, but have free liberty of Hunting & Fishing as usual.' The only complicating factor was whether other articles of the treaty might limit where, when, or how the Mi'kmaq hunted. Establishing a connection between Sylliboy and the treaty, however, was more difficult. Sylliboy was from Cape Breton Island, but the chief signatory of the 1752 treaty, Jean-Baptiste Cope was from Shubenacadie, a community about halfway between Halifax and Truro on mainland Nova Scotia. Three other men also signed but their residence is not identified, leading us to believe that they were also from Shubenacadie. Unless Sylliboy therefore could show a connection between Cape Breton and the 1752 Treaty, he could not claim protection from it.

This problem was addressed by Ben Christmas, the youngest of the six men to testify. Unlike the other five men, Christmas was from a later generation. Born in 1894 in Sydney, Christmas had benefited from increased government funding for Indian day schools. And indeed, as his personal papers demonstrate, he was able to read and write English.[6] Christmas was the last Mi'kmaw person to testify and took the stand after MacDonald had formally submitted to the court six historical documents, one of which included the 1752 Treaty. In direct examination, MacKenzie referred Christmas to the treaty and to the other three men who, in addition to Jean Bapstiste Cope, had signed it. According to Christmas, 'two of chiefs whose signature [sic] appears on the Treaty was Andrew Hadley Martin. He came from Nyanza Victoria Co. And Gabriel Martin. He came from Escasoni.'[7] Although this testimony made a connection between Sylliboy and the right he claimed, it was suspect because the treaty did not record the residence of either Andrew Hadley Martin or Gabriel Martin. Unfortunately, Judge Patterson's notes do not contain more information and so determining how Ben Christmas had come to this conclusion is not possible. The necessity of claiming the connection between Sylliboy and the treaty, however, revealed the difficulties the Mi'kmaq faced once they had decided to mount a legal challenge through the courts.

Once that decision was made, the effect was to alter the basis on which the Mi'kmaq would henceforth make their claims. From then on, the Grand Council and other Mi'kmaq emphasized the written text of the 1752 Treaty to validate their arguments.[8] In *Sylliboy*, this began when the lawyers first had to decide what treaty to use and then to make a link between the defendant and the treaty. As a result, the Grand Council came to exercise less control over treaty interpretation and was forced to give more attention to a text-driven analysis subject to interrogation by common-law procedures. Indeed, although later scholars associated with the Grand Council, such as James Youngblood Henderson, have written about the connection between the council and the 1752 Treaty, the lack of English-language documentation attesting to this relationship renders these interpretations tenuous within the courtroom, and among some historians.[9] In this way, the Mi'kmaq and the Grand Council became prisoners to a court system and to an historical epistemology, which were both foreign and potentially destructive of their ability to sustain a community understanding of the treaty.

Litigation also changed how the men's words were phrased and recorded. Four of the men testified that the community had a *right* to hunt. Christmas said that 'heard according to treaty we had *right* to hunt & fish at any time.' Andrew Bernard spoke about the *right* to fish and to sell the fish while Bernard said that the *right* to fish or shoot at any time of year came from the King. Sylliboy was more explicit when he told Judge Patterson that he had 'Told officer that I had treaty with King and that I had a *right* to furs.'[10]

This phrasing represents a further shift in how the community conceptualized their relationship to government. In earlier petitions, the Mi'kmaq had lamented their exclusion from the land. Although the 1853 petition had mentioned the community's rights, these rights were never identified except in relation to settlers' encroachment onto reserve land. By 1928 the Mi'kmaq had transformed the treaty into a source of rights and a burden that the Crown had a responsibility to fulfil. The treaty, they said, gave them a right to fish and a right to hunt whenever they wanted. It also gave them a right to sell fish. In other words, the government did not have the power to regulate their hunting and fishing, because the treaty governed relationships with non-Mi'kmaw governments. This reasoning implicitly reinforced government policies, which assumed that the Mi'kmaq, like other aboriginal people, occupied a unique legal status within Confederation. However, each party defined the basis of that status differently. The government contended that aboriginal peoples' status as wards of the state was the result of their infantile nature and therefore the 1876 Indian Act was a necessary tool to allow them time to become Canadian. The Mi'kmaq, however, claimed that their status stemmed from the treaties they had made a century and a half before. In other words, policies made on their behalf could not be unilaterally imposed by fiat but were subject to the same negotiating process that had led to the eighteenth-century treaties. Other aboriginal communities' arguments with government officials in the early 1900s were based on similar precepts.[11]

Although we might presume that the men's use of the word 'right' emerged from translating across cultural boundaries or from discussions with Sylliboy's lawyers, it was also the result of how the men perceived themselves and their community. The men's life experiences had revealed a widening chasm between Mi'kmaw and non-Mi'kmaw peoples, which only strengthened the community's identification with the treaty. This memory of the treaty would not have assumed the meanings it did had the Mi'kmaw community grown and prospered in the nineteenth and twentieth centuries. Because the community had not prospered, historical memories of the treaty persisted and became a focal point of a collective historical consciousness. The men who testified at Sylliboy's appeal remembered the treaties, not because their parents had told them, but because their brains had encoded the information with a memory trace or engram and which thereafter they integrated into the narrative they told about their lives. This process of remembering could only have occurred because the conversations with their parents had had some meaning both at the time they occurred, and during their adult years, when their parents were dead. In this way, the men transposed those memories of the treaty into something more: it became a source of rights, which would protect the Mi'kmaq from all the ills that had befallen the men, their families, and their community during their lifetimes.

In describing why the men remembered the treaty, I discussed two aspects of Mi'kmaw history between 1871 and 1925. This was a period when the men would have married, had children, had assumed positions of leadership and when they adapted to living on reserve. These were also years of upheaval, and not just for the Mi'kmaq, but for most other Maritimers, as demographic changes and industrial development led to an exodus from rural areas. It also led to a reduction in Mi'kmaw families' access to off-reserve areas. This constriction, coupled with changes in the region's political economy, including the introduction of day schools and a more aggressive federal attempt to force aboriginal peoples onto reserve, led to overpopulation and a corresponding decline in the average life expectancy. At the same time, and sometimes in conjunction with these developments, some families moved to urban areas in search of employment and markets. The coal-mining belt of northern Cape Breton was one destination and, although families did not always live there permanently, their presence provoked an agitation for their removal. These two events, which we might multiply through examination of other situations where families' lives intersected with urban and rural populations in the late nineteenth and early twentieth centuries, is one context to situate the men's memories. These events cued the men's memory, helping them to recall, however imperfectly, the treaty.

That the six men who testified at the appeal were from Cape Breton had much to do with their willingness to contest Sylliboy's conviction. Unlike the mainland population, the island Mi'kmaq lived almost entirely on reserve, were concentrated in relatively large numbers, were located near to each other, and were less integrated into the wage labour economy. As well, their children were taught on reserve, and families were connected with the Grand Council. All of this made their communities more socially and politically cohesive than the mainland, where populations were more dispersed, where children were more likely to be educated in the public school system, where people were more likely to have intermarried with the non-aboriginal population, and where the Grand Council had less influence. Geography contributed to these differences, but the historical legacies of the nineteenth century had a more lasting influence, creating a more fractured populace. One consequence was that the island Mi'kmaq were also more likely to retain an understanding of the treaties that differed from how other Nova Scotians interpretated the treaty.

How widely did other members of the Cape Breton Mi'kmaw community share the six men's interpretation? On this question, there is little documentation, and so we can only make a reasonable conclusion. From the late 1700s leaders referred to the treaties at the annual gatherings at Chapel Island on St Anne's day, reminding people that they occupied a unique legal status in Nova Scotia society, something that most families would have understood from their daily lives. Even though it is probable that not every adult completely shared the men's understanding, they would have accepted that they had a unique status and so would have seen the treaties as further evidence of this fact.

Significantly, this occurred when colonization and industrialization tore asunder the fabric of European societies, creating national states and a new triumphant nationalism, superseding peoples' affinity to their class, to their community, and to their cultural identity. 'Canadian history,' Professor D.A. McArthur of the University of Toronto wrote in 1924, promotes 'an atititude of intelligent loyalty and even devotion to our nation and its institutions.'[12] Most Mi'kmaw children, however, were schooled separately, illustrating that like other aboriginal people, they were not always included within the new nation. They could be, but only on the terms decided for them, not by them. They might become Canadians if they agreed to shed their 'Indian' other, moving off reserve and living among other Canadians in towns, in cities, or on farms. In other words, Indians were only acceptable if they were no longer Indians.

In lieu of governments and communities that rejected their presence, the Mi'kmaq from the mid-1800s moved to create a concept of citizenship that unified individuals and families scattered the width and breadth of Nova Scotia. These ideas evolved in opposition to how the Mi'kmaq had been treated within the colonial state, initially by dispossession of their lands and later by the segregating influence of the reserve and the moral condemnation they faced in towns and cities. One aspect of this oppositional vision was the community's oral memory of the treaties. This memory became part of Mi'kmaw history and a repository to define the community. In doing so, the Mi'kmaq also created the treaties by defining them as a symbol of identity and as a catalyst for resisting government efforts to remodel and to reform them.

This identification with the treaties also reflected the changing nature of settler governments. In 1760 the British, lacking the power and the financial strength to enforce their will, chose accommodation over confrontation. This meant leaving the Mi'kmaq free to do as they pleased. They lived, as I have argued elsewhere, 'outside the purview of the European fishermen, traders, farmers, soldiers and colonial officials who came to Mi'kma'ki.'[13] However, with industrialization the elasticity implicit in these early years receded. The capitalist ethos implicitly negated alternative forms of economic organization at variance with the principles of private property. Although the Mi'kmaq, like aboriginals elsewhere, were able to maintain their economic independence in the early years of industrialization, this was only possible because of the uneven development of the capitalist economy, which resulted in certain areas, like Nova Scotia, being developed later, and differently, than other regions. From the mid- to late nineteenth century that independence was reduced, forcing families to seek alternative forms of work. Families responded by mostly working in areas familiar to them. However, their employment also reflected the ways elites and ordinary people isolated Mi'kmaw adults from the wage labour economy. This flexibility in how the Mi'kmaq made their living, however, was only possible because of the elasticity still implicit in much of Nova Scotia life and that ordinary people had a common right of access to water, to forests, and to other lands not used or occupied. Ultimately, the use of such common resources conflicted with the expansionary nature of Nova Scotia's burgeoning capitalist economy, leading the Mi'kmaq to agitate for continued access to Crown and private lands. Many Mi'kmaq challenged the government regulations, but only Sylliboy's conviction in 1927 led to a formal hearing before the court. Later in the century, the Mi'kmaq would reinterpret that treaty relationship to include a right to fish and to sell fish outside the federal regulatory system.

Although that reinterpretation occurred in a different historical conjuncture, the community's continued appeal to the treaties illustrates both the flexibility of the Canadian state – and its economic wealth – and its inability to grapple with the unique character of modern aboriginal communities. The treaties would never have assumed the importance they did, either in 1927 or today, if Mi'kmaq had been able to participate equally in the wage labour economy and in the political system that would allow them to influence policies, rather than to be the subject of them. To my mind, this is the crux of the matter and one that governments have been unwilling to recognize until forced to do so.

Mi'kmaw appeals to the treaty, however, ultimately distorted the past and created a vision that was not always reflective of the community's history. There is always a danger of distortion when recourse is made to a document or to a vision that must be sustained in defending a right. Litigation and political grandstanding have created a narrative that places the treaty at the centre of Mi'kmaw history, pushing aside all that does not fit easily into its mould. The story told has often been shaped by what was needed than by what was, and so memories have been tapered and simplified to convey an uncomplicated moral vision to future generations. Section 35 (c) of the 1982 Constitution Act tends towards a burden of proof that forces aboriginal litigants and their 'experts' to conceptualize aboriginal people as 'unique' and 'special' in ways that undermines conceptualizing their active participation in historical events.

In watching the nightly newscasts after the Supreme Court's September 1999 decision in *R.* v. *Marshall,* I was both fascinated and revolted by references to the 'ancient Mi'kmaw treaties,' as if the treaties were some reified artifacts discovered with an archaeologist's trowel. Broadcasters do not usually refer to either the American Constitution or to the BNA Act with similar words. Such turns of phrase would be unthinkable, as these documents contextualize our understanding of contemporary political and legal structures. The American Constitution and the BNA Act are organic documents, forming the basis on which both Canadian and American governments operate, and they inform how those structures should be, or need to be, adjusted. In contrast the treaties signed with the Mi'kmaq are considered to be 'ancient' because they should have no contemporary relevance, a supposition that reflects a cultural perception of aboriginal people as artifacts of the past and not subject to the same historical forces as others.

More than forty years ago, Bruce G. Trigger argued against romanticizing aboriginal people and for understanding them as people who acted rationally and in ways that are discernable.[14] In the 1987 reprinting of his classic history of the Huron people, he wrote

> My primary goal was to demonstrate that native behaviour was based on the rational pursuit of desired ends at least to the same extent as that of Europeans. I had concluded that little was to be gained by eliciting sympathy for native people (as various historians had done in the past) if it was not based on respect for their intelligence and self-discipline. I therefore sought to explain native behaviour as far as possible in terms of rational calculations of how desired ends might be achieved. In doing this I eschewed the alternative romantic approach which views the behaviour of each society as determined by its own particular cultural pattern, or as was once believed, by its own specific biological nature. In relativistic fashion, the romantic view assumes that each culture is a closed system based on its own self-defined rules. Thus the behaviour of one group is unlikely ever to be fully comprehensible to members of another. It is this approach, with its potential for emphasizing the irrational aspects of human conduct, that in various guises has dominated the interpretation of native American behaviour from at least the time of Francis Parkman to the present. Rationalist explanations, by contrast, seek to account for human behaviour in terms of calculations that are cross-culturally comprehensible.[15]

This view has also elicited debate in the study of Oceanic indigenous peoples.[16] In this book, I have adopted a similar approach to understanding Mi'kmaw memories by viewing the descendants of those who made the treaties as historical agents, whose act of remembering occurred within a living context and that affected what they recalled. I have also assumed that the Mi'kmaq were rational and I have approached their memories of the treaties in a similar fashion. What I mean by this is that in understanding aboriginal peoples, we should remember that they, like others, are not imprisoned by their culture, although culture may influence their actions more at certain moments. For most Mi'kmaq of the late nineteenth century, culture was a not a defining point in their lives. What was more important was providing a better life for their families. Men and women who fished, who made baskets, and who trapped for muskrats probably did so because those were things they had learned how to do and could do well, but that work did not render them of incapable of adapting to Nova Scotia's political economy. They, much like the Huron of the seventeenth century, understood that working within the new economy could provide a more dependable and more lucrative source of food and income than a life spent in the bush. However, their efforts to participate in Nova Scotia's wage labour economy were not always welcomed. This made people angry, and in attempting to deal with the injustice of their situations, they turned to the eighteenth-century treaties as one method to combat a government that seemed intent upon destroying their families. That the Mi'kmaq were aboriginal does not mean that they were not subject to same historical forces as everyone else. The only difference is how those historical forces affected them, and how they responded.

Each generation shapes stories about the past, changing the details a little, but just enough to make a difference.[17] We might ask how the men who testified at Sylliboy's trial came to hear about the treaty. Who had told them? What were they actually told? And how did they remember what they heard or what they thought they heard? And for what reasons might the speaker have told the story differently than what he or she had heard? How did the men change what they had heard? And how did they tailor that memory to fit the narrative their lawyers wanted to present? What all this suggests is that there is more complexity to what the men said at Sylliboy's appeal trial than a literal reading of their words would suggest. Their lives help us to understand why they said what they said and what they forgot to say or had already forgotten, or had never been told. The words they speak to us from Judge Patterson's courtroom transmit a vision of Mi'kmaw history that allows us to simplify the past into manageable portions.

In writing about the men, I have also simplified the past by discussing only one aspect of it. I have focused on averages, on what I consider to have been the general trend of the Mi'kmaw population of Nova Scotia from 1794 to 1928. This approach does not give an entirely accurate picture, because it does not always show the diversity of peoples' experiences. Not all non-aboriginals treated the Mi'kmaq harshly. Not all ejected them from their lands. Not all complained to the Department of Indian Affairs about families camping on their lands. Only some did, and we would suppose that others coexisted with the Mi'kmaq, much as their parents and grandparents did. It is also true that not all Mi'kmaw families of the late 1800s lived an itinerant existence. Not all lived by making baskets or other wood products. Not all camped in the woods, not all lived in birch bark camps in the summer, or on reserve. Some families chose to live among, and to integrate into, white communities. They chose respectability, ditching the clothes and attire of their relatives and adopting the suit and tie, the long plaited dresses and a coiffured hairstyle. They were able to do so, I believe, because their skin was whiter and their phonology and syntax approximated the English dialect better than most other Mi'kmaq. This made them acceptable within white communities, in just the same way that my maternal grandfather eventually experienced. He became respectable. Although American border agents at Niagara Falls in February 1912 identified my grandfather as an 'Indian,' his enlistment papers and notice of death did not. Some Mi'kmaq chose similar paths. They chose respectability and all the cultural and social attitudes, values, and beliefs that entails. One of the things it entails, I believe, is a cultural and political separation from others who identified with a different interpretation of their family and community's history. This included a perception of the eighteenth-century treaties not as cultural markers that informed individual consciousness but as emblematic of their integration into Nova Scotian society. The Mi'kmaq, in this interpretation, became subject to English law. They became English. I believe my grandfather did just that when he returned from the war in 1919 and when he did, he began to invoke a narrative of his life that made him more English than Indian, a decision that he reinforced when he applied to become enfranchised in 1920. I think many other Indians who then lived in southwestern Ontario did the same. However, in Nova Scotia and among the Mi'kmaq, I believe that such individuals were a minority before 1914, and most people who were of Gabriel Sylliboy's generation had experienced life in ways similar to the five men who testified at Sylliboy's appeal. Their skin was darker, their syntax and phonology were unmistakably Indian, their clothes were threadbare, and they lacked the mannerisms that would have made them acceptable in white Nova Scotia society. Perhaps, if cities had been larger, if the immigrant population had been greater, then their chances of merging into the urban ghettoes would have been better. But this, in tandem with their historical consciousness, prevented them from being anything other than Mi'kmaq. It is this intangible sense of being that made a Mi'kmaw identity possible and that would lead in 1929, to the building of a residential school at Shubenacadie to accomplish what more than two hundred years of colonization had not.

When Alex Gillis, A.A. Innis, Malcolm MacKinnon, Otto Schierbeck, Magistrate Joseph McDougall, Duncan Campbell Scott, and Judge George Patterson saw and thought about Gabriel Syllbioy, they saw an 'authentic Indian.' As Paige Raibmon writes, 'for aboriginal people, modernity was cast as a process of distancing themselves from their own culture.'[18] They could not fish, they could not hunt, and they could not trap muskrats. When they did those things, they were acting like Indians, and Indianness had to be rooted out to make way for the Canadian that lay buried deep inside of them. When Judge Patterson pronounced Sylliboy's guilt in September 1928, he believed that he was helping Gabriel Sylliboy to become Canadian. The terms on which he was to become Canadian, however, were not ones that he could choose, but would be chosen for him and by imposing a sentence on Sylliboy, Judge Patterson was doing just that. Patterson was operating, like Alex Gillis and Otto Schierbeck, within a cultural framework that used the law to discipline those who either could not or would not adapt.

In listening to what these five men said in 1928, we might interpret those who cite their words as a crass form of opportunism. Today, politicians, judges, and ordinary people do the same when they listen to aboriginal people articulating a version of events at variance with most accounts. What often lies buried within the rhetoric are community memories. The *Sylliboy* case illustrates this precept. What the men said is less important than why they remembered.

What I am suggesting is that Section 35 (c) of Canada's Constitution is a creation of Canada's colonial legacy. This section reads: 'The existing aboriginal and treaty rights of Canada's aboriginal and Metis people are hereby recognized and affirmed.' That aboriginal people felt the inclusion of this section in the Constitution necessary illustrates their aliena-tion from Canadian society. That attitude, it seems to me, was created from a long history of segregation, much in the same way that a similar history of development in Atlantic Canada created the 'Maritime trea-ties.' We should therefore remember, when reflecting upon the number of aboriginals who have used a Section 35 defence, that they did not cre-ate 'aboriginal and treaty rights' alone.

Appendix: Federal and DIA Censuses, 1871 to 1911

Throughout the book, I make use of federal and DIA censuses. In terms of the federal censuses, I use the 1871, 1881, 1901, and 1911 manuscripts. I have not used the 1891 census since people are not specifically identified according to either race or ethnicity. For this reason, the 1891 census is not a dependable source of information since we cannot identify all people of Mi'kmaw ancestry, as is the case with the other censuses.[1]

As is well known, censuses are rarely exact and so some circumspection is warranted when using them. Enumerators make mistakes, as do clerks who compute the names and numbers listed on individual sheets into aggregate figures. Demographers try and overcome these errors by sampling censuses for inaccuracies. In terms of the Nova Scotia Mi'kmaq, the task is much simpler since we are dealing with a relatively small number of people. For the federal censuses we can match every person identified as Mi'kmaq in the manuscript copies of the censuses with the published aggregate figures.

By matching names with figures, we are able to evaluate the reliability of each census. In 1871, the error was relatively minor, over-counting Mi'kmaw totals for Yarmouth by ten and under enumerating the number living elsewhere in the county by eight. This error does not appreciably affect the totals, because the population quoted in the printed census as 1,666 need only be reduced to 1,664. From this total, I have also subtracted an additional thirteen people who are listed as residents of Shelburne County but for whom the manuscript copy of the census is not extant, giving us a total of 1,651, fifteen fewer people than cited in the census's printed copy.[2] The error in the 1881 census is more egregious; statisticians counted 242 more Mi'kmaq than the manuscript copy of the census shows. In most populations, an error of 242 might not make a difference. This is not so when counting a relatively small community where an error of this magnitude translates into over-enumerating the population by 11.4 per cent.[3]

Similar problems abound in the 1901 and 1911 censuses. As with 1871 and 1881, the numbers in the printed and manuscript copies of the 1911 census do not match. The problems are mainly centred in Colchester and King's counties where the printed copy overstates the manuscript totals by 153 giving us 224 Mi'kmaq rather than the published figure of 377.[4] More problematic is the 1901 census. Its numbers are a jarring contrast to censuses taken before and after. In 1881 the census counted 1,883 Mi'kmaq and the 1911 census, 1,758. The 1901 census listed only 1,629.[5] If we accept the accuracy of these figures, then between 1881 and 1901, only twenty years, the population declined by 13.4 per cent.

Department of Indian Affairs (DIA) figures provide an alternative perspective for evaluating the low numbers recorded in 1901. Beginning in the early 1880s, Indian agents included aggregate population totals in their annual reports. DIA figures for 1881 show 2,219 Mi'kmaq, not the 1,870 people enumerated in the federal census, while the 1901 DIA figures show 2,020 people, significantly more than the 1,629 counted by federal census enumerators.[6] This suggests that the federal censuses underestimated the actual Mi'kmaw population. Differences for the censuses conducted in 1881, 1901, and 1911 are summarized in Table 6.1.

Some of these errors in enumeration are not specific to Nova Scotia or to the Mi'kmaq, but reflect problems in enumerating aboriginal individuals and families.[7] Enumerators faced various difficulties in compiling an accurate picture of Canada's aboriginal population, and although by 1901, Indian agents were often enlisted to help, this was done less commonly in the Maritime region. Enumerators therefore were more likely not to have the background to be capable of always perfectly understanding and evaluating each household. Language was always a problem, as enumerators did not speak or understand Mi'kmaq while some Mi'kmaq only spoke English imperfectly. The movement of families on and off reserve also would have presented problems because some families likely were not counted. Mi'kmaw households were also less easily identified than Euro-Canadian ones. Birch bark camps are not log houses and are not always located next to roadways or along town and city streets. Depending on when the census was taken, some families may have been collecting wood or fishing. It is also not untoward to think that a man enumerating the population of a village, town, or city who encountered a group of Mi'kmaq living in a birch bark camp, would not include them in his survey. Finally, there were also problems in identifying who was an Indian and who was not. In American censuses, identity was determined through observation, although other reference points were also used, including 'enrollment in a tribe or agency, community recognition as Indian, and the "degree of Indian blood."'[8] In

Nova Scotia, Indians living off reserve presented special problems. This would have been less of an issue if they occupied an 'Indian dwelling' or lived among a group of families who were known to be Indian. More problematic were single households whose manner of living and skin tone did not immediately signal their racial identity. By 1901, such individuals were more common than in the 1870s, when most Mi'kmaq still lived in rural areas and could be associated with an iconic 'Indian' image. This was less true by the early 1900s when intermarriage into non-Mi'kmaw families and integration into the wage labour economy and the educational system would have made some people less visibly 'Indian.'

We should not suppose that the federal censuses were entirely accurate, but neither should we put absolute faith in DIA figures.[9] As was true for the statistics compiled by the American Bureau of Indian Affairs, so too were there difficulties with DIA censuses. There are two main problems. First, in Nova Scotia agents were part-time employees, much like the game wardens and forest rangers discussed in Chapters One and Two. These men made their principal income from other work and so did not devote as much time to their departmental duties as we might suppose. This inattention is shown by some of the reported figures. For instance, for every year from 1880 to 1898, the Colchester County agent reported the population of his agency to be 100. This static representation suggests that he had little knowledge about his charges. Second, some agents included people in their agency even though they no longer lived there, so some people may have been counted twice. Moreover, we might suspect that agents, as in the United States, had reasons to inflate the numbers, mainly in order to ensure their continued employment.[10] Finally, Indian agents were often patronage appointments and lost their jobs when a new government was elected. After the 1911 election of the Conservatives, for instance, a number of agents and medical officers lost their jobs in Nova Scotia and new individuals were appointed in their places. [11]This turnover further undermined the creation of a competent bureaucracy. In sum, there are likely as many problems with DIA census figures as there are with federal totals.

Ultimately, we cannot resolve the discrepancy between the two sets of figures; the departmental censuses give aggregate totals, making a comparative analysis with the federal nominal census impossible. In this book, I have chosen to use the federal census, mainly because it contains names and therefore provides more opportunity for microanalyses. Regardless of which totals we use, however, both censuses show an increase in population from 1847 to 1881. As well, both sets of figures show a sharp drop in population between 1881 and 1901: in the federal census at a rate of 12.8 per cent and in the DIA census at a rate of 9.0 per cent.

I have also used the censuses to help understand peoples' occupations. While useful, such descriptions also pose interpretative problems. Not all entries noted the multi-occupational aspect of a household, because enumerators tended to simplify men's occupations. For instance, some enumerators might describe one man as a fisherman and another differently, even though both said they had caught similar quantities of fish. To cite one example, in 1871, both Joseph Penall and James Lewis of the Bear River Reserve said they had made 100 gallons of fish oil over the past year. The enumerator, however, reported their occupations differently: James Lewis was described as a cooper/fishermen and Joseph Penall as a hunter.[12] As this example illustrates, occupational descriptions do not give an accurate rendering of each household's economy because more families fished than said they were fishermen, a problem which was also true in how enumerators characterized other households.[13] Second, the guidelines instructed enumerators to list a son's occupation as the same as his father's if the son was associated with the household. Thus, as Darroch and Soltow point out in their study of rural Ontario, a 'farmer's son, working on his father's farm, was to be classified as a farmer.'[14] This classification possibly simplified occupations of males of the younger generation by associating them with their fathers, even though they may have worked for wages or did other types of labour. Third, enumerators rarely recorded a woman's occupation and normally only did so in the case of widows with dependents. This omission reflected the census board's instructions that 'in the case of women, unless they have a definite occupation besides their share in the work of the family or household, the column is to be filled with the sign −; as also in the case of children.'[15] So, even though the occupations expressed in Schedule One are useful, they also simplify male occupations and ignore women's work.

These are just some of the problems in using the census, and they are probably more severe when counting aboriginal people than for the rest of the population. Despite these issues, the census gives a baseline from which to evaluate aborignal communities, and thus adds important information that other sources cannot. When used in tandem with these other sources, the resulting analysis provides a fuller and broader picture than if they were not used. This is the case, for instance, in Chapter Five, which uses Schedules Four and Five to evaluate the agricultural output of Cape Breton Mi'kmaw families. Although we would suspect that the data in these schedules are not precisely accurate, the conclusions reached about the ability of families to supply their income needs from farming accord with what with we know about the lands on which they lived. In a similar way, the figures regarding literacy used in Chapter One, although not precisely accurate, accord with what we know from qualitative records regarding the availability of schooling to families in the mid- to late nineteenth century. In sum, although there are many good reasons to suspect that the censuses do not provide the exactness we would hope, the data do assist in making broader conclusions about the Mi'kmaq than we might otherwise have done. This is particularly true in Chapter Six, which uses the census to compile child/married woman ratios. These data when combined with other material in the DIA records show, I argue, high infant and child mortality. The importance of this is that the DIA records alone only suggest a high incidence. However, when combined with the calculations on child/woman ratios, the DIA material assumes a larger importance and, I would argue, allows me to argue that infant and child mortality spiked in the late nineteenth century.

Notes

ANQR	Archives nationales de Québec à Rimouski
DGSIA	Deputy Superintendent General of Indian Affairs
DPNSHA	Debates and Proceedings of the Nova Scotia House of Assembly
JLA	Journals of the Legislative Assembly
JPHANS	Journals and Proceedings of the House of Assembly of Nova Scotia
LAC	Library and Archives of Canada, Ottawa
MG	Manuscript Group
NSARM	Nova Scotia Archives and Records Management, Halifax, Nova Scotia
NSM	Nova Scotia Museum
PANB	Public Archives of New Brunswick
RG	Record Group
SCR	Supreme Court Reporter
SGIA	Superintendent-General of Indian Affairs

Introduction

1 In this book I am only concerned with aboriginal memories and do not examine how other people conceptualized the past, or how they remembered the history of aboriginal people. This, it it seems to me, would entail another approach and another book. For one recent example of how to approach the issue of how non-aboriginals understood aboriginal history in the mid- to late 1800s, see Jean M. O'Brien, *Firsting and Lasting: Writing Indians Out of Existence* (Minneapolis and London, 2010).

2 *R. v. Syliboy*, 28 July 1928, in William C. Wicken, 'Mi'kmaq Treaty Tradition,' *UNB Law Journal*, 44 (1995), 157–61.

3 *Rex* v. *Syliboy*, 10 September 1928, *Canadian Criminal Cases*, 50 (1928), 390–1, 395–6; N.A.M. MacKenzie, 'Indians and Treaties in Law,' *Canadian Bar Review* 7 (Oct. 1929), 561–8.

4 The literature on conflict over the interpretation of the status of aboriginal peoples is extensive. See e.g., Brian Titley, *A Narrow Vision: Duncan Campbell Scott and the Administration of Indian Affairs in Canada* (Vancouver, 1986), 110–34; on Ontario: Robin Jarvis Brownlie, '"Nothing left for me or any other Indian": The Georgian Bay Anishinabek and Inter-war Articulations of Aboriginal Rights,' *Ontario History* 96, 2 (Autumn 2004), 116–42; Malcolm Montgomery, 'The Legal Status of the Six Nations Indians in Canada,' *Ontario History* 55 (June 1963), 93–101; Constance Backhouse, *Colour-Coded: A Legal History of Racism in Canada, 1900–1950* (Toronto, 1999), 103–31; on aboriginal resistance in British Columbia: Paul Tennant, *Aboriginal People and Politics: The Indian Land Question in British Columbia, 1849–1989* (Vancouver, 1990), 84–113; R.M. Galois, 'The Indian Rights Association, Native Protest Activity and the "Land Question" in British Columbia, 1901–1916,' *Native Studies Review* 8, 2 (1992), 1–34; Douglas C. Harris, *Land, Fish, and Law: The Legal Geography of Indian Reserves and Native Fisheries in British Columbia, 1850–1927* (Toronto, 2005); on the Inuit, Shelagh D. Grant, *Arctic Justice: On Trial for Murder, Pond Inlet, 1923* (Montreal, 2002). On economic expansion onto lands and resources used by aboriginal peoples, Jean Manore, *Cross-currents: Hydroelectricity and the Engineering of Northern Ontario* (Waterloo, 1999).

5 John Leslie and Ron Macguire, eds., *The Historical Development of the Indian Act* (Ottawa, 1979), 120; Titley, *A Narrow Vision*, 59; Revised Statutes of Canada 1927, c. 98, s. 141.

6 *R. v. Simon*, 1985, 2 SCR (1986). *Sylliboy* was cited in case law outside the Maritimes as well, and in Department of Justice opinions regarding the applicability of provincial statutes in relation to aboriginal peoples. For the Maritimes, see PANB, RS 110, Game Law Violations, File 1934 – Victoria County, C.H. Elliot to H.H. Ritchie, 5 April 1934. In the early 1970s, governments still referred to Judge Patterson's 1928 decision when discussing the legality of the eighteenth century treaties. In 1974, Nova Scotia's deputy attorney-general informed the president of the Union of Nova Scotia Indians that 'the law in Nova Scotia would appear to be basically summed up in the decision of R. vs. Syliboy (1929), 50 CCC 389, a decision of the County Court. In that particular case the court decided that the treaties referred to were not made between competent contracting parties and did not extend

to the particular people in question.' NSARM, RG 20/885, doc. 1, G.F. Coles to J. Knockwood, 9 August 1974.

7   Edward W. Said, *Culture and Imperialism* (New York, 1993), 9–10.

8   MacKenzie, 'Indians and Treaties,' 562–5.

9   William C. Wicken, *Mi'kmaq Treaties on Trial: History, Land, and Donald Marshall Junior* (Toronto, 2002).

10   Wicken, *Mi'kmaq Treaties on Trial*, 27.

11   John L. Tobias, 'Protection, Civilization, Assimilation: An Outline History of Canada's Indian Policy,' in Ian A.L. Getty and Antoine S. Lussier, eds., *As Long as the Sun Shines and Water Flows: A Reader in Canadian Native Studies* (Vancouver, 1983), 40–7.

12   Duncan C. Scott, 'Indian Affairs, 1867–1912,' in Adam Shortt and Arthur G. Doughty, eds., *Canada and its Provinces: A History of the Canadian People and Their Institutions* (Toronto, 1914), 622–3. On Scott, see Titley *A Narrow Vision*, esp. chapters 5 and 9.

13   Said, *Culture and Imperialism*, 167.

14   James Belich, 'The Rise of the Angloworld: Settlement in North America and Australasia, 1784–1918,' in Phllip Buckner and R. Douglas Francis, eds., *Rediscovering the British World* (Calgary, 2005), 39–42.

15   On Nova Scotia's growth from the 1740s to the early 1800s, consult Julian Gwyn, *Excessive Expectations: Maritime Commerce and Economic Development of Nova Scotia, 1740–1870* (Montreal and Kingston, 1998), 25–6.

16   This includes such published work as Phillip Buckner, ed., *Canada and the British Empire* (Oxford, 2008); Phillip Buckner and R. Douglas Francis, eds., *Rediscovering the British World* (Calgary, 2005); Hamar Foster, Benjamin L. Berger and A.R. Buck, eds., *The Grand Experiment: Law and Legal Culture in British Settler Societies* (Vancouver, 2008); Catherine Hall, *Civilising Subjects: Metropole and Colony in the English Imagination 1830–1867* (Chicago and London, 2002); Kathleen Wilson, ed., *A New Imperial History: Culture, Identity and Modernity in Britain and the Empire 1660–1840* (Cambridge, 2004).

17   On the effect of empire on Austen's novels, especially *Mansfield Park*, see Said, *Culture and Imperialism*, 80–97.

18   Catherine Hall, 'What Did a British World Mean to the British? Reflections on the Nineteenth Century,' in Buckner and Francis, eds., *Rediscovering the British World*, 36.

19   See John C. Weaver, *The Great Land Rush and the Making of the Modern World, 1650–1900* (Montreal and Kingston, 2003), 81–2.

20   For a suggestive treatment on social networks within the British World, one which has influenced my own thinking, see Elizabeth Elbourne, 'Indigenous Peoples and Imperial Networks in the Early Nineteenth Century: The

Politics of Knowledge,' in Buckner and Francis, eds., *Rediscovering the British World*, 59–85.

21 On Great Britain in this period, Linda Colley, *Britons: Forging the Nation 1707–1837* (New Haven and London, 1992).

22 On this general issue, C.A. Bayly, 'The First Age of Global Imperialism, c. 1760–1830,' *The Journal of Imperial and Commonwealth History* 26, 2 (1998), 42.

23 The theoretical implications of this statement come from Daniel L.Schacter *Searching for Memory: the Mind, the Brain, and the Past* (New York, 1996).

24 Linda Colley, *Captives: Britain, Empire and the World, 1600–1850* (New York, 2002), 227–38; and for a recent attempt which sees the pluralistic nature of British North American colonies, Nancy Christie, 'Introduction: Theorizing a Colonial Past,' in Nancy Christie, ed., *Transatlantic Subjects: Ideas, Institutions, and Social Experience in Post-Revolutionary British North America* (Montreal, 2008), 13–18.

25 Colley, *Captives*, 354–79; and a complementary view, Bayly, 'The First Age of Imperialism,' 38–40.

26 Zoe Laidlaw, '"Aunt Anna's Report": The Buxton Women and the Aborigines Select Committee, 1835–37,' *The Journal of Imperial and Commonwealth History* 32, 2 (2004), 19.

27 For a short overview of this issue, see Martin J. Wiener, *An Empire on Trial: Race, Murder, and Justice under British Rule, 1870-1935* (Cambridge, 2009), 1–4.

28 See A.A. Den Otter, *The Philosphy of Railways: The Transcontinental Railway Idea in British North America* (Toronto, 1997), 3-31.

29 A useful introduction to this complex field of enquiry is Geoffrey Cubitt, *History and Memory* (Manchester and New York, 2007).

30 One such study is Michael Kammen, *Mystic Chords of Memory: The Transformation of Tradition in American Culture* (New York, 1991).

31 Colin M. Coates and Ceclia Morgan, *Heroines & History: Representations of Madeleine de Verches and Laura Secord* (Toronto, 2002); Norman Knowles, *Inventing the Loyalists: The Ontario Loyalist Tradition & the Creation of Usable Pasts* (Toronto, 1997); H.V. Nelles, *The Art of Nation-Building: Pageantry and Spectacle at Quebec's Tercentenary* (Toronto, 1999); Peter E. Pope, *The Many Landfalls of John Cabot* (Toronto, 1997), 173.

32 Jeffrey Olick, *The Politics of Regret: On Collective Memory and Historical Responsibility* (New York, 2007), 23–7; John Bodnar, *Remaking America: Public Memory, Commemoration, and Patriotism, in the Twentieth Century.*(Princeton, 1992), 13–14.

33 Schacter, *Searching for Memory*, 15–97; and also see Schacter, *The Seven Sins*

of Memory: How the Mind Forgets and Remembers (Boston and New York, 2001).

34 Cubitt, *History and Memory*, 68.

35 David Lowenthal, *The Past Is a Foreign Country* (Cambridge, 1995), 194–7.

36 Schacter, *Searching for Memory*, 88-90. Cubitt calls these types of memories 'declarative'and 'episodic.' He defines the former as 'involving the conscious retention or retrieval of data in the form of information that can be articulated.' Episodic memories are those which involve specific events and in which the individual is personally involved. Cubitt, *History and Memory*, 68.

37 A. Irving Halowell, 'Temporal Orientation in Western Civilization and in Pre-Literate Society,' *American Anthropologist* 39 (1937), 666–7.

38 Wicken, 'Mi'kmaq Treaty Tradition,' 157, 159.

39 Cubitt, *History and Memory*, 68.

40 Cubitt, *History and Memory*, 73-4.

41 For a fuller explanation of the trial, see Ken Coates, *The Marshall Decision and Native Rights* (Montreal, 2000), 3–7; Wicken, *Mi'kmaq Treaties on Trial*, 4–13.

42 For a short summary of the principal decisions preceding Marshall, see Coates, *The Marshall Decision*, 83–91.

43 *R. v. Marshall, Canadian Native Law Reporter* 4 (1999), 167–81. The literature on the Marshall case is extensive. See Thomas Isaac, *Aboriginal and Treaty Rights in the Maritimes: The Marshall Decision and Beyond* (Saskatoon, 2001).

44 Peter B. Doeringer and David Terkla, *Troubled Waters: Economic Structure, Regulatory Reform, and Fisheries Trade* (Toronto, 1995), 43–6, 68–75; Anthony Davis (with Leonard Kasdan), 'Modernization in Digby Neck and the Islands,' in Richard Apostle and Gene Barrett, eds., *Emptying Their Nets: Small Capital and Rural Industrialization in the Nova Scotia Fishing Industry* (Toronto, 1984), 168–93.

45 Doeringer and Terkla, *Troubled Waters*, 21–2; Davis, 'Modernization in Digby Neck,' 186: Table 36.

46 For an analysis of the conflict see Coates, *The Marshall Decision*, 135–50.

47 This statement is based on my personal observation when I was doing research for the Royal Commission of Aboriginal Peoples in 1993, while an employee of the Aboriginal Title Project from 1993–94 and later, in other court-related appearances from 1994 to 2001.

48 Some examples from the late nineteenth and early twentieth centuries regarding American court cases include: James E. Goodman, *Stories of Scottsboro* (New York, 1994); Walter Hixson, *Murder, Culture and Injustice: Four Sensational Cases in American History* (Akron, 2000); Suzanne Lesbock, *A*

Murder in Virginia (New York, 2003); David E. Stannard, *Honor Killing: Race, Rape, and Clarence Darrow's Spectacular Last Case* (New York, 2006).

49 Case examinations include Patrick Brode, *Death in the Queen City: Clara Ford on Trial, 1895* (Toronto, 2005); Ken S. Coates and William R. Morrison, *Strange Things Done: Murder in Yukon History* (Vancouver, 2004); Martin L. Friedland, *The Case of Valentine Shortis: A True Story of Crime and Politics in Canada* (Toronto, 1986); Richard Kramer and Tom Mitchell, *Walk Towards the Gallows: The Tragedy of Hilda Blake, Hanged 1899* (Toronto, 2002). Much of the literature that focuses on aboriginal people tends to centre on the legal issues the cases illustrate. For example, Hamar Foster, 'The Queen's Law is Better than Yours: International Homicide in Early British Columbia,' in Jim Philips, ed., *Essays in the History of Canadian Law, Volume V: Crime and Criminal Justice* (Toronto, 1995), 41–111.

50 Shelagh Grant, *Arctic Justice: On Trial for Murder, Pond Inlet, 1923* (Montreal and Kingston, 2002).

51 NSARM, RG 38/15, doc. 41, Inverness County, The King vs. Gabriel Sylyboy, November 1927, Nova Scotia Magistrate's Court.

52 See Wicken, 'Mi'kmaq Treaty Tradition,' 157–61. Another typescript copy is in Ruth Holmes Whitehead, *The Old Man Told Us: Excerpts from Micmac History, 1500–1900* (Halifax, 1991), 327–30. The original copy of the judge's notes is in NSARM, RG 38 (Inverness County), vol. 16: 1916-29.

1 Accounting for Alex Gillis's Actions

1 Coates and Morgan, *Heroines and History*; Nelles, *The Art of Nation-Building*; Pope, *The Many Landfalls of John Cabot*.

2 den Otter, *The Philosophy of Railroads*, 23, 31.

3 NSARM, RG 20/823, file McH-McM 67, Knight to J.D. McKenzie, 11 May 1922; RG 20/827 file #40, J.A. Edwards to Knight, 4 December, 1924.

4 NSARM, RG 38/15, doc. 41, Inverness County, The King vs. Gabriel Sylyboy, November 1927, Nova Scotia Magistrate's Court. A sample copy of the warrant to be used on this occasion is in 11-12 Geo V Cap 2, 'An Act to Consolidate the Acts for the Preservation of Game and the Protection of Woods against Fires,' 28 May 1921, Form D.

5 Tina Loo, *States of Nature: Conserving Canada's Wildlife in the Twentieth Century.* (Vancouver, 2006), 16–21.

6 Some examples include Edward Ives, *George Magoon and the Down East Game War* (Urbana, 1988); Louis S. Hunter, *The Hunter's Game: Poachers and Conservationists in Twentieth-Century America* (New Haven and London, 1997); Karl Jacoby, *Crimes Against Nature: Squatters, Poachers, Thieves, and the Hidden His-*

tory of American Conservation (Berkeley, 2001); on native resistance to wildlife conservation, John Sandlos, *Hunters at the Margin: Native People and Wildlife Conservation in the Northwest Territories* (Vancouver, 2007).

7 NSARM, RG 20/826, file 28, C.C. Burrell to J.A. Knight, 29 May 1925.

8 NSARM, RG 20/820, file 45, C.C. Burrell to J.A. Knight, 20 February 1922.

9 These letters can be found in Lands and Forests files of RG 20, vols. 820–828, which covers the period of 1921 to 1926. Records from before this date are not extant.

10 Bill Parenteau and Richard W. Judd, 'More Buck for the Bang: Sporting and the Ideology of Fish and Game Management in Northern New England and the Maritime Provinces, 1870–1900,' in Stephen J. Hornsby and John G. Reid, eds., *New England and the Maritime Provinces: Connections and Comparisons*, (Montreal and Kingston, 2005), 233–40.

11 Warren, *The Hunter's Game*, 60.

12 Loo, *States of Nature*, 16–17.

13 37 Vic Cap 13, s 1 & 7, 'An Act for the Preservation of Useful Birds and Animals,' 7 May 1874.

14 2 Geo V Cap 19, s 38 (1),'An Act to Amend and Consolidate the Acts for the Preservation of Game,' 3 May 1912; 16-17 Geo V Cap 4, s 143, 'An Act Respecting Lands and Forests,' 4 March 1926; 17-18 Geo V, Cap 55, s 115 (1) (f), 'An Act to Amend Chapter 4, Acts of 1926, "The Lands and Forests Act,"' 11 March 1927. For a fuller history of wildlife legislation in Nova Scotia, see Gillian S. Allen, 'Laws, Logs and Lumber: A History of Forest Legislation,' M.A. thesis, Saint Mary's University, 1993, 117–30.

15 Mr Keefe and Mr Cooper, 4 March 1902 in *Debates and Proceedings of the House of Assembly during the First Session of the Thirty-Third Parliament of the Province of Nova Scotia 1902* (Halifax, 1902), 73–4

16 Parenteau and Judd, 'More Buck for the Bang,' 245–6.

17 Game Commissioners' Report, 30 September 1915, in *JPHANS*, Session 1916, Part II, Appendix 24, 9; and Game Commissioners' Report, in *JPHANS*, Session 1917, Part II, Appendix 24, 9. For the year ending 30 September 1916, $1,730.80 was spent on warden service and expenses while for the year ending 30 September 1914, $3,152.39 was spent. Throughout these years, the annual government appropriation stayed steady at $1,500. The difference was revenue generated from the sale of licenses. For 1913–14, sales amounted to $3,599.02. For 1915–16, sales were $2,390.12, a decrease of $1208.90. In 1915–16, there was $1,421.59 less spent on warden service than in 1913–14. For 1913–14, see Game Commissioners Report, JPHANS, Appendix 24, 12.

18 Game Commissioners' Report, 30 September 1918, in *JPHANS*, Session 1919, Part II, Appendix 24, 10.

19 Despite these problems, Knight's wardens brought several poachers to account, even during the 'bad' years of the war. In 1914–15, $474 was paid in fines to the commission. The following year, $699.80 was paid, and the year after $495.00. These amounts were not much different from before the war when $436.26 had been paid. These figures, however, do not always give the full picture. As Knight himself pointed out in 1909, 'we never look for much net revenue from fines. In many cases, the party goes to jail instead of paying his fine, and when the fine is paid a portion of it often goes to the person giving the information.'

20 Game Commissioner's Report, 30 September 1921, in *JPHANS*, Session 1922, Part II, Appendix 24, 20.

21 Report of the Department of Lands and Forests 1928, in *JPHANS*, Session 1929, Part II, (Halifax, 1929), 55.

22 Parenteau and Judd, 'More Buck for the Bang,' 248–50.

23 Bill Parenteau, 'Angling, Hunting and the Development of Tourism in Late Nineteenth Century Canada: A Glimpse at the Documentary Record,' *The Archivist* 117 (1998), 12.

24 Loo, *States of Nature*, 30

25 *Fishing, Shooting and Canoeing in Nova Scotia: The Summer Vacation Land of America* (Halifax, 1916), 11–12.

26 NSARM, RG 20/747, file 19, 'Licensed Guides in the Province of Nova Scotia, 1927.'

27 Mike Parker, *Guides of the North Woods: Hunting and Fishing Tales from Nova Scotia 1870–1970* (Halifax, 1990), 17–18.

28 G. P. de T. Glazebrook, *A History of Transportation in Canada*, vol. 1 (Toronto and Montreal, 1964; 1st ed 1938), 151–2.

29 Robert MacKinnon, 'Roads, Cart Tracks, and Bridle Paths: Land Transportation and the Domestic Economy of Mid-Nineteenth-Century Eastern British North America,' *Canadian Historical Review* 84 (2003); R. Blake Brown, 'Storms, Roads, and Harvest Time: Criticism of Jury Service in Pre-Confederation Nova Scotia, *Acadiensis* 36, 1 (2006), 101–3.

30 Thomas K. MacCraw, *American Business 1920-2000: How it Worked* (Wheeling, Ill., 2000), 13.

31 Donald F. Davis, 'Dependent Motorization: Canada and the Automobile to the 1930s,' *Journal of Canadian Studies* 21, 3 (1986), 120.

32 For contrasting views of the pace of motorization in one province, G.T. Bloomfield, 'I can See a Car in that Crop: Motorization in Saskatchewan, 1906–1934,' *Saskatchewan History* 37, 1 (1984), 3-24; Rod Banjtes, 'Improved

Earth: Travel on the Canadian Prairies, 1920–50,' *The Journal of Transport History* 13, 2 (1992), 115–40; on rural resistance in P.E.I.: Sasha Mullally, 'The Machine in the Garden: A Glimpse at Early Automobile Ownership on Prince Edward Island, 1917,' *The Island* 54 (Fall/Winter 2003), 16–25. References to Nova Scotia are from George MacLaren, 'Early Automobiles in Nova Scotia,' *The Nova Scotia Historical Quarterly* 4 (1974), 39, 44; on motorcar ownership in Canada, Stephen Davies, '"Reckless Walking Must be Discouraged": The Automobile Revolution and the Shaping of Modern Urban Canada to1930,' *Urban History Review* 18, 2 (1989), 124. Motor vehicle use in Nova Scotia in the 1920s and 1930s was limited to six to seven months of the year.

33 See Ian McKay, *The Quest of the Folk: Antimodernism and Cultural Selection in Twentieth Century Nova Scotia* (Montreal and Kingston, 1994).

34 Bill Parenteau, 'Care Control and Supervision: Native People in the Canadian Atlantic Salmon Fishery, 1867–1900,' *Canadian Historical Review* 79, 1 (1998), 25–6.

35 NSARM, RG 20/824, file 48, Enclosure in R. O. Parker to Knight, 7 April 1921.

36 NSARM, RG 20/823, Knight to J.A. Mulay, 23 February 1923; RG 20/824, file 48, Knight to R. V. Parker, 9 June 1921.

37 NSARM, RG 20/ 820, Blais to Knight, 14 July 1921. Mount Uniacke is now about a half hour drive inland from Halifax, along the Halifax-Windsor road.

38 NSARM, RG 20/820, Blais to Knight, 14 July 1921.

39 NSARM, RG 20/822, Earle Fulton to Knight, 12 September 1921; RG 20/777, file 9, Russell M. Mack to Dept of Forests and Lands, 24 August 1929.

40 'Report of the Department of Lands and Forests 1927' in *JPHANS*, Session 1928, Part II (Halifax, 1928), 55.

41 'Whycocomagh News,' *Inverness County Bulletin and Port Hood Greetings*, 15 September 1928.

42 Records regarding prosecutions have not been found. However, it is clear from DIA records that a number of Mi'kmaq were charged in this period. See for instance, LAC, RG 10/6743, file 420-7, Hipson to McLean, 5 February 1922 and Harris to McLean, 14 July 1923. In addition, other complaints were made to DIA officials. For instance, LAC, RG 10/7832, file 30046-1, A.H.H. Desbarres to Indian Affairs Department, 4 May 1922.

43 NSARM, RG 20/822, J.W. Hattie to Knight, 10 January 1922.

44 NSARM, RG 20/821, Noble Creelman to Knight, 14 March 1922.

45 NSARM, RG 20/747, file 19, 'Licensed Guides in the Province of Nova Scotia, 1927.'

46 Parenteau and Judd, 'More Buck for the Bang,' 242.

47 To cite a few examples of this literature, see: John McLaren, Robert Menzies, and Dorothy E. Chunn, eds., *Regulating Lives: Historical Essays on the State, Society, the Individual and the Law* (Vancouver, 2002); Carolyn Strange and Tina Loo, *Making Good: Law and Moral Regulation in Canada, 1867–1939* (Toronto, 1997); Mariana Valverde, *The Age of Light, Soap, and Water: Moral Reform in English Canada, 1885–1925* (Toronto, 1991). On the relationship between the reforms and creating mass national armies, Desmond Morton, *Fight or Pay: Soldiers Families in the Great War* (Vancouver: UBC Press, 2004), 4–5.

48 Paul Axelrod, *The Promise of Schooling: Education in Canada, 1800–1914* (Toronto, 1997); Susan E. Houston, 'Politics, Schools, and Social Change in Upper Canada,' in Michael S. Cross and Gregory S. Kealey, eds., *Pre-industrial Canada 1760–1849* (Toronto, 1996), 173–4; and on the reasons which led to compulsory school in North America and Western Europe, Pavla Miller, 'Historiography of compulsory schooling: what is the problem?' *History of Education*, 18, 2 (1989), 123–44. For one Upper Canadian perspective on the need to reform the rabble's view of British institutions, see G.M. Craig, ed., 'Comments on Upper Canada in 1836 by Thomas Carr,' *Ontario History* 47, 4 (1955), 171–9.

49 Andy Green, 'Education and State Reformation Revisited,' *Historical Studies In Education* 23, 3 (1994), 1–17.

50 Robert Nicholas Berard, 'Moral Education in Nova Scotia, 1880–1920' *Acadiensis* 14, 1 (1984), 55–62.

51 Ken Osborne, 'Public Schooling and Citizenship Education in Canada, *Canadian Ethnic Studies* 32, 1 (2000), 8–37.

52 Dorothy E. Chunn, 'Sex and Citizenship: (Hetero)Sexual Offences, Law and White Settler Society in British Columbia, 1885–1940, in Robert Adamonski, Dorothy E. Chunn and Robert Menzies, eds., *Contesting Canadian Citizenship: Historical Readings* (Peterborough, 2002), 359–60; Loo and Strange, *Making Good*, 37–43; and on a discussion of the state's influence on life in the Maritimes, Graeme Wynn, 'Ideology, Society, and State in the Maritime Colonies of British North America, 1840–1860,' in Allan Greer and Ian Radforth, eds., *Colonial Leviathan: State Formation in Mid-Nineteenth-Century Canada* (Toronto, 1992), 307–22.

53 Wicken, 'Mi'kmaq Treaty Tradition,' 157. Bernard's illiteracy is shown by his usage of an 'X' to sign his name in a letter sent to the DIA. LAC, RG 10/3103, file 307,576, Andrew Bernard, et al. to DSGIA, 21 January 1907.

54 5 Vic Cap 16 (1842), 'An Act to provide for the Instruction and Permanent Settlement of the Indians'; Marie Battiste, 'Micmac Literacy and Cognitive

Assimilation,' in Jean Barman, Yvonne Hebert and Don McCaskill, eds., *Indian Education in Canada, Volume I: The Legacy* (Vancouver, 1986), 33; L.F.S. Upton, *Micmacs and Colonists: Indian-White Relations in the Maritimes, 1713–1867* (Vancouver, 1979), 90–2.

55 Committee Report, 6 April 1844 in *JPHANS, 1844*, 163. On Mi'kmaw attendance in common schools see Abraham Gesner, 'Report on Indian Affairs,' 21 December 1847 in *JLA* (1848), Appendix no. 24, 120, 122; John W. Johnson, *Life of John Johnson* (Portland, 1861), 32; NSARM, RG 1/431, doc. 62½, Crawley to Howe, 13 February 1852.

56 NSARM, RG 1/431, doc. 121, Petition of James Paul, et al., 14 February 1861.

57 LAC, RG 10/459, Samuel Fairbanks to Hector Langevin, 20 October 1869.

58 LAC, RG 10/3103, file 307,576, Andrew Bernard et al. to DSGIA, 21 Jan 1907.

59 The problem of the conflict between municipal and federal responsibilities toward the Mi'kmaq immediately after 1867 is mentioned in LAC, RG 10/459, 46, Samuel P. Fairbanks to Hector Langevin, 20 October 1869.

60 F.A. Rand to SGIA, 21 August, 1902, *Sessional Papers*, no. 27 (1903), 70; John Lacy to SGIA, 30 June 1902, *Sessional Papers*, no. 27 (1903), 67.

61 John J.E. de Molitor to SGIA, 2 August 1897, *Sessional Papers*, no. 14 (1898), 66. The agent made similar comments in subsequent years.

62 Thomas Butler to SGIA, 30 August 1890, *Sessional Papers*, no. 18 (1891), 28.

63 Quoted in W.D. Hamilton, *The Federal Indian Day Schools of the Maritimes* (Fredericton, 1986), 27.

64 Hamilton, *The Federal Indian Day Schools*, 27.

65 Jean Barman, 'Separate and Unequal: Indian and White Girls in All Hallows School, 1884–1920,' in Jean Barman, Yvonne Hebert, and Don McCaskill, eds., *Indian Education in Canada. Volume I: The Legacy* (Vancouver, 1986), 110.

66 LAC, RG 10/459, 447, Silas Rand to Fairbanks, 31 March 1868.

67 Martha Walls, '"The Maximum, the Minimum or Something in between": The Mi'kmaq and Federal Electoral Legislation, 1899–1951,' Ph.D dissertation, University of New Brunswick, 2006, 87.

68 Barman, 'Separate and Unequal,' 110.

69 J. R. Miller, *Lethal Legacy: Current Native Controversies in Canada* (Toronto, 2004), 232–3.

70 The Tuft's Cove Day School and community was destroyed in the Halifax Explosion of 6 December 1917, and the Cow Bay School closed in 1899

as a result of the population moving off the reserve. The fate of the Sheet Harbour School is unclear. It is referred in the agent's report of 1893: D. O'Sullivan to DGSIA, 16 October 1893, *Sessional Papers* no. 14 (1894), 42.

71 The building program also reflected a shift in government policy towards building residential schools on or near reserves, which had not been true of the industrial school system.

72 Hamilton, *The Federal Indian Day Schools*, 17.

73 Totals have been calculated by adding the number of children between the ages of 6 and 15 inclusive, found in the 1881 Census and 'Census of Indians, ending 31 March 1911,' *Sessional Papers* no. 27 (1912), 26–31. A similar method has been employed for 1911, first referring to the 1911 manuscript copy of the census and then the numbers of children noted in the DIA reports. Because the federal census figures under-estimate the actual number of Mi'kmaq – a point that is covered in Chapter 6 – the actual percentages of children attending were probably slightly lower than shown here.

74 Walls, 'The Maximum, the Minimum,' Table 14, 82.

75 Walls, 'The Maximum, the Minimum,' 80–5.

76 LAC, RG 10/7936, file 32-61, pt. 1, D.K. McIntyre to J.D. Mclean, 16 November 1906; McIntyre to McLean, 22 November 1906; McIntyre to McLean, 7 December 1906.

77 *The Casket* (Antigonish), 11 November 1920, p. 12; LAC, RG 10/7934, file 32-47, pt. 1, R. H. Smith to [ ] 13 January 1919.

78 Walls, 'The Maximum, the Minimum' 162-81, 192-8.

79 Vernon, *Cape Breton Canada*, 97.

80 Harry Piers, 'Brief Account of the Micmac Indians of Nova Scotia and Their Remains,' *Proceedings of the Nova Scotia Institute of Science* (1912), 106; NSM, Harry Piers Papers, 'Micmac Indians,' 18 November 1922.

81 LAC, RG 10/7936, 32-61, pt. 1, D. H. MacAdam to Secretary, 30 June 1902. See Janet Chute, 'Frank G. Speck's Contribution to the Understanding of Mi'kmaq Land Use, Leadership, and Land Management,' *Ethnohistory* 46, 3 (1999), 508–15 for a more extensive analysis of the Grand Council but which also points out that the council assumed more importance from the mid-1800s.

82 Walls, 'The Maximum, the Minimum,' 136–7; Veronica Strong-Boag, '"The Citizenship Debates": The 1885 Franchise Act,' in Robert Adamoski, et.al., *Contesting Canadian Citizenship*, 87.

83 NSARM, RG 38, vol. 15, #41, Magistrate's Court, Port Hood, Nova Scotia, The King vs. Gabriel Sylyboy, et al., 22 November, 1927.

84 Mark S. Weiner, *Black Trials: Citizenship from the Beginnings of Slavery to the End of Caste* (New York, 2004), 12–17.

2 Why Nova Scotia Prosecuted Gabriel Sylliboy

1 NSARM, RG 20/776, file 14, Charles N. Portus to Schierbeck, 5 November 1927; and Congdon to Portus, 10 November 1927; 17-18 Geo V Cap 55, s. 124 (a), 'An Act to Amend Chapter 4, Acts of 1926, "The Lands and Forests Act."'

2 Quoted in James Marshall, *Intention: In Law and Society* (New York, 1968), 6.

3 For an explanation on criminal liability see Phil Harris, *An Introduction to Law*, 3rd ed. (London, 1988), 243–53; Oliver Wendell Holmes, *The Common Law* (Cambridge, 1963; 1st ed. 1881), 7.

4 Harris, *An Introduction to Law*, 253–4.

5 Bill Parenteau and James Kenny, 'Survival, Resistance, and the Canadian State: The Transformation of New Brunswick's Native Economy,' *Journal of the Canadian Historical Association* 13 (2003), 49–71; John G. Reid and William C. Wicken, *An Overview of the Eighteenth Century Treaties Signed Between the Mi'kmaq and Wuastukwiuk Peoples and the English Crown, 1725–1928*. Report Submitted to the Royal Commission on Aboriginal Peoples, 1996.

6 See Ernest R. Forbes, *The Maritime Rights Movement, 1919–1927: A Study in Canadian Regionalism* (Montreal and Kingston, 1979), 54–72.

7 Samuel P. Hays, *Conservation and the Gospel of Efficiency: The Progressive Conservation Movement, 1890–1920* (Pittsburgh, 1999; 1st ed. 1959), 28–35; Stephen Pyne, *Year of the Fires: The Story of the Great Fires of 1910* (New York, 2001), 30–9.

8 H.V. Nelles, *The Politics of Development: Forests, Mines, & Hydro-Electric Power in Ontario, 1849–1941* (Ottawa, 2005; 1st ed. 1973), 183–90, 199–200.

9 Schierbeck's career as chief forester is chronicled in Peter Clancy and L. Anders Sandberg, *Against the Grain: Foresters and Politics in Nova Scotia* (Vancouver, 2000), 42–64.

10 On the Big Lease, see L. Anders Sandberg, 'Forest Policy in Nova Scotia: The Big Lease, Cape Breton Island, 1899–1960, in L. Anders Sandberg, ed., *Trouble in the Woods: Forest Policy and Social Conflict in Nova Scotia and New Brunswick* (Fredericton, 1992), 68–71. A summary of Barnjum's political influence on the pulp and paper industry in the 1920s is in Bill Parenteau and L. Anders Sandberg, 'Conservation and the Gospel of Economic Nationalism: The Canadian Pulpwood Question In Nova Scotia and New Brunswick, 1918–1925,' *Environmental History Review* 19, 2 (1995), 61–5; and Thomas Roach and Richard Judd, 'A Man for All Seasons: Frank John Dixie Barnjum, Conservationist, Pulpwood Embargoist and Speculator!' *Acadiensis* 20, 2 (1991), 129–44.

11 See Doug Owram, *The Government Generation: Canadian Intellectuals and the State 1900–1945* (Toronto, 1986).

12 NSARM, RG 20/719, file 10, Annual Expenditures for Department of Lands and Forests, 1926. The exact numbers of men employed varied from year to year. For instance, for 1928, Schierbeck mentions 75 employees. See 'Report of the Department of Lands and Forests 1928' in *JPHANS*, Session 1929, *Part II* (Halifax, 1929), 65.

13 This included making the chief forester responsible for all Crown lands as well as 'for further reforestation and scientific enquiry.' Some other changes made in the management of forested lands are discussed in Allen, 'Laws, Logs and Lumber,' 59–61, 137–8.

14 NSARM, RG 20/718, file 12, Schierbeck to Douglas, 2 February 1926. For a discussion of Schierbeck's struggles with patronage, see Sandberg and Clancy, *Against the Grain*, 46, 49, and an example of a constituent asking for employment based on political affiliation, NSARM, MG 2/637, letter 32699, Rhodes Papers, James T. d'Entremont to Premier Rhodes, 22 October 1928.

15 16-17 Geo. V Cap 4, s. 98, 'An Act Respecting Lands and Forests,' 19 March 1926.

16 See Bill Parenteau and L. Anders Sandberg, 'Conservation and the Gospel of Economic Nationalism: The Canadian Pulpwood Question in Nova Scotia and New Brunswick,' *Environmental History Review* 19, 2 (1995), 78–9.

17 Forbes, *The Maritime Rights Movement*, 54–64.

18 David Frank, 'The 1920s: Class and Region, Resistance and Accommodation,' in Forbes and Muise, eds., *The Atlantic Provinces*, 242; J. Murray Beck, *Politics of Nova Scotia, 1896–1988* (Tantallon, N.S., 1988), 109.

19 Johnson, *Forests of Nova Scotia*, 141–5.

20 Sandberg and Clancy, 'Property Rights, small woodlot owners'; Parenteau and Sandberg, 'Conservation and the Gospel of Economic Nationalism,' 67.

21 Sandberg, 'Forest Policy in Nova Scotia,' 64–9.

22 NSARM, MG 1/2161, Ralph S. Johnson Papers, 'History of Woodlands,' 1–3; *Halifax Chronicle Herald*, 27 November 1979, 'Prominent Men played crucial role in growth.'

23 Sandberg and Clancy, 'Property Rights, small woodlot owners.'

24 NSARM, RG 20/777, file 29, Edmund Conway to Congdon, 7 October 1929.

25 For some examples, Return of Chief Ranger, E.H. McGregor, Colchester County, 23 December 1904, *JPHANS*, (1905), Appendix no. 9, 11. Motorcars and locomotives were an additional source of fires. The threat of locomotives was recognized in provincial legislation in the late 1800s. 'Of the Protection of Woods Against Fires,' Cap 65, s. 9-11, *The Revised Statutes of Nova Scotia, Fifth Series* (Halifax, 1884).

26 This was part of a longer trend to control forest fires. For earlier references, see 'Remarks by Hon. Mr. Longley,' *DPNSHA* (1904), 151-4; (1905), 26–8.

27 The government's stricter regulation of Crown land is suggested in various letters addressed to Schierbeck's office after 1926. See, for instance, NSARM, RG 20/774, file 32, Roland W. Corbin to Crown Land Department, 27 December 1927; RG 20/774, file 40, William Dixon to Department of Crown Lands, 27 September 1927; RG 20/777, file 2, Anonymous, 22 March 1928.

28 Quoted in Sandberg and Clancy, 'Property Rights, small woodlot owners.'

29 LAC, RG 10/6743, file 420-7, Edward Gillies to Department of Indian Affairs, 2 November 1927.

30 James Kenny and Bill Parenteau, 'Survival, Resistance, and the Canadian State: The Transformation of New Brunswick's Native Economy, 1867–1930,' *Journal of the Canadian Historical Association* 13 (2003), 57–8; Walls, 'The Maximum, the Minimum,' 53–5.

31 'Report of Robert H. Smith, Indian Agent for Colchester County,' *Sessional Papers*, no. 27 (1915), Part II, 33; 'Report of R. A. Harris, Indian Agent for Digby County,' 34; 'Report of Alonzo Wallace, Indian Agent for Shubenacadie Agency, 35; 'Report of Rev. Donald MacPherson, Indian Agent for Inverness County, 35; 'Report of Rev. R. L. McDonald, Indian Agent for Richmond County,' 37.

32 Catherine Parr Traill, *The Backwoods of Canada* (Ottawa, 1997), 120–1.

33 C. Bruce Fergusson, ed., *Uniacke's Sketches of Cape Breton and Other Papers Relating to Cape Breton Island* (Halifax, 1958), 108.

34 On Mi'kmaw baskets, see Ruth Holmes Whitehead, *Micmac Quillwork: Micmac Indian Techniques of Porcupine Quill Decoration, 1600–1950* (Halifax, 1982).

35 The Starr Manufacturing Company was better known for its Acme self-fastening skates, railway and ship spikes, carriage axles, and rotary saw mill machinery. In 1909, the company employed 120 to 200 people. NSARM, MG 100/233: #15.

36 *The Globe* (Toronto), 17 November 1909, 9.

37 Annual Report of the Department of Indian Affairs for the Year Ended March 31 1922, *Sessional Papers, no. 14*, (1923), 28.

38 Significantly the agent called their products the Micmac hockey stick. Alonzo Wallace to SGIA, *Sessional Papers*, no. 27 (1904), 73. Other references on the making of hockey sticks, Lauire C.C. Stanley-Blackwell and R.A. MacLean, *Historic Antigonish: Town and County* (Halifax, 2004), 54.

39 NSARM, RG 39, Halifax County -Supreme Court Records, Series D, vol. 9, B-69a, Newall v. Newall, 1908.

40 Chisholm to SGIA, 29 July 1882, *Sessional Papers*, no. 5 (1883), 27.
41 Walls, 'The Maximum, the Minimum,' 57–9.
42 NSARM, Photographs, J.A. Irvine, Album 35, no. 29, www.gov.ns.ca/nsarm/virtual/irvine/archives.
43 LAC, RG 10/3160, file 363,417-1, H.S. Trefry to DIA, 20 December 1924; 'The Micmac artisans of 60 years ago in camps near Truro,' *Inverness County Bulletin*, 8 October 1927. Two merchants in the Truro area bought these items, Charles Marsh and later Robert Stewart of North River.
44 Roderick MacDonald to SGIA, 1 October 1891, *Sessional Papers*, no. 14 (1892), 42. For instance, LAC, RG 10/7758, file 27048, part 1, J.D. McLean to R.A. Rand, 2 April 1901; LAC, RG 14, D2, vol. 23, 12 Parliament, 7th Session, Unpublished Sessional Papers, no. 157, Hearing before the Court of the Exchequer, Sydney, Nova Scotia, 18 January to 20 September 1917, 333.
45 Charles E. McManus to SGIA, 14 August 1905, *Sessional Papers*, no. 27 (1906), 66; A.J. Boyd to Frank Pedley, 30 April 1912, *Sessional Papers*, no. 27 (1913), 65; Report of R.A. Harris, *Sessional Paper*, no. 27 (1915), 34.
46 In her overview of the Mi'kmaw economy in Atlantic Canada, Martha Walls uses such occuapational descriptions to show the relative importance of coopering and basketmaking in 1901, although she does not compare the data with earlier or later censuses to illustrate changes in household economies. Walls, 'The Maximum and the Minimum,' 55.
47 For the continued dependence on basketmaking in the early 1900s, see Colchester Historical Society, *Historic Colchester: Towns & Countryside* (Halifax, 2000), 12; Mike Parker, *Historic Annapolis Valley: Rural Life Remembered* (Halifax, 2006), 21; Tom Sheppard, *Historic Wolfville: Grand Pre and Countryside* (Halifax, 2003), x; Brian Tennyson and Wilma Stewart-White, *Historic Mahone Bay* (Halifax, 2006), 10; Garth Vaughan, *Historic Windsor* (Halifax, 2006), 114.
48 Roderick MacDonald to SGIA, 28 September 1897, *Sessional Papers*, no. 14 (1898), 64.
49 Bunny McBride, *Our Lives in Our Hands: Micmac Indian Basketmakers* (Halifax, 1990), 10.
50 LAC, RG 10/7934, file 32-47-Part 1, R. Kennedy to McLean, 16 February 1925; NSARM, MG 1/2868 #2, Clara Dennis Notebooks, Interview with Gabriel Sylliboy, [1928], 15.
51 However, the Mi'kmaq could not cut timber for sale. They could only cut wood for manufacture. This, of course, would not have included turning timber into pulp. LAC, RG 10/7833, file 30052-2, Part II, J.D. McLean to Chief Peter L. Paul of Dartmouth, 2 October 1912. Despite this, some communities seem to have regularly cut and sold reserve timber. RG 10/7832,

file 30046-1, Frank Prosper et al. to Department of Indian Affairs, 4 May 1913.

52 'Report of W.H. Walen, Indian Agent for Yarmouth County, *Sessional Papers* no. 27 (1915), Part II, 38.

53 NSARM, MG 100/234, doc. 24, G.G. Campbell, 'History in a Valley,' 2–3.

54 Complaints from outside Colchester and Halifax counties regarding Mi'kmaw squatters can be found in LAC, RG 20/7758, file 27048, part 1, W.A. Hendry to J.D. McLean, 16 July 1899; J. D. Mclean to F.A. Rand, 1 April 1902.

55 Beck, *Politics of Nova Scotia*, 63.

56 LAC, RG 10/6823, file 494-16-5, Part I, D. Sullivan, Mi'kmaq in District 5, 15 February 1894. Windsor Junction is near the present day suburb of Sackville, Nova Scotia, now part of the Halifax Regional Municipality.

57 NSARM, RG 38, Series J, vol. 40, Halifax County Court Records, Evidence Books, The King v. Louis Newall, 9 January 1902, 221–7; 1901 Census, Nova Scotia, Halifax County, Sackville (Windsor Junction), p. 15, line 28.

58 1901 Census, Halifax County, Sackville, Hammonds Plains, Spry Harbour. The Department of Indian affairs counted 51 Mi'kmaq, which under-represents the total counted by federal enumerators. The difference may be due to a higher number present on the day the census was taken. 'Census of Nomadic and Resident Indians,' *Sessional Papers*, no. 11 (Ottawa, 1902), 156.

59 LAC, RG 10/3160, file 363,417-1, H.J. Bury to Deputy Minister of the Interior, 23 April 1919.

60 LAC, RG 10/3119, file 327,352, Jerry Lone Cloud to J.D. McLean, 17 July 1916.

61 NSARM, RG 38, 1993-031/001, A-5154, Lunenburg County Supreme Court, Langille v. Millet, 1918.

62 Susanna Moodie, *Roughing it in the Bush or, Forest Life in Canada* (Toronto, 2000), 297, [Bell and Cockburn edition, 1913].

63 LAC, RG 10/3160, file 363,417-1, Boyd to McLean, 20 April 1918; Daniel Chisholm to McLean, 29 July 1918.

64 LAC, RG 10/3160, file 363,417-1, H.J. Bury to Scott, 21 February 1919.

65 LAC, RG 10/3160, file 363,417-1, McLean to Musgrave, 15 February 1918; Musgrave to McLean, 1 March 1918.

66 LAC, RG 10/3160, file 363,417-1, Bury to Scott, 21 February 1919.

67 LAC, RG 10/3160, file 363,417-1, R.W. McKenzie to Department of Indian Affairs, 27 April 1923.

68 LAC, RG 10/7832, file 30,045, Part 1, P.V. Doyle to DIA, 25 January 1928. This is one of many complaints about the Mi'kmaq in this locality. Other

instances are in RG 10/7832, file 30045, Part I, Hoyt to McLean, 28 January 1918.

69 LAC, RG 10/7759, file 27052-4, Frank Pedley to Nova Scotia Commissioner of Crown Lands, 1 September 1908.

70 LAC, RG 10/7758, file 27048, part 1, Bessie Vieth to Minister of the Interior, 18 March 1901.

71 LAC, RG 10/7832, file 30046-1, A.H.H. DesBarres to DIA, 4 May 1922.

72 LAC, RG 10/3160, file 363,417-1, H. Smith to R.H. Kennedy, 20 December 1923.

73 LAC, RG 10/3160, file 363,417-1, A.J. Boyd to Scott, 9 February 1918.

74 LAC, RG 10/3220, file 536,764-1, Bury to Deputy Minister of the Interior, 23 January 1924.

75 LAC, RG 10/3160, file 363,417-1, Bury to Deputy Minister, 23 April 1919.

76 LAC, RG 10/3119, file 327,352, Census of Indians living at Elmsdale, 1919; RG 10/3160, file 363417-1, Bury to Deputy Minister of the Interior, 23 April 1919. A later letter notes that the homes were lost to fire and not from government action. LAC, RG 10/3119, file 327,352, Bury to DSGIA, 22 November 1926.

77 LAC, RG 10/3119, file 327,352, Petition of Mi'kmaq, 1901; RG 10/3119, file 327,352, A. J. Boyd to J.D. McLean, 16 November 1926; Petition of Mi'kmaq at Elmsdale to H.J. Bury, 21 June 1919.

78 LAC, RG 10/3220, file 536,764, Petition of Halifax County Mi'kmaq, 18 August 1919; Bury to Deputy Minister, 9 January 1920; Petition of Michael Tom and Stephen Knockwood, 21 April 1920.

79 For instance, see F.A. Rand to SGIA, 11 July 1902, *Sessional Papers* no. 27 (1903), 69.

80 NSARM, RG 20/718, file 16, N.J. Beatty to Otto Schierbeck, 30 September 1926.

81 NSARM, RG 20/719, file 53, E.B. Ritchie to H.L. Fenerty, 13 July 1926.

82 David Frank, 'The 1920s: Class and Region, Resistance and Accommodation' in E.R. Forbes and D.A. Muise, eds., *The Atlantic Provinces in Confederation* (Toronto, 1988), 245; Martin V. Melosi, *Coping with Abundance: Energy and Environment in Industrial America* (Philadelphia, 1985), 138–47.

83 See Ernest R. Forbes, *The Maritime Rights Movement*, 38–72.

3 Moving to Appeal

1 NSARM, RG 38/15, doc. 41, Inverness County, The King vs. Gabriel Sylyboy, November 1927, Nova Scotia Magistrate's Court.

2 NSARM, RG 38/16, 1916-29, Inverness County, The King vs. Sylyboy, July 1928, Nova Scotia County Court.

3 John G. Reid and Wiliam C. Wicken, 'An Overview of the Eighteenth Century Treaties Signed Between the Mi'kmaq and Wuastukwiuk Peoples and the English Crown, 1725–1928.' Report Submitted to the Royal Commission on Aboriginal Peoples, 1996; Bill Parenteau and Jim Kenny, 'Survival, Resistance, and the Canadian State,' 67–70.

4 LAC, RG 10/6743, file 420-7, 'At a council of the Indians held on the Bear River Reserve on Feb. 9th 1897.'

5 LAC, RG 10/6743, file 420-7, Robert Logan to DGSIA, 19 February 1903.

6 LAC, RG 10/6743, file 420-7, Petition of Mi'kmaq from Lequille, March 1906.

7 LAC, RG 10/6743, file 420-7, Charles Beckwith to SGIA, 5 March 1906.

8 LAC, RG 10/6743, file 420-7, Scott to Matthews, 10 September 1914; and Matthews to Scott, 14 September 1914.

9 LAC, RG 10/6743, file 420-7, Matthew Francis to SGIA, 30 May 1921.

10 LAC, RG 10/6743, file 420-7, William Paul and Matthew Francis to DSIA, 10 October 1921.

11 LAC, RG 10/6743, file 420-7, Petition of Mi'kmaq of Nova Scotia, 31 October 1921.

12 LAC, RG 10/6743, file 420-7, 'Indians Claim Right to Hunt as They Please,' [November 1922].

13 This is evident from newspaper articles from the 1920s, which published copies of the 1752 treaty or talked about the treaties. For example: *The Casket* (Antigonish), 9 November 1922, 11 January 1923, and 13 December 1928; 'The Micmacs of Canada,' *Inverness County Bulletin*, 6 August 1927, 2.

14 C.W. Vernon, *Cape Breton Canada at the Beginning of the Twentieth Century: A Treatise of Natural Resources and Development* (Toronto, 1903), 98.

15 See James (sakej) Youngblood Henderson, 'Mi'kmaq Tenure in Atlantic Canada,' *Dalhousie Law Journal* 18, 2 (1995), 237–41; Wicken, *Mi'kmaq Treaties*, 55–7, 76–7.

16 Archives de Séminaire de Québec, Universitée 305, no. 42B, 'Collier d'amitée des chief Mohawks du Sault St. Louis aux sauvuages micmack de Ristigouche'; Rimouski, ANQR, Fonds Capucins, contain transcripts of meetings dating from the 1850s with the Mohawk, at least one which is in Mi'kmaq. A photograph of Alek holding a wampum belt, presumably the one he mentions to Dennis, is in William Dennis Collection, P113/73.180.624/N-6107 and is reproduced in Wicken, *Mi'kmaq Treaties on Trial*, 223.

17 NSARM, MG 1/2868, #2, Clara Dennis Notebooks, Transcribed by Ruth Holmes Whitehead and Trudy Sable, 1992; Clara Dennis, *Cape Breton Over* (Toronto, 1942), 51.

18 Wicken, 'Mi'kmaq Treaty Tradition,' 157–9.

19 Wicken, 'Mi'kmaq Treaty Tradition,' 157–9.

20 Wicken, 'Mi'kmaq Treaty Tradition,' 157.

21 For one interpretation of the 1752 Treaty, see Wicken, *Mi'kmaq Treaties on Trial*, 182–8.

22 E. Brian Titley, *A Narrow Vision: Duncan Campbell Scott and the Administration of Indian Affairs in Canada* (Vancouver, 1986), 59.

23 LAC, RG 10/6743, file 420-7, Colin MacKenzie to J.D. McLean, 15 November 1927.

24 LAC, RG 10/6743, file 420-7, J.D. McLean to Colin MacKenzie, 21 November 1927.

25 LAC, RG 10/6743, file 420-7, F. McDormand to Hayter Reed 15 August 1894; and Reed to McDormand, 27 September 1894.

26 LAC, RG 10/6743, file 420-7, Hayter Reed to F. McDormand, 18 March 1897.

27 LAC, RG 10/6743, file 420-7, J.D. McLean to Charles E. Beckwith, 16 March 1906.

28 NSARM, RG 20/821, file 24, Knight to A.H. DesBarres, 4 October 1922. Much of this letter had first been sent to R.S. McKay earlier in the year. RG 20/823, file 67, Knight to R.S. McKay, 5 June 1922.

29 LAC, RG 10/6743, file 420-7, J.D. McLean to B.A. Harris, 25 July 1923.

30 Patterson, 'Indian-White Relations in Nova Scotia, 1749–61,' 43–8.

31 James Oldham, *English Common Law in the Age of Mansfield* (Chapel Hill and London, 2004), 79–85.

32 On the importance of the Protestant faith in influencing Parliament's actions, see Linda Colley, *Britons: Forging a Nation, 1707–1837* (New Haven and London, 1992), 18–30.

33 J.P. Kenyon, *The Stuarts: A Study in English Kingship* (London, 1977; 1st ed., 1958).

34 James Muldoon, 'Discovery, Grant, Charter, Conquest or Purchase: John Adams on the Legal Basis for English Possession of North America,' in Christopher L. Tomlins and Bruce H. Mann, eds., *The Many Legalities of Early America* (Chapel Hill and London, 2001), 28–31; Woody Holton, *Forced Founders: Indians, Debtors, Slaves & the Making of the American Revolution in Virginia* (Chapel Hill, 1999), 6–9; Anthony F.C. Wallace, *Jefferson and the Indians: The Tragic Fate of the First Americans* (Cambridge, 1999), 21–49; Linda Colley, *Captives: Britain, Empire and the World 1600–1850* (New York, 2002), 233–4.

35 Peter Charles Hoffer, *Law and People in Colonial America*, revised edition (Baltimore and London, 1998), 50–75.

36 Peter Karsten, *Between Law and Custom: 'High' and 'Low' Legal Cultures in the Lands of the British Diaspora – The United States, Canada, Australia, and New Zealand, 1600–1900* (Cambridge, 2002), 100–2. This issue is discussed in

more detail in L.F.S. Upton, *Micmacs and Colonists: Indian-White Relations in the Maritimes, 1713–1867* (Vancouver, 1979), 61–78.

37 For one view of the BNA Act, which stresses a dichotomous intepretation, see John Rohr, 'Current Canadian Constitutionalism and the 1865 Confederation Debates,' *American Review of Canadian Studies* 28, 4 (Winter 1998), 41. Also see Christopher Armstrong, *The Politics of Federalism: Ontario's Relations with the Federal Government, 1867–1942* (Toronto, 1981); Norman McI. Rogers, 'The Genesis of Provincial Rights,' *Canadian Historical Review* 14,1 (1933), 9–23; Peter H. Russell, *Constitutional Odyssey: Can Canadians Become a Sovereign People?* (Toronto, 1993), 34–42; Paul Romney, *Getting it Wrong: How Canadians Forgot their Past and Imperilled Confederation* (Toronto, 1999), 33–108.

38 British North America Act, 1867, Section 91 (24), in Derek Smith, ed., *Canadian Indians and the Law: Selected Documents, 1663–1972* (Toronto, 1975), 63. The best example of conflict over Indian land is the *St. Catherine's Milling* case, which came before the Judicial Committee of the Privy Council in 1888. See Harring, *White Man's Law*, 126–47.

39 'Remarks by Mr. Dickey and Attorney-General,' *Debates and Proceedings of the House of Assembly (Nova Scotia), 1870* (Halifax, 1870), 13.

40 A general overview of the issue is discussed in Titley, *A Narrow Vision*, 51–6.

41 LAC, RG 13/A-2, vol. 178, file 1913–589, Memorandum for the Deputy Minister of Justice, 27 August 1913. Also see *R. v. Edward Jim, British Columbia Reports*, vol. XXII (1915), 106–8 on how the courts interpreted the issue of hunting on reserve lands.

42 Anthony J. Hall, 'The St. Catherine's Milling and Lumber Company versus the Queen: Indian Land Rights as a Factor in Federal-Provincial Relations in Nineteenth-Century Canada,' in Kerry Abel and Jean Friesen, eds., *Aboriginal Resource Use in Canada: Historical and Legal Aspects* (Winnipeg, 1991), 269–80.

43 Titley, *A Narrow Vision*, 56.

44 LAC, RG 10/6743, file 420-7, D. C. Scott to Premier Rhodes, 24 March 1928.

45 LAC, RG 10/6743, file 420-7, Scott to Colin MacKenzie, 21 March 1928.

46 LAC, RG 10/6743, file 420-7, Scott to W. Stuart Edward (Deputy Minister of Justice), 22 March 1928; and Edward to Scott, 22 March 1928.

4 Parents, Grandparents, and Great-Grandparents, 1794–1853

1 Daniel L. Schacter, *Searching for Memory: The Brain, the Mind, and the Past* (New York, 1996), 39–71, 101–4. Quote from 45–6; also see Cubitt, *History and Memory*, 81–2.

2 The following relies on the models discussed in Linda Colley, *Captives: Britain, Empire, and the World, 1600–1850* (New York, 2002); Catherine Hall, *Civilising Subjects: Metropole and Colony in the English Imagination 1830–1867* (Chicago, 2002).

3 Andrew Alek: the 1881 census lists Thomas as 52 and Mary as 49. Canada, 1881 Census, Nova Scotia, Richmond County, Red Islands, p. 30, lines 10–11; Christmas: 1871 Census, Nova Scotia, Cape Breton County, Christmas Island, p. 3, lines 1 and 2.

4 See for instance, J.R. Miller, *Compact, Contract, Covenant: Aboriginal Treaty-Making in Canada* (Toronto, 2009).

5 Stuart Banner, *How the Indians Lost Their Land: Law and Power on the Frontier* (Cambridge, 2005); and on the manipulative ways that New York state imposed land surrender agreements on Houdenosaunee peoples after the American Revolution, Alan Taylor, *The Divided Ground: Indians, Settlers, and the Northern Borderland of the American Revolution* (New York, 2006), 142–202.

6 J.M. Bumsted, '1763–1783: Resettlement and Rebellion,' in Phillip A. Buckner and John G. Reid, eds., *The Atlantic Region to Confederation: A History* (Toronto and Fredericton, 1994), 158.

7 Gary M. Walton and James F. Shepherd, *The Economic Rise of Early America* (London, 1979), 64–79; John G. Reid, Pax Brittanica or Pax Indigena? Planter Nova Scotia (1760–1782), and Competing Strategies of Pacification,' *Canadian Historical Review* 85, 4 (2004), 669–92.

8 NSARM, RG 1/430, doc. 23 ½; Upton, *Micmacs and Colonists*, 82–3.

9 Upton, *Micmacs and Colonists*, 80–97, but esp. 80.

10 This statement comes from a reading of Frank Speck's writing, principally, 'The Family Hunting Band as the Basis of Algonkian Social Organization,' *American Anthropologist* (1915), 189–205.

11 LAC, MG 23, G11-19, vol. 3: 1051-3, Monk Papers.

12 In the petition, Jean Baptiste's last name is spelt 'Elexey.' Elsewhere, the family name is spelt 'Alexey,' Alexis, and Alexander. To avoid confusion, I have standardized the spelling and used 'Alexey' throughout. The various spellings that might be attached to Mi'kmaw names are in Ruth Holmes Whitehead, *The Old Man Told Us: Excerpts from Micmac History, 1500–1950* (Halifax, 1991).

13 NSARM, RG 20, A/88, Elexey, John Baptist, Petition to Sir James Kempt, 6 May 1823.

14 NSARM, RG 1/168:155, William Campbell to Francis Alexis, 22 June 1771.

15 See Roland Wright, 'The Public Right of Fishing, Government Fishing

Policy, and Indian Fishing Rights in Upper Canada,' *Ontario History* 86, 4 (1994), 337–8.

16 See Gary Kulick, 'Dams, Fish, and Farmers: Defense of Public Rights in Eighteenth-Century Rhode Island,' in Steven Hahn and Jonathan Prude, eds., *The Countryside in the Age of Capitalist Transformation: Essays in the Social History of Rural America* (Chapel Hill, 1985), 28–9.

17 The court was the local administrative and judicial body whose duties included overseeing minor civil and criminal matters, establishing tax rates and setting laws regarding the fishery. Sitting on the court were the local justices of the peace who met two to four times annually. C.B. Fergusson, 'Local Government in Nova Scotia,' *Bulletin of the Public Archives of Nova Scotia*, no. 17 (Halifax, 1961).

18 NSARM, MG 1/184, doc. 220, Chipman Papers, Kings County, General Sessions of the Peace, June 1791.

19 NSARM, RG 34-324, Record of Sessions, Shelburne County, Yarmouth and Argyle District, 1789–1816, April Term 1791, Regulations for Tusket River.

20 LAC, MG 23-G11-19/3, 819, Monk to Wentworth, 17 November 1793; MG 23 – G11-19/3: 299, Deschamps to Monk, 4 November 1793.

21 LAC, MG 23-G11-19/3, Daniel Hammill to Monk, 13 January 1794.

22 Upton, *Micmacs and Colonists*, 83–4.

23 On equating Protestantism with loyalty and Catholicism with disloyalty, see Linda Colley, *Britons: Forging the Nation 1707–1837* (New Haven and London, 1992), 11–53.

24 LAC, MG 23, G11-19/3, 1046-7, George Henry Monk Letterbook, 10 December 1793, Windsor.

25 LAC, MG 23, G11-19/3, Monk Letterbook, 12 January 1794.

26 NSARM, RG 1/430.

27 Mi'kmaw responses to the American rebellion are detailed in William C. Wicken, 'The 1778 and 1779 Treaties,' Report Submitted to the Mi'gmawei Mawoimi Secretariat (2006), and in Stephen E. Patterson, 'Indian-White Relations in Nova Scotia, 1749–61.' Also see Ernest Clarke, *The Siege of Fort Cumberland: An Episode of the American Revolution* (Montreal and Kingston, 1995), 73–5.

28 The term and idea of the 'thin red line' comes from Linda Colley, *Captives*. This view of the Mi'kmaw position in Nova Scotia, and particularly in relation to the Mi'kmaq in the 1790s approximates the views of John G. Reid, 'Empire, the Maritime Colonies, and the Supplanting of Mi'kma'ki/Wulstuikwik, 1780–1820,' *Acadiensis* 38, 2 (Summer/Autumn 2009), 92–3.

29 Douglas Hay, 'Property, Authority and the Criminal Law,' in Douglas Hay et al., *Albion's Fatal Tree: Crime and Society in Eighteenth-Century England* (New

York, 1975), 17–63. On the resuscitation of the Crown as symbol in British politics during King George III's reign from 1760 to 1821, see Colley, *Britons*, 195–236.

30 A recent examination of this issue is Jack P. Greene, ed., *Exclusionary Empire: English Liberty Overseas, 1600–1900* (Cambridge, 2010).

31 Colley, *Britons*, 43–54; Colley, *Captives*, 303.

32 Generally, see Catherine Hall, *Civilizing Subjects: Metropole and Colony in the English Imagination 1830–1867* (Chicago and London, 2002), 86–115. Regarding Upper Canada, this is a subject that is at the heart of the discussion of educational reform. See, for instance, Alison Prentice, *The School Promoters: Education and Social Class in Mid-Nineteenth Century Upper Canada* (Toronto, 1977), 25–87; and on the Methodist movement in Upper Canada among aboriginal people, Donald B. Smith, *Sacred Feathers: The Reverend Peter Jones (Kahkewaquonaby) and the Mississauga Indians* (Toronto and London, 1987), esp. 34–83.

33 NSARM, RG 34-324, Records of Session, Yarmouth and Argyle District, County of Shelburne, 1789–1816, April term 1800, 1.

34 NSARM, RG 1/430, doc. 117, John Wentworth to Michael Wallace, 28 September 1802.

35 NSARM, RG 34-324, Records of Session, Yarmouth and Argyle District, County of Shelburne, 1789–1816, April term, 1803, p. 1.

36 AN, AC, C11D/4, 85v, 'Memoire des coste de l'acadie, 12 octobre 1701; AC, C11D/10, 'Sur l'acadie,' [1748), [n.p. 4 of 6].

37 Bromley wrote in 1820 that 'You will scarcely meet an Indian but who will tell you that he has cleared and cultivated land some time or other, but that the white men have taken it from him. A Chief told me a few weeks ago, that his father had cleared no less than 200 acres in different parts of the province; but that he had been dispossessed of the whole by the white people.' Walter Bromley, *An Account of the Aborigines of Nova Scotia called the Micmac Indians* (London, 1822), 9–10. On Bromley, see Judith Fingard, 'English Humanitarianism and the Colonial Mind: Walter Bromley in Nova Scotia, 1813–1825,' *Canadian Historical Review* 54 (1973), 125–51.

38 Sharon Block, 'Coerced Sex in British North America, 1700–1820,' Ph.D. dissertation, Princeton University, 1998, 3.

39 Constance Backhouse, 'Nineteenth Canadian Rape Law 1800–92,' in David Flaherty, ed., *Essays in the History of Canadian Law*, vol. II (Toronto, 1983), 204.

40 Block, 'Coerced Sex in British North America,' 138–40.

41 NSARM, RG 34-324, Record of Sessions, Yarmouth and Argyle District, County of Shelburne, 1789–1816, October term, 1807, p. 1. The Vander

Horns lived at Tusket Village on the Tusket River. See Dartmouth, Department of Crowns, Lands and Forests, Yarmouth County Portfolio, doc. 5, Plan of Tusket Village, 1809. The incident involving Jane Alexey was not the only case of assault on a Mi'kmaw woman. In 1815 John Oxley of Cumberland County was indicted for an 'assault' on Molly Tommy who, like the Alexeys, lived on land at the centre of a dispute between local Mi'kmaq and English settlers. NSARM, RG 34-308, Cumberland County, Quarter Sessions, 1808–1833, 31 October 1815, p. 2, The King v. John W. Oxley and John C. Simmon.

42 Susan Brownmiller, *Against Their Will: Men, Women, and Rape* (New York, 1975).

43 Susan Estrich, *Real Rape* (Cambridge, 1987), 10–15; ANQR, Capucins, Article 14, I-9, 4v, 'Kauder's Report of 1862.'

44 On English common law definitions of self-defence and its role in maintaining the King's peace see Richard Maxwell Brown, *No Duty to Retreat: Violence and Values in American History and Society* (New York, 1991).

45 NSARM, RG 20 A/81, Nichols, John, 22 January 1820; also vol. 56, Bonnell, John, 17 April 1815.

46 For instance, John While said he and his sons were 'faithful loyal subjects attached to the British government.' NSARM, RG 20 A/95, While, John, 6 March 1826.

47 Donald Harman Akenson, *The Irish in Ontario: A Study in Rural History* (Kingston and Montreal, 1984), 134–8. For other examples of professed loyalty among immigrants: NSARM, RG 20, A, Corbet, John, 17 April 1815; also vol. 86, Chisolm, Alexander [1820]; NSARM, RG 20, A/68, Hadley, Henry, 1 November 1817; RG 20 A, Umlock, John, 1810.

48 H.C. Darling to Lord Dalhousie, 27 July 1828 in *British Parliamentary Papers. Correspondence and Other Papers relating to Aboriginal Tribes in British Possessions, 1834: Anthropology Aborigines,* vol. 3 (Shannon: Irish University Press Series 1969), 23.

49 See Lord Falkland, 'Memorandum Respecting the Indians of Nova Scotia,' *The Albion*, 13 August 1842, 390; Joseph Howe, 'Annual Report on Indian Affairs for the Year Ending June 30 1872,' *Sessional Papers*, no. 23 (1873), 1–2.

50 John F. Leslie, 'Commissions of Inquiry into Indian Affairs in the Canadas, 1828–1858: Evolving a Corporate Memory for the Indian Department,' M.A. thesis, Carleton University, 1984; Peter Twohig, 'Colonial Care: Medical Attendance among the Mi'kmaq of Nova Scotia,' *Canadian Bulletin of Medical History* 13, 2 (1996), 333–53; Walls, 'The Maximum, the Minimum,' 132–4.

51 NSARM, RG 1/431: 130-1, James Dawson to Joseph Howe, 19 May 1842.

52 See Julian Gwyn, *Excessive Expectations: Maritime Commerce and the Economic Development of Nova Scotia, 1740–1870* (Montreal and Kingston, 1998), 43–89.

53 Andrew Parnaby, 'The Cultural Economy of Survival: The Mi'kmaq of Cape Breton in the Mid-19th Century,' *Labour/Le Travail* 61 (Spring 2008), 83–6. On competition from poor settlers for wildlife and furs, see Julian Gwyn, 'The Mi'kmaq, Poor Settlers, and the Nova Scotia Fur Trade, 1783–1853,' *Journal of the Canadian Historical Association* 14 (2003), 91; and on the economy in the 1840s, T.W. Acheson, 'The 1840s: Decade of Tribulation,' in Buckner and Reid, eds., *The Atlantic Region to Confederation*, 307–14.

54 On Rand's view of the Mi'kmaq, Thomas S. Abler, 'A Mi'kmaq Missionary among the Mohawk: Silas T. Rand and His Attitudes towards Race and "Progress,"' in Celia Haig-Brown and David A. Nock, eds., *With Good Intentions: Euro-Canadian & Aboriginal Relations in Colonial Canada* (Vancouver, 2006), 72–8.

55 *Christian Messenger*, 16 March 1854, 84.

56 Prentice, *The School Promoters*, 66, 82–3.

57 Parnaby, 'The Cultural Economy of Survival.'

58 Clara Dennis, *Cape Breton Over* (Toronto, 1942), 54.

59 NSARM, RG 1/431, doc. 29, Donald McRae, 13 January 1837.

60 Much of this is from Michael Adas, *Machines as the Measure of Man: Science, Technologies and Ideologies of Western Dominance* (Ithaca and London, 1989), quote from 194, 198.

61 Quoted in Ian Radforth, *Royal Spectacle: The 1860 Visit of the Prince of Wales to Canada and the United States* (Toronto, 2004), 209.

62 NSARM, RG 1/431, doc. 29, Kenneth McLeod, John Campbell, Duncan McRae and Roderick Campbell, 4 January 1837; McRae, 13 January 1837.

63 NSARM, RG 1/431, 'Report of Committee of the House to whom the Petition of certain trespassers upon lands reserved for the Indians at Wagmatcook,' 19 April 1838.

64 Edmund M. Dodd and H.W. Crawley to Sir Rupert George, 16 January 1845, *JPHANS* (1845), Appendix 16, 70.

65 Crawley to Joseph Howe, 1 February 1849, *JPHANS* (1849), Appendix 45, 356.

66 Inhabitants of Indian River [Whycocomagh] to Henry Crawley, 27 August 1850; Peter Gougou, John Newel and Gaspar Mense to Crawley, 17 November 1850, *JPHANS* (1850), Appendix 64, 234.

67 W.A. Hendry to S.P. Fairbanks, 8 February 1862, *JPHANS* (1863), Appendix 30, 8.

68 Acheson, 'The 1840s,' in Buckner and Reid, eds., *The Atlantic Region to Confederation* , 307–14; and see Charles Tupper's remarks as reported by Edward Whelan in *The Union of the British Provinces* (Toronto, 1927), 51.

69 On Gesner, see 'Report on Indian Affairs, 21 Dec. 1847,' *JPHANS* (1848), Appendix 24, 117.

70 The views of Bromley, Gesner, and Rand are surveyed in D.G. Bell, 'Was Amerindian Dispossession Lawful? The Response of 19th Century Maritime Intellectuals,' *The Dalhousie Law Journal* 23 (2000), 178–81.

71 *Report of the Select Committee on the Hudson's Bay Company Together with the Proceedings of the Committee, Minutes and Evidence* (London, 1857).

72 Wicken, 'Mi'kmaq Treaty Tradition,' 157, 159. References to this meeting and discussion of the school, see LAC, RG 10/459, Samuel Fairbanks to Hector Langevin, 20 October 1869.

73 For one example, LAC, RG 10/224, part 2, 133735-7; 13 & 14 Vic Cap 42, s. V (Province of Canada), 'An Act for the Better Protection of the Lands and Property of the Indians of Lower Canada,' 10 August 1850; 14 & 15 Vic Cap 59, s. II, 'An Act to repeal in part and to amend an Act, Intituled, An Act for the better protection of the Lands and property of the Indians in Lower Canada,' 30 August 1851.

74 On the conflict, see Janet Chute, *The Legacy of Shingwaukonse: A Century of Native Leadership* (Toronto, 1998), 106–36.

5 Reserve Life, 1850–1881

1 A recent analysis of the treaties is J.R. Miller, *Compact, Contract, Covenant: Aboriginal Treaty-Making in Canada* (Toronto, 2009), 150–221.

2 See for instance, David Lee, 'The Metis Militants of 1885,' *Canadian Ethnic Studies* 21, 3 (1989), 1–19. This is only one example that might be used. There are many more examples of resistance to state policies during this period.

3 Wicken, 'Mi'kmaq Treaty Tradition,' 158.

4 Bill Parenteau and James Kenny, 'Survival, Resistance, and the Canadian State: The Transformation of New Brunswick's Native Economy, 1867–1930,' *Journal of the Canadian Historical Association* 13 (2003), 49–71; Walls, 'The Maximum, the Minimum,' 33–80.

5 Parnaby, 'The Cultural Economy of Survival.'

6 Walls, 'The Maximum, the Minimum,' 142–5.

7 Wm Chisholm to SGIA, 11 October 1881, *Sessional Papers*, no. 6 (1881), 31; Chisholm to SGIA, 25 September 1883, *Sessional Papers*, no. 4 (1883), 40.

8 John Harlow to SGIA, 11 September 1880, *Sessional Papers*, no. 14 (1880), 40.
9 See Parenteau and Kenny, 'Survival, Resistance, and the Canadian State,' esp. 55–6.
10 Bruce Curtis, *The Politics of Population: State Formation, Statistics, and the Census of Canada, 1840–1875* (Toronto, 2001), 314–15.
11 Peter Baskerville and Eric W. Sager, *Unwilling Idlers: The Urban Unemployed and their Families in Late Victorian Canada* (Toronto, 1998), 80–2; Judith Fingard, *The Dark Side of Life in Victorian Halifax* (Porter's Lake, 1989), 16–17; Michael Katz, *The People of Hamilton, Canada West: Family and Class in a Mid-Nineteenth-Century City* (Cambridge, 1975), 94–124.
12 *Manual Containing 'The Census Act' and the Instructions to Officers employed in the Taking of the First Census of Canada* (1871), 13.
13 Canada, 1871 Census, Nova Scotia, Cape Breton, Inverness, Richmond and Victoria Counties. On the census rules regarding de jure residence, see *Manual Containing 'The Census Act,'*, 12–13. For a discussion of this point, Curtis, *The Politics of Population*, 271–2.
14 Data have been compiled using the 1871 manuscript census for the mainland Nova Scotia counties.
15 J.B. Gilpin, 'Indians of Nova Scotia,' *Proceedings and Transactions of the Nova Scotia Institute of Natural Science* IV (1877), 279. Some families also lived in log houses at Bear River and elsewhere in southwest Nova Soctia. See LAC, RG 10/1970, file 5354, John Harlow, 'Census Returns for Annapolis, Digby, Yarmouth and Shelburne Counties,' 1 July 1875.
16 Warner, *Baddeck, and that Sort of Thing*, 110–11; 'Cruising around Cape Breton,' (1884) in Brian Tennyson, ed., *Impressions of Cape Breton* (Sydney, 1986), 187–8. Photos of both types of wigwams are in NSARM, The Mi'kmaq Portraits Collection, 1908, N-2522 and N2523, Pictou Lighthouse Album, 6. Speck mentions the use of tarpaper. Frank G. Speck, *Beothuk and Micmac* (New York, 1925), 113.
17 Reference to framed shanties is in J.E. Beckwith to SGIA, 12 August 1883, *Sessional Papers*, no. 4 (1884), 37.
18 *Manual Containing 'The Census Act,'* xxii, 21–2.
19 For Little Bras d'Or the census district was Sydney Mines. One resident was Andrew Bernard who said at the appeal trial that he had lived at Little Bras d'Or. Silas Rand also makes note of a community there in 1866. Acadia University, Esther Clark Wright Archives, Silas T. Rand journal, 23 July 1866. See 1871 Census, Nova Scotia, Cape Breton County, Sydney Mines, 81-3; Richmond County, River Inhabitants, 58.
20 Canada, 1871 Census, Nova Scotia, Cape Breton, Inverness, Richmond and Victoria Counties.

21 Evidence of Chapel Island families living in 'shanties' in 1871 is surprising because in 1845 Dodd and Crawley had reported thirteen log houses there. Dodd and Crawley to Rupert D. George, 16 January 1845 in *JPHANS, (1845)*, Appendix 16, 69. In contrast, in 1849, Crawley noted that all the families at Wagmatcook lived in wigwams. Crawley to George, 1 February 1849 in *JPHANS*, (1849), Appendix 45, 355. However, by 1859 Moses Perley wrote that 'with respect to Chapel Island, I beg to explain that very few Micmacs reside there.' Perley to Lt.-Gov. Earl of Mulgrave, 8 August 1859 in *JPHANS* (1860), Appendix, Report of Committees, 323.

22 R Grant to SGIA, 5 September 1882, *Sessional Papers*, no. 5 (1882), 29.

23 LAC, RG 14, D2, 12th Parliament, 7th Session, unpublished Sessional Papers, no. 157, Hearings before the Court of the Exchequer, September 1915, Sydney, Nova Scotia, 12. Other mention of birch bark tents are in Acadia University, Special Collections, Silas Rand Diary, entries for 1865 at Kentville, 1866: Antigonish, Little Bras d'Or, Port Mulgrave, North Sydney; 1870: Lower Granville; 1873: Berwick; S.G. W. Benjamin, 'Cruising Around Cape Breton,' (1884) in Brian Tennyson, ed., *Impressions of Cape Breton* (Sydney, 1986), 187–8. Photos of both types of wigwams are in NSARM, The Mi'kmaq Portraits Collection, 1908, N-2522 and N2523, Pictou Lighthouse Album, 6. Speck mentions the use of tarpaper. Frank G. Speck, *Beothuk and Micmac* (New York, 1925), 113.

24 R. Cole Harris and John Warkentin, *Canada before Confederation: A Study in Historical Geography* (New York, 1974), 130. One missionary described the Munsee Indians living on the Thames River in Middlesex County of Upper Canada as covering their houses with birch bark. James Beaven, *Recreations of a long vacation, or, A Visit to Indian missions in Upper Canada* (London, 1846), 75.

25 *Report of the Special Commissioners Appointed on the 8th of September 1856 to Investigate Indian Affairs in Canada* (Toronto, 1858), 53.

26 J. Bernard Gilpin, 'Indians of Nova Scotia,' 272.

27 D. MacIsaac to SGIA, 28 July 1899, *Sessional Papers*, no. 14 (1900), 69.

28 In an earlier period, Abraham Gesner had written, 'few of them who I have been able to establish upon the reserves, would leave their lands were they not compelled by the absolute necessity to seek provisions in the woods, or by begging among the inhabitants.' Abraham Gesner to Lt. Governor John Harvey, 8 February 1849, *JPHANS* (1849), Appendix 36, 337.

29 In his overiew of the Mi'kmaw economy of the Cape Breton in the mid-nineteenth century, Andrew Parnaby briefly carries the story to the late 1860s and points out the distinctions among reserves' agricultural lands. However, this is based on a brief survey of the DIA data. It does confirm,

however, that farming was more important at Eskasoni than at Chapel Island. Parnaby, 'The Cultural Economy of Survival,' 94.

30 I have altered this equation slightly by not including children under the age of two, making the assumption that they continue to get most of their caloric needs through nursing.

31 On milch cows, Province of Quebec, Department of Agriculture, *Dairy Cows: Their Feeding and Care and Improvement of the Herds* (Bulletin No. 1, 1897).

32 *Dairy Cows: Their Feeding and Care.* Figures on lbs per year are on p. 26; and on the difficulties of growing hay, William R. Baron, Anne E. Bridges, 'Making Hay in Northern New England: Maine as a Case Study, 1800–1850,' *Agricultural History* 57, 2 (1983), 165–80.

33 H.W. Crawley to Joseph Howe, 1 February 1849, *JPHANS* (1849), Appendix 45, 355.

34 General references to livestock are made in Dodd and Crawley to Rupert George, 24 December 1845, *JPHANS* (1846), Appendix 18, 66.

35 On exchanges among farmers see Steven Maynard, 'Between Farm and Factory: The Productive Household and the Capitalist Transformation of the Maritime Countryside, Hopewell, Nova Scotia, 1869–1890' in Daniel Samson, ed., *Contested Countryside: Rural Workers and Modern Society in Atlantic Canada, 1800–1950* (Fredericton, 1994), 81.

36 Robert A. MacKinnon, 'The Historical Geography of Agriculture in Nova Scotia, 1851–1951,' Ph.D. dissertation, University of British Columbia, 1991, 137–8, 172; Rebecca Chase Kinsman Ells Diary 1901 in Margaret Conrad, et al. ed., *No Place Like Home: Diaries and Letters of Nova Scotia Women 1771–1938* (Halifax, 1988), 210.

37 Clothing, tobacco, sugar, flour, molasses, farm implements, and fodder are some of the items farmers bought from local merchants. Robert MacKinnon's analysis of one farmer's accounts from Colchester County between 1885 and 1890 showed that 40% of all his purchases were for food, and mostly for flour. MacKinnon, 'The Historical Geography of Agriculture,' 167–167a.

38 Bettina Bradbury, *Working Families: Age, Gender, and Daily Survival in Industrializing Montreal* (Toronto, 1993), 163–7; Bradbury, 'The Home as Workplace,' in Paul Craven, ed., *Labouring Lives: Work & Workers in Nineteenth-Century Ontario* (Toronto, 1995), 437–40.

39 Marjorie Griffin Cohen, 'The Decline of Women in Canadian Dairying,' *Histoire Social/Social History* 17, 34 (Nov. 1984), 310.

40 J.M. Neeson, 'An Eighteenth Century Peasantry,' in John Rule and Robert Malcolmson, eds., *Protest and Survival: Essays for E.P. Thompson* (London and New York, 1993), 36–7.

41 Henry E. Alvord, 'The Village Cow in New England, being the Journal of the Keeper,' in *Keeping One Cow Being the Experience of a Number of Practical Writers in a Clear and Considered Form upon the Management of a Single Milch Cow* (New York, 1880), 36, 39, 42.

42 Cohen, 'The Decline of Women in Canadian Dairying,' 324.

43 Jane Humphries, 'Enclosures, Common Rights and Women: The Proletarialization of Families in the Late Eighteenth and Early Nineteenth Centuries,' *Journal of Economic History* 50, 1 (1990), 24–6; Curtis, *The Politics of Population*, 282–3. My thanks to J.M. Neeson for pointing out the Humphries article.

44 *Dairy Cows: Their Feeding and Care*, 60–1.

45 There is evidence that families sold butter and cream. Rev. Dr H. Standish, 'Life in Nova Scotia,' *Ballou's Monthly Magazine* 55, 2 (February 1882), 163.

46 1871 Census, Nova Scotia, Cape Breton County, Christmas Island Division 2, Schedule 5; and East Bay, Schedule 5.

47 John Harlow to DGIA, 11 September 1880, *Sessional Papers*, no. 14 (1880), 40.

48 A. Cameron to SGIA, 4 October 1904, no. 27 *Sessional Papers* (1905), 68. This was also true of the Fisher Grant Reserve in Pictou County, which was established after 1871. John D. McLeod to SGIA, 20 August 1901, *Sessional Papers*, no. 27 (1902), 68.

49 William Chearnely to Joseph Howe, 4 March 1854, JPNSHA, (1854), Appendix 26, 211.

50 Joseph Chisholm to SGIA, 3 August 1886, *Sessional Papers*, no. 6 (1887), 35.

51 J.E. Beckwith to SGIA, 10 August 1886, *Sessional Papers*, no. 6 (1887), 37.

52 Beckwith to SGIA, 23 July 1881, *Sessional Papers*, no. 6 (1882), 25.

53 'Report of Committee on Indian Affairs, 1859,' *JPHANS* (1860), Appendix – Report of Committees, 214–15; W.A. Henry to Samuel Fairbanks, 25 February 1863, *JPHANS* (1863), Appendix 16, 3–4; NSARM, Indian Land Documents, 'Acct Sales of Indian reserves, N.S.'

54 LAC, RG 10/3220: file 536,764, H.J. Bury, 'The Indian situation in the Province of Nova Scotia as it exists at the present time,' [1925]. Millbrook was only set aside as a reserve in 1881, making Bury's assessement even bleaker.

55 *Manual Containing 'The Census Act*,' 29.

56 See NSARM, RG 1/432, 198-209.

57 However, this also meant that Whycocomagh families were more dependent on off-reserve woodland than other communities like Eskasoni, which had more unoccupied land.

58 Curtis, *The Politics of Population*, 275–8.

59 Julian Gwyn, *Excessive Expectations: Maritime Commerce and the Economic Development of Nova Scotia, 1740–1870* (Montreal and Kingston, 1998), 109–16.

60 Parnaby, 'The Cultural Economy of Survival,' esp. 93. Parnaby reads the occupational data literally, assuming that occupations given in the 1871 Census reflect full time occupations. For the Mi'kmaq, and for others, this was not always true as the rest of this chapter will show.

61 Gilpin, 'Indians of Nova Scotia,' 280; Mike Parker, *Historic Digby* (Halifax, 2002), 144.

62 LAC, RG 10/2134, file 270046-1, J. MacKinnon to Joseph Howe, 22 May 1872.

63 William Chisholm to SGIA, 27 September 1880, *Sessional Papers*, no. 14 (1881), 46.

64 John Fraser to SGIA, 11 September 1900, *Sessional Papers*, no. 27 (1901), 74.

65 The occupations of 257 were recorded. The difference between this figure and the number of households is because often times there was more than one working male and female in a household. Generally, women's occupations were not noted except in cases of widowed households.

66 Digby County: Bear River: 4; Clare: 1; Metaghan: 1; Shelburne County: Louis Head: 3; Queen's County: Port Medway: 2; Caledonia: 1; Lunenburg County: Chester: 2; Guysborough: Molasses Harbour: 5; Hants County: 2.

67 Here, I am using the household as the unit of analysis. More than 314 people declared an occupation, as there was often an adult male in the household. In other cases, the women's occupation was given. In Cape Breton, there were 90 households but 156 people declared occupations.

68 Wicken, 'Mi'kmaq Treaty Tradition,' 158.

69 NSARM, RG 20/823, Alexander MacDonald to J.A. Knight, 3 May 1922.

70 F. McDormand to SGIA, 19 August 1895, *Sessional Papers*, no. 14 (1896), 40. See also F.A. Rand to SGIA, (1896), 59.

71 NSARM, MG 1/2867 #4, Clara Dennis Notebooks, Interview with Chief Louis Luxey of Yarmouth County, p. 13. [n.d].

72 In the late nineteenth and early twentieth centuries, guiding came to form an important source of income. See, Mike Parker, *Historic Annapolis Valley: Rural Life Remembered* (Halifax, 2001), 22–4; Mike Parker, *Historic Digby* (Halifax, 2002), 131.

73 These figures have been compiled through reference to Schedules One and Five of the 1871 Census. For Whycocomagh: Schedule 5, p. 3, lines 12–19; and for Christmas Island: Division #2, Schedule 5, p. 1, lines 14–18.

74 F.A. Rand to SGIA, 5 July 1905, *Sessional Papers*, no. 27 (1906), 64.

75 LAC, RG 14, D2/23, 12th Parliament, 7th Session, Unpublished Sessional Papers, Hearings of the Court of the Exchequer, Sydney, Nova Scotia, September 1915, 344.

76 See the various reports in Game and Inland Fishery Protection Service, Report of the Secretary for 1894.

77 Frank G. Speck, *Beothuk and Micmac: Micmac Hunting Territories in Nova Scotia and Newfoundland* (New York, 1926). I am indebted to Gillian Allen for this insight.

78 For a description of the items made by Mi'kmaw men and women in the mid-1800s, see C. B. Fergusson, ed., *Uniacke's Sketches of Cape Breton and other Papers Relating to Cape Breton Island* (Halifax, 1958), 107–8.

79 Wicken, 'Mi'kmaq Treaty Tradition,' 158.

80 Freeman McDormand to SGIA, 27 August 1883, *Sessional Papers*, no. 4 (1884), 36.

81 M. McKenzie to SGIA, 28 August 1883, *Sessional Papers*, no. 4 (1884), 40.

82 Chisholm to SGIA, 27 September 1880, *Sessional Papers*, no. 14 (1881), 46.

83 J.W. Beckwith to SGIA, 23 July 1881, *Sessional Papers*, no. 6 (1882), 25. Also see Charles Beckwith to SGIA, 3 October 1898, *Sessional Papers*, no. 14 (1899), 64.

84 A. Cameron to SGIA, 7 October 1891, *Sessional Papers*, no. 14 (1892), 44.

85 Beckwith to SGIA, 23 July 1881; R. Grant to SGIA, 5 September 1882, *Sessional Papers*, no. 5 (1883), 29; Margaret Warner Morley, *Down North and Up Along* (New York, 1905), 170; Dennis, *Cape Breton Over*, 50. A photograph of a Mi'kmaq encampment at Baddeck in about 1885 is reproduced in Owen Fitzgerald, *Cape Breton: A Changing Scene, a Collection of Cape Breton photographs ~ 1860–1935* (Sydney, 1986), #3.

86 This issue is discussed in more detail in Chapter 7. On other examples of selling wares in urban areas, see Frederic S. Cozzens, 'A Month with the Blue Noses,' *New York Monthly Magazine*, 49, 1 (January 1857), 61.

87 Larry McCann, '"Living a Double Life": Town and Country in the Industrialization of the Maritimes,' in Douglas Day, ed., *Geographical Perspectives on the Maritime Provinces* (Halifax, 1988), 100–9; Stephen Hornsby, *Nineteenth-Century Cape Breton: A Historical Geography* (Montreal and Kingston, 1992), 139–43, 150–1.

88 Hornsby, *Nineteenth-Century Cape Breton*, 141, 160.

89 LAC, RG 10, F.A. Rand to SGIA, 10 November 1893. For similar comments on Mi'kmaq moving between Millbrook and Halifax County, see LAC, RG 10, file 513,274, Daniel Chisholm to SGIA, 6 September 1918.

6 The Demography of Mi'kmaw Communities, 1871–1911

1 Schacter, *The Brain, the Mind, and the Past*, 80–1, 88.

2 Ibid., 81–7.

3 LAC, RG 10/3220, file 536,736, H.J. Bury, 'The Indian Situation in the Province of Nova Scotia as it exists at the present time,'[1925]. Bury's figures contrast with those compiled in 1931 Census, which show more than 92% of the Mi'kmaq on reserve. Dominion Bureau of Statistics, *Seventh Census of Canada, 1931, vol II: Population by Areas* (Ottawa, 1933), 322–36.

4 Wicken, 'Mi'kmaq Treaty Tradition,' 159.

5 Ibid.

6 Canada, 1891 Census, Nova Scotia, Inverness County, Whycocomagh, p. 12, lines 34–8.

7 To cite just a few examples: Baskerville and Sager, *Unwilling Idlers*; Bettina Bradbury, *Working Families: Age, Gender, and Daily Survival in Industrializing Montreal* (Toronto, 1993); Peter Gossage, *Families in Transition: Industry and Population in Nineteenth-Century Saint-Hyacinthe* (Montreal and Kingston, 1999); Eric W. Sager and Peter Baskerville, eds., *Household Counts: Canadian Households and Families in 1901* (Toronto, 2007).

8 Massimo Livi-Bacci, *A Concise History of World Population* (Cambridge, 1989), 106–13.

9 A general explanation of this point is made for the United Kingdom in Helen I. Cowan, *British Immigration to British North America: The First Hundred Years* (Toronto, 1961; 1st ed., 1928), 18–39.

10 On Southern and Eastern Europe, see Alan M. Kraut, *The Huddled Masses: The Immigrant in American Society, 1880–1921* (Arlington Heights, 1982), 29–41.

11 Norman Stone, *Europe Transformed, 1878–1919* (London, 1983), 22–5; and on general changes in the world economy, Eric Hobsbawm, *Industry and Empire: The Birth of the Industrial Revolution* (London, 1999; 1st ed., 1968), 31–111.

12 Patricia Thornton, 'The Problem of Out-Migration from Atlantic Canada, 1871–1921: A New Look,' in P.A. Buckner and David Frank, eds., *Atlantic Canada after Confederation* (Fredericton, 1988), 47–9.

13 Alan A. Brookes, 'Out-Migration from the Maritime Provinces, 1860–1900: Some Preliminary Considerations,' *Acadiensis* V, 2 (Spring 1976), 39; Alan A. Brookes, 'The Golden Age and the Exodus: The Case of Canning, Kings County,' *Acadiensis* 11, 1 (Autumn 1981), 73–8; Hornsby, *Nineteenth-Century Cape Breton*, 191–6; A.A. MacKenzie, 'Cape Breton and the Western Harvest Excursions 1890–1928,' in Kenneth Donovan, ed., *Cape Breton at 200: Historical Essays in Honour of the Island's Bicentennial 1785–1985* (Sydney, 1985), 82.

14 Calculated from figures given in the 1871 to 1921 censuses.

15 Warden H.C.V. LeVatte, 'Louisbourg addressing the Council, 11 January

1921,' *Minutes and Reports of the County of Cape Breton, January 1921 Session* (Sydney, 1921).

16 Thornton, 'Out-Migration: A New Look,' 54. For Antigonish, Inverness, Pictou, and Victoria counties see tables in D. Campbell and R.A. MacLean, *Beyond the Atlantic Roar: A Study of the Nova Scotia Scots* (Toronto, 1974), 112–13; and for the other counties, Brookes, 'Out-Migration from the Maritime Provinces,' 32.

17 Brookes, 'Out-Migration from the Maritime Provinces,' 36–7; Brookes, 'The Golden Age and the Exodus,' 67–70; Thornton, 'Out-Migration: A New Look,' 55; Hornsby, *Nineteenth Century Cape Breton*, 189.

18 One method to measure this phenomenon is to compare the number of adults 65 years and older per 100 persons under the age of 15; the higher the number, the older the population. Although this method fails to account for variations in life expectancy, it does give a reasonable indication of the relative age of a population. In a period of transition, we would expect urban areas to contain a higher proportion of young people. Analysis of aggregate totals from the 1891 Census confirms this trend, although we should keep in mind that the data gives a static view of urban residency. In 1891, the City of Halifax, a destination for many young people in the 1870s and 1880s, had 12.92 people 65 years of age and older for every 100 people under the age of 15. By comparison, Victoria County had 17.07, Inverness County 17.59, Richmond County 19.08, and Antigonish County 22.14 persons, suggesting that each of these counties had already lost a significant proportion of their youth. Antigonish and Richmond counties were the most seriously affected. Calculated from *Census of Canada 1890–91*, vol. II (Ottawa, 1898), 2–5; D. Campbell and R.A. MacLean, *Beyond the Atlantic Roar: A Study of the Nova Scotia Scots* (Toronto, 1974), 100, 104–5.

19 T.W. Acheson, 'The National Policy and the Industrialization of the Maritimes,' in Michael S. Cross and Gregory S. Kealey, eds., *Canada's Age of Industry, 1849–1896* (Toronto, 1982), 63.

20 Hornsby, *Nineteenth-Century Cape Breton*, 135–6.

21 Terrence Crowley, 'Rural Labour,' in Paul Craven, ed., *Labouring Lives*, 55–6.

22 Hornsby, *Nineteenth-Century Cape Breton*, 121–43.

23 Brookes, 'The Golden Age and the Exodus,' 63–4. For more pessimistic view of the 1870s which sees continuity between the period before and after 1867, see Gwyn, *Excessive Expectations*, 90–125.

24 On this issue, see Michael Katz, *The People of Hamilton, Canada West: Family and Class in a Mid-Nineteenth-Century City* (Cambridge, Mass., 1975), 104–05.

25 Abraham Gesner, 'Report on Indian Affairs,' 21 December 1847, *JLA* (1848), Appendix 24, 116.

26 NSARM, RG 1/454,10, 'Report of the Secretary of the Board of Statistics on the Census of Nova Scotia,' 31 December 1861; Virginia P. Miller, 'The Decline of Nova Scotia Micmac Population, A.D. 1600–1850,' *Culture* 2, 3 (1982), 114; *Census of Canada, 1880–81,* vol. 1, (Ottawa, 1882), 220. Although a census was taken in 1851, officials believed that the census was inaccurate because of Mi'kmaw movement. NSARM, RG 1/454, 10.

27 See Malcolm Potts, *Society and Fertility* (Plymouth, 1979), 194–8.

28 Richard A. Easterlin, 'Factors in the Decline of Farm Family Fertility in the United States: Some Preliminary Research Results,' *The Journal of American History* 63, 3 (1976), 612–14.

29 Elizabeth Cashdan, 'Natural Fertility, Birth Spacing, and the "First Demographic Transition,"' *American Anthropologist* 87, 3 (September 1985), 650; William Englebrecht, 'Factors Maintaining Low Population Density among the Prehistoric New York Iroquois,' *American Antiquity* 52, 1 (1987), 13–27; W. Penn Handwerker, 'The First Demographic Transition: An Analysis of Subsistence Choices and Reproductive Consequences,' *American Anthropologist* 85, 1 (1983), 15.

30 Thomas Chandler Haliburton, *A General Description of Nova Scotia: Illustrated by a New and Correct Map* (Halifax, 1823), 46–7.

31 Marvin Harris and Eric B. Ross, *Death, Sex, and Fertility: Population Regulation in Preindustrial and Developing Societies* (New York, 1987), 6–7; Handwerker, 'The First Demographic Transition,' 15.

32 Jaime S. Ruud and Bonnie Taub-Dix, 'Premenstrual Syndrome: Nutritional Implications,' in Dorothy Klimis-Zaca and Ira Wolinsky, eds., *Nutritional Concerns of Women,* 2nd ed. (Boca Raton, 2004), 61–7.

33 Garry Warrick, *A Population History of the Huron-Petun, A.D. 500–1650* (Cambridge, 2008), 43.

34 On the Catholic missions, see Micheline Dumont-Johnson, *Apôtres ou Agitateurs: la France missionaire en Acadie* (Trois Rivières, 1970).

35 Miller, 'The Decline of Nova Scotia Micmac Population.' The literature on the impact of European-borne diseases is vast and the debate about depopulation rates extensive. For a useful overview of the literature on the Maritime region, see Ralph T. Pastore, 'Native History in the Atlantic Region during the Colonial Period,' *Acadiensis* 20, 1 (Autumn 1990), 200–25.

36 On the general issue of average age at first marriage: Gerhard Ens, *Homeland to Hinterland: The Changing Worlds of the Red River Metis in the Nineteenth Century* (Toronto, 1996), 72–3; and about population growth in Western Canada, Maureen K. Lux, *Medicine That Walks: Disease, Medicine, and Canadian Plains Native People, 1880–1940* (Toronto, 2001), 191.

37 See 'Report of the Deputy Registrar-General Relating the Registration of

Births, Marriages & deaths in Nova Scotia, October 1st to September 30th, 1913,' in *Journals and Proceedings of the Legislative Council of the Province of Nova Scotia*, Session 1914, Part II, Appendix 25, Table I and XIII.

38 See for instance, Bradbury, *Working Families*, 58–66; David Gagan, *Hopeful Travellers: Families, Land, and Social Change in Mid-Victorian Peel County, Canada West* (Toronto, 1981), 72–6; Danielle Gauvreau and Peter Gossage, 'Canadian Fertility Transitions: Quebec and Ontario at the Turn of the Twentieth Century,' *Journal of Family History* 26, 2 (April 2001), 162–88.

39 Tamara K. Hareven and Maris A. Vinovskis, 'Patterns of Childbearing in Late Nineteenth-Century America: The Determinants of Marital Fertility in Five Massachusetts Towns in 1880,' in Hareven and Vinovskis, eds., *Family and Population in Nineteenth-Century America* (Princeton, 1978), 88–94.

40 Warrick, *A Population History of the Huron-Petun*, 172.

41 *Report on the Affairs of the Indians of Canada Submitted to the Legislative Assembly* (Montreal, 1847), Section III, 16.

42 As explained in Chapter 5 the censuses do not adequately reflect residency patterns.

43 This figure is calculated by adding the child/woman ratio for each age cohort from ages 20 to 40. See Hareven and Vinovskis, 'Patterns of Childbearing,' 94.

44 Between 1871 and 1881, the child/woman ratio declined for all age groups (15–49) by 0.099 and for the 20–49 age cohort by 0.087. Similarly, from 1881 to 1901, the child/woman ratio declined for all age groups by 0.178 and for the 20–49 age cohort by 0.175.

45 Marvin McGinnis, 'Canada in the Nineteenth Century,' in Michael R. Haines and Richard H. Steckel, eds., *A Population History of North America* (Cambridge, 2000), 407.

46 Bradbury, *Working Families*, 59–66.

47 'Regular employment' is a relative term and does not signify that individuals worked year round. For a description of urban employment in the 1890s and early 1900s, see Baskerville and Sager, *Unwilling Idlers*, 82–5.

48 Gossage, *Families in Transition*, 171–3.

49 In 1901, eight women living in Sydney had nine children under the age of 5 and in 1911, 15 women had 20 children under the age of 5.

50 Although each of these census districts took their name from a rural village, they also included the surrounding rural area. However, between 1871 and 1911, census districts changed as the population increased and as towns were incorporated. Before 1891, the town of Annapolis Royal was enumerated along with its rural hinterland, but afterward it was counted separately. Similarly, River Hebert, which was enumerated as one district in 1871, was

separated into four districts in 1911, with the new districts called Joggins, Lower Cove, and Shulee (or Shulie as it is spelled today). For this reason, I have tried to select census districts whose boundaries remained stable between 1871 and 1911, except River Hebert. In this case, for 1911 I have added those areas, which had been part of the enumerated district. Peter Gossage and Danielle Gauvreau's sampling of the 1901 Census shows similar figures. Their non-standardized child/woman ratio for Nova Scotia was 0.91. Gauvreau and Gossage, 'Canadian Fertility in 1901: A Bird's Eye View,' in Eric W. Sager and Peter Baskerville, eds., *Household Counts*, Table 2.5, 78.

51 Bill Parenteau and James Kenny, 'Survival, Resistance, and the Canadian State: The Transformation of New Brunswick's Native Economy, 1867–1930,' *Journal of the Canadian Historical Association* 13 (2003), 49–72.

52 J. E. Beckwith to SGIA, 17 July 1884 and Thomas J. Butler to SGIA, 25 August 1884, *Sessional Papers*, no. 3 (1885), 41.

53 LAC, RG 10/2910, file 185,723-8B, L. Vankoughnet, 'Report on Middle River Island Matter,' 18 August 1877.

54 LAC, RG 10/2039, file 8947, R. J. Logan to DGSIA, 25 May 1907.

55 LAC, RG 10/2039, file 8947, N.A. Hendry to H. Austin, 14 December 1882. For other examples on the mainland, see LAC, RG 10/459, [????] to Samuel Fairbanks, 20 August 1869; RG 10/2050, file 9421, Joseph Knockwood to Mr. McLean, 22 February 1909.

56 McLean and his son were jailed under an 1868 Act of Parliament that gave officials the authority to evict squatters from Indian lands. If the squatters attempted to resettle, they could be jailed and would remain in prison without the benefit of a trial, bail, or appeal for a period not longer than thirty days. The act also set out punitive fines against those removing trees, saplings, shrubs, timber, stone, or soil from reserve lands. Under a special provision, the government could order squatters to be jailed for up to three months. This act became legally binding on Nova Scotia after the passage of an Order-in-Council in February of 1872. 31 Victoria (1868), cap 42, 'An Act for the Organization of the Secretary of State, and the management and ordinance of Indian Lands,' in Derek G. Smith, ed., *Canadian Indians and the Law: Selected Documents, 1663–1972* (Toronto, 1975), 67–8; LAC, RG 10/461, 50–3, William Sprague, 'Report from Indian Office recommending issue of a Proclamation, applying certain sections of the Act 31 Victoria, Cap 42 to the Indian Reserves in the Province of Nova Scotia, 28 January 1872.' For an additional explanation of the case, see Sidney L. Harring, *White Man's Law*, 180–1.

57 D. McIsaac to SGIA, September 1880, *Sessional Papers*, no. 11 (1881), 47; McIsaac to SGIA, September 1883, *Sessional Papers*, no. 4 (1884), 39; McIsaac

to SGIA, 9 September 1885, *Sessional Papers*, no. 4 (1886), 41; *McLean* v. *McIsaac et. al.*, 4 August 1885 in *Cases Argued and Determined in the Supreme Court of Nova Scotia 1884–86* (Halifax, 1886), 304–9.

58 LAC, RG 10/2084, file 13,027, J.H. Campbell and others, 29 April 1879.

59 LAC, RG 10/2910, File file 185,723 -8B, Jos. B. McDonald to B.A. Meredith [Deputy Minister of the Interior] 28 Feb. 1877; John Denny to Meredith 12 March 1877; Alexander MacDonald to SGIA, 2 April 1877.

60 For instance, George Wells to SGIA, 1884, *Sessional Papers*, no. 3 (1884), 40.

61 NSARM, RG 1/431, doc. 56, Petition of Newel Joe et al. to Lt. Gov. Murray, 8 December 1849.

62 NSARM, RG 5/P, vol. 8A, doc. 93, Petition of Joseph Gload et al., 20 March 1844.

63 NSARM, RG 1/380, 112-13, Titus Smith, 'General Obserations on the Northern Tour.'

64 A.T. Clark to SGIA, 30 August 1883, *Sessional Papers*, no. 4 (1884), 34.

65 A. MacKenzie to SGIA, 31 August 1883, *Sessional Papers*, no. 4 (1884), 40.

66 George Wells to SGIA, 13 August 1887, *Sessional Papers*, no. 15 (1888), 41.

67 NSARM, MG 1/2867, doc. 4, Clara Dennis, Interview with Chief Louis Luxey, 13.

68 Wells to SGIA, 11 August 1884, *Sessional Papers*, no. 4 (1885), 40.

69 Wells to SGIA, 18 September 1886, *Sessional Papers*, no. 6 (1887), 37–8.

70 See for instance, 'Report of W.H. Venning, Esq., Inspector of Fisheries for Nova Scotia and New Brunswick,' *Sessional Papers*, no. 5 (1872), 122–30.

71 LAC, RG 10/6743, file 420-7, 'Resolution of Bear River Band Council, 9 February 1897.'

72 'Report of W.H. Rogers, Fisheries Inspector, 31 December, 1881,' *Sessional Papers*, no. 5 (1881), 6.

73 Roderick MacDonald to SGIA, 1 October 1891, *Sessional Papers*, no. 14 (1892), 42.

74 Thomas J. Butler to SGIA, 25 August 1884, *Sessional Papers*, no. 3 (1885), 42.

75 'Report of W.H. Rogers, Fisheries Inspector for Nova Scotia,' 31 December 1881, *Sessional Papers*, no. 5 (1882), 3.

76 'Comparative Statement of Production in Each Branch of the Fisheries in Nova Scotia, 1890 and 1891,' *Sessional Papers*, no. 11 (1891), xv.

77 'Of the Yield and Value of the Fisheries of the whole of Nova Scotia for year 1900,' *Sessional Papers*, no. 21 (1902), 96.

78 *Report of the Royal Commission on the Relations of Capital and Labor in Canada, Evidence- Nova Scotia* (Ottawa, 1889), 134–5.

79 Hollingsworth, *The Present State of Nova Scotia*, 63; Joseph Gubbins, *New Brunswick Journals of 1811 & 1813*, Howard Temperley, ed. (Fredericton:

1980), 76; Capt. W. Moorsom, *Letters from Nova Scotia Comprising Sketches of a Young Country* (London, 1830), 114; 'Recollections of Halifax,' *Acadian Recorder*, 4 August 1883, p. 2, col. 4.

80 Max Basque to R.H. Whitehead, 9 March 1984, *Cape Breton's Magazine* (1989), in Whitehead, *The Old Man Told Us*, 318.

81 John Erskine, 'Micmac Notes, 1958,' in Whitehead, *The Old Man Told Us*, 296; Dennis, *Cape Breton Over*, 35.

82 *Halifax Morning Herald*, 23 March 1875.

83 'Report of Secretary for 1894,' *Game and Inland Fishery Protection Service*, 2, 4, 6, 9, 11; Parenteau and Judd, 'More Buck for the Bang,' 242.

84 Parenteau and Judd, 'More Buck for the Bang,' 242–3.

85 See Bill Parenteau, '"Care, Control and Supervision": Native People in the Canadian Atlantic Salmon Fishery, 1867–1900,' *Canadian Historical Review* 79, 1 (1998), 1–35.

86 Report of W.H. Rogers, 31 December 1881, *Sessional Papers*, no. 5 (1881), 5; Report of A.C. Bertram, Fishery Inspector for Cape Breton Island, 31 December 1891, *Sessional Papers*, no. 11 (1892), 5; NSARM, RG 35-317, J2, 'Return of Convictions made by me (C. Godard, J.P) during the year 1893.' Parenteau, '"Care, Control and Supervision,"' 2.

87 On mass production in the woodworking industry, David A. Hounshell, *From the American System to Mass Production, 1800–1932* (Baltimore and London, 1984), 125–51; Parenteau and Kenny, 'Survival, Resistance, and the Canadian State,' 58.

88 RG 14, D2/23 Unpublished Sessional Papers of the 7th Session of the 12th Parliament of Canada, 18 January 1917 – 20 September 1917, Court of the Exchequer, *'Re: Sydney Indian Reserve,' Joseph A. Gillies and His Majesty, the King*, September 1915, (Hereafter *Gillies* v. *R.*) Testimony of Joseph Christmas, September 1915, 333, 344.

89 Freeman McDormand to SGIA, 19 September 1883, *Sessional Papers*, no. 4 (1884), 36.

90 Katz, *The People of Hamilton, Canada West*, 94–134.

91 The higher percentage of off-reserve families on the mainland accounts, as I argue in Chapter 2, for concerns about the Mi'kmaw use of the forest commons. As explained in Chapter 5, these data reflect a static representation of the population.

92 'Report of Committee on Indian Affairs,' [1864], *JPHANS* (1864), Appendix 37, 5.

93 This is suggested by comments about Bedford residents in the early 1920s. Max Basque to R.H. Whitehead and Ronald Caplan, 9 March 1984, *Cape Breton's Magazine* (1989), quoted in Whitehead, *The Old Man Told Us*, 320–1.

94 A. Cameron to SGIA, August 1891, *Sessional Papers*, no. 14 (1892), 44.

95 LAC, RG 10/3103, file 307,576, A.J.Boyd to Duncan C. Scott, 20 June 1917.

96 Table III, *Census of Canada, 1880–81*, vol. 1 (Ottawa, 1882), 221; Table VII, *Fifth Census of Canada 1911*, vol. II (Ottawa, 1913), 187; Table 27, *Sixth Census of Canada, 1921*, vol. 1 (Ottawa, 1924), 385.

97 'Census of Indians, 31 December 1881,' *Sessional Papers*, no. 6 (1882), 220; Census Returns, 30 June 1901, *Sessional Papers*, no. 27 (1902), 156; 'Census of Indians, 31 March 1911,' *Sessional Papers*, no. 27 (1912), 30.

98 Gauvreau and Gossage, 'Canadian Fertility Transitions,' 172. The figures are based on a 5% sampling of the census – 13,674 Ontario women and 9,945 Quebec women between the ages of 15 and 49; 61.9% of the Quebec women and 59.9% of the Ontario women lived in a rural setting. Among this group, the child/woman ratio was 1.25 for Quebec and 0.81 for Ontario.

99 David Gagan, 'Land, Population, and Social Change: The "Critical Years" in Rural Canada West' *Canadian Historical Review* 59, 3 (1978), 308–11.

100 The Cape Breton communities are in the Archdiocese of Antigonish. These records are currently being digitized. Some few registers for the earlier part of the 1800s are available at the Elizabeth Beaton Archives at Cape Breton University.

101 The Mi'kmaw figures have been calculated from the manuscript copy of the 1871 census and the figures for the rest of the population from *Census of Canada, 1870–71*, vol. II, Table VII, 143–65.

102 *Sessional Papers*, no. 27 (1908), Part II, Tabular Statements, 73; *Sessional Papers*, no. 27 (1908), Tabular Statements, 71; *Sessional Papers*, no. 27 (1910), Tabular Statements, 35.

103 LAC, RG 10/2520, file 107,000, pt. 6, J.E. Molitor, 'Location of Indian Families,' Shelburne County, 30 June, 1900; RG 10/2520, file 107,000, pt. 7, Molitor, 'Settlement and Residence of Indians, Shelburne County,' 18 June 1901.

104 William Chisholm to SGIA, 19 August 1887, *Sessional Papers*, no. 15 (1888), 45.

105 J.E. Beckwith to SGIA, 26 July 1882, *Sessional Papers*, no. 5 (1883), 24.

106 R. Ruggles Gates, 'The Blood Groups and Other Features of the Micmac Indians,' *The Journal of the Royal Anthropological Insitute of Great Britain and Ireland* 68 (Jul.-Dec. 1938), 283–98.

107 Brookes, 'Out-Migration from the Maritime Provinces,' 46–7.

108 See Baskerville and Sager, *Unwilling Idlers*, 56, 73–8 for an analysis of factors contributing to people's difficulty in finding work.

109 However, since the outmigration of 100,000 Nova Scotians in this period

has not been factored into our calculations regarding the growth in population between 1881 and 1911, we might also ignore Mi'kmaw emigration as a factor depressing growth rates.

110 For a general discussion of this issue, see Hamilton, 'Anyone not on the list might as well be dead,' 67–72.

111 39 Vict. Cap 18, s. 44. 'An Act to Amend and consolidate the laws respecting Indians,' 12 April 1876. In contrast, men who married non-aboriginal women did not lose their status. Women who married aboriginal men could become status Indians.

112 Up until the 1961, when the federal department created separate bands in Nova Scotia, the government did not maintain band lists. Therefore, there was no concept of 'status' and 'non-status' Mi'kmaq. See Sydney, Cape Breton University, Mi'kmaq Resource Centre, William C. Wicken, 'The Shubenacadie Mi'kmaq and the Lobster Fishery, from First Contact to 1961,' *Provincial Court of Nova Scotia, R. v. Alex MacDonald et al.* (2002).

113 Compiled from the manuscript copy of the 1881 Census.

114 NSARM, St Bernard's Roman Catholic Church, Enfield, Nova Scotia, Baptismals, 1857– ; C-11355.

115 Data for 1918 to 1920 have not been included in Table 6.9 because the departmental numbers for these years simply repeat figures for 1917, as do all the census data for those years. That there should be exactly the same numbers for each of these years seems unlikely, suggesting that officials had recopied data from 1917 in order to include figures from Nova Scotia in their annual reports.

116 The rate was calculated from 1 October to 30 September of the following year. See 'Report of the Deputy Registrar-General Relating to the Registration of Births, Marriages, & Deaths in Nova Scotia,' in *JPHANS (1914–1918)*, Appendix 25.

117 Warren E. Kalbach and Wayne W. McVey, *The Demographic Bases of Canadian Society*, 2nd edition (Toronto, 1979). 69–70.

118 Some Indian agents reported childhood deaths but did not record their ages. F. McDormand to DSGIA, 25 September 1891, *Sessional Papers*, no. 14 (1892), 38; McDormand to DSGIA, 1 September 1892, *Sessional Papers*, no. 14 (1893), 38.

119 The federal census counted 1,758 people, the DIA census 2,026, a difference of 268. In 1911, children under the age of 5 formed 12.2% of the total population. I have multiplied this by 268 to arrive at the approximate number of children who are missing from the 1911 federal census.

120 John L. Tobias, 'Protection, Civilization and Assimilation: An Outline History of Canada's Indian Policy,' in Ian A.L. Getty and Antoine S. Lussier, eds., *As Long as the Sun Shines and Water Flows* (Vancouver, 1983), 43–9.

121 George Smith to SGIA, 1 August 1883, *Sessional Papers*, no. 10 (1884), 39;
McDormand to SGIA, 10 September 1885, *Sessional Papers*, no. 4 (1886),
37; W.C. Chisholm to SGIA, 25 August 1891, *Sessional Papers*, no. 14 (1892),
42; G.W. Boggs to SGIA, 29 September 1890, *Sessional Papers*, no. 18 (1891),
113; 'Report of the Department of Indian Affairs for the Year Ended June
30, 1899,' *Sessional Papers*, no. 14 (1900), xxi; 'Report of Health Officer,
Municipality of Cape Breton, 15 April 1903,' *Minutes and Reports of the
County Council of Cape Breton*, April 1903 (Sydney, 1903), 33.

122 Katherine McCuaig, *The Weariness, the Fever, and the Fret: The Campaign
against Tuberculosis in Canada, 1900–1950* (Montreal and Kingston, 1999),
4–5.

123 On the general issue of overcrowding's impact on the spread of disease,
see 'Report of the Department of Indian Affairs for the Year Ended June
30, 1899,' *Sessional Papers*, no. 14 (1900), xx.

124 Lux, *Medicine That Walks*, 207.

125 The 1881 manual outlined that temporary dwellings could include 'lumbering shanties, public work shanties, fishermen's huts, Indian wigwams,
etc.' Canada, Manual. *Second Census of Canada, 1881*, 26.

126 A.T. Clark to SGIA, 30 August 1883, *Sessional Papers*, no. 4 (1884), 34;
Roderick McDonald to SGIA, 16 September 1898, *Sessional Papers*, no. 14
(1899), 65.

127 Gordon Darroch and Lee Soltow, *Property and Inequality in Victorian Ontario*
(Toronto, 1994), 63, 65.

128 C.W. Vernon, *Cape Breton Canada at the Beginning of the Twentieth Century*
(Toronto, 1903), 98.

7 Moving into the City: The Politics of Relocation

1 Wicken, 'Mi'kmaq Treaty Tradition,' 157, 159; RG 14, D2/23 Unpublished
Sessional Papers of the 7th Session of the 12th Parliament of Canada, 18
January 1917 – 20 September 1917, Court of the Exchequer, *'Re: Sydney
Indian Reserve,' Joseph A. Gillies and His Majesty, the King*, September 1915,
(Hereafter *Gillies* v. *R.*) Testimony of Joseph Christmas, September 1915,
344.

2 For instance, see the comments on cities in Nova Scotia in DPNSHA
(1888), 68–9.

3 Mariana Valverde, *The Age of Light, Soap, and Water: Moral Reform in English
Canada, 1885–1925* (Toronto, 1991), 104–8, 129–39; Carolyn Strange and
Tina Loo, *Making Good: Law and Moral Regulation in Canada, 1867–1939*
(Toronto, 1997), 79–99.

4 For example: David Frank, *J.B. McLachlin: A Biography* (Toronto, 1999).

What is surprising is that academic analyses of the coal miners' union examine the same time as the effort to remove the Mi'kmaq was made. I am not
suggesting that the Mi'kmaq are a central part of the story, but despite this
they are a part of industrial Cape Breton's history. The only academic account of the King's Road removal is found in Sarah A. Brennan, 'Revisiting
the Proverbial Tin Cup: A Study of Political Resistance of the Mi'kmaq of
Nova Scotia, 1900–1969,' M.A. thesis, Saint Mary's University, 2000, 81–98;
see also Geoffrey York, *The Dispossessed: Life and Death in Native Canada* (Toronto: McArthur, 1999), 60-4.

5 See John Sutton Lutz, 'After the Fur Trade: The Aboriginal Labouring Class
of British Columbia 1849–1890,' *Journal of the Canadian Historical Association* 3 (1992); *Makuk: A New History of Aboriginal-White Relations* (Vancouver,
2008).

6 Del Muise, 'The Making of an Industrial Community: Cape Breton Coal
Towns 1867–1900,' in Don McGillvary and Brian Tennyson, eds., *Cape Breton
Historical Essays* (Sydney, 1980), 77, 86–7.

7 'A Year's Progress,' *The Daily Record* (Sydney), 10 August 1900, 2.

8 For a short corporate history of the coal fields, see Hugh Millward, 'Mine
Operators and Mining Leases on Nova Scotia's Sydney Coalfield, 1720 to
the Present,' *Nova Scotia Historical Review* 13, 2 (1993), 67–86.

9 Louis C. Hunter, *Steam Power: A History of Industrial Power in the United States,
1780–1930. Volume Two: Steam Power* (Charlottesville, 1985), 393–5.

10 Larry McCann, 'The 1890s: Fragmentation and the New Social Order,' in
E.R. Forbes and D.A. Muise, eds., *The Atlantic Provinces in Confederation* (Toronto and Fredericton, 1993), 131.

11 Dominion Steel Corporation Limited, 'Memorandum respecting the Sub-
sidiary Companies, 2 February 1912,' 4.

12 C.W. Vernon, *Cape Breton Canada at the Beginning of the Twentieth Century*
(Toronto, 1903), 209. Although initially conceived by Whitney, the company
was sold in 1903 to Ontario interests who, in 1910, also assumed control of
the Dominion Coal Company. Frank, 'Cape Breton Coal,' 213.

13 There were also several small independent coal companies operating in the
region. See Millward, 'Mine Operators and Mining Leases,' 75–6.

14 Vernon, *Cape Breton Canada*, 172–84.

15 *Sixth Census of Canada, 1921, vol IV – Occupations* (Ottawa, 1929), Tables 2,
10, 14. These figures include coal operatives and mine labourers. I have
assumed that most people described as mine labourers worked in the coal
fields. These figures do not include skilled craftsman, office workers, man-
agers, and others who also worked in the coal and steel industries.

16 The exceptions were the coalfields of Cumberland and Pictou counties.

17 Judith Fingard, 'The 1880s: the Paradoxes of Progress,' in Forbes and
Muise, eds., *The Atlantic Provinces*, 89–90.

18 9-10 Geo.V Cap 12, s. 2(1), 'An Act Respecting the Taxation of Certain
Companies,' 17 May 1919; 11-12 Geo.V Cap 3, s. 15 (1), 'An Act to Amend
and Consolidate the Acts to Supplement the Revenue of the Crown and
the Taxation of Certain Companies in the Province of Nova Scotia,' 16 May
1921.

19 J. Murray Beck, *Politics of Nova Scotia 1896–1988* (Tantallon, N.S., 1988), 25,
53–4.

20 For instance, in 1925, the government received $365,391 in mining royal-
ties, a 51% drop from the year before. Public Accounts, Mines Reports,
JPHANS (1926). For a brief overview of these problems, see Ernest R.
Forbes, *The Maritime Rights Movement 1919–1927: A Study in Canadian Regionalism* (Montreal and Kingston, 1979), 57–61; on the 1925 strike and the
election, Beck, *Politics of Nova Scotia*, 110; and on the drop in coal production in 1925, Tables A and B in 'Report of the Royal Commission Respecting the Coal Mines of the Province of Nova Scotia 1925,' *JPHANS* (1926),
Part II.

21 Cozzens, *Acadia; or a month with the Blue Noses*, 171; LAC, RG 10/2911, file
185,723-9A, C.G. Parker to Assistant Deputy and Secretary, Indian Affairs,
20 January, 1913.

22 In 1899, J.D. McLean, the Secretary of Indian Affairs referred to the reserve
'as a common camping ground for all the Indians who visit Sydney.' LAC,
RG 10/2911, file 185,723-9A, J.D. McLean to F. McDonald, M.P, 7 March
1899.

23 Province of Nova Scotia – Pat. 15245, 28 April, 1882 in *Canada, Indian Treaties and Surrenders*, vol. 2 (Saskatoon, 1993), 1st edition, 1891, 236–7; L.A.
Audette, 'In the Matter of the Reference Respecting the Expediency of the
Removal of the Indians from the Reserve at the City of Sydney, Cape Breton, in the Province of Nova Scotia' (Re: Sydney Indian Reserve), 15 March
1916, in *Reports of the Exchequer Court of Canada*, vol. 17 (Toronto, 1918), 519.

24 The site of the reserve is on King's Road where the Sydney Medical Arts
Centre now stands.

25 RG 14, D2/23 Unpublished Sessional Papers of the 7th Session of the 12th
Parliament of Canada, 18 January 1917 – 20 September 1917, Court of the
Exchequer, *'Re: Sydney Indian Reserve,' Joseph A. Gillies and His Majesty, the
King*, September 1915 (Hereafter *Gillies* v. *R.*), Testimony of Joseph Gillies,
September 1915, 12; Testimony of Cecil Sparrow, 234. A photograph of
some residents in about 1890 is in Fitzgerald, *Cape Breton: A Changing Scene*,
no. 4.

26 *Gillies* v. *R.*, Testimony of Joseph Christmas, September 1915, 344.

27 Ron Crawley, 'Off to Sydney: Newfoundlanders Emigrate to Industrial Cape Breton, 1890–1914,' *Acadiensis*, XVII, 2 (1988), 32–9.

28 LAC, RG 10/3022, file 234,951, J.A. MacRae to SGIA, 3 November 1902.

29 Canada, Census of 1881, Nova Scotia, Cape Breton County, Sydney, Division #2, p. 21, lines 7–10; Canada, Census of 1911, Nova Scotia, Cape Breton County, City of Sydney, Indian Reserve, p. 4, lines 1–4.

30 *Gillies* v. *R.*, Testimony of Benjamin Christmas, September 1915, 326; Testimony of Joe Christmas, 333.

31 D.K. McIntyre to DSGIA, 30 June 1905, *Sessional Papers*, no. 27 (1906), 63.

32 *Gillies* v. *R.*, Testimony of Donald McAdam, 257.

33 Cozzens, *Acadia*, 186.

34 Canada, 1871 Census, Nova Scotia, Cape Breton County, Sydney Mines, pp. 81–2; Canada, 1881 Census, Nova Scotia, Cape Breton County, North Sydney, pp. 89–91.

35 D.K. McIntyre to DGSIA, 15 April 1907, *Sessional Papers*, no. 27 (1908), 59; LAC, RG 10/3103, file 307,576, A.J. Boyd to Duncan C. Scott, 20 June 1917.

36 D.K McIntyre to DGSIA, 10 May 1909, *Sessional Papers*, no. 27, (1910) 65; 11 April, 1910, *Sessional Papers*, no. 27, (1911), 65; 4 May 1911, *Sessional Papers*, no. 27, (1912), 70.

37 LAC, RG 10/3103, file 307,576, Petition of Andrew Bernard, et al. to SGIA, 21 January 1907.

38 See LAC, RG 10/3103, file 307,576, 'Squatters at North Sydney photographed by Mr. Scott, September 1909.'

39 Darroch and Soltow, *Property and Inequality in Victorian Ontario*, 215.

40 *Gillies* v. *R.*, Testimony of Donald McAdam, September 1915, 257; Margaret Warner Morley, *Down North and Up Along* (New York, 1905), 170.

41 *Gillies* v. *R.*, Testimony of George Archibald, 146; Beatrice H.Hay Shaw, 'The Indians of the Maritimes,' *The Canadian Magazine*, (January 1922), 346.

42 *Gillies* v. *R.*, Testimony of Donald McAdam, September 1915, 259; Testimony of Gordon G. Spencer, 307–8; Testimony of Ben E. Christmas, 326; Testimony of Joe Christmas, 333–4, 345.

43 LAC, RG 10/2911, file 185,723-9A, Charles Parker letter, 14 April 1912; Report of the Superintendent General Affairs for the year ended March 31 1922, *Sessional Papers*, no. 14 (1923), 28.

44 See for instance the comments by Darlene Ricker, based on oral interviews with Bear River residents. *L'sitkuk: The Story of the Bear River Mi'kmaw Community* (Lockeport, N.S., 1997), 119.

45 LAC, RG 10/3022, file 234,951, J.A. MacRae to SGIA, 3 November 1902.

46 LAC, RG 10/2911, file 185,723-9A, A. Cameron, to J.D. McLean, 29 November 1899.

47 For instance, in August 1901, Gillies was appointed to represent the city in a legal action commenced by R.D. Law. NSARM, Sydney City Council Minutes, 10 August 1901, 294.

48 Sydney Council Minutes, 18 December 1902, 156–7.

49 'Joseph Alexander Gillies,' in J.K. Johnson, ed., *The Canadian Directory of Parliament 1867–1967* (Ottawa, 1968), 230.

50 Indeed, as I point out later in this chapter, Gillies owned several properties around town.

51 *Gillies* v. *R.*, Testimony of Joseph Gillies, September 1915, 13.

52 LAC, RG 13/64, 1887-1088.

53 RG 10/2911, file 185, 723-9A, J.A. Gillies to J.A. Smart, 28 October 1899; *Gillies* v. *R.*, Testimony of Joseph Gillies, 35.

54 LAC, RG 10/2911, file 185,723-9A, John Denny to Dr. Cameron, 25 November 1899; John Denny to Cameron, 13 January 1900; Cameron to Sifton, 16 January 1900; Sifton to Gillies, 20 July 1900.

55 LAC, RG 10/459, 364, Samuel Fairbanks to Hector Langevin, 28 January 1868.

56 DIA, file 201/30-1, vol. 1, 'Surveys and Reserves, General Maritime Region, 1892–1957,' Rimmer Report, 10 July 1901; LAC, RG 10/7833, file 30, 052-2, pt. 2, J. D. McLean to R.E. Rinn, 4 October 1910.

57 LAC, RG 10/2911, file 185,723-9A, C. C. Parker to Ass Deputy, Indian Affairs, 20 January 1913.

58 LAC, RG 10/7936, file 32-61; Wicken, 'Mi'kmaq Treaty Tradition,' 157.

59 *Gillies* v. *R.*, September 1915, 333–44.

60 Titley, *A Narrow Vision*, 21–2.

61 1-2 George V Cap 14, s. 2, 'An Act to amend the Indian Act,' 19 May 1911.

62 Remarks of Mr Oliver, 26 April 1911 in *Debates of the House of Commons of the Dominion of Canada, 3rd Session, 11th Parliament*, 7827.

63 Remarks of Mr Laurier, 26 April 1911 in *Debates of the House of Commons*, 7830.

64 *Gillies* v. *R.*, Testimony of Joseph Gillies, September 1915, 19. The Lekwungen peoples' relocation is briefly discussed in John Sutton Lutz, *Makuk: A New History of of Aboriginal-White Relations* (Vancouver, 2008), 103. For an analysis of how the Lekwungen were thought to pose a threat to white citizens of Victoria in the mid-19th century, see Penelope Edmonds, *Urbanizing Frontiers: Indigenous Peoples and Settlers in 19th Century Pacific Rim Cities* (Vancouver, 2010), 184-229.

65 LAC, RG 10/2911, file 185,723-9A, Parker to Ass Deputy, Indian Affairs, 20 January 1913.

66 Remarks of Mr Borden, 26 April 1911 in *Debates of the House of Commons*, 7832–3.
67 Sydney was incorporated as a city in 1904.
68 LAC, RG 10/2911, file 185,723-9A, Charles Parker to [SGIA], 14 April, 1912; J.D. McLean to Rev. R.L. Macdonald, 24 April, 1913; Remarks of Mr Roche, 11 May, 1914 in *Debates of the House of Commons*, 3535.
69 The Exchequer Court of Canada was a predecessor of the Federal Court of Canada. For a history of the court see Ian Bushnell, *The Federal Court of Canada: A History, 1875-1992* (Toronto, 1997), 27–123.
70 Sparrow to DGSIA, 20 January 1913, in *Gillies* v. *R*, 21–3; *Gillies* v. *R.*, Testimony of Joseph Gillies, 24.
71 *Gillies* v. *R.*, Testimony of Robert McLean, 104.
72 *Gillies* v. *R.*, Testimony of John Knox McLeod, 57.
73 *Gillies* v. *R.*, Testimony of Wilfred Arthur Winfield, 37.
74 *Gillies* v. *R.*, Testimony of John P. Parker, 126.
75 *Gillies* v. *R.*, Testimony of Cecil Sparrow, 230.
76 *Gillies* v. *R.*, Testimony of John McCurdy, 93.
77 *Gillies* v. *R.*, Testimony of Joseph Gillies, 35–6.
78 *Gillies* v. *R.*, Testimony of Cecil Sparrow, 230, 232.
79 *Gillies* v. *R.*, Testimony of Wilfred Arthur Winfield, 38.
80 *Gillies* v. *R.*, Testimony of John McCurdy, 94.
81 *Gillies* v. *R.*, Testimony of Wilfred Winfield, 39.
82 *Gillies* v. *R.*, Testimony of Robert McLean, 106. On this issue in British Columbia, see Jean Barman, 'Taming Aboriginal Sexuality: Gender, Power, and Race in British Columbia, 1850–1900,' *BC Studies* no. 115/16 (1997–98), 237–66.
83 *Gillies* v. *R.*, Testimony of Wilfred Winfield, 47.
84 *Gillies* v. *R.*, Testimony of Major Walter Crowe, 85.
85 'In the Matter of the Reference Respecting the Expediency of the Removal of the Indians from the Reserve at the City of Sydney, Cape Breton, in the Province of Nova Scotia, 15 March 1916,' *Reports of the Exchequer Court of Canada*, vol. 17, 522.
86 LAC, RG 10/7761, file 27061-1A, C.C. Parker to Duncan Campbell Scott, 20 July 1920.
87 LAC, RG 10/7761, file 27061-1A, Petition of Residents of Whitney Pier to Department of Indian Affairs, 30 October 1920.
88 LAC, RG 10/7761, fie 27061-1A, Joe Marshall to DIA, 18 November 1920.
89 LAC, RG 10/7761, file 27061-1A, Duncan Campbell Scott to Deputy Minister of Justice, 14 June 1921.

90 LAC, RG 10/7761, file 27061-1A, Memo to Mr. Roberson, 11 May 1923; Robertson memo, 1924; A.F. MacKenzie to George Ross, 15 July 1925; McLeod to Scott, 1 September 1925.

91 LAC, RG 10/7761, file 27061-1A, John K. MacLeod to Eric McDonald, 30 March 1925; Ben Christmas to Charles Stewart, 16 April 1925; Ben Christmas to MacKenzie King, 18 April 1925.

92 LAC, RG 10/2130, file 25,772, [????] to Francis Bernard, 3 January 1880.

93 LAC, RG 13/A-2, vol. 87, File 1892-850, R. Sinclar, Acting DGSIA to R. Sedgewick, Deputy Minister of Justice, 19 July 1892.

Conclusion

 1 R. Ruggles Gates, 'The Blood Groups and Other Features of the Micmac Indians,' *The Journal of the Royal Anthropological Institute of Great Britain and Ireland* 68 (1938), 283–99.

 2 NSARM, RG 38, vol. 15, #41, Magistrate's Court, Port Hood, Nova Scotia, The King vs. Gabriel Sylyboy, et al., 22 November, 1927.

 3 Alfred F. Young, *The Shoemaker and the Tea Party: Memory and the American Revolution* (Boston, 1999), 87–91.

 4 Cape Breton University, Mi'kmaq Resource Centre, Michael A. Pare, Brief Filed on Behalf of Her Majesty the Queen in R. versus Donald John Marshall, Jr., 23 February 1996; Patterson, 'Indian-White Relations in Nova Scotia, 1749–61.'

 5 Thomas Akins, ed., *Acadia and Nova Scotia: Documents Relating to the Acadian French and the First British Colonization of the Province, 1714–1758* (Cottonport, La., 1972; 1st ed. 1869), 683–5. This is suggested in the other documents filed by the defence lawyers, which included references to the 1760/61 treaties and to the 1727 Casco Bay treaty. Although this latter treaty did not directly involve the Mi'kmaq, it was part of a broader regional treaty, which the Mi'kmaq signed in concert with other Wabanaki peoples. Wicken, *Mi'kmaq Treaties on Trial,* 71–87.

 6 My thinking about Ben Christmas is derived from Sarah Brennan, 'Revisiting the Proverbial Tin Cup,' 101–3. Brennan argues that Ben Christmas represented a linkage between 'the old and new ways, and [was] representative of a new style of leadership.' Ben Christmas's papers are in the Treaty and Aboriginal Rights Research Centre, Shubenacadie First Nation, Shubenacadie, Nova Scotia.

 7 Wicken, 'Mi'kmaq Treaty Tradition,' 160–1

 8 On the conflict between native oral memories and courts see Julie Cruikshank, 'Invention of Anthropology in British Columbia's Supreme Court:

Oral Tradition as Evidence in Dalgamuukw v. B.C.' *BC Studies*, no. 95 (1992), 25–42.

9 James Youngblood Henderson, 'Mi'kmaq Tenure in Atlantic Canada,' *Dalhousie Law Journal*, 18, 2 (1995), 196–294.

10 Wicken, 'Mi'kmaq Treaty Tradition,' 157–9.

11 See for instance, Robin Jarvis Brownlie, '"Nothing left for me or any other Indian": The Georgian Bay Anishinabek and Inter-war Articulation of Aboriginal Rights,' *Ontario History* 96, 2 (2004), 116–42; Malcolm Montgomery, 'The Legal Status of the Six Nations Indians in Canada,' *Ontario History* 55 (June 1963), 93–101; Titley, *A Narrow Vision*, 110–61.

12 D.A. McArthur, 'The Teaching of Canadian History,' *Ontario Historical Society. Papers and Records* 21 (1924), 206.

13 Wicken, *Mi'kmaq Treaties on Trial*, 27.

14 Bruce G. Trigger, *The Children of Aataentsic: A History of the Huron People to 1660*, 2 vols. (Montreal and Kingston, 1976).

15 Bruce G. Trigger, 'Preface to the 1987 reprinting,' *The Children of Aataentsic*, xxvii.

16 Marshall Sahlins, *Islands of History* (Chicago, 1985); *How Natives Think, about Captain Cook, For Example* (Chicago, 1995); Gannath Obeyesekere, *The Apotheosis of Captain Cook: European Mythmaking in the Pacific* (Princeton, 1992).

17 This sentence is inspired from reading Richard White, *Remembering Ahanagran: A History of Stories* (New York, 1998).

18 Paige Raibmon, *Authentic Indians: Episodes of Encounter from the Late-Nineteenth-Century Northwest Coast* (Durham, N.C. and London, 2005), 202.

Appendix: Federal and DIA Censuses, 1871 to 1911

1 While we might be able identify people by name and residency, the names commonly used in the Mi'kmaw community were also used by people of English, Acadian, and German ancestry. This mélange of names renders tenuous any analysis using names to identity people of Mi'kmaw heritage. For an explanation of the decision not to include peoples' origins in the 1891 census, see Chad Gaffield, 'Language, Ancestry and the Competing Constructions of Identity in Turn-of-the-Century Canada,' in Sager and Baskerville, eds., *Household Counts*, 425–6.

2 The printed copy of the census lists eleven Mi'kmaq residents of Carleton Village and two residents of Port La Tour. For some reason, the manuscript copy of the census was not microfilmed or was not retained. Because my purpose is to count only those Mi'kmaq who are listed in the manuscript

copy of the census, I have deleted these thirteen people from the totals used here.

3 The 1881 Census gives a total Mi'kmaw population of 2,125. Statisticians and enumerators made six separate errors. First, the printed census figure includes 230 Mi'kmaq living at Harbour Boucher in Antigonish County. The manuscript copy for Harbour Boucher does not show any Mi'kmaq at that location. Nor does the manuscript copy include an additional 230 Mi'kmaq living in other parts of the county. Second, I did not find four residents of Sydney and two in Dartmouth, all listed in the printed census. Third, four people from Big Pond, Cape Breton County who are identified as Mi'kmaq, clearly are not. Fourth, there are eight people incorrectly identified as Mi'kmaq, confined to jail in Annapolis Royal. These deductions give us an actual Mi'kmaq population of 1,877. Fifth, thirteen people living in Church Point, Digby County are wrongly identified as Indian. This is evident by their family names, Thibodeau and Comeau, and the next page which identifies the Comeaus as French, not Indian. Finally, to this total we should add six people from Berwick, King's County who are identified as Mi'kmaq in the manuscript copy but are not included in the printed copy of the census. This gives us a population of 1,870.

4 Reference to DIA census figures for 1911 confirms an overstatement of the population for both counties. For King's County, the federal census listed 129 on reserve and 109 off reserve. The census shows that off-reserve population in twelve separate communities. The DIA census, on the other hand, does not show anyone on reserve and shows an off-reserve population of eighty-four. Here, I have opted to use the federal census because the manuscript copy lists people by name, and not by aggregate totals, as the DIA census does. The figures for Colchester County show similar problems. The printed copy of the federal census shows ninety-one Mi'kmaq living on reserve at Millbrook and another forty-eight people living off reserve. However, I could not find the off-reserve population in the manuscript copy of the 1911 census. Significantly, the DIA census shows 102 people living at Millbrook and none living off reserve. As is the case with King's County, I have opted for the federal census as the most dependable source of information.

5 Here, I have included people who are identified in the census as 'half-breeds' or Métis. This is the only census in which people were identified in this manner. The printed copy of the 1871 census included a column for half-breeds but enumerators did not record people of mixed blood in their counts for Nova Scotia.

6 For the federal census, I have combined people identified as Indian and

'half-breed' for determining the total Mi'kmaq population. I do this mainly because the federal Department of Indian affairs did not make such a distinction in their own totals. In terms of the DIA totals for 1901, there is an addition error. DIA statisticians counted 2,020 but adding the totals for each community shows a population of 1,943, an error of 73. See 'Census Returns of Resident and Nomadic Indians' in *Sessional Papers*, no. 27 (1902), 154–6.

7 Some of these problems are discussed in Michelle A. Hamilton, '"Anyone not on the list might as well be dead": Aboriginal Peoples and the Censuses of Canada, 1851–1916,' *Journal of the Canadian Historical Association* 18, 1 (2007), 57–79.

8 Nancy Shoemaker, *American Indian Population Recovery in the Twentieth Century* (Albuquerque, 1999), 5.

9 See LAC, RG 10/3022, file 234,950, J.A. MacRae to SGIA, 3 November 1902 for a critical assessment of one agent's reports.

10 Shoemaker, *American Indian Population Recovery*, 5.

11 See for instance, LAC, RG 10/2910, file 185,723-8B, J.D. McLean to F.A. Rand, 13 Aug. 1912 and other related dismissal and appointment letters in this file.

12 1871 Census, Nova Scotia, Digby County, Hillsburgh, Schedule 8.

13 The problem with the 1901 Census is noted in Baskerville and Sager, *Unwilling Idlers*, 84.

14 Darroch and Soltow, *Property and Inequality in Victorian Ontario*, 23; *Manual Containing 'The Census Act,'* 23.

15 *Manual Containing 'The Census Act,'* 23.

Bibliography

Manuscript Sources

Great Britain, Public Record Office
(at Library and Archives Canada)
CO 217: Correspondence of Nova Scotia officials with Board of Trade and Colonial Office

Halifax, Nova Scotia

Nova Scotia Archives and Records Management
  MG 1, Clara Dennis Notebooks
  MG 1, Ralph Johnson Papers
  MG 2, Rhodes Papers
  RG 1, vols. 430–32
  RG 5, House of Assembly Records
  RG 20, Department of Lands and Forests
  RG 34-308, Cumberland County, Quarter Sessions, 1808–1833
  RG 34-324, Record of Sessions, Yarmouth and Argyle District, County of Shelburne, 1789–1816,
  RG 38/15, doc. 41, Inverness County, The King vs. Gabriel Sylyboy.

Nova Scotia Museum
  Harry Piers Papers

Sydney, Nova Scotia
Cape Breton University: Mi'kmaw Resource Centre
  Michael A. Pare, Brief Filed on Behalf of Her Majesty the Queen in R. versus Donald John Marshall, Jr., 23 February 1996

William C. Wicken. 'The Shubenacadie Mi'kmaq and the Lobster Fishery, from First Contact to 1961,' Provincial Court of Nova Scotia, R. v. Alex MacDonald et al. (2002)

Evidence Books (at trial)
  R. v. *Alex MacDonald, et al.* (Nova Scotia Provincial Court: 2002)
  R. v. *Donald Marshall Junior* (Nova Scotia Provincial Court: 1994–95)
  R. v. *Josh Bernard* (New Brunswick Provincial Court: 1999)
  Vaughn Pictou v. *R.* (Federal Tax Court of Canada: 1998)

Wolfville, Nova Scotia

Acadia University, Special Collections
  Silas Rand Diary

Ottawa, Ontario

Library and Archives Canada
  RG 10 Indian Affairs Records
  RG 13 Department of Justice Records
  RG 14, D2, 12th Parliament, 7th Session, unpublished Sessional Papers, no. 157, Hearings before the Court of the Exchequer, September 1915, Sydney, Nova Scotia.
  RG 31, 1871, 1881, 1901, and 1911 Censuses

Rimouski, Quebec

Archives nationales de Québec à Rimouski
  Fonds Capucins

Newspapers

The Casket (Antigonish) 1900–28
The Christian Messenger, 9 and 16 March 1854
Inverness County Bulletin 1927
The Nova Scotian (Halifax) 1820–30

Printed Government Sources

Canada. Parliament. Sessional Papers. Report of the Department of Indian Affairs. 1870–1929.

Debates and Proceedings of the House of Assembly (Nova Scotia).
Journals and Proceedings of the House of Assembly of Nova Scotia, 1865–1930
Journals of the Legislative Assembly (Nova Scotia)
Nova Scotia Statutes, 1759–1926.

Other Printed Sources

Alvord, Henry E. 'The Village Cow in New England, being the Journal of the Keeper,' in *Keeping One Cow Being the Experience of a Number of Practical Writers in a Clear and Considered Form upon the Management of a Single Milch Cow.* New York, 1880.

Bromley, Walter. *An Account of the aborigines of Nova Scotia called the Micmac Indians.* London, 1822.

Cozzens, Frederic. *Acadia; or a month with the Blue Noses.* New York, 1859.

Dennis, Clara. *Cape Breton Over.* Toronto, 1942.

Fergusson, C.B., ed. *Uniacke's Sketches of Cape Breton and Other Papers Relating to Cape Breton Island.* Halifax, 1958.

Fitzgerald, Owen. *Cape Breton: A Changing Scene, a Collection of Cape Breton Photographs 1860–1935.* Sydney, 1986.

Game and Inland Fishery Protection Service, Report of the Secretary for 1894.

Gates, F. Russell. 'The Blood Groups and Other Features of the Micmac Indians,' *The Journal of the Royal Anthropological Institute of Great Britain and Ireland* 68 (1938), 283–99.

Gilpin, J.B. 'Indians of Nova Scotia,' *Proceedings and Transactions of the Nova Scotia Institute of Natural Science* 4 (1877).

Haliburton, Thomas Chandler. *A General Description of Nova Scotia: Illustrated by a New and Correct Map.* Halifax, 1823.

Hollingsworth, S. *The Present State of Nova Scotia with a Brief Account of Canada.* London, 1787.

Johnson, John W. *Life of John Johnson.* Portland, 1861.

Jones, J. Matthew. 'A Fortnight in the Backwoods of Shelburne and Weymouth,' 4 February 1867 in *Proceedings and Transactions of the Nova Scotian Institute of Natural Science for 1867–1870.* Halifax, 1870.

Manual Containing 'The Census Act' and the Instructions to Officers Employed in the Taking of the First Census of Canada. (1871).

Moorsom, Captain W. *Letters from Nova Scotia Comprising Sketches of a Young Country.* London, 1830.

Morley, Margaret Warner. *Down North and Up Along.* New York, 1905.

Piers, Harry. 'Brief Account of the Micmac Indians of Nova Scotia and their Remains,' *Proceedings of the Nova Scotia Institute of Science* (1912).

Province of Quebec, Department of Agriculture. *Dairy Cows: Their Feeding and Care and Improvement of the Herds.* (Bulletin No. 1: 1897).

R. v. *Simon,* 1985, 2 SCR (1986).

R. v. *Sylliboy,* 10 September 1928. *Canadian Criminal Cases* 50 (1928), 390–1, 395–6.

R. v. *Verdi,* Halifax County Court, 5 June 1914. *Canadian Criminal Cases,* 23 (1915).

Re. Indian Reserve, City of Sydney, N.S., Exchequer Court of Canada, 16 March 1916. *Dominion Law Reports* 42 (1916), 314–22.

Rand, Silas T. *A First Reading Book in the Micmac Language Comprising the Micmac Numerals, and the Names of the Different Kinds of Beasts, Birds, Fishes, Trees, &c of the Maritime Provinces of Canada.* Halifax, 1875.

Report of Health Officer. *Minutes and Reports of the County Council of Cape Breton,* April 1903. Sydney, 1903.

Speck, Frank G. *Beothuk and Micmac: Micmac Hunting Territories in Nova Scotia and Newfoundland.* New York, 1925.

– 'The Eastern Algonkian Wabanaki Confederacy.' *American Anthropologist* 17 (1915).

Tennyson, Brian, ed. *Impressions of Cape Breton.* Sydney: University College of Cape Breton Press 1986.

Treaty or Articles of Peace and Friendship, 22 November 1752. Halifax, 1753.

Vernon, C.W. *Cape Breton Canada at the Beginning of the Twentieth Century.* Toronto, 1903.

Waite, P.B., ed. The Confederation Debates in the Province of Canada/1865. Toronto: McClelland and Stewart, 1963.

Warner, Charles Dudley. *Baddeck, and That Sort of Thing.* Boston; 1874.

West, John. *A Journal of a Mission to the Indians of the British Provinces, of New Brunswick, and Nova Scotia, and the Mohawks on the Ouse or Grand River, Upper Canada.* London, 1827.

Whitehead, Ruth Holmes. *The Old Man Told Us: Excerpts from Micmac History 1500–1950.* Halifax: Nimbus, 1991.

Wicken, William, ed. 'Mi'kmaq Treaty Tradition.' *UNB Law Journal* 44 (1995), 157–61.

Secondary Sources

Abler, Thomas S. 'A Mi'kmaq Missionary Among the Mohawk: Silas T. Rand and His Attitudes Towards Race and "Progress."' In Celia Haig-Brown and David A. Nock, eds., *With Good Intentions: Euro-Canadian & Aboriginal Relations in Colonial Canada.* Vancouver: University of British Columbia Press, 2006, 72–86.

Acheson, T.W. 'The National Policy and the Industrialization of the Maritimes.' In Michael S. Cross and Gregory S. Kealey, eds., *Canada's Age of Industry, 1849–1896*. Toronto: McClelland and Stewart, 1982, 62-94.

Augustine, Stephen J. *Mi'kmaq & Maliseet Cultural Ancestral Material: National Collections from the Canadian Museum of Civilization*. Ottawa: Canadian Museum of Civilization, 2005.

Axelrod, Paul. *The Promise of Schooling: Education in Canada, 1800–1914*. Toronto: University of Toronto Press, 1997.

Backhouse, Constance. *Colour-Coded: A Legal History of Racism in Canada, 1900–1950*. Toronto: University of Toronto Press, 1999.

– 'Nineteenth-Century Canadian Rape Law 1800–92.' In David Flaherty, ed., *Essays in the History of Canadian Law*, vol. II. Toronto: University of Toronto Press, 1983.

Banjtes, Rod. 'Improved Earth: Travel on the Canadian Prairies, 1920–50.' *The Journal of Transport History* 13, 2 (1992), 115–40.

Banner, Stuart. *How the Indians Lost Their Land: Law and Power on the Frontier.* Cambridge, Mass.: Harvard University Press, 2005.

Barman, Jean. 'Separate and Unequal: Indian and White Girls in All Hallows School, 1884–1920. In Jean Barman, Yvonne Hebert, and Don McCaskill, eds., *Indian Education in Canada. Volume I: The Legacy*. Vancouver: University of British Columbia Press, 1986, 110–31.

Baron, William R., and Anne E. Bridges. 'Making Hay in Northern New England: Maine as a Case Study, 1800–1850.' *Agricultural History* 57, 2 (1983), 165–80.

Baskerville, Peter, and Eric W. Sager. *Unwilling Idlers: The Urban Unemployed and Their Families in Late Victorian Canada*. Toronto: University of Toronto Press, 1998.

Battiste, Marie. 'Micmac Literacy and Cognitive Assimilation.' In Jean Barman, Yvonne Hebert and Don McCaskill, eds., *Indian Education in Canada, Volume I: The Legacy*. Vancouver, 1986.

Bayly, C.A. 'The First Age of Global Imperialism, c. 1760–1830.' *The Journal of Imperial and Commonwealth History* 26, 2 (1998).

Beck, J. Murray. *The Evolution of Municipal Government in Nova Scotia 1749–1973*. Halifax, 1973.

– *Politics of Nova Scotia 1896-1988*. Tantallon, N.S.: Four East Publications 1988.

Belich, James. 'The Rise of the Angloworld: Settlement in North America and Australasia, 1784-1918.' In Phillip Buckner and R. Douglas Francis, eds., *Rediscovering the British World*. Calgary: University of Calgary Press, 2005, 39–57.

Bell, D.G. 'Was Amerindian Dispossession Lawful? The Response of 19th Century Maritime Intellectuals.' *The Dalhousie Law Journal* 23 (2000), 168–82.

Berard, Robert Nicholas. 'Moral Education in Nova Scotia, 1880–1920.' *Acadiensis* 14, 1 (1984), 49–63.

Bitterman, Rusty. 'Economic Stratification and Agrarian Settlement: Middle River in the early Nineteenth Century.' In Kenneth Donovan, ed., *The Island: New Perspectives on Cape Breton History 1713–1990*. Fredericton: Acadiensis Press, 1990, 72–87.

Bitterman, Rusty, Robert A. MacKinnon, and Graeme Wynn. 'Of Inequality and Interdependence in the Nova Scotian Countryside, 1850–70.' *Canadian Historical Review* 74, 1 (1993), 1–43.

Bloomfield, G.T. 'I Can See a Car in That Crop: Motorization in Saskatchewan, 1906–1934.' *Saskatchewan History* 37, 1 (1984), 3–24.

Bodnar, John. *Remaking America: Public Memory, Commemoration, and Patriotism, in the Twentieth Century*. Princeton: Princeton University Press, 1992.

Bradbury, Bettina. *Working Families: Age, Gender, and Daily Survival in Industrializing Montreal*. Toronto: Oxford University Press, 1993.

Brookes, Alan A. 'The Golden Age and the Exodus: The Case of Canning, Kings County.' *Acadiensis* 11, 1 (Autumn 1981), 57–82.

– 'Out-Migration from the Maritime Provinces, 1860–1900: Some Preliminary Considerations.' *Acadiensis* 5, 2 (Spring 1976), 26–55.

Brown, Richard Maxwell. *No Duty to Retreat: Violence and Values in American History and Society*. New York: Oxford University Press, 1991.

Brownlie, Robin Jarvis. '"Nothing left for me or any other Indian": The Georgian Bay Anishinabek and Inter-war Articulation of Aboriginal Rights.' *Ontario History* 96, 2 (2004), 116–42.

Buckner, Phillip, ed. *Canada and the British Empire*. Oxford, 2008.

Buckner, Phillip and R. Douglas Francis, eds., *Rediscovering the British World*. Calgary, 2005.

Bumsted, J.M. '1763-1783: Resettlement and Rebellion.' In Phillip A. Buckner and John G. Reid, eds., *The Atlantic Region to Confederation: A History*. Toronto and Fredericton: University of Toronto Press and Acadiensis, 1994, 156–83.

Campbell, D., and R.A. MacLean. *Beyond the Atlantic Roar: A Study of the Nova Scotia Scots*. Toronto: McClelland and Stewart, 1974.

Candow, James E., ed. *Industry and Society in Early Nova Scotia: An Illustrated History*. Halifax: Fernwood Publishing, 2001.

Cashdan, Elizabeth. 'Natural Fertility, Birth Spacing, and the "First Demographic Transition."' *American Anthropologist* 87, 3 (Sept. 1985), 650–3.

Christie, Nancy. 'Introduction: Theorizing a Colonial Past,' In Nancy Christie, ed., *Transatlantic Subjects: Ideas, Institutions, and Social Experience in Post-Revolutionary British North America*. Montreal, 2008, 13–18.

Chute, Janet E. 'Frank G. Speck's Contribution to the Understanding of

Mi'kmaq Land Use, Leadership, and Land Management.' *Ethnohistory* 46, 3 (1999), 481–540.

Clancy, Peter, and L. Anders Sandberg. *Against the Grain: Foresters and Politics in Nova Scotia*. Vancouver: University of British Columbia Press, 2000.

Coates, Colin, and Cecilia Morgan. *Heroines & History: Representations of Madeleine de Verchères and Laura Secord*. Toronto: University of Toronto Press, 2002.

Coates, Ken. *The Marshall Decision and Native Rights*. Montreal and Kingston: McGill-Queen's University Press, 2000.

Cohen, Marjorie Griffen. 'The Decline of Women in Canadian Dairying.' *Histoire Social/Social History* 17, 34 (Nov. 1984), 307–34.

Colley, Linda G. *Britons: Forging the Nation 1707–1837*. New Haven: Yale University Press 1992.

– *Captives: Britain, Empire, and the World, 1600-1850*. New York: Anchor, 2004.

Corbett, Mike. 'A Protracted Struggle: Rural Resistance and Normalization in Canadian Educational History.' *Historical Studies in Education* 13, 1 (2001), 19–48.

Cowan, Helen I. *British Immigration to British North America: The First Hundred Years*. Toronto: University of Toronto Press, 1961 (1st ed. 1928).

Crowley, Terrence. 'Rural Labour.' In Paul Craven, ed., *Labouring Lives: Work & Workers in Nineteenth-Century Ontario*. Toronto: University of Toronto Press, 1995, 13–104.

Cruikshank, Julie. 'Invention of Anthropology in British Columbia's Supreme Court: Oral Tradition as Evidence in Dalgamuukw v. B.C.' *BC Studies* 95 (1992), 25–42.

Curtis, Bruce. *The Politics of Population: State Formation, Statistics, and the Census of Canada, 1840–1875*. Toronto: University of Toronto Press, 2001.

Darroch, Gordon, and Lee Soltow. *Property and Inequality in Victorian Ontario: Structural Patterns and Cultural Communities in the 1871 Census*. Toronto: University of Toronto Press, 1994.

Davis, Anthony (with Leonard Kasdan). 'Modernization in Digby Neck and the Islands.' In Richard Apostle and Gene Barrett, eds. *Emptying Their Nets: Small Capital and Rural Industrialization in the Nova Scotia Fishing Industry*. Toronto: University of Toronto Press, 1992, 168–93.

Davis, Donald F. 'Dependent Motorization: Canada and the Automobile to the 1930s.' *Journal of Canadian Studies* 21, 3 (1986), 106–32.

Davies, Stephen. '"Reckless Walking Must Be Discouraged": The Automobile Revolution and the Shaping of Modern Urban Canada to 1930.' *Urban History Review* 18, 2 (1989), 123–38.

Doeringer, Peter B., and David G. Terkla. *Troubled Waters: Economic Structure,*

Regulatory Reform, and Fisheries Trade. Toronto: University of Toronto Press, 1995.

Dunlap, Thomas R. *Nature and the English Diaspora: Environment and History in the United States, Canada, Australia and New Zealand.* Cambridge: Cambridge University Press, 1999.

Easterlin, Richard A. 'Factors in the Decline of Farm Family Fertility in the United States: Some Preliminary Research Results.' *The Journal of American History* 63, 3 (1976), 600–14.

Elbourne, Elizabeth. 'Indigenous Peoples and Imperial Networks in the Early Nineteenth Century: The Politics of Knowledge.' In Phillip Buckner and R. Douglas Francis, eds., *Rediscovering the British World.* Calgary: University of Calgary Press, 2005, 59–85.

Englebrecht, William. 'Factors Maintaining Low Population Density Among the Prehistoric New York Iroquois.' *American Antiquity* 52, 1 (1987), 13–27.

Ens, Gerhard. *Homeland to Hinterland: The Changing Worlds of the Red River Metis in the Nineteenth Century.* Toronto: University of Toronto Press, 1996.

Fergusson, C.B. 'Local Government in Nova Scotia.' *Bulletin of the Public Archives of Nova Scotia,* 17. Halifax, 1961.

Fingard, Judith. 'English Humanitarianism and the Colonial Mind: Walter Bromley in Nova Scotia, 1813–1825.' *Canadian Historical Review* 54 (1973), 125–51.

– 'The 1880s: The Paradoxes of Progress.' In E.R. Forbes and D.A. Muise, eds., *The Atlantic Provinces in Confederation.* Toronto and Fredericton: University of Toronto Press and Acadiensis, 1993, 82–116.

Forbes, Ernest. *The Maritime Rights Movement 1919–1927: A Study in Canadian Regionalism.* Kingston and Montreal: McGill-Queen's University Press, 1979.

Foster, Hamar, Benjamin L. Berger, and A.R. Buck, eds. *The Grand Experiment: Law and Legal Culture in British Settler Societies.* Vancouver, 2008.

Frank, David. 'The Cape Breton Coal Industry and the Rise and Fall of the British Empire Steel Corporation.' In P.A. Buckner and David Frank, eds., *The Acadiensis Reader: Volume Two.* Fredericton: Acadiensis, 1988, 204–35.

– 'The 1920s: Class and Region, Resistance and Accommodation.' In E.R. Forbes and D.A. Muise, eds., *The Atlantic Provinces in Confederation.* Toronto and Fredericton: University of Toronto Press and Acadiensis, 1993, 233–71.

Gaffield, Chad. 'Language, Ancestry and the Competing Constructions of Identity in Turn-of-the-Century Canada.' In Eric W. Sager and Peter Baskerville, eds., *Household Counts: Canadian Households and Families in 1901.* Toronto: University of Toronto Press, 2007, 423–40.

Gagan, David. *Hopeful Travellers: Families, Land, and Social Change in Mid-Victorian Peel County, Canada West.* Toronto: University of Toronto Press, 1981.

– 'Land, Population, and Social Change: The "Critical Years" in Rural Canada West.' *Canadian Historical Review* 59, 3 (1978), 293–318.

Gauvreau, Danielle, and Peter Gossage. 'Canadian Fertility Transitions: Quebec and Ontario at the Turn of the Twentieth Century.' *Journal of Family History* 26, 2 (April 2001), 162–88.

– 'Canadian Fertility in 1901: A Bird's Eye View.' In Eric W. Sager and Peter Baskerville, eds., *Household Counts: Canadian Households and Families in 1901.* Toronto: University of Toronto Press, 2007, 59–109.

Gossage, Peter. *Families in Transition: Industry and Population in Nineteenth-Century Saint-Hyacinthe.* Montreal and Kingston: McGill-Queen's University Press, 1999.

Green, Andy. 'Education and State Reformation Revisited.' *Historical Studies In Education* 23, 3 (1994), 1–17.

Gwyn, Julian. *Excessive Expectations: Maritime Commerce and Economic Development of Nova Scotia, 1740–1870.* Montreal and Kingston: McGill-Queen's University Press, 1998.

– 'The Mi'kmaq, Poor Settlers, and the Nova Scotia Fur Trade, 1783–1853.' *Journal of the Canadian Historical Association* 14 (2003), 65–91.

Hall, Anthony J. 'The St. Catherine's Milling and Lumber Company versus the Queen: Indian Land Rights as a Factor in Federal-Provincial Relations in Nineteenth-Century Canada.' In Kerry Abel and Jean Friesen, eds., *Aboriginal Resource Use in Canada: Historical and Legal Aspects.* Winnipeg: University of Manitoba Press, 1991, 267–86.

Hall, Catherine. *Civilising Subjects: Metropole and Colony in the English Imagination 1830–1867.* Chicago: University of Chicago Press, 2002.

Halowell, A. Irving. 'Temporal Orientation in Western Civilization and in Pre-Literate Society.' *American Anthropologist* 39 (1937), 647–70.

Hamilton, W.D. *The Federal Indian Day Schools of the Maritimes.* Fredericton: Micmac-Maliseet Institute, 1986.

Hamilton, William B. 'Society and Schools in Nova Scotia.' In J. Donald Wilson, Robert M. Stamp and Louis-Philippe Audet eds., *Canadian Education: A History.* Toronto, 1970.

Handwerker, W. Penn. 'The First Demographic Transition: An Analysis of Subsistence Choices and Reproductive Consequences.' *American Anthropologist* 85, 1 (1983), 5–27.

Hareven, Tamara K. and Maris A. Vinovskis. 'Patterns of Childbearing in Late Nineteenth-Century America: The Determinants of Marital Fertility in Five Massachusetts Towns in 1880.' In Hareven and Vinovskis, eds., *Family and Population in Nineteenth-Century America.* Princeton: Princeton University Press, 1978, 82–105.

Harring, Sidney L. *White Man's Law: Native People in Nineteenth-Century Canadian Jurisprudence.* Toronto: University of Toronto Press, 1998.

Harper, Marjory. 'British Migration and the People of the Empire.' In Andrew Porter, ed., *The Oxford History of the British Empire: The Nineteenth Century.* Oxford: Oxford University Press, 1999, 75–85.

Harris, Marvin, and Eric B. Ross. *Death, Sex, and Fertility: Population Regulation in Preindustrial and Developing Societies.* New York: Columbia University Press, 1987.

Hays, Samuel P. *Conservation and the Gospel of Efficiency: The Progressive Conservation Movement, 1890–1920.* Pittsburgh: University of Pittsburgh Press, 1999 (1st ed., 1959).

Henderson, James Youngblood. 'Mi'kmaq Tenure in Atlantic Canada,' *Dalhousie Law Journal* 18, 2 (1995), 196–294.

Hoffer, Peter Charles. *Law and People in Colonial America,* revised edition. Baltimore and London: Johns Hopkins University Press, 1998,

Holton, Woody. *Forced Founders: Indians, Debtors, Slaves & the Making of the American Revolution in Virginia.* Chapel Hill: University of North Carolina Press, 1999.

Hornsby, Stephen. *Nineteenth Century Cape Breton: A Historical Geography.* Montreal and Kingston: McGill-Queen's University Press, 1992.

Houston, Susan E. 'Politics, Schools, and Social Change in Upper Canada.' In Michael S. Cross and Gregory S. Kealey, eds., *Pre-industrial Canada 1760–1849.* Toronto: McClelland and Stewart, 1996, 161–88.

Hunter, Louis C. *Steam Power: A History of Industrial Power in the United States, 1780–1930. Volume Two: Steam Power.* Charlottesville: University of Virginia Press, 1985.

Isaac, Thomas. *Aboriginal and Treaty Rights in the Maritimes: The Marshall Decision and Beyond.* Saskatoon, 2001.

Ives, Edward D. *George Magoon and the Down East Game War.* Urbana and Chicago: University of Illinois Press, 1988.

Jacoby, Karl. *Crimes Against Nature: Squatters, Poachers, Thieves, and the Hidden History of American Conservation.* Berkeley: University of California Press, 2001.

Johnson, Ralph S. *Forests of Nova Scotia.* Halifax, 1986.

Judd, Richard. *Common Lands, Common People: The Origin of Conservation in Northern New England.* Cambridge, Mass.: Harvard University Press, 1997.

Katz, Michael. *The People of Hamilton, Canada West: Family and Class in a Mid-Nineteenth-Century City.* Cambridge, Mass.: Harvard University Press, 1975.

Knowles, Norman. *Inventing the Loyalists: The Ontario Loyalist Tradition & the Creation of Usable Pasts.* Toronto: University of Toronto Press, 1997.

Kulick, Gary. 'Dams, Fish, and Farmers: Defense of Public Rights in Eighteenth-Century Rhode Island.' In Steven Hahn and Jonathan Prude, eds., *The Coun-*

tryside in the Age of Capitalist Transformation: Essays in the Social History of Rural America. Chapel Hill: University of North Carolina Press, 1985, 25–50.

Laidlaw, Zoe. '"Aunt Anna's Report": The Buxton Women and the Aborigines Select Committee, 1835–37.' *The Journal of Imperial and Commonwealth History* 32, 2 (2004)

Lanning, Robert. 'Awakening a Demand for Schooling: Educational Inspection's Impact on Rural Nova Scotia, 1855–74.' *Historical Studies in Education* 12, 1/2 (2000), 129–42.

Livi-Bacci, Massimo. *A Concise History of World Population.* Cambridge: Cambridge University Press 1989.

Loo, Tina. 'Making a Modern Wilderness: Conserving Wildlife in Twentieth-Century Canada.' *Canadian Historical Review* 82, 1 (2001), 92–121.

– *States of Nature: Conserving Canada's Wildlife in the Twentieth Century.* Vancouver: University of British Columbia Press, 2006.

Lowenthal, David. *The Past Is a Foreign Country.* Cambridge: Cambridge University Press, 1985.

Lux, Maureen K. *Medicine That Walks: Disease, Medicine, and the Canadian Plains Native People, 1880–1940.* Toronto: University of Toronto Press, 2001.

MacDonald, Ochiltree. *The Coal and Iron Industries of Nova Scotia.* Halifax, 1909.

MacKenzie, A.A. 'Cape Breton and the Western Harvest Excursions 1890–1928.' In Kenneth Donovan, ed., *Cape Breton at 200: Historical Essays in Honour of the Island's Bicentennial 1785–1985.* Sydney: University College of Cape Breton Press, 1985, 71–84.

MacKenzie, N.A.M. 'Indians and Treaties in Law.' *Canadian Bar Review* 7 (Oct. 1929), 561–8.

MacKinnon, Robert. 'Roads, Cart Tracks, and Bridle Paths: Land Transportation and the Domestic Economy of Mid-Nineteenth-Century Eastern British North America.' *Canadian Historical Review* 84, 2 (2003), 177–216.

McLaren, John, Menzies, Robert and Chunn, Dorothy E. eds., *Regulating Lives: Historical Essays on the State, Society, the Individual and the Law.* Vancouver: University of British Columbia Press, 2002.

Marshall, Donald Sr., Denny, Alexander, and Marshall, Simon. 'The Mi'kmaq: The Covenant Chain.' In Boyce Richardson, ed., *Drumbeat: Anger and Renewal in Indian Country.* Toronto: Summerhill Press, 1989, 71–104.

Martell, J.S. *Immigration to and Emigration from Nova Scotia, 1815–1838.* Halifax, 1942.

Maynard, Steven. 'Between Farm and Factory: The Productive Household and the Capitalist Transformation of the Maritime Countryside, Hopewell, Nova Scotia, 1869–1890.' In Daniel Samson, ed., *Contested Countryside: Rural Work-*

ers and Modern Society in Atlantic Canada, 1800–1950. Fredericton: Acadiensis, 1994, 70–104.

McBride, Bunny. *Our Lives in Our Hands: Micmac Indian Basketmakers.* Halifax: Nimbus, 1990.

McCann, Larry. '"Living a Double Life": Town and Country in the Industrialization of the Maritimes.' In Douglas Day, ed., *Geographical Perspectives on the Maritime Provinces.* Halifax: Saint Mary's University, 1988.

– 'The 1890s: Fragmentation and the New Social Order.' In E.R. Forbes and D.A. Muise, eds., *The Atlantic Provinces in Confederation.* Toronto and Fredericton: University of Toronto Press and Acadiensis, 1993, 119–54.

McCreath, P.L. 'Charles Tupper and the Politics of Education in Nova Scotia.' *Nova Scotia Historical Quarterly* 1, 3 (1971), 203–22.

McCuaig, Katherine. *The Weariness, the Fever, and the Fret: The Campaign Against Tuberculosis in Canada, 1900–1950.* Montreal and Kingston: McGill-Queen's University Press, 1999.

McGinnis, Marvin. 'Canada in the Nineteenth Century.' In Michael R. Haines and Richard H. Steckel, eds., *A Population History of North America.* Cambridge: Cambridge University Press, 2000, 371–432.

Melosi, Martin V. *Coping with Abundance: Energy and Environment in Industrial America.* Philadelphia: Temple University Press, 1985.

Miller, J.R. *Shingwauk's Vision: A History of Native Residential Schools.* Toronto: University of Toronto Press, 1996.

Miller, Virginia. 'The Decline of Nova Scotia Micmac Population, A.D. 1600–1850.' *Culture* 2, 3 (1982), 107–20.

Milloy, John. *'A National Crime': The Canadian Government and the Residential School System, 1879 to 1986.* Winnipeg: University of Manitoba Press, 1999.

Millward, Hugh. 'Mine Operators and Mining Leases on Nova Scotia's Sydney Coalfield, 1720 to the Present.' *Nova Scotia Historical Review* 13, 2 (1993), 67–86.

Morgan, R.J. 'Poverty, Wretchedness, and misery: The Great Famine in Cape Breton, 1845–1851.' *The Nova Scotia Historical Review* 6, 1 (1986), 88–104.

Mullally, Sasha. 'The Machine in the Garden: A Glimpse at Early Automobile Ownership on Prince Edward Island, 1917.' *The Island* 54 (Fall/Winter 2003), 16–25.

Muise, Del. 'The Making of an Industrial Community Cape Breton Coal Towns 1867–1900.' In Don Mcgillivary and Brian Tennyson, eds., *Cape Breton Historical Essays.* Sydney: University College of Cape Breton Press 1980, 76–94.

Muldoon, James. 'Discovery, Grant, Charter, Conquest or Purchase: John Adams on the Legal Basis for English Possession of North America.' In Christopher L. Tomlins and Bruce H. Mann, eds., *The Many Legalities of Early America.* Chapel Hill and London: University of North Carolina Press, 2001, 25–46.

Nelles, H.V. *The Art of Nation-Building: Pageantry and Spectacle at Quebec's Tercentenary*. Toronto: University of Toronto Press, 1999.

– *The Politics of Development: Forests, Mines & Hydro-Electric Power in Ontario, 1849–1941*. Montreal and Kingston: McGill-Queen's University Press, 2005 (1st ed., 1973).

Olick, Jeffrey. *The Politics of Regret: On Collective Memory and Historical Responsibility*. New York: Routledge, 2007.

Osborne, Ken. 'Public Schooling and Citizenship Education in Canada.' *Canadian Ethnic Studies* 32, 1 (2000), 8–37.

Parenteau, Bill. 'Angling, Hunting and the Development of Tourism in Late Nineteenth Century Canada: A Glimpse at the Documentary Record.' *The Archivist* 117 (1998), 11–19.

– 'Care Control and Supervision: Native People in the Canadian Atlantic Salmon Fishery, 1867–1900.' *Canadian Historical Review* 79, 1 (1998), 1–35.

– and Richard W. Judd. 'More Buck for the Bang: Sporting and the Ideology of Fish and Game Management in Northern New England and the Maritime Provinces, 1870–1900.' In Stephen J. Hornsby and John G. Reid, eds., *New England and the Maritime Provinces: Connections and Comparisons*. Montreal and Kingston: McGill-Queen's University Press, 2005, 232–51.

– and James Kenny. 'Survival, Resistance, and the Canadian State: The Transformation of New Brunswick's Native Economy, 1867–1930.' *Journal of the Canadian Historical Association* 13 (2003), 49–71.

– and L. Anders Sandberg. 'Conservation and the Gospel of Economic Nationalism: The Canadian Pulpwood Question in Nova Scotia and New Brunswick, 1918–1925.' *Environmental History Review* 19, 2 (1995), 55–83.

Parker, Mike. *Guides of the North Woods: Hunting and Fishing Tales from Nova Scotia 1870–1970*. Halifax: Nimbus, 1990.

Parnaby, Andrew. 'The Cultural Economy of Survival: The Mi'kmaq of Cape Breton in the Mid-19th Century.' *Labour/Le Travail* 61 (Spring 2008), 69–98.

Pastore, Ralph T. 'Native History in the Atlantic Region during the Colonial Period.' *Acadiensis* 20, 1 (Autumn 1990), 200–25.

Patterson, Stephen E. 'Indian-White Relations in Nova Scotia, 1749–61: A Study in Political Interaction.' *Acadiensis* 23, 1 (Autumn 1993), 23–59.

– '1744–1763: Colonial Wars and Aboriginal Peoples.' In Philip A. Buckner and John G. Reid, eds., *The Atlantic Region to Confederation: A History*. Toronto and Fredericton: University of Toronto Press and Acadiensis, 1994, 125–55.

Perry, George. 'A Concession to Circumstances: Nova Scotia's Unlimited Supply of Women Teachers, 1870–1960.' *Historical Studies in Education* 15, 2 (2003), 327–60.

Pope, Peter E. *The Many Landfalls of John Cabot*. Toronto: University of Toronto Press, 1997.

Potts, Malcolm. *Society and Fertility*. Plymouth: Macdonald and Evans, 1979.

Prentice, Alison. *The School Promoters: Education and Social Class in Mid-Nineteenth Century Upper Canada*. Toronto: McClelland and Stewart, 1977.

Prins, Harald E.L. *The Mi'kmaq: Resistance, Accommodation and Cultural Survival*. Fort Worth: Harcourt Brace College Publishers, 1996.

Price, Richard. *The Spirit of the Alberta Indian Treaties*. Montreal: Institute of Policy Studies, 1979

Pyne, Stephen. *Awful Splendour: A Fire History of Canada*. Vancouver: University of British Columbia Press, 2007.

– *Year of the Fires: The Story of the Great Fires of 1910*. New York: Penguin, 2001.

Reid, John G. 'Pax Britannica or Pax Indigena? Planter Nova Scotia (1760–1782) and Competing Strategies of Pacification.' *Canadian Historical Review* 85, 4 (2004), 669–92.

Ricker, Darlene A. *L'sitkuk: The Story of the Bear River Mi'kmaw Community*. Lockeport, N.S.: Roseway Publishing, 1996.

Robertson, Ian Ross. 'The 1850s: Maturity and Reform.' In Phillip A. Buckner and John G. Reid, eds., *The Atlantic Region to Confederation: A History*. Toronto and Fredericton: University of Toronto Press and Acadiensis, 1994, 333–59.

Rogers, Norman McL. 'The Genesis of Provincial Rights,' *Canadian Historical Review* 14, 1 (1933), 9–23.

Rohr, John. 'Canadian Constitutionalism and the 1865 Confederation Debates.' *American Review of Canadian Studies*, 28, 4 (Winter 1998), 413–44.

Russell, Peter H. *Constitutional Odyssey: Can Canadians Become a Sovereign People?* Toronto: University of Toronto Press, 1993.

Sager, Eric, and Gerald Panting. *Maritime Capital: The Shipping Industry in Atlantic Canada, 1820–1914*. Montreal and Kingston: McGill-Queen's University Press, 1990.

Sahlins, Marshall. *Islands in History*. Chicago: University of Chicago Press, 1985.

– *What Natives Think, about Captain Cook, For Example*. Chicago: University of Chicago Press, 1997.

Said, Edward W. *Culture and Imperialism*. London: W.W. Norton, 1993.

Sandberg, L. Anders 'Forest Policy in Nova Scotia: The Big Lease, Cape Breton Island, 1899–1960. In L. Anders Sandberg, ed., *Trouble in the Woods: Forest Policy and Social Conflict in Nova Scotia and New Brunswick*. Fredericton: Acadiensis, 1992, 65–89.

Sandberg, L. Anders, and Peter Clancy. 'Property Rights, Small Woodlot Owners and Forest Management in Nova Scotia.' *Journal of Canadian Studies* 31, 1 (1996), 25–47.

Schacter, Daniel L. *Searching for Memory: The Mind, the Brain, and the Past*. New York, 1996.

– *The Seven Sins of Memory: How the Mind Forgets and Remembers.* Boston and New York: Houghton Mifflin, 2001.

Schmidt, David L., and Murdeena Marshall. *Mi'kmaq Hieroglyphic Prayers: Readings in North America's First Indigenous Script.* Halifax: Nimbus, 1995.

Shoemaker, Nancy. *American Indian Population Recovery in the Twentieth Century.* Albuquerque: University of New Mexico Press, 1999.

Stoler, Ann Laura. *Carnal Knowledge and Imperial Power: Race and the Intimate in Colonial Rule.* Berkeley: University of California Press, 2002.

Strange, Carolyn, and Tina Loo. *Making Good: Law and Moral Regulation in Canada, 1867–1939.* Toronto: University of Toronto Press, 1997.

Strong-Boag, Veronica. '"The Citizenship Debates": The 1885 Franchise Act.' In Robert Adomski, Dorothy E. Chunn, and Robert Menzies, eds., *Contesting Canadian Citizenship: Historical Readings.* Peterborough, 2002, 69–94.

Tennant, Paul. *Aboriginal People and Politics: The Indian Land Question in British Columbia, 1849–1989.* Vancouver: University of British Columbia Press, 1990.

Thornton, Patricia. 'The Problem of Out-Migration from Atlantic Canada, 1871–1921: A New Look.' In P.A. Buckner and David Frank, eds., *Atlantic Canada after Confederation.* Fredericton: Acadiensis, 1988, 34–65.

Titley, Brian. *A Narrow Vision: Duncan Campbell Scott and the Administration of Indian Affairs in Canada.* Vancouver: University of British Columbia Press, 1986.

Tober, James A. *Who Owns the Wildlife? The Political Economy of Conservation in Nineteenth-Century America.* Westport: Greenwood Press, 1981.

Tobias, John L. 'Protection, Civilization, Assimilation: An Outline History of Canada's Indian Policy.' In Ian A.L. Getty and Antoine S. Lussier, eds., *As Long as the Sun Shines and Water Flows: A Reader in Canadian Native Studies.* Vancouver: University of British Columbia Press, 1983, 39–55.

Trigger, Bruce G. 'Preface to the 1987 reprinting.' *The Children of Aataentsic: A History of the Huron People to 1660.* Montreal and Kingston: McGill-Queen's University Press, 1987.

Upton, L.F.S. *Micmacs and Colonists: Indian-White Relations in the Maritimes, 1713–1867.* Vancouver: University of British Columbia Press, 1979.

Valverde, Mariana. *The Age of Light, Soap, and Water: Moral Reform in English Canada, 1885–1925.* Toronto: Oxford University Press, 1991.

Wallace, Anthony F.C. *Jefferson and the Indians: The Tragic Fate of the First Americans.* Cambridge, Mass.: Harvard University Press, 1999.

Warren, Louis S. *The Hunter's Game: Poachers and Conservationists in Twentieth-Century America.* New Haven and London: Yale University Press, 1997.

Warrick, Gary. *A Population History of the Huron-Petun, A.D. 500–1650.* Cambridge: Cambridge University Press, 2008.

Weaver, John C. *The Great Land Rush and the Making of the Modern World, 1650–1900*. Montreal and Kingston: McGill-Queen's University Press, 2003.

Weiner, Mark S. *Black Trials: Citizenship from the Beginnings of Slavery to the End of Caste*. New York: Alfred A. Knopf, 2004.

White, Richard. *Remembering Ahanagran: A History of Stories*. New York: Hill and Wang, 1998.

Whitehead, Ruth Holmes. *Micmac Quillwork: Micmac Indian Techniques of Porcupine Quill Decoration, 1600–1950*. Halifax: Nimbus, 1982.

Wicken, William C. *Mi'kmaq Treaties on Trial: Land, History and Donald Marshall Junior*. Toronto: University of Toronto Press, 2002.

– 'Mi'kmaq Land in Southwestern Nova Scotia, 1771–1823.' In Margaret Conrad, ed., *Making Adjustments: Change and Continuity in Planter Nova Scotia, 1759–1800*. Fredericton: Acadiensis, 1991, 113–22.

Wiener, Martin J. *An Empire on Trial: Race, Murder, and Justice under British Rule, 1870–1935*. Cambridge, 2009.

Wright, Ronald. 'The Public Right of Fishing, Government Fishing Policy, and Indian Fishing Rights in Upper Canada.' *Ontario History* 86, 4 (1994), 337–62.

Worster, Donald. *Nature's Economy: A History of Ecological Ideas*. Cambridge: Cambridge University Press, 1977.

Young, Alfred F. *The Shoemaker and the Tea Party: Memory and the American Revolution*. Boston: Beacon Press, 1999.

Unpublished Materials

Allen, Gillian S. Laws. 'Logs and Lumber: A History of Forest Legislation in Nova Scotia.' M.A. thesis, Saint Mary's University, 1993.

Block, Sharon. 'Coerced Sex in British North America, 1700–1820.' Ph.D. dissertation, Princeton University, 1998.

Brennan, Sarah A. 'Revisiting the Proverbial Tin Cup: A Study of Political Resistance of the Mi'kmaq of Nova Scotia, 1900–1969.' M.A. thesis, Saint Mary's University, 2000.

Leslie, John F. 'Commissions of Inquiry into Indian affairs in the Canadas, 1828–1858: Evolving a corporate memory for the Indian Department.' M.A. thesis, Carleton University, 1984.

– and Ron Macguire, eds., *The Historical Development of the Indian Act* . Ottawa: 1979.

MacKinnon, Robert A. 'The Historical Geography of Agriculture in Nova Scotia, 1851–1951.' Ph.D. dissertation, University of British Columbia, 1991.

Reid, John G., and William C. Wicken. 'An Overview of the Eighteenth Century

Treaties Signed Between the Mi'kmaq and Wuastukwiuk Peoples and the English Crown, 1725–1928.' Report Submitted to the Royal Commission on Aboriginal Peoples, 1996.

Walls, Martha. '"The Maximum, the Minimum or Something in Between": The Mi'kmaq and Federal Electoral Legislation, 1899–1951.' Ph.D. dissertation, University of New Brunswick, 2005.

Wicken, William C. 'The 1778 and 1779 Treaties.' Report Submitted to the Mi'gmawei Mawoimi, 2006.

Index